Criminal Genius

Criminal Genius

A Portrait of High-IQ Offenders

———

James C. Oleson

UNIVERSITY OF CALIFORNIA PRESS

University of California Press, one of the most distinguished university presses in the United States, enriches lives around the world by advancing scholarship in the humanities, social sciences, and natural sciences. Its activities are supported by the UC Press Foundation and by philanthropic contributions from individuals and institutions. For more information, visit www.ucpress.edu.

University of California Press
Oakland, California

Library of Congress Cataloging-in-Publication Data

Names: Oleson, James C., author.
Title: Criminal genius : a portrait of high-IQ offenders / James C. Oleson.
Description: Oakland, California : University of California Press, [2016] | Includes bibliographical references and index.
Identifiers: LCCN 2016006683 | ISBN 9780520282414 (cloth : alk. paper) | ISBN 9780520282421 (pbk. : alk. paper)
Subjects: LCSH: Criminal behavior—Case studies. | Genius—Case studies.
Classification: LCC HV6080 .O625 2016 | DDC 364.3—dc23
LC record available at http://lccn.loc.gov/2016006683

25 24 23 22 21 20 19 18 17 16
10 9 8 7 6 5 4 3 2 1

For Jameson

CONTENTS

FIGURES AND TABLES

FIGURES

TABLES

With respect to the study of intelligence and crime, there are—broadly speaking—two ideological camps. The first camp is positivist, even materialist, in its orientation. Its adherents are often politically conservative (Walsh & Ellis, 1999). This camp understands intelligence as an important characteristic and accepts intelligence tests and intelligence quotient (IQ) scores as meaningful measures of human intelligence. It is mindful of a century of research that demonstrates a negative correlation between IQ and crime (Ellis & Walsh, 2003; Herrnstein & Murray, 1994; Hirschi & Hindelang, 1977; Wilson & Herrnstein, 1985). It rejects the myth of the blank slate (Pinker, 2002) and insists that our physical bodies, as well as our social institutions, shape human behavior. The biosocial approach to the study of intelligence and crime is exciting because it promises a bridge between neuroscience and criminal conduct (Beaver, Barnes, & Boutwell, 2015; Raine, 1993, 2013). For, whether stemming from genetic inheritance or environmental cause, brain abnormalities appear to be related to (at least some forms of) criminal behavior. For example, an emerging body of work connects traumatic brain injury to violent crime (e.g., León-Carrión & Ramos, 2003). Similarly, a recent wave of articles, both scholarly (e.g., Levitt, 2004; Nevin, 2000) and popular (e.g., Drum, 2013; Hamblin, 2014), purport a robust relationship between lead emissions from automobiles and subsequent crime rates. Neuroscientist Adrian Raine has concluded, "I think there's no longer any question, scientifically, that there's an association between the brain and criminal behavior. We're beyond the point of debating that" (Fischman, 2011). But this same positivist camp invokes the memory of Cesare Lombroso's biological anthropology (1876/2006), is criticized for overstating the influence of biology (Burt & Simons, 2014), and is condemned for treating crime as an innate and immutable problem that cannot be solved (Ferguson & Beaver, 2009).

It is also difficult to disentangle modern crime and intelligence research from its origins in the long, dark history of eugenics (Kevles, 1985; Rafter, 1997, 2008). Although the natural criminal might deserve pity, not blame, such pity is often earned at the cost of personhood (Lewis, 1953); and in order to protect state interests, incorrigible offenders (or potential offenders) have been detained (Katz & Abel, 1984), sterilized (e.g., Buck v. Bell, 1927; Skinner v. Oklahoma, 1942), and killed (Barefoot v. Estelle, 1983; Mucchielli, 2006; Murdoch, 2007).

The second camp is critical in its orientation. Its adherents are often political liberals or radicals (Walsh & Ellis, 1999). They often eschew positivism's fetish for quantification (Young, 2011). Within this second camp, many criminologists (usually trained as sociologists), for various reasons, view IQ as a suspect measure (Kamin, 1974). Intelligence, it is claimed, is culturally constructed (Cohen, 1955; Gould, 1981). There is not one general intelligence *(g)*—if indeed something called intelligence truly exists—but multiple intelligences (Gardner, 1983, 1993; Sternberg, 1985). Indeed, several within this camp believe that IQ operates as a signifier of racist scholarship (e.g., Platt & Takagi, 1979). Intelligence tests are dismissed as arbitrary and unreliable (Kanazawa, 2012), as well as instruments of oppression used to deny agency to the poor, the dispossessed, and the downtrodden (Gould, 1981). While progressives within this camp may be willing to employ IQ measures when they can be used to exculpate offenders, as in *Atkins v. Virginia* (2002) and *Hall v. Florida* (2014), most remain unwilling to accept IQ as an explanation for crime. Instead, many sociologically oriented criminologists cling to the social-structural traditions of strain (Agnew, 1992), labeling (Becker, 1963), subcultural (Cohen, 1955), and radical (Taylor, Walton, & Young, 1973) theories. Mass incarceration is not a rational response to an epidemic of antisocial behavior, but political pacification, an attempt to quell the boil of social unrest that accompanies expanding social inequality (Wilkinson & Pickett, 2009). Crime—*real* crime—has nothing to do with low-IQ delinquents peddling drugs. *Real* crime is colonialism, globalization, and neoliberalism. *Real* crime is climate change (White, 2012), shock doctrine governance (Klein, 2007), and unending war (Simpson, 2008). Of course, because these crimes are the métier of the affluent and powerful, they are not even regarded as crimes (Reiman & Leighton, 2013): if governments wanted to wage a war on *real* crime, they would target too-big-to-fail corporations and too-big-to-jail plutocrats (Taibbi, 2014), even states themselves (Rothe & Friedrichs, 2006).

These two ideological camps operate in a kind of cold war and rarely speak. They take up different units of analysis—the study of individual differences versus the study of societal institutions—and pretend that the other camp simply does not exist. For years, I have resided—somewhat uncomfortably—between these two camps. I *do* believe in general intelligence, *do* believe that cognitive differences are measured by IQ tests, and *do* believe that IQ is associated with life opportunities (Firkowska-Mankiewicz, 2002; Strenze, 2007) and well-being (Fergusson, Horwood, & Ridder, 2005). But I also acknowledge that social environments influence IQ (Brinch & Galloway, 2012; Sharkey, 2010) and believe that high IQ does not necessarily produce lawfulness. After all, William James Sidis, probably the most intelligent person to ever live—with an IQ estimated between 250 and 300—was sentenced to 18 months of hard labor for leading a riot and assaulting a policeman (Wallace, 1986). Notorious serial killers have possessed high IQ scores (Aamodt, 2014; Calder, 2013), and most white-collar criminals are able to commit their offenses *because* above-average intelligence affords them the opportunity (Raine et al., 2012). White-collar crime is far more pernicious, costly, and injurious than all street crimes combined (Coleman, 2005). Thus, I believe that some form of détente is possible: the tools of the positivist camp are commensurable with the concerns of the critical camp.

When I first read about the association between low IQ and crime, I was puzzled. Many people I had encountered—including bright people with high IQ scores—had violated the law, often with impunity. Perhaps because they did not seem like "criminals," they had not been treated as such. Thus, when I read Wallerstein and Wyle's 1947 article, "Our Law-Abiding Law-Breakers," their conclusion—that 99% of their anonymous subjects had engaged in at least one of their listed criminal offenses and that many had committed a felony—seemed somehow reassuring. *They* (the criminals) are us. Similarly, when I read Porterfield's 1946 book, *Youth in Trouble,* his finding that Texas Christian University students were involved in the same offenses as delinquents in a local court, up to and including homicide, was strangely comforting. They are us. And when I read Murchison's 1926 book, *Criminal Intelligence,* I was not at all surprised to learn that the IQ scores of the prisoners surpassed those of their keepers. These researchers challenged the comforting myth of the criminal type (Sarbin, 1969). Our jails and prisons may be filled with poor "rabble" (Irwin, 1985), but this does not mean that the wealthy do not commit crimes. The affluent and the powerful *do* commit crimes—crimes great and small—although they rarely go to prison (Reiman & Leighton, 2013). "Law is like a cobweb; it's made for flies and the smaller kinds of insects, so to speak, but lets the big bumblebees break through" (Drew, in Sutherland, 1940, pp. 8–9). Research suggesting that a small percentage of chronic offenders are responsible for a disproportionate volume of crime (Farrington, Ohlin, & Wilson, 1986; Wolfgang, Figlio, & Sellin, 1972) may be true, especially when it comes to street crime, but most of us dabble in wrongdoing. Almost *all* of us engage in offending, usually in adolescence (Moffitt, 1993). We "get drunk and fall down, use drugs, take a leak in an alley, take a shortcut through someone's yard, fall asleep in a subway car, scream at a boyfriend or girlfriend, hop a fence" (Taibbi, 2014, p. xxi).

Research suggests that the relationship between IQ and crime is not negative and linear, but curvilinear (Mears & Cochran, 2013; Schwartz et al., 2015): prevalence rates fall precipitously below IQ 50 and above IQ 100 (Jensen, 1980). Thus, research suggesting that crime and delinquency are associated with below-average IQ scores is, in part, a function of the frequency of different types of crime. High-frequency crimes such as petty theft, assault, disorderly conduct, and vandalism tend to be associated with low IQ, while low-frequency crimes such as counterfeiting, insider trading, embezzlement, and other corporate crimes tend to be associated with high IQ (Wilson & Herrnstein, 1985). Different kinds of crimes also carry different risks of detection. Low-IQ crimes are often committed in public view, while high-IQ crimes are often committed behind closed (and expensive) doors. In terms of seriousness, however, the criminals with high IQs are the ones capable of offenses that victimize hundreds, thousands, or millions of people. "Kill a man, one is a murderer; kill a million, a conqueror; kill them all, a God" (Rostand, 1962, p. 68).

Despite a century of research on intelligence and crime, criminologists know almost nothing about high-IQ crime. Of course, high-IQ offenders, both real and imagined, have achieved a kind of celebrity (Oleson, 2003): thus, "the Unabomber," Theodore Kaczynski, exists in a pantheon of criminal genius along with Nathan Leopold and Richard Loeb, "Red-Light Bandit" Caryl Chessman, and "Mensa Murderer" George Trepal, as well as James Bond's nemesis (Ernst Stavro Blofeld), Sherlock Holmes's archrival Professor Moriarty, and Hannibal "the Cannibal" Lecter.

Modern psychologists are more likely to describe high-IQ offenders as "gifted" than as "geniuses" (Kreuter, 1962), but the label *genius* invokes a conceptual history that can shed light on the understanding of intelligence and crime. One approach to the study of adult offenders possessing genius-level (98%+) IQ scores would be to scrutinize infamous cases of high-IQ crime. Instead, however, I used a self-report questionnaire to measure the rates of incidence, prevalence, arrest, and conviction for 72 different offenses, including a range of drug crimes, justice system crimes, professional misconduct, property crimes, sex crimes, vehicular crimes, violent crimes, and white-collar crimes. I also derived key themes from follow-up interviews with self-reported offenders, many of whom claimed to have never been caught. Thus, using a traditional measure of individual differences—IQ—I have attempted to move beyond traditional self-report studies to reveal something about the criminological world of "intellectual elites" (Herrnstein & Murray, 1994, p. 25). I hope that both the positivist and critical camps of criminology will discover something of value in the research.

ACKNOWLEDGMENTS

This book was realized through the efforts of many people. I began to study high-IQ crime at the University of Cambridge in 1995, and Professor David Farrington was an exceptional PhD supervisor. My PhD cohort—Nick Baylis, Sarah Fitzharding, Jason Moore, and Michael Rice, all overseen by Loraine Gelsthorpe—was another valuable resource. Professors Andrew Von Hirsch and Hans Eysenck provided me with insights along the way, and Professors Gisli Gudjonsson and Adrian Grounds transformed my viva voce examination into a learning opportunity.

Of course, the research was possible only because hundreds of anonymous individuals took the time and trouble to complete my self-report questionnaires, and I remain deeply grateful to them. I am especially thankful to the participants who volunteered for follow-up interviews, or otherwise invested significant attention in the project, and to the research assistants who helped distribute questionnaires or assisted with data entry. It mattered.

Old Dominion University supported the research, providing me with a summer research fellowship in 2002. The University of Auckland offered welcome institutional support as well. The Faculty Research Development Fund Grant allowed me to draw upon the expertise of the staff at Auckland's Centre of Methods and Policy Application in the Social Sciences: Professor Peter Davis, Gerald Cottrell, Dug Yeo Han, Roy Lay-Yee, and Martin von Randow. Two funded summer scholars—Rachael Chappell and Sam Jeffs—also assisted with the project. A period of leave granted in 2015–16 gave me time to complete the book as a Visiting Fellow in Law at the University of Groningen.

I would like to thank the scholars who reviewed the manuscript: Professors J. C. Barnes, Kevin Beaver, and Matt DeLisi. The work benefited from their generous comments. I am also grateful to the editorial staff at the University of California Press—particularly Maura Roessner, Jack Young, and Cindy Fulton—as well as to my copyeditor, Julie Van Pelt, my indexer, Jim Fuhr, and to Ron Mandelbaum at Photofest. The *George Mason Law Review* authorized me to draw upon my 2009 article, "The Insanity of Genius," for a section of chapter 5, and the *Qualitative Report* permitted me to adapt portions of my 2004 article, "Sipping Coffee with a Serial Killer," for a section of chapter 6.

For their patience and understanding, I would like to thank my family (Jennifer, John, and Patricia Oleson) and my partner, Clare Wilde, as well as her family. For their various contributions at various stages of the project, I would also like to thank Christine Baiko, Mira Bernstein, Wayne Billheimer, Peter Bogdanoff, Meriko Borogove, Kendal Bushe, Erin Chanfrau, Bruce Curtis, Eric Flesher, Becki Fogerty, Randy Gainey, Jenn Garnett, Dmitry Green, Aaron Haggarty, Jen Heung, Heather Klaubert, Emery Lee, Daniel McDougall, Elizabeth Monk-Turner, Tom Nicholls, Brian Payne, Karen Roller, Jon Sorenson, James Temple, and Chris Warne.

Introduction

This book provides a glimpse into a rarely seen world of criminal behavior. Most of what people know of crime is learned from offenders who have been apprehended: the failures of the criminal world. Little is known about the "dark figure" of crime—offenses that go undetected, unreported, and unsolved (Biderman & Reiss, 1967; Skogan, 1977). The research described here examines the offending of a rarely studied population: adults with intelligence quotient (IQ) scores of 130+ (98%+), at or above the level of borderline genius (Simonton, 1994). It constitutes groundbreaking work, for, despite society's long-standing preoccupation with the criminal genius—from Socrates to Hannibal—almost nothing is known about this population (Blackburn, 1993).

DARK FIGURES

Crime is recognized as an immense social problem: indeed, the burden of crime is estimated to exceed $1 trillion per year in the United States alone (Anderson, 1999). Thus, one of the important contributions of criminology lies in the accurate measurement of delinquency and crime. Beyond guesswork, researchers typically measure the volume of crime with official crime statistics, victimization studies, or self-report studies (Hood & Sparks, 1970). Many jurisdictions report official crime rates—measures of the number of offenses recorded by law enforcement officials. For example, in the United States, the Federal Bureau of Investigation (FBI) collects information from 18,000 municipalities to provide an aggregate view of 8 index crimes and 18 other offenses, known as the Uniform Crime Reports (UCR; FBI, 2015). The Crimes Detected in England and Wales reports provide analogous data in the United Kingdom (Smith, Taylor, & Elkin, 2013). Official statistics provide a useful measure of crime, but they often reveal more about social attitudes, law enforcement priorities, and the exercise of discretion than the actual amount of crime (Kitsuse & Cicourel, 1963). Many crimes simply go unreported (Skogan, 1977). Even when offenses are reported, between one-fifth and one-third of reported crimes are dismissed by law enforcement (for lack of evidence of crime or because informal police activity resolved the matter) and omitted from final statistics (Hough & Mayhew, 1985). Criminologists estimate the "dark figure" of crime to be approximately four times greater than that reported in official statistics (Hood & Sparks, 1970).

Victimization studies provide an alternative to official statistics. In the United States, the National Crime Victimization Survey (NCVS) gathers data from 90,000 households each year about rape, robbery, assault, burglary, motor-vehicle theft, and theft (Truman & Langton, 2014); the Crime Survey for England and Wales (formerly the British Crime Survey) provides analogous information in the United Kingdom (Office for National Statistics, 2014); and the International Crime Victim Survey collects this kind of information from countries around the world (van Dijk, van Kesteren, & Smit, 2007). Victimization studies consistently reveal that crime is far more common than suggested by official statistics—depending upon offense, NCVS rates range between 60% and 500% greater than UCR rates (McDowall & Loftin, 2007). Victimization studies, however, suffer from their own limitations: sexual and domestic-violence crimes are still underreported; "victimless" crimes such as tax evasion, gambling, and illegal drug consumption go unmeasured; and, for crimes such as price fixing, political corruption, and environmental pollution, victims seldom realize they have been victimized (Coleman, 2005).

Self-report studies are another means of measuring crime. Self-reporting is the most commonly employed methodology in criminology (Hagan, 1993). Like victimization studies, self-report studies suggest that criminal behavior is far more common than official statistics indicate (e.g., West & Farrington, 1973). Yet self-report studies suffer from limitations as well. Most self-report studies employ junior- or high-school boys (who may or may not have official records as delinquents) as subjects and they often focus on petty crime and status offenses (behaviors that are not illegal when committed by an adult; Wolfgang, 1976). This is understandable, given that adolescent subjects usually lack the opportunity and means to commit serious, adult crimes. It is possible, however, to use self-report instruments to measure serious offending. Self-report instruments can be used to "study up" (Gusterson, 1997; Nader, 1974). Self-report techniques can be employed with adult subjects to reveal the landscape of white-collar, organized, state, and other serious crime (Box, 1981).

It is disturbing to contemplate what such studies might reveal. White-collar crime dwarfs the harm of all known street crimes combined, whether measured in terms of financial costs or physical injuries and wrongful deaths (Coleman, 2005). Self-report studies of criminal elites could present a much-altered view of crime from what is presented by official statistics. Reiman (2001) explains,

> The acts defined legally as crimes, the acts treated seriously as crimes, tend to be the acts committed by poor people, often poor nonwhite people. Harmful acts of the well-off—refusal to make the workplace safe, which results in thousands of deaths and injuries each year; ongoing pollution of the atmosphere, which increases the rates of lung disease and a variety of deadly cancers; tax cheating and the savings & loan debacle, which cost citizens far more than all the robberies reported to the police each year; and much more—tend rarely to be defined as crimes, and when they are so defined, tend not to be treated as serious crimes. (p. xi)

The most serious—the most harmful—crimes are not even conceived of as crimes: "the devil's best trick is to persuade you that he doesn't exist" (Baudelaire, 1864/1980, p. 191). Criminologists know even less about the dark figure of white-collar crime than they do about the dark figure of street crime (Burdis & Tombs, 2012). Thus, self-report studies of the powerful, the affluent, and the influential could shed valuable light on the nature of white-collar and other elite crimes. The revelations from such studies might also prompt criminologists to reevaluate the nature of "the criminal" (Sarbin, 1969) and reconsider familiar relationships between crime and its correlates. For example, researchers have demonstrated that the rich, defying stereotypes, are more likely to cheat and steal than the poor (Piff, Stancato, Côté, Mendoza-Denton, & Keltner, 2012). If criminologists administered a self-report questionnaire to measure the white-collar offenses that produce financial harm, physical injuries, and negligent deaths on a massive scale, instead of counting petty delinquency and high-visibility street crimes, they might record positive—not negative—correlations between crime and educational achievement, socioeconomic status, and age.

Self-report research of elites also has the potential to contribute to the research on intelligence and crime. A substantial body of research indicates that below-average intelligence (an IQ of about 92, or half a standard deviation below the population average of 100) is a long-established correlate of delinquency and crime (e.g., Herrnstein & Murray, 1994; Hirschi & Hindelang, 1977; West & Farrington, 1973; Wilson & Herrnstein, 1985). Lynam, Moffitt, and Stouthamer-Loeber (1993) characterize the relationship between low IQ and offending as "one of the most robust findings across numerous studies of juvenile delinquency" (p. 187). However, others (e.g., Murchison, 1926; Sutherland, 1931) reject the association between low IQ and crime as spurious. McCord, McCord, and Zola (1959) suggest that low IQ is associated, not with crime and delinquency, but with an increased likelihood of being detected and punished. Barnes and Teeters (1959) reason that because "we seldom arrest and convict criminals except the poor, inept, and friendless, we can know very little of the intelligence of the criminal world. It is possible that it is, by and large, superior" (p. 7). Certainly, there are criminals with high IQs, but researchers know little about them: they are enigmas.

ENIGMAS

History remembers the great men (and women) of history for their achievements, forgiving or forgetting their indiscretions. Most of these individuals, however, "committed crimes just as grave as those of the men who are now serving sentences in our penitentiaries, and yet these are the men who have given to the world its laws, its philosophies, its literature, its poetry, its art and its music" (Gemmill, 1915, p. 90). In fact, in their times, many of history's greatest thinkers were persecuted and prosecuted, incarcerated and executed. Lange-Eichbaum (1931) notes, "[W]e love most of all to see a genius wearing the martyr's crown" (p. 20). Currie (1974) describes an analogous shift, from genius-as-hero to genius-as-martyr-and-victim. Geniuses often threaten the establishment. They may "treat other great, even sacred interests, inconsiderately . . . trample down many an innocent flower—crush to pieces many an object in its path" (Hegel, 1837/1956, p. 32). After all, revolutionaries, visionaries, and iconoclasts are inherently rebellious; by definition, they challenge the establishment. Shaw (1957) quips, "If a great man could make us understand him, we should hang him" (p. 258). In a similar vein, Rhodes (1932) writes,

> [T]he genius and the criminal type are fundamentally one and the same thing. This is not an original opinion. It has been endorsed for thousands of years by society itself. Society punishes the genius while he lives, even if its laws do not permit it to put him in gaol or execute him. . . . The ordinary man comes to terms with society. The . . . genius will not. Those who will not are, when all is said and done, actual or potential criminals. It is the aim of the genius, although it may not be more than subconscious, to overthrow society and rebuild it upon lines that would bring it into harmony with *him*. (pp. 37, 59, emphasis in original)

The case of Napoleon Bonaparte is illustrative. Simonton (1994) writes that Napoleon's eminence stemmed from a willingness to sanction millions of murders: "Yet, owing to the scope and drama of this homicidal enterprise, Napoleon has gone down in the records as a 'great man'" (p. 312; cf. Lombroso, 1902). This echoes the views of Locke (1689/2002): "Great robbers punish little ones, to keep them in their obedience; but the great ones are rewarded with laurels and triumphs, because they are too big for the weak hands of justice in this world" (p. 81). Crowned in triumphs and laurels, the murderer Napoleon qualified as one of Carlyle's (1841/1966) great heroes, as *the* most eminent man in history (Cattell, 1903), and as the greatest genius the world has ever known (Cox, 1926). He was imprisoned on St. Helena from 1815 until his death in 1821 (Giles, 2001).

Although the public may not conceive of them as such, Socrates, Christ, and Galileo were all criminals. Socrates, one of the most important figures in Western philosophy, was identified as the "most dangerous man in Athens" (Lindsay, 1918, p. x). In 399 BCE, he was tried before a jury of 500 citizens on charges of impiety and corrupting the youth of Athens, found guilty, and executed by poison (Stone, 1988). Jesus of Nazareth was arrested for violating Roman sedition laws in 30 CE, tried before the Jewish Sanhedrin, and transferred to Roman jurisdiction for execution by crucifixion (Winter, 1961). Linder (2002) states, "[N]o other trial in human history has so significantly affected the course of human events." Scientist and mathematician Galileo Galilei is known for his writings on pendulums, the speed of falling bodies, and—in *Dialogue Concerning the Two Chief World Systems* (Galilei, 1632/1953)—the heliocentric model of the solar system. It is his 1633 trial, however, that lionizes him in the mind of the public (Finocchiaro, 1989). Summoned to Rome for trial by the Inquisition, Galileo was arrested, threatened with torture, and forced to recant his claim that the earth revolved around the sun. Legend says that, after recanting, Galileo muttered, "Eppur si muove" (And yet it moves; Brecht, 1966). He was condemned to life imprisonment for suspicion of heresy, and although the sentence was quickly commuted to a relatively comfortable house arrest, Galileo died a heretic and a prisoner in his own home.

As further described in chapter 1, many famous figures in history have been persecuted as criminals (Oleson, 1997). Their ranks include political leaders (e.g., Benazir Bhutto, Mahatma Gandhi, Adolf Hitler, Nelson Mandela, Josef Stalin, and Leon Trotsky), religious leaders (e.g., Joan of Arc, Mani, Martin Luther, and Martin Luther King Jr.), scientists (e.g., Antoine Laurent Lavoisier, Timothy Leary, Wilhelm Reich), and artists (e.g., Fyodor Dostoevsky, Jean Genet, Aleksandr Solzhenitsyn, Henry David Thoreau, and Oscar Wilde). These individuals were geniuses *and* criminals.

In *The Faces of Crime and Genius: The Historical Impact of the Genius-Criminal* (1970), Lipton defines criminal geniuses as satisfying three criteria: their genius and their crime must be unquestionable, their crimes must have been crimes in their own times (not just under contemporary standards), and their imprint on history must be indelible: "it must have mattered that they had lived" (p. 12). Lipton describes eight criminal geniuses (table 1).

Lipton's subject is inherently intriguing. The public is fascinated by both the criminal (Duncan, 1996; Kooistra, 1989) and the genius (Currie, 1974; Murray, 1989). Simultaneously playing upon the public's admiration of the genius and its ambivalence for the outlaw, the criminal genius carries a deep cultural resonance.

There is a celebrity of infamy. It is no coincidence that we are as interested in Al Capone as Albert Einstein, as interested in Ted Bundy as Teddy Roosevelt, and as interested in John Wayne Gacy as John Wayne. . . . [B]oth the genius (a social personification of that which is divine in our human faculties) and the criminal (a social personification of the antisocial and malevolent impulses that psychologist Carl Jung said constitute the

TABLE 1 Criminal geniuses

Name	Description
Gilles de Rais	Classic hero and classic monster
Catherine de Medici	Mistress of genocide
William Dampier	Pirate, writer, scientist
John Law	Convicted murderer, gambler, financial genius
Edward Gibbon Wakefield	Architect of colonialism and kidnapper
Paul Verlaine	Poet and social outcast
O. Henry	Short story writer and embezzler
Jack London	Author and oyster pirate

SOURCE: Drawn from Lipton, 1970.

"shadow archetype") are powerful icons. While they seem different from us, there is something strangely familiar about both the genius and the criminal. In them, we see alienated aspects of ourselves, refined and magnified, and reflected back with a kind of majesty. The genius and the criminal fascinate us, and when a rare individual exists as *both* genius and criminal, we struggle to reconcile his divinity (of genius) with his wickedness (of crime). (Oleson, 2003, pp. 407–408, emphasis in original)

Others have commented upon the divine/diabolical duality. Lipton (1970) describes the genius-criminal as "a man touched in great ways by the fingertips of the gods whose soul was at the same time branded deeply with an animal's mark" (p. 8). Curry (1902) writes, "Geniuses of all the nations bear a striking resemblance in type, and it is so with criminals. The born criminal usually possesses ignoble features, while geniuses possess noble and often almost superhuman features. The criminal is devil-like, the genius God-like" (p. 17). Landy (2012) argues that the master criminal is an analogue of the devil, lending deeper meaning to human experience. Playing upon the tension between the divine and diabolical, a number of authors have examined elites of the criminal world.

CRIMINAL ELITES

Criminal Masterminds: Evil Geniuses of the Underworld (Grieg, 2005) describes 50 criminal geniuses—not creative or scientific geniuses who coincidentally violated the laws of their societies, but offenders who achieved notoriety through the commission of shocking crimes (cf. Bankston, 2007). *Criminal Masterminds (True Crime): Evil Geniuses of the World of Crime* (Williams, Head, & Prooth, 2010) includes 33 of Grieg's masterminds but adds 29 additional offenders and organizes them into different categories. The offenders identified in these books are noteworthy (table 2), but 4 genius criminals merit particular attention: Nathan Leopold, Richard Loeb, Theodore Kaczynski, and Caryl Chessman.

TABLE 2 Criminal masterminds by offense type

Grieg ($n = 50$)		Williams, Head, & Prooth ($n = 62$)	
Offense Category	Offenders	Offense Category	Offenders
Ruthless Robbers	Jonathan Wild	Bank Robbers	Butch Cassidy
	Brinks Mat Robbers		Dillinger
	The Great Train Robbers		Willie "the Actor" Sutton
	Antony "Fats" Pino		Great Train Robbery
	Willie "the Actor" Sutton		Mesrine
			Anthony Pino
Devious Drug Barons	Pablo Escobar	Female Fiends	Countess Bathory
	The Arellano-Felix Brothers		Lucretia Borgia
	George Jung		Belle Guinness
	Howard Marks		Nannie Doss
			Phoolan Devi
			Maria Licciardi
Ingenious Escape Artists	Jacques Mesrine	Fictional Masterminds	Blofeld
	Papillon		Raffles
	Joseph "Whitey" Riordan		Moriarty
	Jack Sheppard		Fantômas
			Hannibal Lecter
			Don Vito Corleone
			Fu Manchu
Unflappable Fraudsters	Frank Abagnale Jr.	Swindlers and Forgers	Victor Lustig
	D. B. Cooper		Elmyr de Hory
	Martin Frankel		Frank Abagnale Jr.
	Elmyr de Hory		Han van Meegeren
	Joyti De-Laurey		Clifford Irving
	Han van Meegeren		Joyti De-Laurey
	Clifford Irving		Martin Frankel
	Count Victor Lustig		Nick Leeson
Cold-Blooded Killers	Charles Manson	Ancient Murderers	Attila the Hun
	Jack Unterweger		Genghis Khan
	The Menendez Brothers		Caligula
	Mark Hoffman		Vlad the Impaler
			Gilles de Rais
			Marquis de Sade
Maverick Mobsters	Al Capone	Organized Crime	The Mafia
	John Gotti		Triads
	Lucky Luciano		Lucky Luciano
	The Kray Twins		Arnold Rothstein
	Meyer Lansky		Benjamin "Bugsy" Siegel
	Dutch Schultz		Dutch Schultz
	Arnold Rothstein		Micky Cohen
	Bugsy Siegel		John Gotti
	Mickey Cohen		The Kray Twins
	Erminia Guiliano		The Blood Brothers
			The Medellin Cartel

(continued)

TABLE 2 *(continued)*

Grieg (*n* = 50)		Williams, Head, & Prooth (*n* = 62)	
Offense Category	Offenders	Offense Category	Offenders
Audacious Outlaws	Butch Cassidy and the Sundance Kid	Murderers, Outlaws, and Thieves	Jack Sheppard
	Bonnie and Clyde		Machine Gun Kelly
	John Dillinger		Bonnie and Clyde
	Charles "Pretty Boy" Floyd		"Pretty Boy" Floyd
	George "Machine Gun" Kelly		Ned Kelly
	Ned Kelly		Charles Manson
Covert Spies	Aldrich Ames	Spies and Double Agents	Mata Hari
	Christopher Boyce and Andrew Daulton Lee		Aldrich Ames
			Klaus Fuchs
	The Cambridge Spies		The Cambridge Spies
	Klaus Fuchs		"Falcon" and "Snowman"
Terrorist Masterminds	Osama bin Laden	Terrorists	Abu Nidal
	Abu Nidal		Baader-Meinhof Gang
	Carlos the Jackal		Osama bin Laden
	Theodore "the Unabomber" Kaczynski		Carlos the Jackal
	Timothy McVeigh		Oklahoma Bomber
			Theodore "the Unabomber" Kaczynski
			Abimael Guzmán

SOURCE: Drawn from Grieg, 2005, and Williams, Head, & Prooth, 2010.

Nathan Leopold and Richard Loeb

Nathan Leopold and Richard Loeb were tried for murder in "the trial of the century" (Geis & Bienen, 1998; Higdon, 1999), which "stirred the entire English speaking world as no other [trial] in modern times" (McKernan, 1989, p. 1). Both sons of Chicago millionaires, Leopold and Loeb were child prodigies: Loeb graduated from the University of Michigan with a bachelor degree at 17 and Leopold graduated from the University of Chicago at 18. Both were brilliant: Loeb had an IQ of 160, and Leopold's IQ (210) surpassed that of Albert Einstein (Oleson, 2003). Loeb was fascinated by crime. "He fantasized about being a master criminal. He often imagined himself as the 'mastermind' of a gang of expert crooks" (Kurland, 1994, p. 214). In addition to ornithology and linguistics, Leopold was keenly interested in philosophy. In particular, he was fascinated by Nietzsche's (1911) concept of the *übermensch,* and believed that Loeb, his lover, was its living embodiment. On May 24, 1924, they set out to commit "the perfect crime." They lured 14-year-old Bobby Franks into an automobile, killed him with a chisel, disfigured his face with acid, and then concealed his body in a culvert. They sent a ransom note to the dead boy's father. They nearly got away with it too; police cracked the case only because

FIGURE 1. Nathan Leopold, Richard Loeb, and attorney Clarence Darrow in the Chicago courtroom. Source: Photofest.

Leopold's eyeglasses (constructed with a new kind of hinge) had slipped out of his pocket and were located near the body.

After their arrest, both young men confessed, characterizing the murder as "an experiment" (Proper, 2004), and the Illinois state's attorney announced that he had "a hanging case" (Higdon, 1999, p. 112). Leopold and Loeb were represented by Clarence Darrow, the "attorney for the damned" (Darrow, 2012), whose remarkable closing argument filled 11 hours and spanned 3 days (figure 1). Alan Dershowitz wrote, "No lawyer, indeed no civilized person, should go through life without reading . . . Darrow's eloquent defense of young human life" (in McKernan, 1989, p. i). When Darrow finished, the judge was weeping and the stricken courtroom stood in silence for two minutes.

It worked: the jury spared the lives of Leopold and Loeb. Both young men were sentenced to life imprisonment for murder plus 99 years for kidnapping (Higdon, 1999). Loeb was murdered in prison, but in 1958, after learning a total of 37 languages, organizing the Joliet Prison library, writing his autobiography (Leopold,

1958), and spearheading a prison malaria project, Leopold was granted a special parole. He immigrated to Puerto Rico, married, earned his master's degree, and established a foundation for emotionally retarded young people. When he died in 1971, his brain was harvested and studied for clues to genius (Oleson, 2003).

Theodore Kaczynski

Theodore Kaczynski (figure 2), better known as "the Unabomber," was "America's most-wanted serial killer" (Douglas & Olshaker, 1996). Kaczynski's childhood IQ was 167 (Chase, 2003). Like Leopold and Loeb, Kaczynski was a prodigy: he enrolled at Harvard at 16 (Gibbs, Lacayo, Morrow, Smolowe, & Van Biema, 1996). By 20, he had completed his bachelor's degree in mathematics and went on to earn his PhD at the University of Michigan before accepting a teaching post at the University of California, Berkeley. But on June 30, 1969, without explanation, Kaczynski tendered his resignation and moved to the outskirts of Lincoln, Montana. For 25 years, like a modern Thoreau (Oleson, 2005), Kaczynski lived in a primitive 10-by-12-foot shack. There, on the periphery of society, Kaczynski's reclusiveness curdled into misanthropy: he vandalized the property of noisy neighbors, set booby traps in the woods, and fired a rifle at a passing helicopter. In the fall of 1977, Kaczynski wrote in his diary, "I think that perhaps I could now kill someone" (Chase, 2003, p. 206). Then, beginning with a package bomb delivered to the University of Illinois, Chicago, in 1978 (Duffy, 1996), Kaczynski waged a 17-year campaign of terror that involved 16 more bombs, killed 3 victims, wounded 23 others, and cost the US government $50 million in "the nation's longest and most costly manhunt" (Douglas & Olshaker, 1996).

For years, the Unabomber's motives were unclear, but with the controversial publication of the Unabomber manifesto, *Industrial Society and Its Future* (Kaczynski, 2010), it became clear that the author was a Luddite who blamed computers and technology for the evils of modern society (Yancy, 2007). The Unabomber case was cracked because Kaczynski's brother, David, recognized phrases from Ted's letters in the manifesto and contacted authorities. When the FBI raided Kaczynski's shack in April of 1996, they discovered a trove of damning evidence: notebooks filled with sketches of bombs, materials for making bombs, a partially constructed pipe bomb, a carbon copy of the manifesto, and a handwritten diary detailing the Unabomber attacks. On April 15, 1996, Kaczynski appeared on the covers of both *Time* and *U.S. News and World Report,* his bedraggled image pasted below headlines that read "Twisted Genius" and "Odyssey of a Mad Genius."

The legal proceedings that followed were convoluted. Mello (2000) characterizes them as "the non-trial of the century." Kaczynski's court-appointed federal defenders believed that a mental-health defense was the only way to save their client's life (Luban, 2005). This was unacceptable to Kaczynski, however, even though it meant a death sentence: Kaczynski was terrified that his campaign against technology would be discounted as the work of a "sickie" (Mello, 2000, p. 452). Thus,

FIGURE 2. Theodore Kaczynski escorted by law enforcement agents. Source: AP Images.

when the judge would not allow him to represent himself, Kaczynski agreed to a coerced plea bargain—accepting responsibility for the Unabomber crimes—rather than accept the mental-illness defense foisted upon him by his lawyers. Kaczynski was sentenced to eight life sentences and remains incarcerated in ADX Florence, the federal supermax prison in Colorado.

Caryl Chessman

Convicted in 1948 of robbery, kidnapping, and attempted rape, Caryl Chessman (figure 3) was sentenced to death under California's "Little Lindbergh" law (authorizing capital punishment in kidnapping cases if victims suffered bodily harm; Kunstler, 1961). When he was convicted, Los Angeles newspapers gleefully reported that the "criminal genius" had been sentenced to death (Machlin & Woodfield, 1962). Chessman initially scored a 178 on an IQ test, although later IQ tests produced scores in the 130–140 range, but Chessman was unquestionably intelligent. From his cell on death row, he produced four books (1954, 1955, 1957, 1960) and managed his appeals for nearly 12 years. He insisted that he was not the "Red-Light Bandit" and maintained that he had been framed for robbing bookies who paid protection money to the Los Angeles police. While on death row, Chessman became a cause célèbre among death-penalty abolitionists: Brigitte Bardot, Marlon Brando, Aldous Huxley, Albert Schweitzer, and many others took up his cause. A Brazilian industrialist

FIGURE 3. Promotional photograph of Caryl Chessman.
Source: Photofest.

collected more than 2 million signatures demanding mercy; 60,000 more signatures came from Uruguay. Nevertheless, Chessman was executed in San Quentin's gas chamber on May 2, 1960. A 60-day stay of execution that might have changed the course of his appeal arrived moments too late.

Leopold, Loeb, Kaczynski, and Chessman are emblematic criminal geniuses, possessing superior intelligence and psychopathic personality traits, but they are not unique. Blanco (1996) reports that 7% of Cambridge University students regularly engage in criminal activity "to supplement their grants or their allowances from pater" (p. 7). Numerous physicians and nurses, generally intelligent and highly educated, have been convicted of murdering their patients (Iserson, 2002; Leaves-

TABLE 3 Select criminal geniuses from history

Offender	Description	Key Scholarship
Frank Abagnale	Forger, fraud, and later, FBI consultant, with 136 IQ (Adams, 1980)	Abagnale & Redding, 1980
Amy Bishop	University of Alabama professor with 180 IQ (Dewan, 2010), murdered three colleagues during departmental meeting	Keefe, 2013
Edward Bunker	Robber, drug dealer, and forger, as well as screenwriter and novelist; played Mr. Blue in *Reservoir Dogs*	Bunker, 2000
Caryl Chessman	"The Red-Light Bandit" and death-row novelist became a cause célèbre for death-penalty abolition	Bisbort, 2006 Chessman, 1954 Chessman, 1955 Chessman, 1957 Hamm, 2001 Kunstler, 1961 Machlin & Woodfield, 1962 Parker, 1975
William Coday	Polyglot murderer	Sands, 2009
Robert Ferrante	University of Pittsburgh professor, wife murderer	Botelho, 2014
Daniel Gajdusek	Nobel laureate with 180 IQ, child molester	McCarthy, 1997
Karoly Hajdu (aka Charlotte Bach)	Transgender con man	Wheen, 2004
Jim Jones	Jamestown cult leader, with IQ between 115 and 118	Reiterman & Jacobs, 1982
Theodore Kaczynski	"The Unabomber"	Chase, 2003 Douglas & Olshaker, 1996 Finnegan, 1998 Gibbs, Lacayo, Morrow, Smolowe, & Van Biema, 1996 Graysmith, 1997 Kaczynski, 2010 Luban, 2005 Mello, 1999 Waits & Shors, 1999
Ivar Kreuger	"The Match King" (industrialist-financier-tycoon), fraud and swindler	Shaplen, 1960
Timothy Leary	Harvard professor, sentenced to 10 years for drugs, escaped from prison, described by President Richard Nixon as "the most dangerous man alive" (Snider, 1990, p. 49)	Leary, 1983
Paul Calder Le Roux	Computer programmer, cartel kingpin involved in smuggling narcotics, gold, arms, and in contract murders; DEA informant	Ratliffe, 2016

(continued)

TABLE 3 *(continued)*

Offender	Description	Key Scholarship
Nathan Leopold and Richard Loeb	"Trial of the century" for murder of Bobby Franks	Baatz, 2008
		Darrow, 1924
		Fass, 1993
		Higdon, 1999
		Leopold, 1958
		McKernan, 1989
		Sellers, 1926
		Theodore, 2007
Bernard Madoff	Fraud who ran $65 billion pyramid scheme	LeBor, 2009
George L. Leslie	Architect, safecracker, and "King of the Bank Robbers"	Asbury, 1928
		Conway, 2009
William Chester Minor	Surgeon and contributor to the *Oxford English Dictionary* confined in Broadmoor Hospital for murder	Winchester, 1998
Herman Webster Mudgett (aka H. H. Holmes)	19th-century con man and serial killer who confessed to 23 murders	Larson, 2003
		Lombroso, 1902
		Schechter, 1994
John Nash	Nobel laureate, schizophrenic subject of *A Beautiful Mind,* arrested for indecent exposure in 1954	Nasar, 1998
George I. Norman Jr.	Swindler, bank fraud, fugitive	Solotaroff, 1997
Arnold Rothstein	Loan shark, bookmaker, thief, racketeer	Pietrusza, 2003
Jimmy Savile	BBC celebrity with a 150 IQ, serial sexual abuser and rapist	BBC, 2014
		Greer & McLaughlin, 2013
Sylvan "Cherry Hill Fats" Sconick	Fraud, thief	Adleman, 1973
Joseph Silver	Burglar, gun runner, jewel thief, and human trafficker	Van Onselen, 2007
Edward Snowden	NSA contractor with 145+ IQ, leaked classified documents about US surveillance programs, described as "the most wanted man in the world"	Bamford, 2014
Garrett Brock Trapnell	Bank robber and aircraft hijacker	Asinof, 1876
George Trepal	"Mensa Murderer"	Good & Goreck, 1995
		Trepal v. State, 1993
Alan Turing	Cryptanalyst who cracked Nazi Enigma device, namesake of the Turing test in artificial intelligence; convicted of homosexuality	Hodges, 1983
		Leavitt, 2006
Ross Ulbricht	Creator of darknet Silk Road, hacker, money launderer, drug trafficker, contracted hit men to carry out murders; sentenced to life in prison without parole	Bearman & Hanuka, 2015a
		Bearman & Hanuka, 2015b
John Webster	Harvard professor, murderer	Stone, 1990
Jonathan Wild	"The Thief-Taker General" who commanded a posse of thief catchers, the eighteenth-century equivalent of Britain's Criminal Investigative Division, and who used this role as a front to orchestrate a vast network of criminal activity	Howson, 1970
Adam Worth	"The Napoleon of Crime" (master thief)	Macintyre, 1997

ley, 2010). History is peppered with offenders who possess superior intelligence (Sturtz, 1995). Table 3 identifies a number of them.

Although research suggests that the average IQ for serial killers is only 94.7 (Aamodt, 2014), many infamous mass murderers and serial killers possess superior intelligence:

IQ 170: "Boston Strangler" Albert DeSalvo (Aamodt, 2015)

IQ 170: "Dating Game Killer" Rodney Alcala (Miller, 2010)

IQ 160: Charlene Gallego (Van Hoffman, 1990)

IQ 152: Caroll Edward Cole (Calder, 2013)

IQ 148: Wakefield massacre killer Michael "Mucko" McDermott (Haskell, 2002)

IQ 147: Andrew Cunanan (Aamodt, 2015)

IQ 145: Cannibal killer Jeffrey Dahmer (Aamodt, 2015)

IQ 136: "Co-Ed Killer" Edmund Kemper (a childhood IQ score; also scored 145 as adult according to Russell, 2002)

IQ 130: Gary Heidnik (Aamodt, 2015)

IQ 130: Harvey Glatman (Aamodt, 2015)

IQ 126: Oklahoma City bomber Timothy McVeigh (Michel & Herbeck, 2001)

IQ 126: David Copeland (Aamodt, 2015; alternatively reported as IQ 136 by Calder, 2013)

IQ 124: Ted Bundy (Aamodt, 2015)

IQ 118: "Killer Clown" John Wayne Gacy (Calder, 2013)

IQ 118: David "Son of Sam" Berkowitz (Calder, 2013)

In their study of 77 death-row defendants, Hanlon, Rubin, Jensen, and Daoust (2010) found that murderers who killed more than one victim scored significantly higher on IQ tests than those with a single victim. Genocide might also be associated with above-average intelligence. At the 1945 Nuremberg trials, all 21 defendants who completed an IQ test had above-average IQ scores, ranging from 106 to 143, averaging 128 (Gilbert, 1950). Hitler is purported to have had an IQ of 141 (Trost & Kravetsky, 2013).

Perhaps the most intelligent human being ever to live was a criminal. Child prodigy William James Sidis had an IQ score estimated between 250 and 300 (Wallace, 1986), a score between 10 and 13.3 standard deviations above the mean. Statistically speaking, even an IQ of 200—far more common than an IQ of 250—should occur in only 1 in 76 billion people. In comparison, there are only 7.3 billion people in the world. Published tables of the normal statistical distribution typically extend to only four standard deviations and cannot be used to calculate the frequency of 250–300 IQ scores, but it is clear that—if they were anywhere close to accurate—

Sidis's scores represent a superhuman intelligence (Colman, 1993). He completed primary school in six months (Montour, 1977). At 3 years old, he learned Latin and Greek, teaching himself. By 6, he also knew Russian, French, German, Hebrew, Turkish, and Armenian. At 8, he passed the MIT admissions test, developed a base-12 logarithm table, and invented a universal language—Vendergood. He passed the Harvard admissions test at nine, but the university did not admit him until he was 11; he graduated cum laude at 15. At 21, Sidis was arrested in Boston for his involvement in a 1919 May Day riot. Most of the rioters received a sentence of 6 months, but the judge—holding Sidis responsible for the disturbance—imposed a sentence of 18 months at hard labor, 6 months for rioting and a year for assaulting an officer (Wallace, 1986). Sidis appealed, was cleared, and dropped out of sight. In obscurity, he lived a double life. Hiding from the press (e.g., Manley, 1937) in a series of menial jobs, Sidis wrote several books, even anticipating the existence of black holes 14 years before the publication of the pioneering work on the subject. He died—destitute, unemployed, and living in a boarding house—in 1944 (Wallace, 1986).

MYTHS

Long before the advent of intelligence testing or the phenomenon of "crimes of the century," people told stories about criminal genius. Around the world, societies recounted myths about rebellious gods who opposed patriarchal authority and orthodoxy (Camus, 1956; Walker, 1983). Lévi-Strauss (1955) claims that myths are universal because they express and mediate antagonistic concepts; Kierkegaard suggests that myths are timeless and universal because they provide externalized representations of ongoing internal relationships (in May, 1975). Perhaps this is why "[f]iction lives longer than fact" (Van Ash & Rohmer, 1972, p. 3).

The story of Lucifer and the rebel angels, enshrined in Milton's *Paradise Lost* (1667/1998), captures the crux of criminal genius. In Milton's epic, the archangel Lucifer is "great in power, in favour, and pre-eminence" (ll. 5.660–5.661). Lucifer is ambitious because he is great, and when God favors Christ (the Son) over the angels, Lucifer suffers a sense of "injur'd merit" (l. 1.98). His arrogance erupts when God decrees that the angels should glorify the Son. Lucifer mocks his fellow angels with scorn: "Will ye submit your necks, and choose to bend / The supple knee?" (ll. 5.787–5.788). Remarkably, a third of the angels side with Lucifer, waging war in Heaven for three days before being cast out. Plunging into Hell, Lucifer is transformed into Satan, the nemesis of God (figure 4). Banished, Satan embraces his exile: "Better to reign in Hell, than serve in Heav'n" (l. 1.263). Because he cannot defeat God, he attacks God's creation. Of course, tempting Adam and Eve in the Garden of Eden is abhorrent to Satan, even while damned, but Satan does so because he is so desperate to defy God. He seeks to ease his own suffering by inflicting misery.

Of course, "[l]ong before Satan, [the ancient Greeks] created a touching and

FIGURE 4. Gustave Doré, *The Fall of Satan*, from John Milton's *Paradise Lost*.

noble image of the Rebel and gave us the most perfect myth of the intelligence in revolt" (Camus, 1956, p. 26). According to legend, Prometheus and the other Titans (gigantic immortals who predated the Olympian gods) were denied status as gods and imprisoned beneath the earth. After Prometheus stole fire from heaven and shared the secret with mankind, he was chained to a mountain where each day his regenerating liver was torn out and consumed by an eagle (Griffith, 1983). However, the theme of "intelligence in revolt" is limited neither to classical myth nor to Abrahamic tradition. The criminal genius pervades literature and film to the current day. Table 4 identifies some representative characters.

MAD SCIENTISTS AND MASTER CRIMINALS

In 1818, approximately 150 years after the publication of *Paradise Lost*, Shelley reinvented the myth of Prometheus in *Frankenstein; or, The Modern Prometheus*. Her

TABLE 4 Select representations of the criminal genius in literature and film

Character	Bibliography	Filmography
Frank Abagnale Jr.	Abagnale & Redding, 1980	Spielberg, 2002
Harrison Bergeron	Vonnegut, 1968	Pittman, 1995
Ernst Stavro Blofeld	Fleming, 1961	Gilbert, 1967
	Fleming, 1963	Glen, 1981
	Fleming, 1964	Hamilton, 1971
		Hunt, 1969
		Kershner, 1983
		Mendes, 2015
		Young, 1963
		Young, 1965
John Doe	N/A	Fincher, 1995
Fantômas˙	Souvestre & Allain, 1916	Feuillade, 1913a
	Souvestre & Allain, 1917a	Feuillade, 1913b
	Souvestre & Allain, 1917b	Feuillade, 1913c
	Souvestre & Allain, 1918a	Feuillade, 1914a
	Souvestre & Allain, 1918b	Feuillade, 1914b
Dr. Victor Frankenstein	Shelley, 1869	Branagh, 1994
		Whale, 1931
		Whale, 1935
Dr. Fu-Manchu	Rohmer, 1913/1997	Adreon & Witney, 1956
	Rohmer, 1916	Brabin, 1932
	Rohmer, 1931	Haggard, 1980
	Rohmer, 1936	Sharp, 1965
	Rohmer, 1960	Witney & English, 1940
John Galt	Rand, 1957	Johansson, 2011
		Manera, 2014
		Putch, 2012
Gordon Gecko	N/A	Stone, 1987
Auric Goldfinger	Fleming, 1959	Hamilton, 1964
Bridget Gregory (aka Wendy Kroy)	N/A	Dahl, 1994
Cyrus "the Virus" Grissom	N/A	West, 1997
Hans Gruber	N/A	McTiernan, 1988
Simon Gruber	N/A	McTiernan, 1995
HAL 9000	Clarke, 1968	Hyams, 1984
	Clarke, 1982	Kubrick, 1968
Billy "Dr. Horrible"	N/A	Whedon, 2008
Eleanor Iselin	Condon, 1959	Demme, 2004
		Frankenheimer, 1962
Henry Jekyll	Stevenson, 1886	Fleming, 1941
		Frears, 1996
		Mamoulian, 1931
		Robertson, 1920
Johnny	N/A	Leigh, 1993

John "Jigsaw" Kramer	N/A	Bousman, 2005
		Bousman, 2006
		Bousman, 2007
		Greutert, 2009
		Greutert, 2010
		Hackl, 2008
		Wan, 2004
Kurtz	Conrad, 1902	Coppola, 1979
		Roeg, 1993
Hans Landa	N/A	Tarantino, 2009
Dr. Hannibal "the Cannibal" Lecter	Harris, 1981	Demme, 1991
	Harris, 1988	Fuller, 2013
	Harris, 1999	Mann, 1986
	Harris, 2007	Scott, 2001
		Ratner, 2002
		Webber, 2007
Nathan Leopold and Richard Loeb†	Leopold, 1958	Kalin, 1992
Dr. Mabuse	Jacques, 1923	Chabrol, 1990
		Lang, 1922
		Lang, 1933
		Lang, 1960
		Reinl, 1966
Dr. Moreau	Wells, 1896	Frankenheimer, 1996
		Kenton, 1932
		Taylor, 1977
Dexter Morgan	Lindsay, 2004	Manos, 2006
	Lindsay, 2005	
	Lindsay, 2007	
	Lindsay, 2009	
	Lindsay, 2010	
	Lindsay, 2011	
	Lindsay, 2013	
Professor James Moriarty	Doyle, 1892–1893/2005	Doherty, 2013
	Doyle, 1897–1915/2006	McGuigan, 2010
		Neill, 1942
		Neill, 1945
		Ritchie, 2011
		Theakston, 2002
		Werker, 1939
Dr. Julius No	Fleming, 1958	Young, 1962
John Roe O'Neill	Herbert, 1982	N/A
Elijah Price	N/A	Shyamalan, 2000
Arthur J. Raffles	Hornung, 1899	Irving, 1917
	Hornung, 1901	Wood, 1939
	Hornung, 1905	
	Hornung, 1909	

(continued)

TABLE 4 *(continued)*

Character	Bibliography	Filmography
Rodion Raskolnikov	Dostoevsky, 1866/1950	Golan, 2002
		Sargent, 1998
		von Sternberg, 1935
Thomas Ripley	Highsmith, 1955	Cavani, 2002
	Highsmith, 1970	Clément, 1960
	Highsmith, 1974	Minghella, 1999
	Highsmith, 1980	Spottiswoode, 2005
	Highsmith, 1992	Wenders, 1977
Rotwang	N/A	Lang, 1928
Lisbeth Salander	Lagercrantz, 2015	Alfredson, 2010a
	Larsson, 2008	Alfredson, 2010b
	Larsson, 2009a	Fincher, 2011
	Larsson, 2009b	Oplev, 2009
Brandon Shaw and Charles Granillo[†]	Hamilton, 1929	Hitchcock, 1948; characters renamed Brandon and Philip
Tony Soprano	N/A	Chase, 1999
Keyser Söze	N/A	Singer, 1995
Judd Steiner and Arthur Straus[†]	Levin, 1956	Fleischer, 1959
	Levin, 1959	
Dr. Strangelove	N/A	Kubrick, 1964
Walter Hartwell White Sr., aka. "Heisenberg"	N/A	Gilligan, 2008
Whit Whittier	Chessman, 1954	Sears, 1955
Henry Winter	Tartt, 1992	N/A

NOTE: The list of books and films in this table is illustrative, not comprehensive. Many of the film characters in this table were also identified by Leistedt and Linkowski (2014) as cinematic depictions of psychopaths (though many of these "elite psychopaths" deviate from actual clinical etiology of psychopathy). Despite the mystique of the elite psychopath, verbal intelligence is inversely related to psychopathy (DeLisi, Vaughn, Beaver, & Wright, 2010).

* The first five Fantômas novels are collected as Ballantine's *Fantômas* (Allain & Souvestre, 1986); the five Fantômas films by Feuillade are collected on Kino Lorber's 2010 DVD, *Fantômas: The Complete Saga*.

† The fictional characters in *Rope* and *Compulsion* are based on real-life offenders Nathan Leopold and Richard Loeb.

novel recounts Dr. Victor Frankenstein's creation—and rejection—of a creature assembled from cadavers and electricity. It is explicit in its allusions to *Paradise Lost*. When the creature addresses Frankenstein, it explains that it would have been Frankenstein's Adam but is instead his "fallen angel" (Shelley 1818/1869, p. 78), his "demon" (p. 23). The creature's voice could very well be that of Lucifer, accusing God:

> I am malicious because I am miserable. Am I not shunned and hated by all mankind?
> You, my creator, would tear me to pieces and triumph; remember that, and tell me

why I should pity man more than he pities me? . . . Shall I respect man when he contemns me? Let him live with me in the interchange of kindness, and instead of injury I would bestow every benefit upon him with tears of gratitude at his acceptance. But that cannot be; the human senses are insurmountable barriers to our union. Yet mine shall not be the submission of abject slavery. I will revenge my injuries; if I cannot inspire love, I will cause fear. (pp. 114–115)

Bloom (2004) also links the monster to the figure of Satan: "Kierkegaard remarks that Satan's despair is absolute because Satan, as pure spirit, is pure consciousness, and for Satan (and all men in his predicament) every increase in consciousness is an increase in despair. Frankenstein's desperate creature attains the state of pure spirit through his extraordinary situation and is racked by a consciousness in which every thought is a fresh disease" (p. 9). Bloom notes that "the monster is *more human* than his creator. This nameless being, as much a Modern Adam as his creator is a Modern Prometheus, is more lovable than his creator and more hateful, more to be pitied and more to be feared" (p. 4, emphasis in original). Like Milton's Lucifer, the monster in *Frankenstein* is sympathetic and intelligible. In contrast, Dr. Frankenstein is inscrutable and, in many ways, villainous. Victor Frankenstein, a "godlike yet tormented genius" (Stiles, 2009, p. 322), cleared the way for generations of mad scientists (Haynes, 2016; Skal, 1998). Classic examples include Dr. Moreau (Wells, 1896) and Henry Jekyll (Stevenson, 1886), but the genre extends to criminally minded scientists such as Dr. Mabuse (Jacques, 1923), Dr. Fu-Manchu (Rohmer, 1913/1997), Ernst Stavro Blofeld (Fleming, 1961), Fantômas (Souvestre & Allain, 1916), Professor Moriarty (Doyle, 1892–1893/2005), Walter White (Gilligan, 2008), and Dr. Hannibal Lecter (Harris, 1981).

Novelist Charles Stross (2006) identifies Dr. Mabuse as the first literary supervillain. A psychologist, hypnotist, master of disguise, and archcriminal, Mabuse does little directly; rather, he orchestrates a gang of criminal agents who operate as his principals. His crimes include counterfeiting and manipulating the stock market. Brilliant and manipulative, Mabuse hypnotizes, blackmails, and deceives others, using mind control to make them cooperate with his nefarious schemes. Although the character of Mabuse never achieved the name recognition in the United States that it did in Germany (Kalat, 2001), Fritz Lang's trio of Mabuse films placed the character (figure 5) among the ranks of leading mad scientists (Mack, 2012).

Rohmer's Chinese archvillain, Dr. Fu-Manchu, has a "giant intellect" (Rohmer, 1913/1997, p. 13) and holds doctoral degrees from four western universities including Heidelberg, the Sorbonne, and Edinburgh (Rohmer, 1960). As an agent (and later, leader) of the Si-Fan, a secret criminal network involved in drug trafficking and white slavery, Fu-Manchu is "the yellow peril incarnate" (Rohmer, 1913/1997, p. 13). He frequently employs unusual weapons to murder his enemies: his secret army of

FIGURE 5. Rudolf Klein-Rogge as Dr. Mabuse, from *The Testament of Dr. Mabuse.*
Source: Photofest.

agents, poisonous snakes, spiders, or bacteria. He was also a fantastically popular character (Van Ash & Rohmer, 1972): between 1913 and 1959, 13 different Fu-Manchu novels were published; the franchise was continued even after Rohmer's death; and the character spawned comic strips, comic books, radio programs, more than a dozen feature films (figure 6), and a television series.

The French archvillain Fantômas has much in common with Mabuse and Fu-Manchu. He, too, commands an invisible army of spies and street criminals—"Apaches"—who carry out his crimes. He, too, is a master of disguise. Unlike Mabuse, however, the diabolical Fantômas engages directly in crime. He *enjoys* blood on his hands. In Allain and Souvestre's novels, the sociopathic Fantômas replaces perfume with sulfuric acid in department stores, releases plague-infected rats on an ocean liner, and strips the gold from the dome of the Hôtel National des Invalides. A darling of the surrealist movement (Walz, 2000), Fantômas appeared in comic strips, radio programs, silent and feature films (figure 7), and television programs.

Ernst Stavro Blofeld (figure 8) is the best known of the James Bond villains. Stross (2006) traces his literary origins to Mabuse, while Mack (2012) traces his beginnings to Fu-Manchu. Whatever his pedigree, Blofeld is a brilliant master

FIGURE 6. Christopher Lee as Dr. Fu-Manchu, from *The Face of Fu-Manchu*. Source: Photofest.

criminal who leads a global crime organization known as SPECTRE (SPecial Executive for Counterintelligence, Terrorism, Revenge, and Extortion), in which he is known as Number One.

In the films *From Russia with Love* and *Thunderball*, Blofeld's face is not shown. Instead, the camera focuses on the villain's trademark white cat. In later films, Blofeld's face is revealed, although—ostensibly through surgical reconstructions—the actors portraying the character change from film to film. Like Fantômas and Mabuse, Blofeld is capable of radically changing his appearance, gaining or losing hundreds of pounds and undergoing radical plastic surgeries. What does not change, however, is Blofeld's determination to destroy his nemesis, James Bond, and to seize world domination. Blofeld represents not mere criminality, but primordial evil:

FIGURE 7. Fantômas in promotional poster.

> One is strongly tempted to say that such schemes are totally absurd and such crimi-
> nals quite as totally divorced from real super-criminals like those of the Cosa Nostra.
> But this is of course precisely the point: Blofeld, Dr. No, and Hugo Drax belong to a
> far more ancient organization than the Cosa Nostra. They are members of the syndi-
> cate of evil magicians and sorcerers, witches and warlocks who have appeared in
> myths and fairy-tales since the beginning of time. Their colleagues are not the likes
> of Vito Genovese and Joe Bananas but Mephistopheles and Loki and Sauron, the evil
> wizard of Tolkien's *Lord of the Rings*. (Carpenter, 1967, p. 83)

Blofeld is the exemplar for a league of evil film geniuses that followed. Indeed, the
figure of Blofeld has become so inextricably tied to the stereotype of the criminal
genius that the character was parodied as "Dr. Evil" in the *Austin Powers* spy com-
edies (Roach, 1997, 1999, 2002)—down to his Nehru-style suit and his coddled
hairless cat, Mr. Bigglesworth.

Professor Moriarty (figure 9), the enigmatic nemesis of Sherlock Holmes,
appears in only two of Arthur Conan Doyle's stories, but he is succinctly painted
as a brilliant and exceedingly dangerous figure. In *The Valley of Fear* (Doyle, 1887–
1915/2006), Holmes describes Moriarty as

> [t]he greatest schemer of all time, the organizer of every deviltry, the controlling
> brain of the underworld, a brain which might have made or marred the destiny of

FIGURE 8. Donald Pleasence as Ernst Stavro Blofeld, from *You Only Live Twice*.
Source: Photofest.

FIGURE 9. Sidney Paget, Professor Moriarty,
from *The Strand* magazine.

nations—that's the man! But so aloof is he from general suspicion, so immune from criticism, so admirable is his management and self-effacement, that for those very words that you have just uttered he could hale you to a court and emerge with your year's pension as a solatium for his wounded character. Is he not the celebrated author of *The Dynamics of an Asteroid,* a book which ascends to such rarefied heights of pure mathematics that it is said that there was no man in the scientific press capable of criticizing it? (p. 636)

In "The Final Problem" (1893/2005), Doyle provides his readers with additional information. When Dr. Watson explains that he has never heard of Moriarty, Holmes exclaims,

The man pervades London, and no one has heard of him. That's what put him on a pinnacle in the records of crime. . . . He is a man of good birth and excellent education, endowed by nature with a phenomenal mathematical faculty. At the age of twenty-one he wrote a treatise upon the binomial theorem, which has had a European vogue. On the strength of it he won the mathematical chair at one of our smaller universities, and had, to all appearances, a most brilliant career before him. But the man had hereditary tendencies of the most diabolical kind. A criminal strain ran in his blood, which, instead of being modified, was increased and rendered infinitely more dangerous by his extraordinary mental powers. Dark rumours gathered round him in the university town, and eventually he was compelled to resign his chair and to come down to London, where he set up as an army coach. (p. 718)

Holmes compares Moriarty to a dangerous spider that lies motionless at the center of a web. He confesses that his own horror at Moriarty's crimes is dwarfed by his admiration for the ex-professor's mental ability, and he admits that in Moriarty he has met an intellectual equal. Like Raffles, the gentleman thief (Hornung 1899, 1901, 1905, 1909), Moriarty is an inversion of Holmes. He is the consulting criminal to Holmes's consulting detective:

> He is the Napoleon of crime, Watson. He is the organizer of half that is evil and of nearly all that is undetected in this great city. He is a genius, a philosopher, an abstract thinker. He has a brain of the first order. . . . He does little himself. He only plans. But his agents are numerous and splendidly organized. Is there a crime to be done, a paper to be abstracted, we will say, a house to be rifled, a man to be removed—the word is passed to the professor, the matter is organized and carried out. The agent may be caught. In that case money is found for his bail or his defence. But the central power which uses the agent is never caught—never so much as suspected. (Doyle, 1892–1893/2005, p. 719)

Some Holmes scholars (e.g., Starrett, 1943) believe that Arthur Conan Doyle modeled Moriarty on Adam Worth (Macintyre, 1997); others on the vituperative astronomer, Simon Newcomb (Schaefer, 1993), or Carl Friedrich Gauss, who *did* write a paper on the dynamics of an asteroid (Gauss, 1907/1963). In *The Valley of Fear* (Doyle, 1887–1915/2006, p. 653), Doyle himself contrasts Moriarty with Jonathan Wild, an eighteenth-century master thief characterized as "the world's first super-criminal" (Howson, 1970).

Since their introduction in 1887, the 56 short stories and 4 novels featuring Sherlock Holmes have proven to be enduringly popular. "[T]he idea of Sherlock Holmes has become far larger, and now means far more, than the letter of the texts that inspired it" (Barnes, 2004, p. 8). Indeed, Holmes is the world's most frequently portrayed movie character (*Guinness World Records News,* 2012). As the oeuvre's central villain, Professor Moriarty also looms as a preeminent criminal genius in the public imagination.

Walter "Heisenberg" White (figure 10) is another scientist who embraces crime. When viewers of *Breaking Bad* (Gilligan, 2008) first meet Walter White, he is a

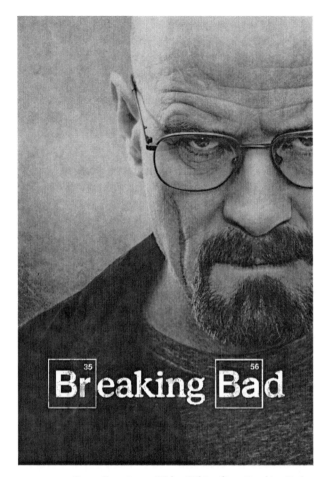

FIGURE 10. Bryan Cranston as Walter White, from *Breaking Bad*.
Source: Photofest.

meek high school chemistry teacher who works part-time at a car wash to provide
for his family. But when he is diagnosed with inoperable lung cancer, something
changes in White. He abruptly quits his car-wash job and contacts a former student who operates as a small-time drug dealer, offering to use his knowledge of
chemistry to produce methamphetamine. White, after all, was a graduate of Cal
Tech and—before choosing his life as a high school teacher and family man—
worked on X-ray crystallography research that earned a Nobel Prize and made two
of his colleagues into science millionaires. White's "blue sky" meth is 99.1% pure
and is highly sought after. Throughout five seasons of *Breaking Bad*, protagonist

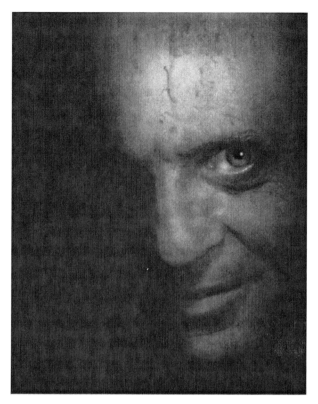

FIGURE 11. Anthony Hopkins as Dr. Hannibal Lecter, from
Hannibal. Source: Photofest.

Walter White changes from a laboratory nerd who looks like *The Simpsons'* Ned
Flanders into a diabolical narcotics kingpin. He transforms himself from a man
who is frightened of life—who feels victimized by life—into a ruthless opponent
with nothing to lose, a man who boasts that he is not afraid of danger: "I *am* the
danger!" Heir to the throne of Mabuse and Fantômas, White lies and manipulates
like a sociopath; he operates clandestine drug labs, steals laboratory equipment
and precursor chemicals, launders money, plants a car bomb, blows up a drug
lord's headquarters, kidnaps, allows the girlfriend of his partner to die in front of
his eyes, and kills business associates as well as his enemies—he even poisons an
innocent child.

The American Film Institute (AFI) selected Hannibal "the Cannibal" Lecter
(figure 11) as its number one villain of all time, eclipsing iconic figures like Darth
Vader, the Wicked Witch of the West, and *2001*'s HAL 9000 (AFI, 2003). In 2010,

Entertainment Weekly ranked Lecter at number 8 in its list of the 100 greatest characters from the last 20 years (Vary, 2010). A brilliant and urbane physician who is also a cannibalistic serial killer, Lecter occupies only a small, oblique role in Thomas Harris's *Red Dragon* (1981), but he assumes greater significance in the books that followed. Along the way, Lecter transforms from an organized serial killer, first to a genius criminal whose IQ is "not measurable by any means known to man" (Harris, 1988, p. 190), and then to a vampire-devil with red eyes, a sixth finger on his left hand, unnaturally sharp senses, superhuman strength, and power over wild animals (Oleson, 2006b). Other cerebral serial killers in this vein include Dexter Morgan (e.g., Lindsay, 2004), John "Jigsaw" Kramer (Oleson & MacKinnon, 2015), and John Doe (Fincher, 1995).

Some criminal geniuses from literature and film are not scientists but are nevertheless criminal masterminds. *The Sopranos* mafia boss, Tony Soprano, boasts of a 136 IQ; his hit man cousin has an IQ of 158 (Chase, 1999). In *Crime and Punishment* (Dostoevsky, 1866/1950), Rodion Raskolnikov murders an old pawnbroker, Alyona Ivanovna, to prove that he is an "extraordinary man"—above the law, beyond good and evil. He kills her because he wants to be a Napoleon (pp. 329–330). Raskolnikov describes his theory:

> An extraordinary man has a right—not officially, be it understood, but from and by his very individuality—to permit his conscience to overstep certain bounds, only so far as the realisation of one of his ideas may require it. . . . [A]ll legislators and rulers of men, commencing with the earliest down to Lycurgus, Solon, Mahomet, Napoleon, etc. etc., have one and all been criminals, for, whilst giving new laws, they have broken through older ones which had been faithfully observed by society and transmitted by its progenitors. These men most certainly never hesitated to shed blood, as soon as they saw the advantage of doing so. It may even be remarked that nearly all these benefactors and teachers of humanity have been terribly bloodthirsty. Consequently, not only all great men, but all those who, by hook or by crook, have raised themselves above the common herd, men who are capable of evolving something new, must, in virtue of their innate power, be undoubtedly criminals. (193–194)

Others have asserted Raskolnikov's view (cf. Rhodes, 1932). Aristotle (350 BCE/1941), in the *Politics*, suggests that "legislation is necessarily concerned only with those who are equal in birth and capacity; and that for men of pre-eminent virtue there is no law—they are themselves a law" (p. 1195). The Roman maxim, *quod licet Jovi, non licet bovi* (what is permitted to Jupiter is forbidden to an ox), expresses the sentiment somewhat more bluntly.

The belief that extraordinary ability justifies crime precipitated the crime of Leopold and Loeb and figures prominently in the dramatizations of their offense (Mason, 2013). In Hitchcock's adaptation of the 1929 play *Rope*, Wyndham Brandon explains, "The few are those men of such intellectual and cultural superiority that they're above the traditional 'moral' concepts. Good and evil, right and wrong, were invented for the ordinary average man, the inferior man, because he needs them" (San Juan & McDevitt, 2013, p. 67). The poster for Fleischer's 1959 film *Compulsion* reads, "You know why we did it? Because we damn well felt like doing it!"

Other writers have explored the relationship between extraordinary ability and the right to defy the law. Rand's *Atlas Shrugged* (1957) begins with the question, "Who is John Galt?" Throughout the novel, characters pose this question as a sort of Zen koan, but when magnates of industry begin to vanish, taking their assets with them and leaving their parasitic underlings behind, it is Galt—the man who once vowed to stop the motor of the world—who is responsible. Incompetents try to assume the seats of power where great men once sat, but they lack ability: the nation unravels in a slow-motion apocalypse. When Galt seizes the airwaves, he begins his three-hour objectivist manifesto:

> This is John Galt speaking. . . . I am the man who has deprived you of victims and thus has destroyed your world, and if you wish to know why you are perishing—you who dread knowledge—I am the man who will now tell you. . . . You have cried that man's sins are destroying the world and you have cursed human nature for its unwillingness to practice the virtues you demanded. Since virtue, to you, consists of sacrifice, you have demanded more sacrifices at every successive disaster. . . . You have sacrificed justice to mercy. You have sacrificed independence to unity. You have sacrificed reason to faith. You have sacrificed wealth to need. You have sacrificed selfesteem to self-denial. You have sacrificed happiness to duty. . . . Why, then, do you shrink in horror from the sight of the world around you? That world is not the product of your sins, it is the product and the image of your virtues. . . . You have fought for it, you have dreamed of it, and you have wished it, and I—I am the man who has granted you your wish. (p. 928)

Galt is captured by government agents and ordered to assume the role of Economic Director, to place the nation's economy back on track. Galt replies that they can force him to sit at a desk, but they cannot force him to find a solution to their problem. No threat, no weapon, can force a man who is determined to be free. Nevertheless, they try. They electrocute Galt, severely, raising the shock levels higher and higher until their machine malfunctions. A mechanic is summoned, but he cannot determine what is wrong. It is Galt, still out of breath from torture, who tells them how to repair it. Galt is liberated by a number of like-minded partisans and, in the closing pages of the novel, begins the task of rebuilding a nation that lies in ruin.

Vonnegut's pithy "Harrison Bergeron" (1968) explores similar themes. In 2081 America, everyone is finally equal (thanks to the tireless efforts of the Handicapper General and her army of H-G men). To enforce equality, those possessing natural ability or talent are handicapped. Athletes wear encumbering weights, the toobeautiful wear masks, and the too-clever wear earpieces that blast distracting radio signals. Harrison Bergeron, a brilliant and handsome 14-year-old who stands seven feet tall, is heavily handicapped. He wears 300 pounds of metal, huge earphones to disrupt his thoughts, thick eyeglasses to impair his vision and give him headaches, and a red rubber nose to make him ugly. When Harrison rebels, refusing to live a handicapped life, he is taken to prison, but escapes. Like Galt, Harrison seizes a television studio. He strips away his handicaps and proclaims himself emperor. He selects the first woman brave enough to stand—a beautiful ballerina—as his empress. Unencumbered by their weights, Harrison and his empress dance, leaping 30 feet into the air, defying gravity, but the Handicapper General, who has entered the studio with a shotgun, kills them on live television. The story ends with Harrison's parents, watching TV, sad, but prevented by their handicaps from remembering exactly what happened. Vonnegut's story provides an interesting counterpoint to *Crime and Punishment*. What *is* allowed to the great? What laws *can* they rightly spurn? *Do* the ends of genius justify criminal means?

Answers to these questions are proffered in the acclaimed graphic novel *Watchmen* (Moore & Gibbons, 1987) and its film adaptation. Set in an alternate 1985 where Richard Nixon is serving his fifth presidential term and Cold War tensions between the United States and the Soviet Union are high, masked heroes have been outlawed through passage of the 1977 Keene Act. When a former superhero, the Comedian, is found murdered, the masked vigilante Rorschach uncovers a plot to eliminate superheroes. He warns four former colleagues: Dr. Manhattan (a godlike blue quantum being), Nite Owl (a retired Batman-style hero), Silk Spectre (a retired heroine), and Ozymandias ("the world's smartest man," now a successful industrialist; figure 12). Nite Owl and Rorschach uncover evidence linking Ozymandias to the Comedian's death and confront him at his Antarctic fortress. There, Ozymandias reveals his plan: to save humanity from nuclear annihilation by staging a hoax extraterrestrial invasion of New York City that will kill half of the city but simultaneously unite all nations, ending war. It is a bold form of radical necessity (Oleson, 2007b). Nite Owl and Rorschach vow that they cannot allow him to do it, but they are too late. "I did it thirty-five minutes ago" (Moore & Gibbons, 1987, chap. 11, p. 27). The smartest man in the world has killed more than three million innocent people. *Watchmen* swept the 1987 Kirby Awards for best new series, best writer, and best writer/artist; it won the 1988 Will Eisner Awards for best finite series, best graphic album, best writer, and best writer/artist; it was selected for a 1988 Hugo Award; it was the only graphic novel to be included in *Time*'s all-time 100 greatest novels list (Grossman & Lacayo, 2005); and it was ranked 13 in *Entertainment Weekly*'s top 100 novels of the last 25 years (*Entertainment Weekly*, 2008).

Of course, other comic book villains have also shaped popular understandings of the criminal genius. Early antiheroes like Fantômas and Fu-Manchu were popularized in comic strips and comic books and fueled moral panics about real-life crime in the 1950s (e.g., Wertham, 1954). Contemporary supervillains from the DC

FIGURE 12. Matthew Goode as Ozymandias, from *Watchmen.*
Source: Photofest.

universe (Beatty, Greenberger, Jimenez, & Wallace, 2008; Wallace, 2014), the Marvel universe (De Falco et al., 2006), and other comics pantheons have continued the work of Fantômas and Fu-Manchu, antagonizing new generations of heroes. The real-world influence of fictional supervillains—depicted in comic books, film, and video games—should not be underestimated. Heath Ledger's performance as the Joker (figure 13) earned him a posthumous Academy Award for best supporting

FIGURE 13. Heath Ledger as the Joker, from *The Dark Knight*. Source: Photofest.

actor in 2009. It also impressed James Eagan Holmes, a "brilliant" doctoral student at the University of Colorado. Extrapolated from his GRE scores (Meyer, 2012), Holmes's IQ is approximately 151. Possessing a "superior" IQ, Holmes harbored a long-standing hatred of humanity, having "decided to dedicate his life to killing others" when he was still young (Bates, 2015). On July 20, 2012, Holmes exclaimed, "I am the Joker" before opening fire on a movie-theater audience in Aurora, Colorado, killing 12 and injuring 58 others (Kellner, 2013).

The aforementioned criminal geniuses from fiction and film shape our assumptions about high IQ and crime. In the absence of relevant scholarship, fictional representations are among the only ways we can know the criminal genius. And given that the influence of Hollywood on public attitudes and beliefs about crime dwarfs the influence of academic criminological scholarship (Rafter & Brown, 2011), it is hardly surprising that the criminal genius looms as our most cherished villain.

THE PLAN OF THE BOOK

This book attempts to shed light on the underresearched population of criminal geniuses. It provides some of the first empirical information about offenders possessing IQ scores of 130 (98%) and higher. This is the threshold for admission to the high-IQ society Mensa and the IQ threshold at which people are described as "borderline genius" (Simonton, 1994). Comparing data from 465 high-IQ subjects with data from 756 controls, the book describes the self-reported patterns of respondents offending from three different categories of geniuses: members of a high-IQ society with a 99.9% (IQ 150+) admission threshold, US and UK university students with genius-level (IQ 130+) scores; and geniuses (IQ 130+) incarcerated in US and UK prisons.

It describes the rates of prevalence, incidence, recency, arrest, and conviction for 72 offenses. It also describes the key themes derived from 44 follow-up interviews and examines some of the jurisprudential dimensions of high-IQ crime.

The book is organized into an introduction and seven numbered chapters. This introduction has used the criminological concept of the "dark figure" to note that researchers know far more about the criminal behavior of some groups (e.g., the poor, the uneducated, and the young) than other groups (e.g., the wealthy, the powerful, and those who possess the means to obstruct research access). While little is known about the crimes of those possessing above-average IQs, the concept of the criminal genius holds long-standing popular appeal and helps explain the allure of criminals like Leopold, Loeb, Kaczynski, and Chessman, as well as fictional villains such as Mabuse, Fu-Manchu, Blofeld, Fantômas, Moriarty, Lecter, Galt, and Ozymandias.

Chapter 1 traces the evolution of the idea of "genius" from its origins as a Roman tutelary spirit to later conceptions of eminence, creativity, and intelligence. Galton (1892) linked genius to eminence and noted that eminent parents gave birth to eminent offspring. Galton did not examine the criminality of genius, but comparing rates of imprisonment for the 100 most influential people in history to the imprisonment rates for countries belonging to the Organization for Economic Cooperation and Development indicates that eminent geniuses are criminalized at rates greater than in the general population. Genius became associated with creativity (and madness) during the Renaissance, and the association endures today. Genius then became associated with intelligence in the early twentieth century, prompted by the rise of IQ testing and Terman's (1926) longitudinal study of 1,470 children with 135+ IQ scores. The nature of human intelligence is described and related to criminal behavior. Those who have studied intelligence and crime have generally adopted one of three approaches: (1) most researchers have argued that delinquency and crime are associated with below-average IQ, (2) some researchers have suggested that IQ is distributed equally across criminal and noncriminal populations, and (3) a few researchers have suggested that criminals possess higher IQs than noncriminals. Little research on high-IQ offenders has been published, however, and what published work there is has compared gifted and average delinquents. Until the research described in this book, no criminological self-report study of adult offenders with genius-level IQs had been conducted.

Chapter 2 describes the methodology of the research. Little is known about high-IQ criminals because they are statistically rare. Only 2% of the general population has an IQ score of 130+ and only 1 in 2,000 possess an IQ of 150+. Another reason little is known is that few are caught. The differential detection hypothesis suggests that people with high IQs are less likely to be detected, arrested, prosecuted, convicted, and incarcerated than others. Prison studies, therefore, are of limited utility, and self-reporting is essential in order to examine elite crime.

Of course, there is little advantage for high-IQ individuals to participate in self-report research and potentially much to lose. High-IQ individuals often possess the means to block research inquiries. This chapter describes some of the ethical and legal challenges associated with self-report research. It describes the study's sampling, the design of the self-report questionnaire, the rationale and logistics of the follow-up interviews, and the structure of the revised Eysenck Personality Questionnaire (EPQ-R).

Chapter 3 describes the index and control group respondents. It describes their demographics (e.g., sex, age, race, education, occupation, IQ score, and so forth) and relates these variables to self-reported offending. The characteristics of the most criminal 20% (using measures of crime seriousness) are compared with those of the least criminal 20% (including abstainers, those who claim to have committed no offenses). This chapter also describes respondents' personality traits (as measured by the EPQ-R) and their experiences with mental illness and mental-health treatment, as well as the books, movies, and famous figures that shaped the respondents' thinking and influenced their behavior.

Chapter 4 describes the findings related to 72 offenses. Self-reported prevalence, incidence, and recency data are described, organized into nine crime types, ranging from minor infractions to capital felonies: (1) sex crimes, (2) violent crimes, (3) drug crimes, (4) property crimes, (5) white-collar crimes, (6) professional misconduct, (7) vehicular offenses, (8) justice system offenses, and (9) a handful of miscellaneous offenses. Contrary to prevailing theories of IQ and crime, high-IQ index respondents reported higher prevalence rates for 50 of the 72 offenses and reported higher incidence rates than controls.

Chapter 5 describes the criminal justice consequences of the offenses. Using the same nine offense types, this chapter describes the arrest and conviction rates of the index and control groups. The data are consistent with the differential detection and differential reaction hypotheses: index respondents reported more successful (no arrests) offenses than controls. Building upon the US Supreme Court's logic in *Atkins v. Virginia* (prohibiting the execution of mentally retarded defendants), chapter 5 then explores the culpability of high-IQ offenders. Noting that people with genius-level IQ scores are as statistically abnormal as the mentally handicapped defendants protected under *Atkins,* it asks whether criminal geniuses, vis-à-vis normal offenders, are equally, less, or more culpable. If it is true that people separated by 30 IQ points cannot communicate meaningfully, then gifted defendants might be functionally insane because of social isolation. This chapter also describes several challenges associated with punishing high-IQ offenders.

Chapter 6 describes the qualitative analyses derived from the 44 follow-up interviews. It describes the life history of "Faulkner," an offender with a 162 IQ who claims to have killed 15 people. This chapter also describes the analysis of qualitative materials in light of Hirschi's (1969) theory of social bonds, noting that the interviews were consistent with explanations of crime related to weakened dimensions of attachment, commitment, involvement, and belief. The chapter asks whether high IQ is always a protective factor or whether, at some levels and under some circumstances, it might begin to operate as a criminogenic risk factor.

Chapter 7 reviews the core findings from the research, describes some of its key limitations, and identifies some of its strengths. This chapter also discusses the implications of the work. The link between IQ and crime is contentious because it has fundamental implications for criminal justice and public policy. If IQ is unrelated to crime and everyone has the same propensity to follow or defy the law, crime is a choice and punishment operates as a price for antisocial behavior. But if IQ differences make it harder for some people to follow the law than others, then claims of "equal justice under law" are harder to sustain. And if social interventions cannot change IQ, difficult questions of when and how to absolve defendants of criminal culpability must be confronted. This chapter sketches out some of these conceptual issues and calls for additional research on the IQ-crime relationship.

1

Crime, Genius, and Criminal Genius

The lower classes feel for the criminal very much the same reverence that the educated feel for the man of genius. He has always been the hero, and often almost the saint of the degenerate and the low born.

CHARLES CURRY, "CRIMINALS AND THEIR TREATMENT," P. 11

Early criminology was founded in philosophy and medicine and sought to locate the origins of criminal behavior within the biology of the criminal (e.g., Hartl, Monnelly, & Elderkin, 1982; Hooton, 1939; Lombroso, 1876/2006; Sheldon, 1949). Throughout the latter part of the twentieth century, however, criminology was transformed into an essentially sociological discipline (Hirschi & Hindelang, 1977), often to the exclusion of the investigation of individual differences (Pinker, 2002). Biological explanations of crime remain taboo (Wright & Miller, 1998) and psychological explanations are disavowed. Many sociologically oriented criminologists deny the role played by intelligence in crime, although even researchers critical of the IQ-crime linkage acknowledge low intelligence as a significant criminological variable (e.g., Caplan, 1965). Low intelligence ranked 19th in the list of factors identified by criminologists to explain serious and persistent offending (Ellis & Walsh, 1999).

Dozens of studies have examined the relationship between IQ and offending (e.g., Binder, 1988; Bower, 1995; Burt, 1955; Caplan, 1965; Hirschi, 1969; Hirschi & Hindelang, 1977; Rutter & Giller, 1983; West & Farrington, 1973; Woodward, 1955), but with few exceptions, these investigations have focused upon only below-average or average individuals. The few studies of bright offenders (e.g., Gath, Tennant, & Pidduck, 1970) have examined juvenile subjects with IQ scores only one standard deviation above normal. This book represents the first systematic criminological investigation of adult subjects with genius-level IQs (two standard deviations above the mean, as distant from the mean as mental retardation). To understand the crimes of genius, however, it is necessary to begin by defining *genius*.

DEFINING GENIUS

Genius is notoriously difficult to define (Howe, 1999) and is a concept that evolved over 2,000 years (McMahon, 2013). At different moments in history, *genius* has signified (1) an attendant spirit, (2) exceptional creative ability, (3) eminence, and (4) exceptional intelligence (Ball, 2014). For each of these definitions, genius followed the zeitgeist of the age, reflecting what man felt was divine within man. In the ancient world, genius was a procreative force; in the Renaissance, it was creativity tempered by judgment; in the Romantic period, it was creativity triumphant over reason; in the Darwinian nineteenth century, it was hereditary eminence; and in the twentieth and twenty-first centuries, it is psychometric IQ. These varied definitions are not entirely unrelated. Ochse (1990) writes, "People tend to agree that 'creativity', 'intelligence' and 'wisdom' have something in common, and that creativity is closer to intelligence than to wisdom. . . . Some take it for granted that a [creative] genius is intellectually 'brilliant' in most respects" (p. 108). Csikszentmihalyi (1996) suggests that genius denotes a person who is both brilliant and creative. Others argue that intelligence and creativity are both necessary, but not sufficient, for genius. "[W]hatever . . . genius is, it is something more than I.Q. A high I.Q. may be one of the necessary attributes, but it is only one" (Rockwell, 1927, p. 380; cf. Galton, 1892).

Genius as Tutelary Spirit

The etymology of the word *genius* may provide clues to its deep meaning (Nitzsche, 1975). Although Sprenger (1861) suggests that *genius* is derived from *jinn*, the Arabic spirit associated with lamps and wishes, most scholars trace the term's etymology to the Latin *gignere* (to sire). But a thorough genealogy actually begins not with the Latin, *gignere*, but with the cognate Greek concept of the *daimon* (δαιμον).

In Homer, *daimon* describes all supernatural phenomena that cannot be attributed to Olympian gods (Murray, 1989), but by the time Hesiod wrote *Works and Days* in 700 BCE, *daimones* were more precisely rendered as dead men from the Golden Age who acted as beneficent guardians to men on earth. Plato describes *daimones* both as intermediaries between men and gods and as guardian spirits allotted to each man at birth. In the *Apology*, Socrates describes the *daimonion* that occasionally spoke to him, guiding him in decision making: "I am subject to a divine or supernatural experience . . . a sort of voice, which comes to me and when it comes it always dissuades me from what I am proposing to do, and ever urges me on" (Hamilton & Cairns, 1989, p. 17). This version of the *daimon* most resembles the Roman *genius*, the procreative spirit of paternal ancestry allotted to each Roman man at birth. The concept was expanded later: *genius* referred to a tutelary spirit who determined both a man's character and his accomplishments. Birthday sacrifices were made to geniuses, and oaths sworn by one's genius were sacred (Becker, 1978). The concept was further modified so that every existing entity—whether individual, house, town, or nation—had an attendant spirit. For example, the Genius Populi Romani, the guardian of Rome, was especially important (Fears, 1978). Although later men of exceptional abilities were said to possess genius, in the ancient world it was the other way around. "Talent is what you possess; genius is what possesses you" (Cowley, in Peter, 1977, p. 211). Every man had a genius, which acted upon him as an external agent.

Genius as Creativity

For more than 1,000 years, the concept of genius was abandoned in Europe. Early Christians transformed *daimones* into demons (Walker, 1983). Joan of Arc described the voices she heard as saintly—not daimonic—but in the fifteenth century, hearing voices (even the voices of saints) was sufficient to justify her excommunication as a heretic. After one of the most famous trials in history (Barrett, 1991), Joan of Arc was executed.

With the arrival of the Italian Renaissance, however, the notion of genius as a possessing force reemerged. The Florentine Ficino popularized the notion of *genios,* men of exceptional creative ability known both for their talents and their *pazzia* (Becker, 1978). *Pazzia,* loosely interpreted as insanity, drew from two classical sources: Plato's idea of divine madness and Aristotle's notion of melancholia.

Plato suggests that the poet, while composing poetry, is mad, literally out of his mind *(ekstatikoi),* creating by divine dispensation without being personally aware of what he is doing (Murray, 1989). In the *Phaedrus,* Plato argues that man's greatest blessings come through four varieties of divine madness: Apollo's prophetic madness, Dionysus's telestic or ritual madness, the poetic madness of the Muses, and the erotic madness of Aphrodite and Eros. Plato writes, "There is a third form of possession or madness, of which the Muses are the source. This seizes a tender, virgin soul and stimulates it to rapt passionate expression, especially in lyric poetry. . . . But if any man comes to the gates of poetry without the madness of the Muses, persuaded that skill alone will make him a good poet, then shall he and his works of sanity with him be brought to nought by the poetry of madness" (Hamilton & Cairns, 1989, p. 492).

The Aristotelian notion of melancholia also helped shape Renaissance conceptions of genius. Aristotle explains the inspiration of the poet as a function of shifts within the body's four Hippocratic humors: "[T]hose who are full of hot black bile become frenzied *(manikoi)* or brilliant *(euphueis)* or amorous or easily moved to anger and desire, and some become more talkative. Many too, if this heat approaches the seat of the intellect, are affected by fits of frenzy or possession" (in Murray, 1989, p. 20).

Pazzia, in linking Platonic possession-states to Aristotelian melancholia, articulated a new and enduring relationship between genius and madness. Although *pazzia* encompassed everything from mere strangeness to clinical insanity, it typically referred to melancholic traits such as moodiness, sensitivity, solitariness, and eccentricity. Becker (1978) argues that Renaissance geniuses remained fundamentally rational. While there was something irrational about the generative powers of genius, it was generally agreed that the mental faculty of judgment restrained the imagination from actual madness.

With the ascendance of the Romantic movement, however, the primacy of judgment was usurped by the irrational imagination. Kessel (1989) argues that at this time, originality supplanted reason as the chief attribute of the great man. Scientists were no longer described as geniuses. Their accomplishments were described in impersonal terms (Raskin, 1936). Men no longer venerated the sage, but glorified the poet. Carlyle (1841/1966) writes that our heroes first manifested as gods, then prophets, and next emerged as poets. Romantic genius was liberated from the shackles of reason: organic, impulsive, creative, and artistic. A sort of ecstatic *Geniekult* celebrated the Dionysian ideal of the maddened genius (Becker, 1978).

> "There is no great genius without some touch of madness." (Seneca, in
>   Sanderlin, 1979, p.38)
>
> "Between genius and madness there is often not the thickness of a hair." (Sand,
>   in Herschman & Lieb, 1988, p. 8)
>
> "The lives of men of genius show how often, like lunatics, they are in a state of
>   continuous agitation." (Schopenhauer, in Herschman & Lieb, 1988, p. 9)
>
> "Great wits are sure to madness near allied / And thin partitions do their
>   bounds divide." (Dryden, in Kessel, 1989, p. 197)

In 1836, Lélut published *Du demon de Socrate,* in which he suggests that the daimon of Socrates was an auditory hallucination, mistaken as the voice of a supernatural agent. Lélut concludes that Socrates was mad. In *L'amulette de Pascal* (1846), Lélut arrives at similar conclusions in the case of Pascal.

Inspired by the revolutionary paradigm in *On the Origin of Species* (Darwin, 1859/1870), researchers applied concepts of evolution in their own pioneering research on genius. For example, Moreau (1859) insists that the originality of genius can be traced to the same degenerative organic causes that are responsible for madness or idiocy, a claim developed more fully by Lombroso in *Genio e follia* (1872). Lombroso (1891) maintains that genius is rooted in hereditary degeneration of the nervous system: "We may confidently affirm that genius is a true degenerative psychosis belonging to the group of moral insanity, and may temporarily spring out of other psychoses, assuming their forms, though keeping its own special peculiarities, which distinguish it from all others" (p. 333; cf. Mora, 1964). Others shared Lombroso's conception of genius as pathological (e.g., Bett, 1952; Hirsch, 1896; Hyslop, 1925; Jacobson, 1926; Kretschmer, 1931; Lange-Eichbaum, 1931; Madden, 1833; Marks, 1926; Nisbet, 1900; Tsanoff, 1949; Türck, 1914). Nordau (1895) suggests that the genius hails from the same degenerate stock "as criminals, prostitutes, anarchists, and pronounced lunatics" (p. vii). On the other side of the debate, other commentators insisted the genius was healthy (e.g., Carroll, 1940; Freud, 1964; Padovan, 1902; Schlesinger, 2012; Stevenson, 1886). In *The Sanity of Art* (1908), Shaw wryly asks, "What in the name of common-sense is the value of a theory that identifies Ibsen, Wagner, Tolstoy, Ruskin, and Victor Hugo with the refuse of our prisons and lunatic asylums? . . . I could prove Nordau to be an elephant on more evidence than he has brought to prove that our greatest men are degenerate lunatics" (pp. 91–92).

Table 5 identifies some of the key publications on both sides of the mad-genius controversy (Becker, 1978; Chan, 2001; Sirotkina, 2002). The debate between the degenerationists and their opponents waned after World War II. Nevertheless, many researchers continue to equate genius with creative ability (Andreasen, 2005; Bloom, 2002; Briggs, 1988; Eysenck, 1995; Ochse, 1990; Root-Bernstein & Root-Bernstein, 1999). The MacArthur Foundation continues to award its "genius grants" on the basis of exceptional creativity and the promise of great contributions. The relationship between genius and madness also continues to attract scholarly interest (Kinnell, 1983; Missett, 2013; Schlesinger, 2012). Juda (1949) studied 113 German artists, architects, composers, writers, and their relatives and found that artists and their first-degree relatives had higher rates of psychiatric abnormality than would be expected in a general population. Andreasen (1987) examined 30 creative writers and found dramatically elevated rates of mood disorders. In the general population, only 1% suffer from manic depression, only 3% from cyclothymia (an attenuated form of manic depression), and only 5% from major depression (American Psychiatric Association, 2013); yet 80% of Andreasen's writers experienced one or more episodes of mania, cyclothymia, or major depression. Ludwig (1995) studied mental illness in 1,004 eminent geniuses and found elevated rates of mental disorder and substance abuse, particularly among artists. Jamison (1993) concurs, citing numerous studies indicating elevated incidence rates of major depression, manic depression, cyclothymia, and suicide in artists, writers, and poets. She reports that artists experience up to 18 times the suicide rate of the general population, 8–10 times the rate of depression, and 10–20 times the rate of manic depression and cyclothymia (Jamison, 1995).

Genius as Eminence

In 1869, Galton—Darwin's second cousin—published *Hereditary Genius*. It differed from earlier works on the subject of genius by including statistical analyses instead of biographical accounts. Serebriakoff (1985), a founding member of the high-IQ society, Mensa, writes, "Previous writers about genius, ability, and talent had wondered to what extent they were hereditary. Galton started the first objective studies to establish the facts. . . . Galton was the first in the field of individual psychology, as he put it, 'To treat the subject in a statistical manner and arrive at exact numerical results'" (p. 171).

TABLE 5 Select references on the genius-madness relationship

Genius as pathological	Genius as nonpathological
Andreasen, 2005	Bloom, 2002
Bett, 1952	Briggs, 1988
Ellis, 1927	Burks, Jensen, & Terman, 1930
Herschman & Lieb, 1988	Cox, 1926
Hirsch, 1896	Csikszentmihalyi, 1996
Hyslop, 1925	Eysenck, 1995
Jacobson, 1926	Holahan & Sears, 1995*
Jamison, 1993	Hollingworth, 1926
Kretschmer, 1931	Howe, 1999
Lange-Eichbaum, 1932	Ludwig, 1995
Lombroso, 1891	Ochse, 1990
Ludwig, 1927	Padovan, 1902
MacDonald, 1902	Root-Bernstein & Root-Bernstein, 1999
Madden, 1833	Shenk, 2010
Marks, 1926	Simonton, 1994
Nisbet, 1900	Terman, 1926
Nordau, 1895	Terman & Oden, 1947
Schwarz, 1947	Terman & Oden, 1959

NOTE: The dichotomy is based on table 3.1 in Becker (1978), which revealed a shift between 1836 and 1950 from understanding the genius as pathological to viewing the genius as healthy.

* Holahan and Sears (1995) identify *The Gifted Group in Later Maturity* as volume 5—not 6—in *Genetic Studies of Genius*, because Cox's contribution to the series (volume 2) was based on historiometric data, not on the materials from Terman's longitudinal study.

In *Hereditary Genius* (1892), Galton makes three related claims. First, he suggests that people vary in terms of their natural abilities. At one end of the intellectual distribution, there are the very dull; at the other end, there are geniuses. Second, he suggests that the naturally enabled genius will rise, almost without exception, to achieve distinction. Third, he suggests that these natural abilities are heritable and that genius runs within families. Galton sought to demonstrate his tripartite thesis by examining the pedigrees of almost 1,000 geniuses (defined as men who achieved what only 250 in 1 million can hope to achieve: "On the most brilliant of starlight nights there are never so many as 4,000 stars visible to the naked eye at the same time; yet we feel it to be an extraordinary distinction to a star to be accounted as the brightest in the sky" [p. 9]) selected from dictionaries and encyclopedias based on the space allotted to them, including judges, generals, poets, painters, and scientists. Galton then looked at their relatives, trying to assess the likelihood that an eminent individual would be related to another eminent individual. Galton concludes that a genius's son is 129 times as likely to be a genius himself as the child of an ordinary father. Galton attributes the achievement of genius to three necessary factors: capacity, zeal, and the tendency to work hard. In the second edition of *Hereditary Genius,* he writes, "I do not mean capacity without zeal, nor zeal without capacity, nor even a combination of them without an adequate power of doing a great deal of very laborious work. But, I mean a nature, which when left to itself, will, urged by an inherent stimulus, climb to the path that leads to eminence and has strength to reach the summit—one which, if hindered or thwarted—will fret and strive until the hindrance is overcome, and it is again free to follow its labouring instinct" (p. 33).

Galton's work was challenged by Kroeber (1944), who examined 5,000 creative individuals living between 700 BCE and 1900 CE and concluded that creativity levels oscillate in society much faster than its biological foundations. Kroeber himself adopted Galton's nomothetic method, using eminent creators selected from encyclopedias. The practice extends into the present.

Yoder (1894) uses biographies to select 50 subjects for his analysis of the childhoods of great men. Cattell (1903) ranks the top 1,000 eminent people by measuring the space their biographical entries filled in American, English, French, and German biographical dictionaries. For his *A Study of British Genius* (1927), Ellis drew 1,030 subjects from the *Dictionary of National Biography.* Eisenstadt (1978) utilized the *Encyclopaedia Britannica* in selecting 699 subjects for his study of parental loss and genius. Roe (1952) selected 64 US scientists for analysis based on eminence. In *Cradles of Eminence,* Goertzel, Goertzel, and Goertzel (1962) selected as subjects those 400 twentieth-century figures who had two or more biographies (or one biography, if born outside the United States) in the Montclair, New Jersey, public library. In *300 Eminent Personalities* (1978), they used the same approach, excluding the early sample and using the Menlo Park, California, public library. De Bono (1976) identifies the 30 greatest thinkers who have "shaped our civilization," and Michael Hart (1992) compiled a list of history's 100 most influential persons, using eminence as an index of influence. More recently, Lazar, Karlan, and Salter (2006) assembled a similar list of the 101 most influential characters "who never lived," and Pollard-Gott (2009) uses analogous techniques to rank the 100 most influential characters in fiction.

Many scholars continue to associate eminence (or "greatness") with genius (e.g., Albert, 1992; Feist, 2014; Simonton, 1976, 1994). Simonton, in particular, has used historiometric techniques (1990, 1998, 2003) to examine leadership (1984, 2006), scientific achievement (1988, 2013), and creativity (1999, 2011). Simonton is the world's leading expert on genius, and his *Wiley Handbook of Genius* (2014) stands as the high-water mark in the scientific study of genius.

Landrum (1993, 1994, 1997) relates eminence to genius in a series of books. In *Profiles of Genius* (1993), he describes the characteristics of 13 successful entrepreneurs, including leaders of Domino's Pizza, FedEx, Apple, and Honda Motor Company; in *Profiles of Female Genius* (1994), Landrum describes the characteristics of 13 eminent women, including Ayn Rand, Margaret Thatcher, Oprah Winfrey, and

Madonna; and in *Profiles of Black Success* (1997), he outlines the contributions of 13 others, including Bill Cosby, Nelson Mandela, Michael Jordan, and Thurgood Marshall. While some might not recognize industrialists, singers, and sports figures as geniuses, Landrum (1994) defends their inclusion. "One publisher told me he had difficulty 'equating mere celebrity and financial success with "genius."' Au contraire! Too many people, including this particular publisher, confuse genius with IQ or some mysterious aptitude or talent" (p. 16). Other researchers concur, characterizing genius as something within everyone's grasp (e.g., Shenk, 2010; Siler, 1999; Weisberg, 1986).

Genius as Intelligence

Today, when the term *genius* is used, it often denotes high intelligence (especially intelligence as measured by IQ tests). Antecedents of the IQ test can be traced to early measures of ability, like the civil service examinations administered in Imperial China (Bowman, 1989; DuBois, 1970), but the modern intelligence test originates with the work of a French educator, Binet (Kaufman, 2009). Intrigued by his own daughters' intellectual maturation, Binet collaborated with colleagues to develop a standardized scale of cognitive ability. In 1905, the Binet-Simon intelligence scale was introduced in France and used to separate retarded children from normal children (ensuring that classrooms would not be slowed down). Early intelligence testing was refined in 1912 by Stern, who developed the intelligence quotient (IQ), a ratio of mental to chronological age that yielded a single number. The quantification of IQ reified psychometric intelligence. Thorndike (1914) observed, "If a thing exists, it exists in some amount . . . and if it exists in some amount, it can be measured" (p. 141). Lord Kelvin wrote, "One's knowledge of science begins when he can measure what he is speaking about, and expresses it in numbers" (in Eysenck, 1995, p. 4). Today, "[i]ntelligence is the most studied human characteristic in the world" (Wright & Boisvert, 2009, p. 93).

Terman popularized the IQ in the United States. In 1916, he published the "absolutely seminal" American version of the Binet-Simon scale, the Stanford-Binet (Cravens, 1992, p. 183). One year later (1917), he used documentary sources to examine Galton's precocity, estimating Galton's childhood IQ at 200. These two projects, the Stanford-Binet and the assessment of a posthumous IQ, anticipated the first two volumes of the six-volume *Genetic Studies of Genius*.

In 1921, Terman and his testing staff began sifting through 250,000 California schoolchildren, selecting 1,470 boys and girls with IQs of 135 or greater from grades three through eight. Terman set out to challenge pathological explanations of genius, hoping to demonstrate that claims of "early ripe, early rot" were unfounded (Goleman, 1980; Seagoe, 1975). Terman challenged this myth by collecting exhaustive data. In 1925, he published the first installment of his results in *Mental and Physical Traits of a Thousand Gifted Children*, volume 1 of *Genetic*

TABLE 6 Original and adjusted IQ ratings for Cox's groupings in childhood
(AI) and youth (AII)

Grouping	AI IQ		AII IQ	
	Original	Adjusted	Original	Adjusted
Soldiers	115	125	125	140
Artists	122	140	135	160
Musicians	130	145	140	160
Statesmen	135	155	142	165
Fiction writers	141	160	149	165
Religious Leaders	132	150	145	170
Revolutionary Statesmen	140	160	144	170
Nonfiction Writers	139	160	148	170
Scientists	135	155	152	175
Philosophers	147	170	156	180

SOURCE: Adapted from Cox, 1926.

Studies of Genius. The book includes chapters on demographics, physical and educational history, personality traits, specialization of abilities, and the interests of the subjects (scholastic, play, reading, and social). In this volume, he concludes that geniuses are actually healthier, more popular, and more accomplished than average children (Terman, 1926). Cox's *The Early Mental Traits of Three Hundred Geniuses,* volume 2 of *Genetic Studies of Genius,* was published in 1926. Employing Cattell's (1903) list of 1,000 eminent persons, Cox eliminates those born before 1450, aristocrats, and others whose eminence cannot be unquestionably attributed to their own accomplishments, reducing the group to 301 subjects. Five raters, using Terman's (1917) technique for assessing a historic IQ, calculated two indices of IQ: AI and AII. The AI scores reflected IQ before the age of 17, as determined by the age at which the individual mastered universal cognitive tasks such as reading and writing. The AII scores reflected IQ between 17 and 26 and were based upon academic and early professional accomplishments. Because many of the original estimates appeared too low, Cox adjusted the IQ estimates. The original and adjusted ratings are presented in table 6.

Gould (1981) criticizes Cox's study for its adjustments, noting that when documentary evidence is good, IQ estimates are high. For example, John Stuart Mill had an adjusted AI IQ of 190 and an AII IQ of 170. But Cervantes was rated at a mere 105 and 110, respectively, and Copernicus was rated at 105 and 130, since little was known of their lives before the age of 17. Eysenck (1995), however, inverts Gould's argument, suggesting that an unremarkable IQ might explain the absence of documentary evidence. Nevertheless, although Cox's study was visionary, later volumes in *Genetic Studies of Genius* eschewed historiometrics and followed the approach of volume 1. In what Serebriakoff (1985) describes as "the biggest, long-est term and most thorough research in the whole field of the social sciences" (p. 219), the 1,470 geniuses—called "Terman's Termites"—were tracked across their lifetimes. In 1928, Terman added 58 new Termites, siblings of the original geniuses, raising the total number to 1,528: 857 boys and 671 girls (Goleman, 1980). The follow-up data were published in volume 3 of *Genetic Studies of Genius, The Promise of Youth: Follow-Up Studies of a Thousand Gifted Children* (Burks, Jensen, & Terman, 1930). Volume 4, *The Gifted Child Grows Up: Twenty-Five Years Follow-Up of a Superior Group* (Terman & Oden, 1947); volume 5, *The Gifted at Mid-Life: Thirty-Five Years of the Superior Child* (Terman & Oden, 1959); and volume 6, *The Gifted Group in Later Maturity* (Holahan & Sears, 1995), providing additional support for the claim that geniuses often enjoy satisfying, successful lives. Interest-ingly, Wirthwein and Rost (2011) found no significant differences between gifted and average adults in terms of subjective well-being. The study is ongoing—the longest-running longitudinal study in the world—and will continue until the last Termite dies or withdraws from the study.

Although the gifted sample did not include a single revolutionary genius of the caliber of an Einstein or Newton (Shurkin, 1992), the group demonstrated remark-able achievement. While still in their 40s, Terman's women had published 5 novels, 5 volumes of poetry, 32 scholarly books, 4 plays, more than 150 essays, and more than 200 scientific papers. Seven were listed in *American Men of Science,* two in *Who's Who in America,* and two in the *Directory of American Scholars.* Terman's men did even better. Seventy appeared in *American Men of Science,* 31 in *Who's Who in America,* and 10 in the *Directory of American Scholars.* They produced 60 schol-arly books, 33 novels, 375 short stories and plays, 230 patents, and almost 2,000 sci-entific papers. While the Termites' rates of death, delinquency, divorce, and insanity were all below average, their salaries were higher, their jobs better, and their profes-sional achievements greater than those of comparable Americans with average IQs. They were satisfied by their careers, friends, and families (Sears, 1977). More than past acts, the Termites regretted inactivity, and not getting enough education was their most common regret (Hattiangadi, Medvec, & Gilovich, 1995). Terman's origi-nal claim—suggesting that genius is not pathological—has been replicated (Sub-otnik, Karp, & Morgan, 1989). Other researchers report average or superior levels of psychosocial adjustment among high-IQ populations (e.g., Cornell, Delcourt, Bland, Goldberg, & Oram, 1994; Gallucci, Middleton, & Klein, 1999; Garland & Zigler, 1999; Neihart, 1999; Norman, Ramsay, Martray, & Roberts, 1999).

Nevertheless, the evidence for high levels of psychosocial adjustment is mixed. Other researchers have reported elevated rates of psychosocial maladjust-ment among the exceptionally gifted (e.g., Dauber & Benbow, 1990; Gross, 1993; Kincaid, 1969). Grant and Schwartz (2011) argue that excessive levels of knowledge and wisdom actually undermine well-being: these virtues follow an inverted-U distribution; people appear happiest when they possess moderate levels of these traits. Janos, Fung, and Robinson (1985) found that gifted children who report feeling "different" have lower levels of self-esteem than those who do not feel different. Hollingworth (1942) agrees that many gifted children are well adjusted and healthy but warns that exceptionally gifted children (IQ of 150+) are especially vulnerable to problems of social adjustment (cf. Bridges, 1973). Hollingworth advanced a theory of optimum intelligence: while children with IQ scores between 125 and 150 have much in common with their average peers and can establish satisfying relationships, children with IQ scores of 150+ struggle to find others with whom they can form attachments. Winner (1996) writes, "Even Terman admitted that children with very high IQs faced acute social problems. Terman's subjects who scored 170 or higher on IQ tests were said to have 'one of the most difficult problems of social adjustment that any human being is ever called upon to meet.' At age fourteen, 60 percent of the boys with such high IQs and 73 percent of the girls were described by their teachers as solitary and poor mixers" (p. 225).

In volume 6 of *Genetic Studies of Genius* (1995), Holahan and Sears report that, by late maturity, 7% of the male deaths and 4% of the female deaths in the study were by suicide, a rate much higher than the 10.5 in 100,000 rate of suicide in the general US population (McKeown, Cuffe, & Schulz, 2006). Other researchers also link high IQ to suicide (Farrell, 1989; Voracek, 2004; but see Lajoie & Shore, 1981). Nevertheless, despite social hardships reported by many highly gifted students (Montour, 1977; Runnion, 1982), many parents go to lengths to improve the IQ scores of their children (Quart, 2006). The preoccupation with improving psychometric scores has been criticized as a symptom of a testing culture (Sacks, 1999) and a cult of IQ (Sharp, 1972).

Is giftedness really a gift (Davidson, 2012)? In a small survey I conducted in 2002, a convenience sample of 148 adult subjects from a range of ages and occupations was provided with a brief statement about genius and psychosocial adjustment, derived from the findings of Terman and Hollingworth (Grossberg & Cornell, 1988; Neihart, 1999). I stated, "There is conflicting research on genius. Some researchers have indicated that geniuses are often successful and happy. They are healthier, more popular, and earn more money than average people. Other researchers have indicated that geniuses are often lonely and socially alienated. Especially when they are very gifted, geniuses feel different from other people, may suffer from a variety of mental disorders, and may become embittered and reclusive. Given these two possibilities, would you choose to be a genius if you had the choice?" The results revealed deep ambivalence about the prospect of genius. Three respondents (2.0%) indicated that they were not sure, 73 (49.3%) indicated that they would choose to be a genius, and 72 (48.6%) indicated that they would not choose to be a genius. Although the respondents identified luminaries like Einstein, da Vinci, Michelangelo, Mozart, Jefferson, Franklin, and Bill Gates as geniuses, almost half of the sample indicated that they would decline the gift of genius-level intelligence.

The notion that IQ, an innate mental trait, should be responsible for the outcomes in one's life—not unlike a Roman spirit of genius—is controversial. Pinker (2002) has described the social sciences' resistance to the idea of an innate human nature, and this antipathy can be particularly acute when framed as a modern myth of the metals. In the *Republic* (Hamilton & Cairns, 1989), Plato recommends the creation of a lie to enhance social stability: a creation myth claiming that rulers are made of gold, soldiers of silver, and farmers of iron and brass. But the idea that some people are born good, others bad (Sudiker, 2003); that some are born to lead while others, although blameless, are born to serve, violates our belief that good deeds are rewarded and wicked acts are punished (Lerner, 1980). It offends conceptions of equity and justice that might be hardwired into the human brain (Tabibnia, Satpute, & Lieberman, 2008).

Some critics are suspicious of the very construct of IQ (e.g., Kamin, 1974; Lippmann, 1922a, 1922b), and much of the controversy surrounding IQ relates to its biological foundations. Whether the physical basis of IQ is related to brain size (Willerman, Schultz, Rutledge, & Bigler, 1991), the dopaminergic system (Previc, 1999), neural networks (Vakhtin, Ryman, Flores, & Jung, 2014), efficient nerve velocity (Miller, 1994), or the ability to suppress irrelevant sensory inputs (Melnick, Harrison, Park, Bennetto, & Tadin, 2013), many researchers are suspicious of innate sources of behavior that cannot be influenced by social interventions (Pinker, 2002; Rowe, 1994). "[N]o known social intervention has successfully increased IQ scores over the life course. Programs designed to increase IQ and thus reduce crime and violence are likely to fail" (Wright & Boisvert, 2009, p. 98; cf. Beaver et al., 2014).

Some social scientists are also wary of claims of IQ heritability. When examining the variance in human characteristics, behavioral geneticists distinguish between genetic factors (h^2), shared environmental factors (c^2; shared by all family members), and nonshared environmental factors (e^2; unique to individuals) (Falconer, 1989). IQ differences are shaped by all three of these factors, but genetics (Nisbett et al., 2012) and intrauterine conditions (Devlin, Daniels, & Roeder, 1997) appear to play a dominant role in determining IQ. Multiple genes appear to be implicated in IQ and cognitive ability (Beaver, Vaughn, Wright, DeLisi, & Higgins, 2010; Beaver, Wright, DeLisi, & Vaughn, 2012; Plomin, 1999), but "the influence of genetic factors on the development of intelligence is indisputable" (Nedelec, Schwartz, & Connolly, 2015, p. 470). Hunt (2011) summarized the data, writing, "Additive genetic heritability accounts for 40–80% of the variance in virtually all cognitive traits" (p. 243). Wright and Boisvert (2012) suggest an even higher figure: "Estimates of the heritability of intelligence generally range between 60% and 80%, with some studies finding that intelligence is almost 100% heritable" (p. 94). Based on such data, researchers have rejected claims that IQ is a mere social construction. "The anti-hereditarian position that there are no genetic influences on IQ has crumbled for want of any empirical data that would support such a radical view" (McGue, 1997). Gottfredson (1997) and 51 other experts on intelligence conclude, "[G]enetics plays a bigger role than does environment in creating IQ differences among individuals" (p. 14). While the same can be said of many inherited human characteristics (e.g., height, weight, or eye color), this finding is noteworthy because IQ is relatively stable from childhood into adulthood (Deary, Pattie, & Starr, 2013) and correlated positively with desirable social outcomes such as academic achievement and employment (Ferguson, Horwood, & Ridder, 2005) and socioeconomic success (Marioni et al., 2014; Strenze, 2007).

The association between biology and intelligence also has racial implications. Of course, the very concept of "race" is contentious (Wade, 2014). The American Anthropological Association (1994) has resolved that differentiating humans "into biologically defined 'races' has proven meaningless and unscientific as a way of explaining variation (whether in intelligence or other traits)," a social-constructivist understanding of race that is supported by the American Sociological Association (2003). Nevertheless, in the United States, race continues to operate as an enforced legal category (e.g., Grutter v. Bollinger, 2003; Johnson v. California, 2005) and is integral to the lived identity of many persons (e.g., Coates, 2015). Consumers can purchase at-home DNA ancestry kits that provide ethnicity results. Biological race also continues to inform modern social science scholarship (Morning, 2014). Indeed, "in the years following the completion of the Human Genome Project, race has vigorously resurfaced as a prominent topic of scientific, and especially of genetic, research" (Rich, 2014, p. 1). Although biological race is widely dismissed as unscientific (Krimsky & Sloan, 2011), genetic alleles are distributed into clusters in humans. Some researchers claim these population clusters approximate classical race typologies (e.g., Risch, Burchard, Ziv, & Tang, 2002).

The study of race vis-à-vis IQ is doubly fraught. Rose (2009) suggests that scientists should not study race and IQ, arguing that society cannot possibly benefit from such research. Gottfredson (1994), however, says that to ignore race and IQ is to enforce an "egalitarian fiction." After all, most researchers who have studied the topic have reported racial IQ differences. Specifically, they have identified an American black-white IQ difference of approximately 15 IQ points (Gottfredson, 1997; Herrnstein & Murray, 1994; Neisser et al., 1996). Hispanics have mean scores that lie between those of blacks and whites; and Asian Americans have IQ scores equal to whites, although some studies report that Asians in Asia possess IQ scores 1 to 10 points above whites (Neisser et al., 1996). These racial IQ deficits correspond with overrepresentation in the criminal justice system, prompting some to argue for a race-IQ-crime linkage (Rushton & Templer, 2009).

Analyses of big data reveal that IQ scores also vary between nations (Lynn & Vanhanen, 2002, 2006) and US states (Kanazawa, 2006). Bartels, Ryan, Urban, and Glass (2010) report an inverse association between average state IQ and FBI crime statistics for violence and property offenses (cf. Templer & Rushton, 2011), and other researchers, disaggregating official data to the county level, report significant negative associations between county IQ and county crime rates (Beaver & Wright, 2011). Rushton and Templer (2009) report similar associations between national differences in IQ and official crime rates.

The suggestion that differences in academic achievement, socioeconomics, or crime rates can be explained by racial IQ differences is taboo. When Jensen (1969) suggested that Project Head Start initiatives had failed to boost African American IQ scores because 80% of IQ is biologically based, public reaction was explosive. "The University of California had to provide him with a bodyguard after he had received numerous death threats and after radical students interfered with his classes and speeches" (Murdoch, 2007, p. 224). When Shockley (1972) suggested compensating low-IQ persons who would agree to voluntary sterilization, he too was denounced as a racist. When Rushton mailed unsolicited, abridged copies of *Race, Evolution, and Behavior* (1995), a book that applies biological R/K theory to human racial groups, suggesting, inter alia, that Asians concentrate their parenting resources in few offspring while blacks produce numerous offspring and invest fewer resources per child, he incited terrific animosity (Tucker, 2002). Herrnstein and Murray's 1994 book, *The Bell Curve,* also was controversial. They argued that income, job performance, child illegitimacy, and involvement in crime are more related to IQ than to parental socioeconomic status or education. Backlash against *The Bell Curve* was dramatic. Seligman published *A Question of Intelligence: The IQ Debate in America* (1994); Gould issued a new edition of *The Mismeasure of Man* (1996); Jacoby and Glauberman edited *The Bell Curve Debate* (1995); and Fraser edited *The Bell Curve Wars: Race, Intelligence, and the Future of America* (1995). But while publications about "bell curve wars" imply a bellicose and fractionated approach to intelligence and IQ testing, there is actually a remarkable consensus about the structure of human intelligence (e.g., Gottfredson, 1997; Hunt, 2011; Neisser et al., 1996, Nisbett et al., 2012).

What *is* intelligence? Boring (1923) employs a glib tautology ("Intelligence is what the tests test" [p. 35]), and Gay (1948) demonstrates that the definitions people offer for "intelligence" have more to do with their own life experiences and values than any scientific understanding. However, mainstream researchers agree that "[i]ntelligence is a very general mental capability that, among other things, involves the ability to reason, plan, solve problems, think abstractly, comprehend complex ideas, learn quickly and gain from experience" (Gottfredson, 1997, p. 13). In fact, in their survey of 1,020 experts in the field of intelligence, Snyderman and Rothman (1987) found that 96.0% agreed that intelligence is related to the capacity to acquire knowledge, 97.7% agreed that it is related to problem solving, and 99.3% agreed that it is related to abstract thinking or reasoning. Intelligence, as measured by IQ tests, has profound real-world consequences: "IQ is strongly related, probably more so than any other single measurable human trait, to many important educational, occupational, economic, and social outcomes. Its relation to the welfare and performance of individuals is very strong in some arenas in life (education, military training), moderate but robust in others (social competence), and modest but consistent in others (law-abidingness). Whatever IQ tests measure, it is of great practical and social importance" (Gottfredson, 1997, p. 14).

Intelligence, however, is not monolithic. Many researchers distinguish fluid from crystallized intelligence (e.g., Cattell, 1963; McGrew, 2009). Fluid intelligence *(gf)* relates to novel, dynamic reasoning while crystallized intelligence *(gc)* reflects acquired information and skills, indicating the "breadth and depth of acquired knowledge of the language, information and concepts of a specific culture" (McGrew, 2009, p. 5). Another way of parsing full-scale intelligence is to distinguish verbal intelligence (VIQ) from performance intelligence (PIQ). Most people have closely matched VIQ and PIQ scores, and a difference of 12+ points is significant (Kaufman, 1976). Intellectual asymmetry is of great interest to criminologists. While VIQ > PIQ patterns are predictive of prosocial behavior in adults (Walsh, Taylor, & Yun, 2015), PIQ > VIQ patterns are associated with delinquency and crime. Andrew (1977) describes "the classic Wechsler 'P > V' sign for delinquency" (p. 99), and many researchers have confirmed this finding as robust (e.g., Ellis & Walsh, 2003; Prentice & Kelly, 1963; Walsh, Petee, & Beyer, 1987). The "PIQ > VIQ relationship was found across studies, despite variations in age, sex, race, setting, and form of the Wechsler scale administered, as well as in differences in criteria for delinquency" (Miller, 1987, p. 120).

Another approach to parsing cognitive ability is to distinguish intellectual function (IQ) from executive function (EF) controlled in the prefrontal lobe (Stuss & Benson, 1986). IQ operates like the raw horsepower of a car engine, while EF—involving the control and organization of cognition, decision making, memory, inhibitory control, and regulation of behavior—operates like the transmission, directing the power of the engine. IQ is strongly associated with academic achievement, but EF characteristics (such as self-control, focus, and attention)—also with strong genetic foundations (Jackson & Beaver, 2013)—collectively play an equal role (Krapohl et al., 2014). Even though intelligence and executive function are related, etiologically and functionally they are discrete activities (Antshel et al., 2010; Friedman et al. 2006), to the extent that "frontal [executive function] damage does not result in evident deficits in psychometric intelligence tests" (Ardila, Pineda, & Rosselli, 2000, p. 32). One can possess a high IQ yet have EF deficits, and vice versa. Executive function is particularly implicated in criminal behavior (Beaver, Wright, & DeLisi, 2007; DeLisi, 2015; Ogilvie, Stewart, Chan, & Shum, 2011), although, as Beaver and his colleagues (2013) note, it can be terrifically difficult to disentangle the influences of IQ from those of EF when studying crime.

Some experts believe in multiple intelligences. For example, Sternberg (1985) posits a triarchic theory, claiming that there are analytic, creative, and practical intelligences. He has augmented his theory by adding a wisdom-based intelligence (Sternberg, 2003). He criticizes conventional IQ testing for tapping analytic abilities while overlooking the importance of practical problem solving and creativity. Gardner (1983) echoes Sternberg's criticism and argues that the linguistic and logical-mathematical intelligences measured by most IQ tests are but two varieties of human intelligence. He suggests that bodily-kinesthetic, spatial, musical, interpersonal, and intrapersonal intelligences also should be acknowledged. Goleman's (1995) concept of emotional intelligence (EQ) resembles Gardner's interpersonal intelligence, and other researchers have argued that EQ is a bona fide intelligence (Mayer, Caruso, & Salovey, 1999). But Snyderman and Rothman (1987) found that only 13% of their experts believed in a multiple abilities model, while 58% believed in a general intelligence (g) model. Although reducing all cognitive abilities down to a single value necessarily obfuscates differences between people, individuals who score highly on one test tend to score highly on other tests, even those that tap different cognitive abilities. Spearman (1927) concludes that a fundamental mental property is at work. Some have argued that g is a statistical artifact of factor analysis (e.g., Gould, 1981), but g is staunchly defended by others (Jensen, 1998). In the American Psychological Association's review of intelligence research, Neisser and his colleagues (1996) write that a common contemporary view is of a hierarchy of intellectual abilities, with something like g at the apex and increasingly specialized abilities spread below it. This view resembles the Cattell-Horn-Carroll (CHC) theory, positing a hierarchy of three strata (with g at the top, about 9 broad abilities below it, and 70+ narrow abilities below them; Schneider & McGrew, 2012).

By definition, the average IQ score is 100. Despite rapid gains in intelligence scores around the world (Flynn, 1987, 2012; Trahan, Stuebing, Fletcher, & Hiscock, 2014), IQ tests are periodically renormed to maintain a population mean of 100 and to conform scores to a normal (bell-curve-shaped) distribution. Most common IQ tests have robust measures of reliability (the extent to which the test produces consistent results) and validity (the ability to measure what the test purports to measure; Franzen, 2000). Indeed, Kanazawa (2012) explains, "Arthur R. Jensen, probably the greatest living intelligence researcher, claims that IQ tests have higher reliability than the measurement of height and weight in a doctor's office. He says that the reliability of IQ tests is between .90 and .99 (meaning that random measurement error is between 1% and 10%), whereas the measurement of blood pressure, blood cholesterol and diagnosis based on chest X-rays typically has reliability of around .50" (p. 44).

Different IQ tests employ different scoring schemes. For example, the Wechsler Intelligence Scale for Children (WISC) and the Wechsler Adult Intelligence Scale (WAIS) use a standard deviation of 15 points whereas early versions of the Stanford-Binet used a standard deviation of 16 points (Kaufman, 2009). The Army Alpha

TABLE 7 Frequency of IQ scores between 100 and 200

IQ	X = μ(100) + σ(15)	Percentile	Frequency: 1/X
200	$\mu + 6.6666666667\sigma$	99.9999999987%	76,017,176,740
190	$\mu + 6\sigma$	99.9999999010%	1,009,976,678
180	$\mu + 5.3333333333\sigma$	99.9999951684%	20,696,863
170	$\mu + 4.6666666667\sigma$	99.9998467663%	652,598
160	$\mu + 4\sigma$	99.9968313965%	31,560
150	$\mu + 3.3333333333\sigma$	99.9570883466%	2,330
140	$\mu + 2.6666666667\sigma$	99.6169574875%	261
130	$\mu + 2\sigma$	97.7249937964%	44
120	$\mu + 1.3333333333\sigma$	90.8788718026%	11
110	$\mu + 0.6666666667\sigma$	74.7507532660%	3.96051419092
100	μ	49.9999999782%	1.99999999913

NOTE: For each IQ score in column one, the second column represents how many standard deviations (σ) above the population mean (μ) the score is. The third column represents the percentage of the population that has an IQ below the listed score. The fourth column indicates how many people would need to be present for one of them to possess the listed IQ score by chance.

produced scores between 0 and 212 (Yoakum & Yerkes, 1920). Different tests have different scoring frameworks, but IQ tests produce scores that translate into standard frequencies on the bell curve. By virtue of the shape of the intelligence distribution, approximately half of all IQ scores fall between 90 and 110. Almost everyone (99.7%) falls within three standard deviations (e.g., a WISC IQ between 55 and 145). Table 7 provides basic information about the frequency of IQ scores between 100 and 200.

Various labels are associated with IQ ranges (figure 14). In the left tail of the distribution, individuals with scores of 70 (two standard deviations below the mean) or less are characterized as *intellectually handicapped*. During the early twentieth century, this population was called *feebleminded* (the feebleminded population was divided into *idiots* [IQs below 20], *imbeciles* [IQs of 20–50], and *morons* [IQs of 50–70]; Barclay, 1999). These terms, since incorporated into the common lexicon, soon fell out of favor with psychometricians. *Mentally defective* was the preferred nomenclature during the 1940s; and today, the term *mental retardation* (or *developmental disability*) is used when an IQ score of 70 or less is accompanied by other diagnostic criteria. There are four degrees of severity of mental retardation: *mild* (IQ of ~50–70), *moderate* (IQ of ~35–50), *severe* (IQ of ~20–35), and *profound* (IQ below ~20; American Psychiatric Association, 2013). In the center of the curve, average intelligence ranges from about 90 to 110.

In the right tail of the distribution, many researchers eschew the term *genius* (Kreuter, 1962). For example, Wechsler (1939) cautioned, "[W]e are rather hesitant about calling a person a genius on the basis of a single intelligence test score" (p. 45). Modern psychometric testers prefer labels of *giftedness,* using standard

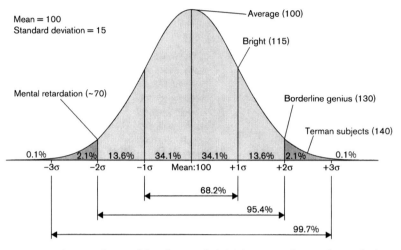

FIGURE 14. Annotated normal distribution of IQ. With a mean of 100 and a standard deviation of 15, more than 95% of the population scores between 70 and 130 on IQ tests, and more than 99% score between 55 and 145.

deviations as threshold values (Wasserman, 2003). An IQ score of 115 qualifies one as *bright;* at 130, one is *moderately gifted;* at 145, *highly gifted;* at 160, *exceptionally gifted;* and at 175, *profoundly gifted.* Those who *do* link genius to IQ have proposed different qualifying thresholds. Terman uses a threshold IQ score of 140, later expanding his study to include IQ scores of 135. Eysenck (1995) defines "the typical genius as having an IQ some three to four standard deviations above the mean" (p. 59). Galton (1892) describes the genius as 250 in a million. Hollingworth defines genius as a 180 IQ. Simonton (1994) defines "borderline genius" as a 130 (98%+) score. This score mirrors the threshold for mental handicap in a symmetrical normal distribution. Thus, the borderline genius is as far from the population mean as the borderline mentally retarded person (Oleson, 2009; Robinson, Zigler, & Gallagher, 2000). Furthermore, the genius with a 160 IQ is as divergent from the borderline genius with an IQ of 130 as that borderline genius is from the norm (IQ 100). But because they are so rare, little is known about the profoundly gifted (but see Feldman, 1984; Gross, 1993; Hollingworth, 1942; Kearney, 1990; Lubinski, Webb, Morelock, & Benbow, 2001). A number of high-IQ societies exist, with various admissions thresholds. At IQ 130, an individual is eligible to join Mensa (Serebriakoff, 1995), the High Potentials Society, and the Mysterium Society; at IQ 99%, Intertel, the Top One Percent Society, and Chorium; at 99.9%, the Triple Nine Society, the International Society for Philosophical Enquiry, and the Iquadrivium Society; at 99.997%, the Prometheus and Epimetheus Societies; at 99.9999% (one in a million), the Mega Society; and at 99.9999999% (one in a billion), the Giga Society.

These quantitative IQ differences are important because they can also produce qualitative differences in human potential. Of course, alone, high IQ does not guarantee the realization of genius. IQ is likely a necessary but not sufficient correlate of genius. Unless it is combined with executive function, personality traits, and appropriate habits cultivated over time, high IQ might not even produce success in life. But high IQ unlocks hitherto unknown possibilities:

> General intelligence, for example, is undoubtedly quantitative in the sense that it consists of varying amounts of the same basic stuff (e.g., mental energy) which can be expressed by continuous numerical measures like Intelligence Quotients or Mental-Age scores, and these are as real as any physical measurements are. But it is equally certain that our description of the difference between a genius and an average person by a statement to the effect that he has an IQ greater by this or that amount, does not describe the difference between them as completely or in the same way as when we say that a mile is much longer than an inch. The genius (as regards intellectual ability) not only has an IQ of say 50 points more than the average person, but in virtue of this difference acquires seemingly new aspects (potentialities) or characteristics. These seemingly new aspects or characteristics, in their totality, are what go to make up the "qualitative" difference between them. (Wechsler, 1955, p. 134)

Hirsch goes even further: "The genius differs in kind from the species, man. Genius can be defined only in terms of its own unique mental and temperamental processes, traits, qualities, and products. Genius is another psychobiological species, differing as much from man, in his mental and temperamental processes, as man differs from the ape" (in Hollingworth, 1942, p. 4).

GENIUS AND CRIME

Darwin believed that criminal traits were innate and heritable (Baschetti, 2008). In *The Descent of Man and Selection in Relation to Sex* (1875), he reasons, "In regard to the moral qualities, some elimination of the worst dispositions is always in progress even in the most civilized nations. Malefactors are executed, or imprisoned for long periods, so that they cannot freely transmit their bad qualities" (p. 137). Although Darwin is rarely invoked in contemporary explanations of crime, his influence upon the formation of criminological thought should not be underestimated. Evolutionary thinking lies at the heart of the pioneering work of Lombroso. In *Criminal Man* (1876/2006), Lombroso broke from Beccaria's (1764/1995) classical school of penology (which assumed criminals to be rational agents, responsible for their actions) and argued instead that the offender is a product of reverse evolution, an "atavistic being, a relic of a vanished race" (Lombroso-Ferrero, 1911, p. 135). Crime inheres in his nature. Fortunately, the criminal can be identified by the presence of physical stigmata: powerful jaws, high cheekbones, and handle-shaped ears

(Lombroso, 1876/2006). *Criminal Man* made Lombroso a household name and earned him the appellation "father of criminology" (Gibson, 2002). However, few people—even few criminologists—realize that 12 years earlier, Lombroso had advanced a similar theory of degeneration to explain the phenomenon of genius (Lombroso, 1891). Intriguingly, the father of criminology proposed analogous theories to explain both genius and crime (Lombroso, 1902; Mora, 1964). Other theorists built upon this foundation, drawing connections between crime, madness, and genius:

> You have all noticed the odd boy of the family; the doubtful character; the precocious prodigy; the black sheep of the flock. For example, let us take a respectable farmer's family of four or five children. The parents are healthy, sober, poor but respectable people. The children, with one exception, resemble one or the other parent. Their mental endowments do not exceed mediocrity. But this odd boy—this variation from the family likeness, is the one who interests us. He differs from the others greatly and is willful, perverse, moody, impulsive, and perhaps frail and sickly. Marked precocity is his only redeeming characteristic. The ordinary pleasures of childhood which interest his brothers and sisters have no charm for him. He plays alone or wanders off in the fields, seeking solitude in the passivity of nature. He is such a strange boy. His parents do not understand him, and his associates look upon him with awe. As he reaches the adolescent period, he becomes dissatisfied and restless, reluctantly gaining his parents consent to leave home, or failing in that, runs away and turns his face toward some near-by large city. Here his interesting career commences and if followed up is found to attain one of four terminations. *First,* and most prominent in the order of frequency is an early death. *Second,* he may help swell the criminal ranks. *Third,* he may become mentally deranged and ultimately find his way into a hospital for insane. *Fourth,* and least frequently, he startles the world by an invention or discovery in science or by an original composition of great merit in art, music or literature. He is then styled a genius. (Babcock, 1895, p. 752, emphasis in original)

Little has been written on the relationship between crime and the classical conception of genius (genius as attendant spirit), but preclassical explanations for crime frequently relied upon the devil, demons, witches, and evil spirits (Farrington, 1996). The records from the notorious Salem witchcraft trials of 1692 provide some insight into the practice (Norton, 2002), but another estimated 200,000 to 500,000 witches were executed in Europe between 1300 and 1650 CE (Ben-Yehuda, 1980). Today, demonic explanations for crime have been supplanted by scientific theories of crime, even though some offenders insist that they have been controlled by evil spirits (Oleson, 2006).

Similarly, the relationship between creative genius and crime has been little studied. Certainly, if creative people are more willing to violate conventions, norms, or rules (Cropley & Cropley, 2011; Cropley, Kaufman, & Runco, 2010; Gino

& Wiltermuth, 2014), they may run a greater risk of criminal sanction. Many celebrated writers have been jailed (Oleson, 1997). Yet creativity is generally regarded to be a positive force (e.g., May, 1975), and the suggestion that there is a "dark side" to creativity is an idea of recent vintage (McLaren, 1993). In *Creativity and Crime* (2013), Cropley and Cropley note, "Crime and creativity fuse when . . . people generate useful and effective novelty in order to make their statutorily prohibited actions serve their illegal purposes better" (p. 2). Creative genius can make a criminal exceptionally successful. After all, it enabled Frank Abagnale to flourish as a confidence artist and forger for years (Abagnale & Redding, 1980). There may be an association between creativity and crime. Kanazawa (2003) notes that the age-crime curve (revealing a universal general decline in criminal behavior after the teens and early 20s) closely resembles the age-creative genius curve associated with jazz musicians, painters, and authors. He posits a common generative force that underlies both art and crime.

The relationship between eminence and crime has also attracted oblique attention. When Simonton (2009) analyzed historiometric eminence and rated morality, he found a U-shaped function: "In other words, the greatest monarchs were either good or evil, famous or infamous. More mediocre rulers were less extreme in their moral behavior. So if you can't go down in history as a saint, at least you can leave your mark as a sinner" (p. 30). In *A Study of British Genius* (1927), Ellis analyzes 1,030 subjects drawn from the *Dictionary of National Biography* and reports that over 16% of the men studied had been imprisoned on one or more occasions, while others had escaped imprisonment only by voluntary exile. Among the 100 most influential figures in history identified in *The 100: A Ranking of the Most Influential Persons in History* (Hart, 1992), at least 16 were arrested, imprisoned, or executed; another 8 faced voluntary or involuntary exile; and others were engaged in unlawful revolutionary conduct. Certainly, there is empirical support for Rhodes's (1932) assertion that "[s]ociety punishes the genius while he lives, even if its laws do not permit it to put him in gaol or execute him. . . . The ordinary man comes to terms with society. The . . . genius will not" (pp. 37, 59).

In summary, little research exists on the linkage between crime and genius, as such. A handful of studies have attempted to relate crime to incorporeal spirits, creativity, or eminence. There is, however, an immense body of research that attempts to relate intelligence to propensities for crime (for overviews, see Baxter, Motiuk, & Fortin, 1995; Ellis & Walsh, 2003; Farrington & Welsh, 2007; Hirschi & Hindelang, 1977; Loeber et al., 2012; Lynam, Moffitt, & Stouthamer-Loeber, 1993; Wilson & Herrnstein, 1985). Stretching back a century, some of the research on intelligence and crime distinguishes *g* from executive functions, personality traits, and other genetic influences, but much of it does not, thereby confounding careful analysis. Much of the research is deliberate about psychometric assessment, but some of it—especially some of the early research on IQ and crime—is not. Accordingly, "[c]riminologists have treated the relationship between IQ and delinquent behavior with a curious mixture of faith, indifference, and contempt" (McGloin, Pratt, & Maahs, 2004, p. 604).

However, three logical possibilities exist. First, criminals may have below-average IQ scores. Most researchers examining the topic have concluded that there is an association between *below-average* intelligence and crime (e.g., Goddard, 1914; Goring, 1919; Herrnstein & Murray, 1994; Hirschi & Hindelang, 1977). Below-average verbal intelligence appears to be particularly implicated in criminal behavior. Second, criminals may possess *average* IQ scores, with the same distribution as the general population. Some researchers have reached this conclusion (e.g., Sutherland, 1931) and some have suggested that low IQ scores observed in the criminal justice system are artifactual. Third, criminals may have *above-average* IQ scores (Murchison, 1926; Stone, 1921; Weber & Guilford, 1926). After all, even Lombroso—a firm believer in the atavism of the natural criminal—acknowledged, "Intelligence is feeble in some [criminals] and exaggerated in others" (Lombroso-Ferrero, 1911, p. 41, emphasis omitted). Barnes and Teeters (1959), for example, speculated that criminal IQ might, in fact, be superior. Indeed, one study of gifted delinquents indicates that IQ is positively correlated with number of admitted prior offenses (Gath, Tennent, & Pidduck, 1971). Each of these three possibilities is discussed below, along with the implications of a curvilinear relationship (Mears & Cochran, 2013).

Below-Average Intelligence: Feebleminded Criminals

"Low intelligence was, perhaps, the first variable to be linked to offending" (Maguin & Loeber, 1996, p. 152). This association between low intelligence and crime can be traced to anthropometric research conducted in the tradition of Lombroso and eugenic family studies (Rafter, 1988). In *The American Criminal* (1939), Hooton describes the data from 107 different physical and social measurements drawn from 13,873 criminals and 3,203 controls. He concludes that criminals are distinguishable from noncriminals, both in terms of social position and morphology. Others, however, argue that it is not biological atavism that distinguishes the criminal, but inferior mental ability (Bondio, 2006). In *The English Convict: A Statistical Study* (1919), Goring compares the anatomy of 3,000 English convicts to large numbers of noncriminal citizens and concludes that it is not atavism that distinguishes the convict from the citizen, but low intelligence. Goring claims a minimum correlation of .66 between mental defectiveness and crime.

In the United States, Goddard took up the study of low intelligence. He built upon Dugdale's (1910) eugenic study of the "Jukes" family—a lineage riddled with 200 years of "pauperism, prostitution, exhaustion, disease, fornication, and illegitimacy" (Vold & Bernard, 1986, p. 68). The cost of maintaining the Jukes family on benefits and in institutions, by Dugdale's reckoning, exceeded $1.3 million.

He believed that both environmental and hereditary factors played a role in the transmission of crime and disease. In 1916, Estabrook expanded the Jukes study to include 2,820 subjects and concluded that since 1800, the Jukes had cost the New York public at least $2 million ($45 million in 2016 dollars). Estabrook emphasized the hereditary causes of social problems, viewing the Jukes as "unredeemed," and proposed that such families be prevented from reproducing because environmental changes cannot alter their heredity. Estabrook's research played an important role in justifying the involuntary sterilization of many feebleminded persons in the United States, as upheld in *Buck v. Bell* (1927). Writing for the majority of the US Supreme Court, Justice Holmes famously reasons,

> We have seen more than once that the public welfare may call upon the best citizens for their lives. It would be strange if it could not call upon those who already sap the strength of the State for these lesser sacrifices, often not felt to be such by those concerned, in order to prevent our being swamped with incompetence. It is better for all the world if, instead of waiting to execute degenerate offspring for crime or to let them starve for their imbecility, society can prevent those who are manifestly unfit from continuing their kind. The principle that sustains compulsory vaccination is broad enough to cover cutting the Fallopian tubes. Three generations of imbeciles are enough. (p. 207)

Although *eugenics* is a dirty word in contemporary parlance (Lynn, 2001), there was terrific enthusiasm for it in the first half of the twentieth century (Gould, 1981; Stern, 2005). US state fairs held "better baby" and "fitter family" contests (Pernick, 2002) and the US Congress held hearings on bills to establish a laboratory for "the study of the criminal, pauper, and defective classes" (MacDonald, 1902).

Thus, Goddard's eugenic family study, *The Kallikak Family: A Study in the Heredity of Feeblemindedness* (1912), squared with the American zeitgeist. Goddard traced a family of criminals back to its origin: a revolutionary soldier by the name of Martin Kallikak who met a feebleminded barmaid on his way home from battle and fathered a feebleminded son by her. Tracing the parents' lineage revealed 480 direct descendants, including 36 illegitimate offspring, 33 sexually immoral people, 24 confirmed alcoholics, and 8 brothel keepers; 143 of the 480 were feebleminded and others possessed questionable intelligences. But, Goddard observed, when this same man married a "worthy girl" from a good family, they created a line of 496 upstanding individuals—doctors, lawyers, educators, and merchants—none of whom were illegitimate. This second line included no immoral women, no brothel keepers, only one sexually immoral man, and two alcoholics. Only 3 members of this second line were feebleminded and none were criminal.

Goddard then published *Feeble Mindedness: Its Causes and Consequences* (1914) and *The Criminal Imbecile* (1915), establishing himself as the preeminent authority on feeblemindedness in America. Goddard divided society into three discrete groups: a natural aristocracy of the highly intelligent; the swollen ranks of the simple and harmlessly dull; and the alcoholics, prostitutes, and natural criminals of the moron class. Estimating that between 25% and 50% of the people in American prisons were mentally defective and that *all* feebleminded people were potential criminals (Goddard, 1914), Goddard campaigned for the involuntary sterilization of the feebleminded. One of the clear and present dangers to American society, Goddard believed, was immigration. Goddard used early IQ tests to demonstrate that 40% to 50% of the immigrants arriving in America belonged to the moron class. He acknowledged the detrimental effects of language bias and adverse testing conditions but ignored them and insisted that the "morons" be deported. "Because of Goddard's efforts, the rate of deportation increased 350 percent in 1913 and 570 percent in 1914" (Hergenhahn, 1986, p. 193).

There was no doubt in Goddard's mind that a robust link existed between feeblemindedness and criminality. Others concurred (e.g., Erickson, 1929). Goddard (1914) presented data from 16 different reformatories and institutions for delinquents, reporting that the percentage of feebleminded juveniles ranged from a low of 40% to a high of 89%. Goddard even claimed that "the percentage of defectives increased with the skill of the examiner, it being inferred that a completely perfect examiner would find that all criminals were mentally defective" (Murchison, 1926, p. 18). Many of the leading intelligence researchers of the early twentieth century agreed with Goddard's claims, including Terman (1916):

> Morality depends on two things: (a) the ability to foresee and to weigh the possible consequences for self and others of different kinds of behavior; and (b) upon the willingness and capacity to exercise self-restraint. That there are many intelligent criminals is due to the fact that (a) may exist without (b). On the other hand, (b) presupposes (a). In other words, *not all criminals are feeble-minded, but all feeble-minded persons are at least potential criminals.* That every feeble-minded woman is a potential prostitute would hardly be disputed by anyone. Moral judgement, like business judgement, social judgement, or any kind of higher thought process, is a function of intelligence. (p. 11, emphasis added)

Indeed, Terman, citing Dugdale (1910) and Goddard (1912, 1914), suggested that intelligence was the needle in man's moral compass and that individuals possessing only subnormal mental faculties could not be expected to make independent moral decisions. The abundant evidence for natural criminality in the feebleminded, combined with the relative lack of evidence for crime among persons of average or superior intelligence, conveyed a two-part message. First, it suggested that crime and immorality were blights incurred upon society by the shortcomings of the feebleminded. Second, it implied (more through what was left unsaid than through any explicit claim) that intelligent people did not commit crimes.

Although Terman and his coauthors produced more than 6,000 pages in the first five volumes of *Genetic Studies of Genius,* they devote less than 1 page to their subjects' involvement in crime. In volume 5—the last volume to which Terman contributed—the authors write,

> As shown in our earlier report, the incidence of crime and delinquency is very low. Three subjects (all boys) had youthful records of delinquency that resulted in their being sent to a juvenile reformatory. In addition, one man served a term of several years in prison for forgery. All four of these are married, employed, and fulfilling their duties as responsible citizens. Three other boys came before the Juvenile Court for behavior difficulties but after brief detention were released to their parents. Among the gifted women only two are known to have had encounters with the police. Both were arrested for vagrancy and one served a jail sentence. Although each of these women has a history of several marriages, both seem to have become much more stable in recent years, and to have made normal behavioral adjustments." (Terman & Oden, 1959, p. 46)

In 1968, Oden updated the findings with four sentences: "The incidence of crime and delinquency has remained extremely low. Prior to 1940 one man had served a prison term for forgery and three boys had been sent to reformatories briefly. Two women in their youth were arrested for misdemeanors. So far as known, there have been no further serious breaches of the law" (p. 10).

While it is remarkable that Terman's subjects had almost no contact with the criminal justice system (West & Farrington, 1973; cf. Beaver et al., 2013), the paucity of deviance and crime in the analysis is striking. Margolin (1993) described the carefully constructed depiction of gifted children in the early twentieth century as "goodness personified." For example, the photographs of gifted children in Hollingworth's *Gifted Children: Their Nature and Nurture* (1926) depicted her young subjects as well groomed, well dressed, smiling, and handsome. On the other hand, the photographs in *The Kallikak Family* (Goddard, 1912) contained retouched photos in which heavy, dark lines traced the eyes and mouths of its subjects, making simplicity appear dangerous and sinister—perhaps deliberately (Gould, 1981).

Research on feeblemindedness and crime began to be challenged during the 1920s and 1930s (Zeleny, 1933), along with medicobiological criminology generally. "During the 1930s, American sociologists waged a successful turf war against biologists, psychologists, and physicians, wresting criminology from its biological roots, to make the growing field a specialty within the larger discipline of sociology" (Wright & Miller, 1998, p. 2). Race and class—not intelligence—became the presumptive causes of crime. With the revelations of World War II, interest in intelligence and crime, connoting the taboo of eugenics, further waned from the 1940s through the 1970s (Wilson & Herrnstein, 1985). In 1977, however, the topic was reinvigorated.

In their landmark article, "Intelligence and Delinquency: A Revisionist View" (1977) Hirschi and Hindelang argue that IQ is at least as important a correlate of delinquency as race or class, and they suggest that it is "reasonable to expect that samples of delinquents would differ from the general population by about eight IQ points" (p. 581). Their conclusion accorded with the findings of other researchers who reported an average offender IQ of 92, approximately one half of one standard deviation below the population mean (e.g., Caplan, 1965; Merrill, 1947; Quay, 1987; Woodward, 1955). Wilson and Herrnstein (1985) suggest that the IQ gulf might be slightly larger. Because the mean population IQ is 100, as the true percentage of offenders increases, the nonoffender average IQ must also increase to compensate. Thus, Wilson and Herrnstein estimate a gap of 10, rather than 8, IQ points. Other researchers have examined the gap by disaggregating petty offenders from serious persistent offenders (Moffitt, 1993; but see Donnellan, Ge, & Wenk, 2000). Since a pioneering 1972 study by Wolfgang and his colleagues, many researchers have reported that a minority (5% or 6%) of offenders are responsible for a disproportionate volume (often more than 50%) of offending: "Across social and behavioral science literatures and spanning a range of constructs, including life-course-persistent offenders, serious, violent, and chronic delinquents, psychopaths, and career criminals, this 5% group is characterized by a disproportionate contribution to crime and related social problems, by a sharply disproportionate contribution to serious violence, by evidence of life-long psychopathology, and by the imposition of extreme social burden and other collateral costs" (Vaughn et al., 2011, p. 75). Although petty offenders differ from nonoffenders by only about 1 IQ point, serious persistent offenders differ from nonoffenders by approximately 17 points (Moffitt, Caspi, Silva, & Stouthamer-Loeber, 1995).

Precisely *how* low IQ relates to crime remains unknown. "In light of the evidence that the relationship between intelligence and offending is real, it is somewhat surprising to find how few theoretical attempts have been made to explain the relationship" (Ellis & Walsh, 2003, p. 351; see also Jolliffe & Farrington, 2010). The low IQ-crime relationship is probably not a matter of street criminals failing to learn math skills or being poorly read; rather, the relationship pertains to fundamental cognitive capacities: slow executive functioning, limited verbal IQ (i.e., difficulty articulating thoughts and feelings), impaired empathy and foresight (Farrington & Welsh, 2007), and low self-control (Felson & Staff, 2006; Gottfredson & Hirschi, 1990; Jensen, 1998). Possessing poor attention skills and limited ability to defer gratification (Shoda, Mischel, & Peake, 1990), as well as *g*-based difficulties in understanding concepts, young people with low IQ might turn to delinquency and crime via school failure (Hirschi, 1969; McGloin et al., 2004; Menard & Morse, 1984; Simons, 1978; Ward & Tittle, 1994), a possibility explored in chapter 6.

Low IQ appears to be exacerbated by low parental socioeconomic status (Levine, 2011). Some have suggested that a delinquent or criminal lifestyle might lead to low IQ, rather than vice versa, either through traumatic brain injury from fights or drug abuse (e.g., León-Carrión & Ramos, 2003) or through antiauthoritarian or subcultural attitudes that undermine subjects' test motivation (e.g., Tarnopol, 1970), but most researchers have rejected the temporal order critique. Low IQ in early childhood (even as young as three and four years old) significantly predicts later delinquency and adult arrests (Denno, 1990; Hogh & Wolf, 1983; Lipsitt, Buka, & Lipsett, 1990; McCord & Ensminger, 1997; Stattin & Klackenberg-Larsson, 1993; West & Farrington, 1973) and cannot plausibly be attributed to a criminal lifestyle. Similarly, even after statistically controlling for test motivation, a significant IQ-delinquency relationship endures (Lynam et al., 1993; but see Block, 1995).

The association between low IQ and crime also has been bolstered by epidemiological research on environmental toxins. Since the 1990s, US crime rates have fallen unexpectedly and precipitously, and researchers have struggled to understand why (Levitt, 2004). Reductions in exposure to paint- and gasoline-based lead (Nevin, 2000) may help explain both rising IQ scores (Flynn, 1987, 2012) and falling crime rates. "Gasoline lead may explain as much as 90 percent of the rise and fall of violent crime over the past half century" (Drum, 2013). Lead, however, is not the only neurotoxin to depress IQ. Bellinger (2012) estimates that exposure of pregnant women to just three toxins (lead, methylmercury, and organophosphate pesticides) cost an aggregate 41 million IQ points in the US population. Other chemicals produce similar reductions in IQ (Hamblin, 2014). Research associating traumatic brain injury and violent crime also points to a cognitive cause of crime. According to Burhan and his colleagues (2014), increases in national IQ exert a powerful suppressing effect on crime, particularly through increased efficacy of the intellectual class (i.e., those in the 95th percentile of IQ) in setting crime policy and providing effective governance.

Sociologically oriented criminologists remain skeptical of research on IQ and crime (Walsh & Wright, 2015), but Lynam and his colleagues (1993) insist that the negative IQ-delinquency relationship "is difficult to deny; it is one of the most robust findings across numerous studies of juvenile delinquency" (p. 187). Indeed, West and Farrington (1973) count the negative IQ-delinquency relationship as a primary background factor leading to delinquency; Jensen (1998) describes it as "a well-established empirical fact" (p. 298); Eysenck and Gudjonsson (1989) describe the relationship as "undisputed" (p. 50); and Caplan (1965) identifies an eight-point difference as a "first class" relationship (p. 104). Beaver and his colleagues (2013) state the matter even more forcefully: "There is likely not another individual level variable that is so consistently associated with crime and other forms of antisocial behaviors than IQ. . . . [R]esearch examining the etiology of crime and antisocial behaviors is likely misspecified if a measure of IQ is not included in the statistical models" (p. 285).

Average Intelligence: Rejecting Feeblemindedness

Not all researchers concur that crime is negatively correlated with intelligence. Murchison (1926) warns, "[G]reat harm has been done and is being done by the propaganda which creates the impression that the criminal is feebleminded" (p. 38). Murchison's *Criminal Intelligence* challenges Lombroso's study of the criminal man, Dugdale's study of the Jukes, and—especially—Goddard's analyses of feeblemindedness. Murchison notes that the actual number of cases was never revealed in Goddard's work, only percentages, and observes that Goddard neither identified the means of selecting his cases nor defined "mental defectiveness," the criterion by which Goddard evaluated his cases. All of Goddard's cases were juveniles, the majority were female, and not a single report came from a penitentiary. Murchison seeks to remedy these flaws by assessing the intelligence of *real* criminals: adult male criminals in penal institutions. He compares the IQ scores of 94,004 enlisted soldiers from World War I with scores from 3,368 prisoners at Leavenworth penitentiary and concludes that the inmates are actually *more intelligent* than the soldiers. His conclusion is that criminals are at least as intelligent as law-abiding citizens. Murchison (1926) also examines the IQ scores of guards in a certain penitentiary (probably Leavenworth) and compares them to the inmates' scores: "[T]he average score of the criminals was . . . 75 per cent higher than the average score of the guards" (p. 28).

Other prison studies produced similar results. For example, after controlling for nationality and race, Doll (1920) concludes, "[T]he mental constitution of the [New Jersey State] prison as a whole corresponds very closely to the average intelligence of adult males of the State as a whole" (p. 195). In Illinois, Tulchin (1938) found that the intelligence of two state penitentiaries mirrored that of those registered with the state draft. Murphy and D'Angelo (1963) found that incarcerated women scored in the low-average to average IQ range.

Like Murchison, Sutherland (1931) attacks the link between feeblemindedness and crime, with devastating effect. In his meta-analysis of 50 studies of feebleminded delinquents, he notes that as psychometric testing improved, the intellectual deficits of the offenders dwindled. Looking at the same trend in the IQ-crime research, Wootton (1959) later observes, "[A]s the techniques for more accurate measurement of intelligence have been refined, the foundations of the once widely held belief in the existence of a negative correlation between intelligence and criminality have crumbled away" (p. 302). Accordingly, Sutherland (1931) interprets the result as signifying that IQ differences between delinquents and controls are a function of the tests or testers, not the abilities of the tested. He therefore concludes, "[F]eeblemindedness . . . seems to be a relatively unimportant factor. . . . It appears to be of some significance in determining the general type of crimes and of a few specific types of crimes" (p. 373). Others, too, suggested that delinquents and criminals have IQ scores approximating those of the general population (e.g., Baker, Decker, & Hill, 1929; Black & Hornblow, 1973; Lichtenstein & Brown, 1938; Maller, 1937; Rutter, Tizard, & Whitmore, 1970; Valliant & Bergeron, 1997). Samenow (1984) distinguishes IQ and crystallized intelligence from cunning:

There has also been a theory that criminals are inherently less intelligent than the general population, but this has been laid to rest. Empirical studies of criminals and noncriminals simply do not support such a proposition. Criminals may score low on IQ tests and lack basic information that most people acquire in the primary grades of school. However, their mental acumen and resourcefulness are striking to anyone who is privy to their complex, well-thought-out schemes. Criminals are remarkable in their capacity to size up their environment in order to pursue objectives important to them. (p. 19)

Some researchers (e.g., Doleschal & Klapmuts, 1973; Feldman, 1977; Rutter & Giller, 1984; Stark, 1975; Tennenbaum, 1992) suggest that criminals as a class have average IQ scores but individual criminals with low IQ are more likely to be detected and caught by the police. "In other words, individuals with higher intelligence may be committing crimes at the same rate as individuals with lower intelligence, but only the less intelligent ones are getting caught by the police" (Wright & Boisvert, 2009, p. 96). Alternatively, it may be that criminals have average IQ but criminal justice officials, enjoying enormous discretion (Stuntz, 2011), react differently to low-IQ offenders than to average- or high-IQ offenders. A full discussion of the differential detection and differential reaction hypotheses can be found in chapter 5, but in general, while there is evidence to indicate that IQ is negatively correlated with increased penetration into the criminal justice system (e.g., advancing from detection to arrest to prosecution to conviction to incarceration; Beaver et al., 2013; Cullen, Gendreau, Jarjoura, & Wright, 1997; Herrnstein & Murray, 1994; McCord, McCord, & Zola, 1959), low IQ is also associated with self-reported offending (Farrington, 1992; West & Farrington, 1973). Supported by the findings of Moffitt and Silva (1988), most researchers reject the hypotheses. "The [IQ-crime] relationship does not appear to be attributable to the possibility that low-IQ offenders are more likely to be apprehended" (Ellis & Walsh, 2003, p. 353).

Other critics of the IQ-crime relationship believe that it is not IQ that leads to delinquency and crime, but class and/or race. "[S]ocial class and race are considered important correlates of official delinquency by almost everyone" (Hirschi & Hindelang, 1977, p. 573; cf. Ellis, Beaver, & Wright, 2009). Critics of the IQ-crime relationship argue that IQ tests actually measure the assimilation of middle-class values (e.g., Cohen, 1955) or suggest that the disadvantage of class and/or race operates as a third variable that both depresses IQ (i.e., via middle-class conformity) and increases the risk of criminal justice involvement. Menard and Morse (1984), for example, conclude that delinquency is related not to IQ but to institutional structures, and the authors note that the weak support they *did* find for an association between IQ and delinquency "might arguably be eroded were race and social class controlled" (p. 1375). In a study by Lynam and his colleagues (1993), however, class and race *were* controlled, and the IQ-delinquency relationship was still significant.

Above-Average Intelligence: Bright Delinquents

Lombroso (1902) suggests that great intelligence has the power to magnify under-lying criminality: "[I]ntelligence is the soul of things; it is such a lever that it can raise a little criminal, an individual with scarcely the tendencies to crime, simply through a diminution of the moral sense, to the most terrible heights of wrong-doing; intelligence is a wind which can transform a small spark into a great fire" (p. 237). In *The Young Delinquent* (1955), Burt agrees, describing the juvenile offender as typically dull, although not technically feebleminded. Burt's finding accords with the prevailing 8- to 10-point IQ deficit model (e.g., Hirschi & Hinde-lang, 1977). But Burt also finds that approximately 2.5% of his London delinquents possessed intellectual talents of scholarship level. Burt (1955) writes that these bright delinquents, "tactfully and wisely handled . . . are among the most hopeful cases that the psychologist is called upon to study," but he cautions that "[w]rongly treated, they turn into criminals of the most dangerous and elusive type" (p. 182). Cloward and Ohlin (1960) write, "Some persons who have experienced a marked discrepancy between aspirations and achievements may look outward, attributing their failure to the existence of unjust or arbitrary institutional arrangements which keep men of ability and ambition from rising in the social structure. Such persons do not view their failure as a reflection of personal inadequacy but instead blame a cultural and social system that encourages every-one to reach for success while differentially restricting access to the success-goals" (p. 111).

Harvey and Seeley (1984) also find gifted students in a delinquent population. Bright delinquents *do* exist, although little is known about them (Cohn, 2009; Mahoney, 1980; Seeley, 1984). While hundreds of studies of juvenile delinquency exist, only a fraction of them include IQ as a variable, and just a handful employ high-IQ delinquents as subjects. When high-IQ subjects *are* used, they typically report IQ scores that lie above the population mean but fall below the 98th per-centile (i.e., the threshold of borderline genius). Table 8 describes the samples and summarizes some of the key findings from a number of studies of gifted delinquents.

Some researchers (e.g., Anolik, 1979; Cornell, 1992; Lajoie & Shore, 1981) sug-gest that gifted and average delinquents share common social and criminological characteristics. Caplan (1964) and Powell, however, argue that "delinquents are not a unitary class" (p. 317) and can be divided meaningfully into average and high-IQ groupings.

Simmons (1956) argues that bright delinquents tended to offend for different reasons than normal or dull delinquents. He suggests that high IQ acts as a protec-tive factor against offending and that only severe emotional disturbance is enough to overcome this factor and turn gifted youngsters to crime. Simmons's findings are supported by the research of Cowie, Cowie, and Slater (1968), who studied

TABLE 8 Select references on gifted/bright delinquents (1944–2009)

Investigators	Year	Key Findings
Anolik	1979	Compared 30 bright delinquents (IQ ≥ 115) to 30 matched controls with average IQ (90–104); index and controls did not differ meaningfully in terms of personality, family, educational, or criminological characteristics.
Brooks	1980	Compared 67 gifted nonoffenders, 68 gifted offenders, and 135 controls with average IQ scores.
Burt	1955	Descriptive research: "In a few cases the intelligence of the young delinquent is not below normal but above it; and, paradoxically enough, that in itself may lead to his undoing" (p. 180).
Caplan & Powell	1964	Compared 100 superior delinquents (IQ ≥ 120) to average-IQ delinquents (IQ 90–109) on 83 different measures; found superior delinquents differ from average delinquents in terms of delinquency, school, and family measures.
Cohn	2009	Descriptive research: Discusses biological bases of crime, identification of gifted delinquents, risk factors, and treatment interventions.
Cornell	1992	Studied 157 adolescents convicted of violence or larceny: Most delinquents had below-average (86.6) IQ scores; only 2 subjects had full-scale IQ scores over 130; for 13 delinquents with 120+ IQ, family disturbance and adjustment difficulties preceded offense; for all subjects, PIQ > VIQ.
Cowie, Cowie, & Slater	1968	Studied 318 delinquent girls: Girls with highest intelligence had severe psychiatric disturbances; girls with intermediate intelligence had intermediate psychiatric disturbance; girls with lowest intelligence had no psychiatric symptoms.
Gath & Tennent	1972	Descriptive research: Survey of extant literature suggests that bright delinquents share criminological, educational, and social characteristics with other delinquents but are less often identified, are treated differently by the courts, and are more often presented as emotionally disturbed.
Gath, Tennent, & Pidduck	1970	Compared 50 bright delinquent boys (IQ ≥ 115) to 50 matched controls (IQ 90–105): 18 of the 50 gifted delinquents committed offenses for psychological reasons; only 8 of the 50 boys with average IQ scores committed offenses for psychological reasons.
Gath, Tennent, & Pidduck	1971	Compared 50 bright delinquent boys (IQ ≥ 115) to 50 matched controls (IQ 90–105). Gifted delinquents commit offenses for psychological (not financial) reasons: gifted offenders gained £69 profit per offender; average-IQ offenders gained £1,151 profit per offender.
Haarer	1966	Measured IQ of 665 boys and 470 girls in Michigan facilities for delinquents; only 29 boys and 11 girls had gifted (120+) IQ scores.
Lajoie & Shore	1981	Descriptive research: Summary of research concludes that bright delinquents are uncommon; use of full-scale IQ scores and presence of learning disabilities may obfuscate gifted delinquents.
Mahoney	1980	Descriptive research: Summary of research indicates that bright delinquents are uncommon and likely to come from broken homes; theorized that bright youth are protected by IQ except under extreme family circumstances.

(continued)

TABLE 8 *(continued)*

Investigators	Year	Key Findings
Merrill	1947	Descriptive research: Bright delinquents (IQ ≥ 120) better at avoiding detection and, if caught, are able to avoid prosecution.
Neihart	2009	Descriptive research: High-IQ delinquency related to criminal thinking; discussion of episodic dyscontrol as explanation for single acts of heinous acts of violence.
Seeley	1984	Studied 268 delinquents in two-year study: Gifted youth were underrepresented in delinquent populations.
Simmons	1956	Descriptive research: Offenses of high-IQ delinquents were "not light-hearted mischief but the result of deep-seated internal compulsion" (p. 271).
Simmons	1962	Descriptive research: High-IQ delinquents generally suffer from emotional disturbance—such disturbance is usually more severe than would be necessary to trigger delinquency in less intelligent boys.
Simmons & Davis	1953	Descriptive research: Describes operating principles of Kneesworth Hall, a UK school for bright delinquents.
Tennent & Gath	1975	Compared 50 bright delinquent boys (IQ ≥ 115) to 50 matched controls (IQ 90–105); although recidivism rates were high for both groups (74–80%), no differences in recidivism were detected between bright and average delinquents.
West & Farrington	1973	Longitudinal study of 411 working-class boys: Boys with IQ > 110 were underrepresented in the delinquent group and had much lower recidivism rates (2%) than boys with average IQ (7%) or IQ < 90 (20%).

318 delinquent girls and concluded that delinquent girls demonstrating the highest intelligence also demonstrated severe psychiatric disturbances, while delinquent girls with intermediate intelligence showed intermediate levels of psychiatric disturbance, and girls demonstrating the lowest levels of intelligence showed no psychiatric symptoms. Simmons's findings also find support in the work of Brooks (1967, 1972, 1980), who studied boys at Kneesworth Hall (a home for British delinquents with 120+ IQ scores).

Gath and his colleagues (1970) compared the psychiatric characteristics of 50 bright delinquent boys with IQ scores of 115+ (mean IQ of 126.2) against the psychiatric characteristics of 50 delinquent boys with IQ scores between 90 and 105 (mean IQ of 96.8) and drew several conclusions. They found support for earlier claims that bright delinquents tend to offend for psychiatric reasons. While 22 average boys committed their offences for subcultural rather than psychological reasons (e.g., they stole something from a shop to impress their peers versus damaging property after fighting with parents), only 17 of the bright boys offended for this reason. Sometimes, psychological factors were also at work, but subcultural factors actually determined the offense; this was true for 20 average boys and 15 bright boys. While psychological factors were predominant in the offending of only 8 average boys, they were predominant in 18 bright delinquents. Gath and his colleagues (1971) found additional support for the idea that bright delinquents offended for emotional or psychological reasons, reporting that gifted delinquents averaged only £69 profit per offender, while those offenders of average intelligence averaged £1,151 profit each. The authors also found that bright delinquents asked for more offenses to be "taken into consideration," admitting to more prior offenses than delinquents of average intelligence.

Although bright offenders admitted more crimes, they were treated more leniently by the criminal justice system. Consistent with later research emphasizing the importance of verbal IQ (Beaver, DeLisi, Vaughn, Wright, & Boutwell, 2008; Bellair, McNulty, & Piquero, 2016; Walsh, Taylor, & Yun, 2015), Neihart (2009) concludes that "high verbal ability may protect against the development of antisocial cognition, perhaps by mediating the accelerated development of prosocial moral reasoning" (p. 323). Gath and his colleagues (1970) suggest that "a greater ability of the bright boys to communicate" (p. 158) might facilitate greater feelings of empathy in criminal justice officials. Gath and Tennent (1972) also indicate that the high value placed upon intelligence by society could lead to excuse making, probably through psychiatric explanations. Certainly, psychiatric explanations are sometimes invoked to make intelligible otherwise inexplicable crimes (Prins, 1986); psychological excuses could be especially attractive in explaining delinquency that cannot be explained with traditional constructs of race, class, or low IQ. Whether the studies of bright delinquents are generalizable to adult offenders remains unknown: studies of gifted offenders have employed juveniles as subjects. Only a handful of articles have examined adult offenders with high IQs (e.g., Monk-Turner et al., 2006; Oleson, 2002, 2004; Oleson & Chappell, 2012).

IQ and Crime: A Curvilinear Relationship

Researchers often presume a negative linear relationship between IQ and crime, despite other studies that describe nonlinear associations (e.g., Hirschi & Hindelang, 1977; Mears & Cochran, 2013). If the presumption of a linear association is wrong, then "prior research may have consistently misestimated the relationship and, in so doing, potentially understated the extent of association between IQ and offending" (Mears & Cochran, 2013, p. 18). The actual IQ-delinquency relationship is not an absolutely linear one, but curvilinear. Schwartz and his colleagues (2015) reported mostly linear patterns, with curvilinear associations at the highest and lowest ends of the spectrum. Similarly, Jensen (1980) reported the highest rates of delinquency in the 70–90 IQ range, falling off sharply below IQ 50 and above IQ 100. Langdon, Clare, and Murphy (2011) reported low rates of offending among mentally handicapped subjects. At *very* low IQs, defendants are deemed incompetent for criminal prosecution (Nicholson & Kugler, 1991).

The relationship also varies according to the type of crime being considered (Fox, 1946). West (1967) indicates that many offenses require significant intelligence to execute. Feldman (1993) notes that IQ scores increase as "we move away from street crimes to organized crime and corporate crime, both of which require considerable skills" (p. 156). Wilson and Herrnstein (1985) agree: "It has been found that such crimes as forgery, bribery, securities violations, and embezzlement are associated with higher IQs than is the average for the offender population in general, whereas assaults, homicide, rape, and sex offenses in females are associated with lower IQs. . . . Because these are high frequency offenses, they naturally weigh heavily in determining the average offender's characteristics, such as IQ" (p. 165).

Reducing the IQ-crime relationship to a simple 8- to 10-point gap overlooks any distinctive patterns of offending. Ellis and Walsh (2003) note, for example, that while most of the self-report evidence supports a robust negative relationship between IQ and crime, the relationships between IQ and self-reported drug use and between IQ and recidivism are less clear. Thus, disentangling the link between IQ and crime, by offense type, might reveal distinct patterns. To shed light on this issue, the next chapter outlines this book's study of self-reported criminal behavior in adults with genius-level (130+) IQ scores.

2

———

The Study

My theory is that criminology is the easiest science in the world. One has only to let the criminal talk—sooner or later he will tell you everything.

—AGATHA CHRISTIE, *APPOINTMENT WITH DEATH,* P. 156

One reason so little is known about criminal genius is that geniuses are rare. Only 2% of the population possesses an IQ score of 130 or more. Only 1 in 2,000 possesses an IQ of 150 or more. Consequently, few high-IQ offenders are caught. Furthermore, as discussed in chapter 5, some research suggests that high-IQ offenders are even less likely to be detected, arrested, prosecuted, convicted, or incarcerated. Prison studies, therefore, are of limited utility, and self-reporting is essential in the study of elite crime. This, however, presents its own challenges, as there is little reason for high-IQ individuals to participate in self-report research and many incentives to reject research overtures.

This chapter describes the negotiation of research access and outlines some of the ethical and legal challenges associated with self-report research (e.g., how to protect the identity of subjects who self-report felony or capital crimes for which they have not been caught?). The chapter also describes the sampling of three distinct categories of genius, the construction of the self-report questionnaire, the rationale for follow-up interviews, and the measurement of personality variables.

RESEARCH ACCESS AND ETHICS

Research access presents few difficulties when criminologists choose to study the poor and the vulnerable—the offenders who populate the world's prisons. The processes of arrest and conviction compromise the privacy of citizens, and social scientists are free to access volumes of information through official statistics (skewed although such statistics may be). However, to "study up" (Nader, 1972) in criminology—to study not the vulnerable but the powerful, to study not the failures of the criminal world but its successes—is extraordinarily difficult. The most serious crimes are invisible (Reiman, 2001).

Scholars often downplay the vicissitudes of blocked research access, possibly to maintain the appearance of competence (Lareau & Shultz, 1996), but *access matters*. The research that is produced in criminology is a function of the research access that can be negotiated. The most compelling social research is blocked by individuals who possess the wealth, means, and power to obstruct it (Fussell, 1983; Mills, 1956; Moyser, 1988). Other research efforts are frustrated by institutional gatekeepers who react to requests for access in the manner of an immune response (Wolff, 2004). For example, Broadhead and Rist (1976) note that although researchers frequently want to study the "dark side" of bureaucracies, "in negotiating for entry, these interests are more than likely to be at odds with the gatekeeper. The common result, therefore, is for the gatekeeper either to reject the investigator's bid to do research, or for the researcher to reformulate the research problem within boundaries that are acceptable" (p. 328).

Certainly, criminologists can learn a great deal about serious dark-figure crime from elites who work within the justice system, such as policy makers, politicians, lawyers, and judges (Richards, 2011). Ideally, though, criminologists should heed the advice of Chicago School theorist Robert Park and enter the field. Park enjoined his students to escape from libraries and study life, as it is actually lived, in the metropolis:

> You have been told to go grubbing in the library, thereby accumulating a mass of notes and a liberal coating of grime. You have been told to choose routine problems wherever you can find musty stacks of routine records based on trivial schedules prepared by tired bureaucrats and filled out by reluctant applicants for aid or fussy do-gooders or indifferent clerks. This is called "getting your hands dirty in real research." Those who counsel you are wise and honorable; the reasons they offer are of great value. But one more thing is needful: first-hand observation. Go and sit in the lounges of the luxury hotels and on the doorsteps of the flophouses; sit on the Gold Coast settees and on the slum shakedowns; sit in the Orchestra Hall and in the Star and Garter Burlesk. In short, gentlemen, go get the seat of your pants dirty in real research. (in Bulmer, 1986, p. 97)

Like sociologists, criminologists must immerse themselves in the field (Ferrell & Hamm, 1998; Parnell & Kane, 2003). Doing so, however, may mean adopting unconventional, even extreme, methods (Miller & Tewksbury, 2001). To know dark-figure crime, criminologists may need to interview contract killers (Carlo, 2006), hang out with homeless drug users (Bourgois & Schonberg, 2009), do ethnographic fieldwork with active burglars (Wright, Decker, Redfern, & Smith, 1992), or live within fugitive society (Goffman, 2014). And to understand the crimes of the powerful, criminologists must negotiate access into rarefied circles of elites that most researchers will never glimpse. Criminologists interested in elite dark-figure offending should understand, however, that such research will be ethically complicated and might be hazardous. Researchers of dark-figure crime may be confronted by very real physical, moral, and legal dangers.

Fieldwork can be physically dangerous (Lee, 1995; Williams, Dunlap, Johnson, & Hamid, 1992). Lee (1995) writes, "Any list of potential dangers is likely to be lengthy, but a short list would surely include the hazards of assault, rape, and robbery; the risks of infection, accident, and disease; the possibilities of arrest, harassment, verbal abuse, and violent confrontation" (p. vi). Howell's 1990 study of anthropologists suggests that accidents are relatively common—70% of those surveyed had been forced to cope with an accident. She notes that falls and motor-vehicle accidents are common for fieldworkers, as are malaria and hepatitis A. Some physical dangers are a function of the dangerous setting in which fieldwork takes place—such as in a war zone (e.g., Sluka, 1995). Lee (1995, p. 3) calls these "ambient" dangers. Other dangers, precipitated by the researcher's presence, such as exposure to drug-induced violence (e.g., Williams et al., 1992) or physical assaults by gang members (Gilbert, 2013), are "situational" (Lee, 1995, p. 3). Both ambient and situational dangers can be lethal. Sluka (1995) notes that 60 anthropologists have died in (ambient) fieldwork mishaps, and that at least 3 anthropologists have been murdered in episodes of situational violence.

Moral dangers are also commonplace. The conduct of social research presents criminologists with an ethical minefield (Israel & Hay, 2011). Since development of the Nuremberg Code of 1945 (Weindling, 2001), researchers have been expected to take reasonable steps to safeguard the mental and physical well-being of their subjects. Professional societies such as the Academy of Criminal Justice Sciences (2000) and the British Society of Criminology (2015) have established codes of ethics to implement these obligations). But even strict adherence to these codes does not resolve all moral questions. By studying crime without condemning it, the criminological fieldworker at some level assents to it (Polsky, 1969; Yablonsky, 1965). Klockars (1979) argues that moral compromises are unavoidable: "I do not believe it is possible to do good fieldwork with deviant subjects and not, morally speaking, get one's hands dirty" (p. 265).

Moral dangers are aligned with legal dangers. Promises of anonymity and confidentiality are essentially moral, but they quickly can become legal when organizations (e.g., universities, professional associations) and institutions (e.g., law enforcement, the judiciary) become interested in criminological research. In a powerful passage, Polsky (1969) explains,

> If one is effectively to study law-breaking deviants as they engage in their deviance in its natural setting, i.e., outside of jail, he must make the moral decision that in some ways he will break the law himself. He need not be a "participant observer" and

commit the deviant acts under study, yet he has to witness such acts or be taken into confidence about them and not blow the whistle. That is, the investigator has to decide that when necessary he will "obstruct justice" or be an "accessory" before or after the fact, in the full legal sense of those terms. *He will not be enabled to discern some vital aspects of criminally deviant behavior and the structure of law-breaking subcultures unless he makes such a moral decision, makes the deviants believe him, and moreover convinces them of his ability to act in accord with his decision.* The last-mentioned point can perhaps be neglected with juvenile delinquents, for they know that a professional studying them is almost always exempt from police pressure to inform; but adult criminals have no such assurance, and hence are concerned not only with the investigator's intentions but with his sheer ability to remain a "stand-up guy" under police questioning. (p. 138, emphasis added)

Methodological mechanisms can be employed to minimize legal risk (e.g., Astin & Boruch, 1970; Oleson, 1999; Traynor, 1996), and researchers can obtain privacy certificates from the National Institute of Justice (28 C.F.R. § 22.23), but the statutory shield protections enjoyed by journalists typically do not extend to academics (Palys & Lowman, 2002).

Teitelbaum (1983) considers three theories of liability—accessorial liability, misprision of a felony, and obstruction of justice—and concludes that researchers who do not affirmatively engage in felony crimes are not at risk. First, accessorial liability and misprision apply only to felony offenses, not misdemeanor crimes. Second, misprision of a felony, the crime of failing to report a known felon, has been abandoned as a prosecutable offense in most US and UK jurisdictions. The modern interpretation of misprision is equivalent to accessory after the fact. Third, both accessorial liability and obstruction of justice require proving both an *actus reus* (affirmative conduct) and a *mens rea* (intent to hinder the felon's apprehension, conviction, or punishment) component.

Teitelbaum's conclusion, however, might be cold comfort to the criminologist who *is* subpoenaed to produce documents or testimony. If one's research is seized (Sonenschein, 2001), professional codes of ethical conduct do little to protect a researcher from compelled disclosure. In 1993, the FBI subpoenaed PhD student Rik Scarce to provide information about an Animal Liberation Front break-in on the Washington State University campus. When Scarce refused to comply, citing the researcher's duty of confidentiality as codified in the American Sociological Association's code of ethics, he was jailed for contempt of court. Scarce (1995, 2005) was jailed—not as punishment, but as coercion—for 159 days.

Similarly, after making promises of confidentiality, PhD student Richard Leo negotiated phenomenal access to the Laconia Police Department. He was the "first sociologist ever granted entrée into American police interrogation rooms" (Leo, 1996, p. 127). When one defendant, a man charged with armed robbery, claimed that his confession had been coerced and subpoenaed Leo's field notes, Leo had to decide between honoring his promise of confidentiality and complying with the subpoena. In the end, Leo (1995) produced his notes, prompting the judge to suppress the confession and dismiss three of the four felony counts against the defendant. Erikson (1995) later excoriated Leo for unethical conduct, accusing him of at least three forms of wrongdoing: lying and deceit, failure to protect the privacy of his subjects, and spoiling the field for future generations of researchers. The lesson to be gleaned from the experiences of Scarce and Leo is clear: criminologists who undertake fieldwork on dark-figure crime proceed at their own risk.

The research described in this book was nearly blocked. I had devised a self-report study to examine the prevalence (the percentage of the sample who reported committing the offense at any time) and incidence (the total number of offenses reported) of high-IQ crime across 72 offenses, including serious felonies like rape and murder. Instead of focusing on gifted delinquents, as some studies had done (e.g., Gath, Tennent, & Pidduck, 1970), I wanted to study adult offenders with IQ scores that were borderline genius or higher. I also wanted to conduct follow-up interviews with a sample of the respondents. Having read about the risks of subpoena, I developed a link-file system to establish a firewall between self-report data and the contact details of interview participants (Astin & Boruch, 1970; Boruch, 1976). Believing in the fundamental importance of the work, I resolved to protect the confidentiality of my subjects, even if it meant contempt of court. Confidently, I conveyed this determination (along with a description of the research design) to the gatekeeper of a high-IQ society that I had joined in the hopes of conducting insider ("emic") research (Headland, Pike, & Harris, 1999).

This first gatekeeper ("Albert") responded professionally and formally, identifying the necessary documents to assess my request. As I prepared those materials, I also contacted the representative for a second high-IQ society ("Bob") about access there. Initially, I received a letter indicating that the request could not be honored, as I was not a member of the organization (hinting that an insider approach might have succeeded); but Bob soon followed up with a friendly letter, conferring access, even offering to assist in the construction of the sampling frame. Unfortunately, shortly after I received a membership roster from Bob, I also received Albert's response, denying access to his organization's membership lists. The principal bases for rejection were related to my lack of a control group, the lack of subject anonymity, and the potential for legal liability. Albert characterized my plan to protect the identity of self-reported offenders with a link-file system as "one of the most unethical statements . . . ever received in support of a potential research project" (personal communication, July 25, 1996). I was notified that Albert's organization would never undertake steps to impede the legal system and would not condone such behavior. Albert's letter was also distributed to more than 10 other people, including Bob. After receiving the letter, Bob contacted me to rescind the research access that had been granted.

As a self-funded doctoral student, I did not know if I could afford to continue. I seriously considered abandoning the topic altogether. A third gatekeeper from Albert's society, "Charlie," sent me a letter, helpfully suggesting other sources of data. Charlie identified six bases for Albert's withdrawal of access. These included concerns about the potential for litigation, concerns about newsworthiness of the subject matter, and an obligation to safeguard the good name of the high-IQ society. Charlie's letter also included this paragraph: "The special significance of this kind of misbehavior, in a culture that depends upon deceit and hypocrisy for its stability, should not be underestimated: one sows the seeds of distrust of one's own kind; one violates those most revered mutual understandings and sources of trust that dare not speak their name; one betrays all those who have given one their support; in effect, one forcibly asserts one's right to pariah status among one's peers" (personal communication, May 29, 1996).

Charlie's letter suggested that I had a responsibility to perpetuate the myth of a noncriminal intellectual elite, like Plato's myth of the metals (Hamilton & Cairns, 1989). *Don't pull on this loose thread,* the letter seemed to say, *or the entire sweater will come unraveled.* Society will be put at risk. The language of "sources of trust that dare not speak their name," evocative of Oscar Wilde's trial for gross indecency (Holland, 2004), suggested that outing "our" criminality would be a betrayal of those who join high-IQ societies. At the time, the reference to "one's right to pariah status" seemed menacing, but, given the generous tone of the letter, was almost certainly intended to serve as a benevolent note of caution.

I was fortunate. I was able to locate another high-IQ society that was cooperative with the broad goals of my research, and I was able to secure membership in the society (allowing me, once again, to pursue an emic approach). Without access to this sample, however, the research described in this book would never have been conducted.

SAMPLING

Investigators of gifted delinquency have traditionally drawn upon remand home samples (e.g., Gath et al., 1970), but this strategy would not satisfy the demands of a study of adults. The identification of research participants through high-IQ societies was an obvious choice.

The high-IQ society sampled in this research requires an IQ score at or above the 99.9% mark. Sampling from the membership of this group conferred several advantages. First, it ensured that participants possessed an elite IQ. Membership is offered only to those who qualify at 99.9% (~150 IQ) on psychometrically approved tests. This eliminated the need to verify IQ scores. In addition, using this high-IQ society meant that the IQ scores of the respondents in this study surpassed the adult scores of the 1,528 geniuses who participated in Terman's (1926) study. Second, the society's commitment to research suggested that at least a fraction of its members would cooperate with my research. Finally, membership rosters provided an immediate sampling frame. This simplified the distribution of postal questionnaires (Oppenheim, 1992; Scott, 1961).

Self-report instruments were mailed to 728 current and former members of the high-IQ society. Each of the surveyed members received a cover letter explaining the research project, a paper copy of the self-report instrument, a short form to complete if the participant wanted to volunteer for an optional follow-up interview, two questionnaires measuring personality variables, and a self-addressed stamped envelope to return the questionnaires and interview form.

However, sampling error presented a real concern. To what extent did members from the high-IQ society accurately represent other high-IQ individuals? Would they differ even from other individuals with 150+ IQs in some fundamental way? This has profound implications for the generalizability of this study. Towers (1990) suggests that there are three distinct types of gifted individuals:

1. Conformists who follow a "committed strategy," finding gratifying niches in academia or the professions and surrounding themselves with gifted friends and colleagues.
2. Socially estranged outsiders who follow a "marginal strategy," turning to elite high-IQ societies for the intellectual stimulation they lack in menial jobs and social lives.
3. "Dropouts" who withdraw from society, incapable of using their own prodigious intellects to overcome their severe social maladjustments.

Towers argues that the first group—gifted individuals who have found outlets for their abilities in their socially conforming careers—rarely join high-IQ societies and that high-IQ societies are magnets for the second group. Therefore, to better approximate the population of all individuals possessing genius-level IQs, two additional groups were sampled via snowball sampling (Biernacki & Waldorf, 1981): students from elite universities and high-IQ prisoners.

Students at elite universities typically have IQ scores that meet or exceed the 130+ threshold of borderline genius. For example, using a standard IQ test (with a mean of 100 and a standard deviation of 15), Jensen (1980) notes that high school graduates have a mean IQ score of 110, students from average four-year universities score a 115 IQ, and doctoral students average a 130 IQ. Average students in the elite professions such as law, medicine, dentistry, engineering, or chemistry score a 120 IQ (Herrnstein & Murray, 1994). Herrnstein & Murray (1994) report that graduates from the top 12 US universities (e.g., Harvard, Stanford, Yale, Princeton, Cal Tech, MIT, Duke, Dartmouth, Cornell, Columbia, Chicago, and Brown) possess IQ scores averaging 2.7 standard deviations above the mean (~140 IQ). Students at foreign institutions such as Cambridge, Oxford, or the Sorbonne are presumably of the same caliber as these elite American students and like their US counterparts, usually go on to successful professions. Individuals at these world-ranked institutions, therefore, are Towers's first category of the gifted: people who find gratifying niches in challenging careers and surround themselves with gifted friends and colleagues. Using snowball sampling, 900 self-report instruments were distributed in blocks of 30, 60, 90, or 120 to former classmates and colleagues who agreed to serve as research associates, distributing the surveys to undergraduates, postgraduates, postdoctorates, professionals, and professors at prestigious academic institutions, including Cal Tech, Cambridge, Cornell, Dartmouth, École Centrale, Harvard, Harvey Mudd, Leeds, Notre Dame, Oxford, the Sorbonne, Stanford, Tehran University, UC Berkeley, UC Davis, UC Irvine, UCLA, UC San Diego, UC Santa Cruz, University of North Carolina (Chapel Hill), University of Southern California, University of Arizona, University of Georgia, University of Sydney, University of Washington, University of Wisconsin (Madison), and Yale.

For example, I mailed a bundle of 60 surveys to my former classmate Zack, who was attending Harvard University. Zack, in turn, gave bundles of 10 surveys to six of his Harvard classmates, who in turn shared them with *their* classmates. Most university students did not know their IQ scores but were able to report their SAT or GRE scores (often accepted for admission purposes by high-IQ societies because of their high psychometric loading of general intelligence, or g; Frey & Detterman, 2004). Scores on standardized academic tests were translated into IQ scores using conversion tables published by high-IQ societies; when test scores were not available, the student's university was used to impute an average IQ score. These scores, derived from undergraduates, likely underestimate the true IQ scores of respondents (a mixture of undergraduate and graduate students) and are conservative measures. Details on the imputation of IQ can be found in the appendix A.

I identified a third sample of high-IQ respondents, comprised of 62 individuals incarcerated in the United States or United Kingdom, with IQ scores at or above the 98% mark, through both snowball sampling and notices published in the prison publications *Prison Writing* and *Inside Time*. Many of these people had learned of their IQ scores through prison intake procedures. This small sample tapped Towers's (1990) third category of the gifted: "dropouts." Oversampling an incarcerated population ensured that even serious offenses would be represented in self-reported results (Cernkovich, Giordano, & Pugh, 1985; Junger-Tas & Marshall, 1999); it also helped limit the impact of heteroschedacity (i.e., unequally distributed data) and facilitated comparisons between participants who avoided detection and others who were caught and punished for their offenses.

In total, 1,690 surveys were distributed on January 20, 1997, and 424 (25.1%) viable surveys were returned. Specifically, 260 (35.7%) of the 728 high-IQ society questionnaires were returned, 30 (48.4%) of the 62 incarcerated questionnaires, but only 134 (14.9%) of the 900 university questionnaires. Some commentators have suggested that testing for statistical significance is inappropriate if nonresponse rates are high. "The employment of significance tests on such a sample is nonsensical as there is no way that only random error has affected the statistics calculated from the sample" (Henkel, 1976, p. 80). As nonresponse bias was a concern (Kanuk & Berenson, 1975), I contacted my research associates who had volunteered to distribute questionnaires At least 320 of the university surveys had never been distributed. Assuming that the entirety of the remaining 580 *were* circulated, the 134 returned questionnaires represent a response rate of 23.1% in the university sample and increase the overall response rate to 30.9%.

Data from the first three groups were collected between December 1996 and June 1997 (and compared to previously published self-report data; see Oleson, 2002). On March 20, 2004, self-report data from fourth group—a control group—were collected, using the same questionnaire. Students enrolled in a distance-learning course at a large urban university were offered extra credit for their assistance in creating a control group. Students printed the self-report instrument from a .PDF file posted online and returned up to five questionnaires gathered from family and friends. This netted a total of 797 viable self-report questionnaires for the control group. Because the questionnaires were downloaded and printed remotely, the response rate for the control group is not known. Most (85%) questionnaires in the control group did not include IQ scores, and IQ estimates were imputed.

After the control group data were collected, I made adjustments to the composition of high-IQ and control groups. A small number (n = 43) of self-report questionnaires collected during 2004 reported IQ scores greater than the 98% IQ threshold for genius. I redistributed these questionnaires to the high-IQ group, increasing that group to 465. Inversely, I removed 2 questionnaires reporting above-average but less than 98% IQ scores from the high-IQ group and added them to the control group, increasing that group to 756.

SELF-REPORT QUESTIONNAIRE

While it may seem counterintuitive, there is strong evidence indicating that subjects provide accurate research information about offending behaviors when presented with a self-report questionnaire (Junger-Tas & Marshall, 1999; Krohn, Thornberry, Gibson, & Baldwin, 2010). Self-reporting, the most commonly used methodology in criminology (Hagan, 1993), boasts impressive measures of validity and reliability (Thornberry & Krohn, 2000). In terms of validity, Huizinga and Elliott (1986) noted that both the content validity (successfully tapping the range of behaviors with relevant and plausible self-report questions) and the criterion validity (comparing scores to a known external criterion, such as police records or peer reports) of self-reporting are robust. Self-reports of arrests have greater than

80% correspondence with official arrest records (Pollock, Menard, Elliott, & Huizinga, 2015). Junger-Tas and Marshall (1999) reported that US samples "have produced prevalence and incidence rates at least as valid as those from official or victimization data" (p. 293). Self-reporting also produces robust measures of reliability. Hindelang, Hirschi, and Weis (1979) reported test-retest and split-half reliabilities on the order of 0.9 and argued that once the domain of behavior under investigation is considered (i.e., not validating self-report scales of petty noncriminal offending against official criminal statistics), the self-report instrument has "considerable validity" (p. 1009). Similarly, Huizinga and Elliott (1986) reported that test-retest assessments of reliability (using intervals from less than one hour to over two months) typically produced reliabilities in the 0.85–0.99 range. Scales of serious offences (e.g., felony assault or theft) produced the highest reliabilities, while scales containing less-serious offenses (e.g., property damage or petty theft) appeared to be less reliable. They concluded that the self-report methodology is not only legitimate but unique in its power to shed light on both the character and causes of offending: "We believe that self-report measures are among the most promising of our measures of criminal behavior and are, perhaps, the only measures capable of meeting the needs of both descriptive and etiological research efforts" (Huizinga & Elliott, 1986, p. 324).

The earliest self-report studies were more akin to attitude measures than behavioral inventories (Junger-Tas & Marshall, 1999). They used "have you ever?" style questions, overlooking the dimensions of frequency and recency, thereby failing to distinguish adolescent-limited offenders from life-course persistent offenders (Moffitt, 1993). They also focused on juvenile delinquent males, using a schoolroom population that is vulnerable to research (May, 1993) but that fails to include some of the most serious offenders: school dropouts and adults involved in adult-level crimes (Wilson & Herrnstein, 1985). As a function of the juvenile populations being sampled, self-report studies have also overrepresented trivial offenses. For example, Short and Nye's (1957) groundbreaking self-report questionnaire of delinquency consisted of seven final items that asked respondents if they had ever (1) driven a car without a driver's license or permit, (2) skipped school without a legitimate excuse, (3) defied parents' authority (to their face), (4) taken little things (worth less than $2), (5) bought or drank beer, wine, or liquor, (6) purposely damaged or destroyed public or private property, or (7) had sexual relations with a person of the opposite sex.

While there is indisputable value in comparing self-reported prevalence rates against official delinquency figures, and while childhood delinquency may help to predict adult criminality (e.g., Farrington, 1992), Short and Nye's offenses are so trivial that that they scarcely constitute "offending" (Hindelang, Hirschi, & Weis, 1979). Several are status offenses, behaviors that are not even illegal when committed by an adult. Wolfgang (1976) notes, "[M]ost previous studies in the United States have been conducted with junior and senior high-school students who reported in mostly anonymous questionnaires or protected interviews relatively trivial and innocuous juvenile status offenses, like stealing from their mothers' pocketbooks, being truant, or committing petty larceny" (p. 27). The problems with this are obvious: as juveniles, delinquents—even the brightest of delinquents—rarely engage in tax evasion, draft dodging, or insider trading. Criminology's focus on delinquency and street crime produces a particular kind of knowledge: "[T]he obsession with juvenile self-reported delinquency and the limited number of items in the one adult self-reported crime study have resulted in rendering invisible the massive contribution to crime by government and corporate officials: this is ironic, considering that one purpose of such studies was to make good the deficiencies of the official statistics" (Box, 1981, p. 87).

Of course, if a criminologist was interested not in high-frequency petty delinquency and high-visibility street crimes but in the white-collar offenses that produce financial harm, injury, and negligent deaths on a massive scale (Coleman, 2005), then a self-report questionnaire might produce positive—not negative—relationships between crime and education, socioeconomic status, income, and IQ. While self-reporting has not been used to directly assess the crimes of elites, several studies have shed important light on offending behavior. Porterfield (1946) compared 337 students at Texas Christian University to a group of 2,049 delinquents processed by a local juvenile court, measuring 55 offenses ranging in seriousness from creating a disturbance in church or shooting staples to negligent homicide and murder. He concluded that the crimes perpetrated by students were every bit as serious (though not as frequently committed) as the crimes committed by the official delinquents. Porterfield argued that university students committed their crimes for the same reasons as the delinquents, and he attributed the difference in outcomes to family disorganization and lower socioeconomic status in the delinquent group. Porterfield even reported one homicide from the university group, but subsequent researchers rejected this finding as straining credulity. Hindelang, Hirschi, and Weis (1979) wrote, "Subsequent self-report researchers have excluded the homicide item and have uncovered no murderers in their samples" (p. 996). Yet when Wolfgang, Figlio, and Sellin (1972) included a homicide item ("killed someone not accidentally") in their self-report study of 10,000 Philadelphia boys, 4 of their subjects reported a criminal homicide.

Wallerstein and Wyle (1947) surveyed 1,698 adults in the New York metropolitan area and asked them about their involvement with 49 different offenses, including serious crimes like larceny, automobile theft, burglary, robbery, perjury, conspiracy, and fraud. They reported that 99% of respondents indicated committing at least 1 listed offense. Men averaged 18 offenses each, and women averaged 11 offenses. Almost two-thirds of the 1,020 men (64%) reported committing at least 1 felony—an offense that was grounds for the loss of citizenship rights under New York law; almost one-third (29%) of the 678 women reported committing such a felony. The authors characterized the "principal conclusion to be drawn from this study . . . [as] the revelation of the prevalence of lawlessness among respectable people" (Wallerstein & Wyle, 1947, p. 118).

Smithyman interviewed 50 men from the greater Los Angeles area who had committed rape (i.e., nonconsensual penetration of vagina, anus, or mouth) but had never been arrested. Smithyman's (1979) portrait of the rapist was different than that painted by official statistics: his subjects were better educated and more and better employed, and far fewer of them were black.

Winslow and Gay (1993) asked 1,035 students at a large American university to describe their involvement in acts of low-consensus deviance (e.g., early sexual intercourse, frequent or casual sex, and regularly using alcohol, marijuana, cocaine, or other drugs). The authors found that although minorities and the poor were overrepresented in official criminal statistics (acts that reflect high-consensus deviance, behaviors earning the approbation of the bulk of society), white and affluent students "were uniformly more likely than non-whites and students with relatively low incomes to have engaged in early sex, to be sexually active now, and to be more inclined to drink alcohol and use drugs" (Winslow & Gay 1993, p. 23). Thus, in addition to providing valuable information about the prevalence and incidence of crime, the self-report instrument has the potential to reveal new aspects of crime.

While the self-report methodology is hailed as one of the most promising techniques available to criminologists, it does have its limitations. For example, most self-report studies employ written questionnaires, which, as Hirschi and Hindelang (1977) note, can undermine accurate responses if the samples are illiterate or suffer from impaired mental capacity. Since many delinquency studies have assessed "at-risk" groups, these authors' warning is particularly noteworthy. On the other hand, these concerns are largely obviated when surveys are administered to high-IQ subjects. With this population, it is possible to ask subjects to complete detailed and complicated tasks. While closed and precoded questions reduce the effort needed to complete a self-report survey and simplify data analysis, closed questions force respondents to answer in the researcher's terms. Data can assume an unrealistically sanitized appearance that fails to reflect the real-world context of offending. Hughes (1980) writes, "The open-textured quality of ordinary language which the investigator tries to remedy, in part at least, by the provision of forced-choice answers and such like, places a question mark against the assumption that the researcher and respondent share 'the same community of meaning structures for assigning cultural significance' to the items" (p. 96).

This problem of interpretation and meaning can be problematic in self-report research. For example, while an employee who steals a notepad from her office might be legally guilty of larceny, it is possible that neither she nor her employers would define the behavior as criminal. Hence a ticked box on her self-report inventory creates the illusion of an antisocial behavior that may have little to do with the reality of her situation. Alternatively, since this employee might not consider the theft of a notepad as criminal, she may therefore fail to record it on the self-report instrument; this would introduce inaccuracies in the researcher's data, since—at least technically—an offense had occurred. The high rates of serious offending reported by Wallerstein and Wyle (1947) almost certainly reflected the wide range of behaviors encompassed by offense categories. For example, malicious mischief included such "offenses" as removing flowers or vegetables from other people's property, intentionally damaging property, or opening mail without permission. Indecency included "showing or giving an obscene, lustful or passion-provoking picture, object or writing" (p. 109). Elliott and Huizinga (1983), acknowledging the problem, recalculated National Youth Survey offenses into three categories: inappropriate, appropriate but trivial, and appropriate and nontrivial. Incidence estimates changed dramatically when only offenses in the appropriate and nontrivial category were measured.

Since self-report questionnaires are retrospective instruments, telescoping (the tendency to think of events as happening more recently than they really did) can obscure facts. While telescoping is less problematic in questionnaires about prevalence, it can be a serious limitation in self-report studies evaluating temporal dimensions of offending. Victim surveys have demonstrated that bounding events with meaningful anchors (e.g. "How many times did you kill a person *since last Christmas?*") can ameliorate the effects of telescoping (Sudman & Bradburn, 1973).

Although the value of self-reporting can be limited by telescoping and literacy effects, by variations in how questions are interpreted, and by unsophisticated sampling or design, the self-report instrument is also, as Hood and Sparks (1970) note, one of the only means of studying hidden offending. While victim surveys such as the Crime Survey for England and Wales (Office for National Statistics, 2014) or the American National Crime Victimization Survey (Truman & Langton, 2014) do reveal unseen aspects of the dark figure, offender-based self-report instruments can also describe details about hidden crimes that seldom lead to arrest, are consensual in nature, or lack individual victims. Given the differential detection literature, suggesting that high-IQ subjects avoid detection, prosecution, and punishment, self-reporting was an obvious choice for the present study of high-IQ crime.

After reviewing a variety of self-report questionnaires, adopting questions from a number of them and adding additional items after studying penal codes, I constructed a new self-report instrument in 1995. I pilot-tested the instrument on 15 graduate students from the University of Cambridge and then revised it. After revision, the new self-report instrument consisted of a 17-item demographics section, a self-report section containing 72 offenses, and an open-ended section asking respondents to describe the three books, films, and people that had most influenced them (see appendix B for a copy of the questionnaire). The 72 offenses involved nine different offense types: sex, violence, drugs, property, white-collar, professional misconduct, vehicular, justice system, and miscellaneous. The 72 offense items are listed, by category, in table 9.

TABLE 9 Self-report items by offense type

Sex

Been paid for having sexual relations with someone
Paid someone for sexual relations
Had (or tried to have) sexual relations with someone against their will
Had sexual relations with someone under the legal age of consent (while over the age of consent yourself)
Made sexual comments or advances toward someone that you knew were unwanted
Had sexual relations in a public place
Made obscene telephone calls, such as calling someone and saying dirty things

Violence

Used violence or the threat of violence to rob someone
Carried a hidden weapon other than a plain pocketknife
Made a serious threat that you meant to carry out
Beaten someone up seriously enough that they required medical attention of any kind
Killed another human being (excluding wartime situations)
Constructed a bomb or similar explosive device
Held someone against their will (kidnapping)
Attempted suicide

Drugs

Used marijuana, cannabis, or hashish
Bought marijuana, cannabis, or hashish
Sold marijuana, cannabis, or hashish
Used hard drugs, such as heroin, cocaine, LSD, or ecstasy
Bought hard drugs, such as heroin, cocaine, LSD, or ecstasy
Sold hard drugs, such as heroin, cocaine, LSD, or ecstasy
Manufactured or cultivated a controlled substance (drugs)
Taken pharmaceuticals prescribed for someone else
Smuggled alcohol, tobacco, or food items (e.g., avoiding duty when crossing federal borders)
Smuggled illegal drugs or drug paraphernalia
Bought or provided liquor for a minor
Been drunk in a public place

Property

Purposely damaged or destroyed property that did not belong to you
Stolen (or tried to steal) a motor vehicle, such as a car or motorcycle
Stolen (or tried to steal) things worth $5 or less (including petty shoplifting)
Stolen (or tried to steal) things worth between $5 and $50
Stolen (or tried to steal) something worth more than $50
Picked someone's pocket or stolen (or tried to steal) from someone's purse
Knowingly bought, sold, or held stolen goods (or tried to do any of these things)
Damaged property or real estate by lighting a fire (arson)
Avoided paying for things such as movies, bus or subway rides, or food
Used another person's telephone or telephone card without their permission
Used another person's ATM (cashpoint) card without their permission
Broken into a building or vehicle (or tried to break in) to steal something or just to look around

White-Collar

Used privileged information in making investment decisions
Manipulated financial accounts in an illegal manner
Sold or traded government or industrial secrets
Intentionally misreported income information on your tax forms
Broken into another computer (hacked)
Made unauthorized copies of commercial computer software
Made copies of copyrighted records, tapes, or videocassettes
Used an electronic device to eavesdrop or spy on someone
Tricked (or tried to trick) a person, group, or company for financial gain (fraud)
Forged another person's signature on an official document, prescription, or bank check

Professional Misconduct

Violated safety or environmental standards
Abused work privileges (e.g., personal telephone calls, personal e-mail, or personal use of the copy machine)
Plagiarized another person's work (used it without giving them credit)
Invented or altered research data
Cheated on an examination or test

Vehicular

Consumed enough alcohol to put you over the legal limit and then driven a car
Driven a car without a license
Taken a vehicle for a ride (drive) without the owner's permission
Driven a car at unsafe speeds or in a reckless manner

Justice System

Taken steps to evade (dodge) a military draft or selective service
Instigated acts of rebellion against the government or agencies of the government
Made an agreement with other people to commit a criminal act
Resisted arrest
Violated the conditions of your parole
Knowingly lied while under oath
Failed to appear in court when ordered to do so by summons

Miscellaneous

Counterfeited fine art or currency
Spread false and injurious statements about someone, either orally or in print
Fished or hunted without a license where one is required
Blackmailed someone
Intentionally trespassed on private or government property
Been loud, rowdy, or unruly in a public place (disorderly conduct)
Gambled where it is illegal to do so

NOTE: Self-report items are organized by offense type; see appendix B for the 72 items in their original questionnaire order.

		Nvr.	Lyr.	Evr.	Arr.	Con.
16.	Used violence or the threat of violence to rob someone	☐	☐	☐	☐	☐
17.	Carried a hidden weapon other than a plain pocketknife	☐	☐	☐	☐	☐
18.	Made a serious threat that you meant to carry out	☐	☐	☐	☐	☐
19.	Beaten someone up seriously enough that they required medical attention of any kind	☐	☐	☐	☐	☐

FIGURE 15. Layout of self-report questionnaire items.

In the questionnaire, five empty boxes accompanied each listed offense (figure 15). Respondents were asked to record (1) the number of times they had committed the offense in the last year, (2) the number of times they had ever committed the offense (including those in the last year), (3) the number of times they had been arrested for the offense, and (4) the number of times they had been convicted for the offense. If respondents had never committed the listed offense, they were asked to mark a "never" box to indicate this. The instrument generated a dense field of information in a small space (important in suppressing the costs associated with international postal questionnaires): prevalence (the percentage of the sample who reported committing the offense at any time), incidence (the total number of offenses that offenders reported), recency (the percentage of total offenses that were committed in the previous year), and likelihood that offenses resulted in an arrest/conviction.

The instrument was a postal questionnaire (Scott, 1961). It could be completed and returned anonymously, although each respondent was also invited to return an enclosed follow-up slip, volunteering for an interview. Most of the 1,690 questionnaires distributed between December 1996 and June 1997 also contained the full-scale revised Eysenck Personality Questionnaire (EPQ-R) and the Impulsiveness Questionnaire (IVE; Eysenck & Eysenck, 1996). The 62 questionnaires administered to the prison sample, however, did not include these personality instruments.

Although the self-report instrument for the current study was effective in obtaining prevalence and incidence data (as well as data on recency, arrests, and convictions), an effective means of comparing offending at the individual level of analysis was still lacking. Theoretically, individuals could be compared by counting the percentage of the 72 offenses they had committed, or by summing the number of offenses they had committed, but these are blunt measures. They equally weight a homicide and an abuse of work privileges, treat petty shoplifting and automobile theft as equivalents. Trying to weight different crimes, however, is difficult (Nye & Short, 1957). "Is one homicide to be equated with 10 petty thefts?

TABLE 10 Scale for seriousness of offending

Element	Score Value
Minor injury to victim	1
Victim treated and discharged	4
Victim hospitalized	7
Victim killed	26
Victim of forcible sex intercourse	10
Intimidated by weapon, add	2
Intimidation of persons in connection with theft, etc.	
(other than in connection with forcible sex acts):	
Physical or verbal only	2
By weapon	4
Forcible entry of premises	1
Value of property stolen and/or damaged:	
Under $10	1
$10–250	2
$251–2,000	3
$2,001–9,000	4
$9,001–30,000	5
$30,001–80,000	6
Over $80,000	7
Theft of motor vehicle (recovered, undamaged)	2

SOURCE: Drawn from Sellin & Wolfgang, 1964, p. 298.

100? 1,000? We may sense that these are incommensurables and so *feel* that the question of comparing their magnitude is a nonsense question" (Merton, 1961, p. 703, emphasis in original). Fortunately, Sellin and Wolfgang provided a means of weighting self-report items by seriousness in their *The Measurement of Delinquency* (1964). Many of the offenses in the current study were directly comparable to Sellin and Wolfgang's scaling analysis; other scores were extrapolated as needed from their scales (see table 10). Seriousness scaling is discussed in the technical appendix (appendix A).

Seriousness coefficients weighted each individual's incidence profile. For example, if a person reported 3 acts of vandalism (10 crime points per offense) and 1 use of marijuana (53.81 points per offense), this yielded a crime score of 83.81. If another person reported 1 act of shoplifting (46.46 points per offense) and 30 abuses of work privileges (1.00 point per offense), this yielded a crime score of 76.46. Thus, the first offender would be considered a (slightly) more serious offender.

There are difficulties in using seriousness coefficients to generate individual crime scores. While assigning a crime score to each individual permits the comparison of heterogeneous offenders, these coefficients fail to account for context, intentionality, or the relationship between the offender and the victim. Table 10, drawn from Sellin and Wolfgang's study, indicates that killing someone is 2.6 times as serious as a rape, 3.7 times as serious as an assault leading to hospitalization, and 13 times as serious as an automobile theft. This may be so. Since the scale defines seriousness strictly in terms of social harm, however, it fails to distinguish between the pub brawl and the attempted assassination that lead to equivalent injuries. The seriousness coefficients also reflect the biases of the participants in Sellin and Wolfgang's study. University students, for example, rated marijuana use as more serious than heroin use (Sellin & Wolfgang, 1964, p. 393). Police officers rated kidnapping as a more serious offense than stabbing someone to death (p. 393). Perhaps law enforcement personnel perceived high-profile crimes as more serious than serious but commonplace offenses. Changing social norms also undermine the reliability of the ratings. Some behaviors rated as serious offenses in 1964—homosexual sex and abortion, for example—have been decriminalized. Therefore, although Sellin and Wolfgang's results have been replicated (e.g., Normandeau, 1970), the crime scores of individuals in the current study should be treated with caution.

PERSONALITY QUESTIONNAIRES

Fortuitously, Hans Eysenck, one of the leading experts on human intelligence (e.g., Eysenck 1962, 1966), also wrote on the psychology of crime (Eysenck, 1977; Eysenck & Gudjonsson, 1989). Eysenck and Gudjonsson (1989) suggest that crime is a function of personality, which can be described with four higher-order factors: intelligence, psychoticism, extraversion, and neuroticism. Intelligence consists of general intelligence (g), as measured by standard IQ tests. Psychoticism is an expression of emotional independence or "tough-mindedness." It is a subclinical expression of the characteristics that constitute psychopathy (e.g., Cleckley, 1982; Hare, 1980) or antisocial personality disorder (American Psychiatric Association, 2013). Individuals with high psychoticism possess the following traits: "(1) solitary, not caring for other people; (2) troublesome, not fitting in; (3) cruel, inhumane; (4) lack of feeling, insensitive; (5) lacking in empathy; (6) sensation-seeking, avid for strong sensory stimuli; (7) hostile to others, aggressive; (8) liking for odd and unusual things; (9) disregard for dangers, foolhardy; (10) likes to make fools of other people, and to upset them" (Eysenck, 1977, p. 58).

Extraversion is a measure of one's orientation to the outer, objective world. Its opposite is introversion, the measure of one's orientation to the inner, subjective world (Eysenck & Gudjonsson, 1989). Eysenck (1977) contrasts the qualities of the extravert with the qualities of the introvert:

> The typical extravert is sociable, likes parties, has many friends, needs to have people to talk to, and does not like reading or studying by himself. He craves excitement, takes chances, acts on the spur of the moment, and is generally an impulsive individual. He is fond of practical jokes, always has a ready answer, and generally likes

change; he is carefree, easygoing, optimistic, and likes to "laugh and be merry." He prefers to keep moving and doing things, tends to be aggressive and loses his temper quickly; his feelings are not kept under tight control and he is not always a reliable person. The typical introvert is a quiet, retiring sort of person, introspective, fond of books rather than people: he is reserved and reticent except with intimate friends. He tends to plan ahead, "looks before he leaps," and distrusts the impulses of the moment. He does not like excitement, takes matters of everyday life with proper seriousness, and likes a well-ordered mode of life. He keeps his feelings under close control, seldom behaves in an aggressive manner, and does not lose his temper easily. He is reliable, somewhat pessimistic, and places great value on ethical standards. (pp. 51–52)

Neuroticism is a measure of emotional stability or emotionality. Individuals with high neuroticism tend to be neurotic, unstable, and emotional, while those with low neuroticism tend to be unemotional and stable.

Eysenck believes that personality is largely shaped by genetics. He estimates that approximately 80% of intelligence is heritable and that 60% to 80% of personality traits are heritable (Eysenck, 1977, p. 103). These genetic influences produce neurological variations that explain personality types: high N (neuroticism) scores reflect greater autonomic nervous system lability, high E (extraversion) scores reflect strongly inhibited central nervous system function (requiring greater amounts of stimulation to maintain a comfortable level of arousal that Eysenck calls "hedonic tone"), and high P (psychoticism) scores reflect a weakening of central nervous system homeostasis, due to impaired cortical regulation of subcortical arousal mechanisms (q.v., Claridge, Robinson, & Birchall, 1985).

Eysenck believes that, as a general matter, antisocial behavior is associated with high P, high E, and high N scores, relative to controls matched for sex and age, and that the same is true of criminals. Data from two studies demonstrate the relationship in male prisoners. The data suggest a robust relationship between elevated P, E, and N scores and serious criminal offending. Nevertheless, acknowledging the heterogeneity of the criminal world, Eysenck (1977) also reports that in a study of five different kinds of prisoners—"confidence tricksters, property offenders, violent criminals, inadequate criminals, and a residual group which included prisoners who had not specialized in one type of crime, but had been guilty of several different varieties" (p. 60)—it was possible to construct a typology of offenders based on P, E, and N scores. "[T]he particular direction of criminal activity is partly determined by personality" (p. 61; see also table 11).

The three axes of personality linked to temperament—psychoticism, extraversion, and neuroticism—can be assessed using the revised Eysenck Personality Questionnaire (Eysenck & Eysenck, 1996). The EPQ-R is a powerful instrument to augment studies of self-reported offending. It is a fairly short scale (106 yes/no items) and simple to score. It has been validated against a number of research

TABLE 11 Psychoticism, extraversion, and neuroticism scores of adult male prisoners and controls

	n	Psychoticism	Extraversion	Neuroticism
Study 1				
Prisoners	1301	6.55 ± 3.16	12.51 ± 3.63	11.39 ± 4.97
Controls	1392	4.10 ± 2.53	11.65 ± 4.37	9.73 ± 4.71
		$p < 0.001$	$p < 0.001$	$p < 0.001$
Study 2				
Prisoners	569	6.65 ± 3.12	12.47 ± 3.67	11.77 ± 4.98
Controls	595	4.38 ± 2.32	11.54 ± 3.62	8.82 ± 4.50
		$p < 0.001$	$p < 0.001$	$p < 0.001$

NOTE: Drawn from Eysenck, 1977, p. 60. Data are from two independent investigations. The n indicates sample size, and p is the probability that the observed result occurred by chance.

populations. The EPQ-R includes a lie (L) scale (indicating both conformity and dissimulation) and subscales to measure criminality and addiction. The addition of the 54-item Impulsiveness Questionnaire (Eysenck & Eysenck, 1996) made it possible for the current study to assess impulsiveness, venturesomeness, and empathy. Impulsiveness encompasses the abnormal or pathological aspects of risk taking, while venturesomeness represents healthy risk taking. Using the EPQ-R and IVE, along with IQ measures, facilitated the investigation of all four dimensions of personality (g, P, E, and N) as they relate to self-reported offending.

FOLLOW-UP INTERVIEWS
AND ADDITIONAL MATERIALS

While the survey is a quantitative technique, assuming a social reality that can be empirically measured, the interview assumes a social reality that is not fundamentally quantifiable; the latter emphasizes the phenomenological meanings that people ascribe to their experiences (Bryman, 1988; Tewksbury, 2009). The self-report instrument utilized in the current research efficiently captured prevalence and incidence data, but it did not collect details about the contexts in which criminal activity took place. Nevertheless, questions of *how* and *why* are every bit as important as questions of *how much* and *when* (Katz, 1988), and follow-up interviews made it possible to explore these questions. It is impossible to completely convey the sense experience of crime—the bark of a gunshot, the perfume of marijuana smoke, or the adrenaline rush of "getting away with it"; and while it may be inappropriate to dwell on such dramatic elements in academic research, it is important to recollect—even momentarily—that these constitute the authentic elements of crime. Accordingly, self-report questionnaires from individuals who volunteered for a follow-up interview were examined, and a purposive sample of 44 participants was drawn and contacted for interview. These interviews were used to gather narrative details about the offenses and to illustrate the full range of offending in the study, from innocent angels who denied ever committing any offense to hardened career criminals. The interviews also made it possible to seek themes that explain the origins of high-IQ offending. Analysis of the interview data can be found in chapter 6.

The interviews conducted were semistructured in nature, which is to say they used a single standard protocol of questions (reproduced in appendix C) but afforded the latitude to clarify ambiguous answers or to probe for more details. Because of the international character of the research, several interviews were conducted by telephone, e-mail, or postal correspondence. Most, however, were conducted face-to-face and took place in a number of settings: cafés, diners, and microbreweries; dormitories, apartments, and city parks. Some interviews were conducted in prison settings, but most were conducted on the outside, with people who may or may not have been caught for their crimes: "I visited an incarcerated child molester, talking with him for two full days, and interviewed a retired gentleman, who claimed to have never committed any of my 72 listed offenses—not even abusing work privileges or hedging on his taxes. I interviewed a marijuana harvester, an armed robber, and a car thief. Another man had once been on the FBI's ten most wanted list, and yet another had been arrested for building bombs in preparation for a 'war against society'" (Oleson, 2004, p. 194). Follow-up interviews lasted approximately 2 hours, although some were as brief as 1 hour, and two of the interviews extended over several meetings (each of these was approximately 14–15 hours long).

While the research design originally included only postal self-report responses and follow-up interviews, documentation and materials from several other sources ultimately contributed to the study. In *Let Us Now Praise Famous Men* (1969), Agee writes, "If I could do it, I'd do no writing at all here. It would be photographs; the rest would be fragments of cloth, bits of cotton, lumps of earth, records of speech, pieces of wood and iron, phials of odors, plates of food and excrement. . . . A piece of the body torn out by the roots might be more to the point" (12–13). In addition to their self-report questionnaires and interviews, the research participants also provided many other forms of documentation. Letters were common (including both notes of praise and critiques of the research), autobiographical sketches, and impressions of the topic of high-IQ offending. More than 20 individuals wrote about the alienating effects of high intelligence. Some sent reprints of published articles, others sent unpublished essays on penological themes, some sent poetry or artwork, and others sent photographs. These artifacts provided supplemental information about high-IQ crime and the participants.

3

The Participants

Criminals share with geniuses a type of degeneration that produces not only evil but also new virtues.

—CESARE LOMBROSO, *CRIMINAL MAN*, P. 352

As described in chapter 1, Terman's *Genetic Studies of Genius* provides an extraordinarily rich longitudinal portrait of a gifted cohort (Terman, 1926). It is hailed as the single greatest study in the history of the social sciences (Serebriakoff, 1985). The current study neither attempts to replicate Terman's study nor to match it in terms of its astonishing duration and depth. Rather, the current inquiry seeks to extend the examination of giftedness in a new and underresearched direction (i.e., the relationship between high IQ and offending).

This chapter describes the respondents in the index and control groups. It identifies their key demographics, such as sex, age, occupation, IQ, and the like. It also relates the relationships between several of these variables and the prevalence and incidence of offending. Additionally, the chapter compares the characteristics of the most criminal quintile of the sample (as measured by crime scores) with the traits of the least criminal quintile (including abstainers, those who denied committing offenses of any kind). The chapter then outlines the respondents' experiences with mental illness and its treatment and, using the revised Eysenck Personality Questionnaire (EPQ-R), describes the personality traits of some respondents. Finally, this chapter reports the books, movies, and famous figures that shaped the respondents' thinking and influenced their behavior.

DEMOGRAPHICS

The questionnaire produced an enormous volume of data. In addition to collecting prevalence, incidence, recency, arrest, and conviction data for 72 offenses (described in chapter 4), it collected self-report information about key demographic variables including IQ, sex, age, ethnicity, nationality, religion, education, occupation, income, sexual orientation, and marital status. These variables were analyzed using prevalence and incidence data, although homogeneity in the data and/or small frequency counts limited the ability to do so for all measures. The data are summarized in Table 12 and a discussion follows.

IQ Score

IQ was the independent variable in this study. Specifically, the study asked whether differences in intelligence correlate with self-reported offending, even in the right asymptote of the IQ distribution. Because self-assessed IQ has low measures of validity (Paulhus, Lysy, & Yik, 1998), all sample means were based either upon (self-reported) scores of previously administered tests or upon imputed scores. Many respondents, particularly those in the high-IQ society sample, were versed in psychometric testing, knew their IQ score(s), and provided detailed information about the tests they had taken. Some, however, particularly students, were able to report ACT, SAT, or GRE scores—academic achievement tests with high general intelligence (g) loadings (Frey & Detterman, 2004) used for admissions purposes into high-IQ organizations—but did not know their IQ scores. Others, particularly respondents in the control group, did not know their IQ scores (in which case scores were estimated on the basis of educational achievement and employment, as explained in appendix A). Because scores were reported from more than a dozen IQ and achievement tests, measures of intellectual ability were standardized into z-scores and transformed into generic IQs (with a mean of 100 and a standard deviation of 15 points, per the Wechsler Adult Intelligence Scale).

The high-IQ society sample had a mean IQ score of 158.5. This IQ score would place an individual at the 99.994 percentile, qualifying him or her for membership in IQ societies such as Mensa, Intertel, and the Triple Nine Society. Only 1 person in approximately 20,000 possesses such an IQ score. This sample's mean score is higher than the mean 147 IQ in Terman's longitudinal study of genius described in chapter 1, and more than one standard deviation higher than his 135 IQ threshold (Holahan & Sears, 1995). The mean IQ for the university sample was 142.9; the mean IQ for the incarcerated sample was 145.2; and the mean IQ for participants reassigned from the control group to the index group was 142.8. These samples all had lower mean scores than the high-IQ sample, but they still exceeded Terman's admissions threshold. The mean IQ for the aggregated index group was 148.7 (slightly higher than the mean in the Terman study). The control group had a mean IQ of 115.4. Although the control group is employed as a contrast to the high-IQ samples in the study, even this group had a mean IQ more than one standard deviation above average. This means that those with IQs in the below-average range associated with delinquency and crime (e.g., 90–92) remain

TABLE 12 Demographic data for high-IQ society sample, university sample, incarcerated sample, reassigned high-IQ sample, cumulative index group, and control group

	High IQ (n = 260)	University (n = 132)	Incarcerated (n = 30)	Reassigned (n = 43)	Cumulative Index (n = 465)	Control (n = 756)
Mean IQ	158.5 ± 10.8	142.9 ± 4.8	145.2 ± 9.3	142.8 ± 9.6	148.7 ± 16.6	115.4 ± 6.1
Sex						
Male	213 (82.2%)	66 (50.4%)	29 (96.7%)	27 (64.3%)	335 (72.5%)	288 (38.3%)
Female	46 (17.8%)	65 (49.6%)	1 (3.3%)	15 (35.7%)	127 (27.5%)	463 (61.7%)
Age						
<25	16 (6.5%)	66 (53.2%)	2 (6.7%)	24 (58.5%)	108 (24.4%)	232 (31.8%)
25–44	73 (29.4%)	54 (43.5%)	19 (63.3%)	12 (29.3%)	158 (35.7%)	337 (46.2%)
45–64	93 (37.5%)	4 (3.2%)	9 (30.0%)	5 (12.2%)	111 (25.1%)	145 (19.9%)
65+	66 (26.6%)	0 (0%)	0 (0%)	0 (0%)	66 (14.9%)	16 (2.2%)
Ethnicity						
Asian	8 (3.1%)	28 (21.5%)	0 (0%)	1 (2.4%)	37 (8.0%)	60 (8.0%)
Black	2 (0.8%)	2 (1.5%)	1 (3.3%)	3 (7.1%)	8 (1.7%)	206 (27.3%)
White	249 (96.1%)	100 (76.9%)	29 (96.7%)	38 (90.5%)	416 (90.2%)	488 (64.7%)
Nationality						
US	192 (74.4%)	95 (74.2%)	8 (26.7%)	28 (70.0%)	323 (70.8%)	483 (77.3%)
UK	23 (8.9%)	3 (2.3%)	21 (70.0%)	2 (5.0%)	49 (10.7%)	7 (1.1%)
Other	43 (16.7%)	30 (23.4%)	1 (3.3%)	10 (25.0%)	84 (18.4%)	135 (21.6%)
Religion						
None	97 (38.5%)	54 (43.2%)	7 (23.3%)	5 (13.5%)	163 (36.7%)	43 (7.2%)
Catholicism	40 (15.9%)	29 (23.2%)	3 (10.0%)	5 (13.5%)	77 (17.3%)	42 (7.1%)
Other Christian	74 (29.4%)	24 (19.2%)	11 (36.7%)	21 (56.8%)	130 (29.3%)	463 (77.9%)
Judaism	14 (5.6%)	5 (4.0%)	3 (10.0%)	0 (0%)	22 (5.0%)	10 (1.7%)
Islam	2 (0.8%)	3 (2.4%)	0 (0%)	0 (0%)	5 (1.1%)	4 (0.7%)
Buddhism	3 (1.2%)	2 (1.6%)	3 (10.0%)	1 (2.7%)	9 (2.0%)	3 (0.5%)
Hinduism	0 (0%)	3 (2.4%)	0 (0%)	0 (0%)	3 (0.7%)	0 (0%)
Other	22 (8.7%)	5 (4.0%)	3 (10.0%)	5 (13.5%)	35 (7.9%)	29 (4.9%)
Education						
Some School	7 (2.7%)	0 (0%)	3 (10.3%)	1 (2.4%)	11 (2.4%)	20 (2.7%)
High School	11 (4.3%)	1 (0.8%)	1 (3.4%)	3 (7.1%)	16 (3.5%)	132 (17.6%)
Vocational	5 (1.9%)	1 (0.8%)	4 (13.8%)	0 (0%)	10 (2.2%)	25 (3.3%)
Some College	26 (10.1%)	24 (18.5%)	11 (37.9%)	17 (40.%)	78 (17.0%)	365 (48.6%)
BA/BS	69 (26.7%)	40 (30.8%)	6 (20.7%)	12 (28.6%)	127 (27.7%)	133 (17.7%)
MA/MS	74 (28.7%)	36 (27.7%)	3 (10.3%)	6 (14.3%)	119 (25.9%)	39 (5.2%)
Professional	34 (13.2%)	12 (9.2%)	1 (3.4%)	2 (4.8%)	49 (10.7%)	7 (0.9%)
PhD	32 (12.4%)	16 (12.3%)	0 (0%)	0 (0%)	48 (10.5%)	6 (0.8%)
Other	0 (0%)	0 (0%)	0 (0%)	1 (2.4%)	1 (0.2%)	24 (3.2%)
Occupation						
Unemployed	98 (38.7%)	83 (65.9%)	30 (100%)	8 (20.5%)	219 (49.7%)	167 (23.5%)
Managers	19 (7.5%)	4 (3.2%)	0 (0%)	4 (10.3%)	27 (6.1%)	91 (12.8%)
Professionals	113 (44.7%)	32 (25.4%)	0 (0%)	15 (38.5%)	160 (36.3%)	171 (24.1%)
Technicians	4 (1.6%)	1 (0.8%)	0 (0%)	2 (5.1%)	7 (1.6%)	43 (6.1%)

Clerical Support	2 (0.8%)	0 (0%)	0 (0%)	1 (2.6%)	3 (0.7%)	34 (4.8%)
Service/Sales	13 (5.1%)	6 (4.8%)	0 (0%)	4 (10.3%)	17 (3.9%)	136 (19.2%)
Agriculture	1 (0.4%)	0 (0%)	0 (0%)	0 (0%)	1 (0.2%)	3 (0.4%)
Craft/Trades	0 (0%)	0 (0%)	0 (0%)	0 (0%)	0 (0%)	29 (4.1%)
Machines	2 (0.8%)	0 (0%)	0 (0%)	1 (2.6%)	2 (0.5%)	6 (0.8%)
Elementary	0 (0%)	0 (0%)	0 (0%)	1 (2.6%)	1 (0.2%)	15 (2.1%)
Armed Forces	1 (0.4%)	0 (0%)	0 (0%)	3 (7.7%)	4 (0.9%)	15 (2.1%)
Median Income	$40,000	$15,000	$600	$31,750	$30,000	$26,000
Sexual Orientation						
Heterosexual	238 (93.0%)	123 (96.9%)	24 (80.0%)	38 (90.5%)	423 (93.0%)	712 (95.6%)
Homosexual	9 (3.5%)	1 (0.8%)	4 (13.3%)	3 (7.1%)	17 (3.7%)	15 (2.0%)
Bisexual	9 (3.5%)	3 (2.4%)	2 (6.7%)	1 (2.4%)	15 (3.3%)	18 (2.4%)
Marital Status						
Single	63 (24.5%)	98 (75.4%)	13 (43.3%)	21 (50.0%)	195 (42.5%)	316 (42.0%)
Married	132 (51.4%)	18 (13.8%)	6 (20.0%)	10 (23.8%)	166 (36.2%)	308 (40.9%)
Separated	5 (1.9%)	0 (0%)	0 (0%)	0 (0%)	5 (1.1%)	0 (0%)
Divorced	33 (12.8%)	3 (2.3%)	7 (23.3%)	2 (4.8%)	45 (9.8%)	24 (3.2%)
Living with Partner	20 (7.8%)	11 (8.5%)	4 (13.3%)	2 (4.8%)	37 (8.1%)	44 (5.8%)
Widowed	4 (1.6%)	0 (0%)	0 (0%)	7 (16.7%)	11 (2.4%)	61 (8.1%)

NOTE: Forty-five cases were reassigned between samples based on reported IQ: 2 cases were moved from the university sample to the control group, and 43 cases (the reassigned high-IQ sample) were moved from the control group to the high-IQ (index) group. Sample sizes differ across variables because of missing data. Furthermore, totals within samples may not sum exactly to 100% because of rounding.

underrepresented in the control group. Indeed, the control group mean represents an IQ score more than one standard deviation above the population mean of 100. Individuals possessing this score are identified as "bright" and previously have served as subjects in studies of gifted delinquents (e.g., Anolik, 1979; Gath, Tennant, & Pidduck, 1970).

Is there a relationship between IQ and offending, as the IQ-crime literature suggests, even at very high-IQ levels? Table 13 compares prevalence, incidence, and recency data for self-reported offenses in the index group (consisting of the high-IQ society, university, incarcerated, and reassigned samples) and the control group. Prevalence rates were about 10% higher in the index group than in the control group in both the last year and ever. Incidence rates also were higher in the index group. Among those who reported an offense, a larger percentage of the index group than the control group reported committing six or more offenses. Nevertheless, although the groups are large, making the test for statistical significance fairly sensitive, the data are not sufficient to reject the possibility that differences between the groups are caused by chance. However, it is noteworthy that the data do not demonstrate a statistically significant difference between the index and control groups. If the relationship between IQ and offending is negative and linear,

TABLE 13 Prevalence, incidence, and recency by index and control groups

		High IQ ($n = 465$)	Control ($n = 756$)	χ^2	p
Any offense last year	Once last year	15 (5.4)	29 (7.7)	2.55	.4671
	2 to 5 last year	62 (22.4)	89 (23.7)		
	6 to 9 last year	30 (10.8)	31 (8.3)		
	10+ last year	170 (61.4)	226 (60.3)		
	Missing or None	188 (40.4)	381 (50.4)		
Any offense ever	Once ever	5 (1.1)	8 (1.2)	6.76	.0799
	2 to 5 ever	14 (3.2)	42 (6.5)		
	6 to 9 ever	20 (4.5)	22 (3.4)		
	10+ ever	403 (91.2)	571 (88.8)		
	Missing or None	23 (4.9)	113 (14.9)		

NOTE: The n indicates the number of people in each sample. Numbers outside parentheses are prevalence counts (number of persons in the sample who reported an offense) and numbers inside parentheses are incidence counts (average number of offenses reported by those who report an offense). Recency is indicated by separating the offenses reported in the last year from total offenses reported (which include those from the last year). The χ^2 statistic indicates amount of correspondence between observed and expected values, and p is the probability that the observed result occurred by chance. Probabilities <.05 are deemed statistically significant.

as widely assumed (Mears & Cochran, 2013), one would expect to see respondents in the control group reporting significantly higher rates than respondents in the index group.

Table 14 combines the index and control groups and parses the respondents by IQ level. For both "last year" and "ever" offenses, it compares three groups: (1) individuals with IQ scores of 115 or less, (2) individuals with IQ scores between 116 and 129, and (3) individuals with IQ scores of 130 or more. The table reveals a similar pattern to table 13. Prevalence rates were approximately 10% higher for the 130+ group than for the other groups, both for offenses in the last year and offenses ever committed. Incidence rates were higher among the 130+ group as well. Among those who reported an offense, those with higher IQ scores reported more offenses. Again, the data cannot reject the possibility that observed differences between the groups are caused by chance, but these data do not support a negative, linear relationship between IQ and offending.

Sex

Although males and females have comparable full-scale IQ scores, males tend to outperform females on spatial and mechanical items, while females outperform males on many verbal tasks (Neisser et al., 1996). Given the negative association posited between verbal IQ and criminal activity (Walsh et al., 2015), sex-based IQ differences may help to explain gender differences in crime. Self-report and official statistics both suggest that males participate in delinquent and criminal acts

TABLE 14 Prevalence, incidence, and recency by IQ

		≤115 (n = 563)	116–129 (n = 225)	≥130 (n = 433)	χ²	p
Any offense last year	Once lasts year	23 (8.0)	7 (6.4)	14 (5.5)	5.96	.4278
	2 to 5 last year	61 (21.3)	32 (29.4)	58 (22.7)		
	6 to 9 last year	23 (8.0)	9 (8.3)	29 (11.3)		
	10+ last year	180 (62.7)	61 (56.0)	155 (60.6)		
	Missing or None	276 (49.0)	116 (51.6)	177 (40.9)		
Any offense ever	Once ever	7 (1.5)	2 (1.0)	4 (1.0)	6.46	.3737
	2 to 5 ever	32 (6.7)	10 (5.2)	14 (3.4)		
	6 to 9 ever	15 (3.1)	9 (4.7)	18 (4.4)		
	10+ ever	427 (88.8)	172 (89.1)	375 (91.2)		
	Missing or None	82 (14.6)	32 (14.2)	22 (5.1)		

NOTE: See table 13 for a description of table elements.

with greater frequency than females. Males are also ensnared in the criminal justice system in far greater numbers. "Males are five to fifty times as likely to be arrested as are females" (Wilson & Herrnstein, 1985, p. 104). The US male incarceration rate is currently 14 times the female rate (Carson, 2014). Sociologists often attribute these differences to social influences such as macrosociological power structures, gender socialization, and "chivalry" in the criminal justice system (Daly & Chesney-Lind, 1988; Fagan, 2015), but biosocial criminologists also explain the relationship in terms of testosterone, genetics, and brain differences (Beaver & Nedelec, 2015).

Males were overrepresented in the index group and underrepresented among controls. The high-IQ society sample was 82.2% male, and the reassigned sample was 64.3% male. In the prison sample, males were even more overrepresented: 28 of the 30 prisoners identified as male; only 1 was female; and 1 (housed in a male prison and coded as male) identified as a hermaphrodite. Of course, males were also overrepresented in the membership ranks of the high-IQ society and in US and UK prison systems. Males and females in the university sample were closer to an equal distribution: 66 respondents were male and 65 were female. Although women constitute a majority of university students (National Center for Education Statistics, 2013), there is enormous variation in the male-female ratio across universities and programs. The university sample reasonably approximates the sex distribution of the institutions at the time the sample was drawn. In the control group, females were overrepresented: more than three-fifths of the respondents were female.

Table 15 presents prevalence, incidence, and recency data by sex. Unexpectedly, for offenses reported in the previous year, prevalence and incidence rates were

TABLE 15 Prevalence, incidence, and recency by sex

		Male ($n = 622$)	Female ($n = 588$)	χ^2	p
Any offense	Once last year	20 (6.1)	24 (7.6)	1.67	.6444
last year	2 to 5 last year	80 (24.2)	71 (22.5)		
	6 to 9 last year	34 (10.3)	26 (8.2)		
	10+ last year	196 (59.4)	195 (61.7)		
	Missing or None	292 (46.9)	272 (46.3)		
Any offense	Once ever	5 (0.9)	8 (1.6)	2.10	.5519
ever	2 to 5 ever	26 (4.6)	29 (5.8)		
	6 to 9 ever	23 (4.0)	18 (3.6)		
	10+ ever	518 (90.6)	449 (89.1)		
	Missing or None	50 (8.0)	84 (14.3)		

NOTE: See table 13 for a description of table elements.

both slightly higher for females than males, although these differences were not statistically significant. For all offenses ("ever"), however, males reported somewhat higher prevalence and incidence rates. These differences were not significant either. Observed differences between self-reported male and female offending could be the product of chance variation.

Age

"Criminal behavior depends as much or more on age than on any other demographic characteristic—sex, social status, race, family configuration, etc.—yet examined by criminologists" (Wilson & Herrnstein, 1985, p. 126). Indeed, the "age-crime curve" is one of the most consistent findings on offending across different time periods and jurisdictions (Farrington, 1986). Hirschi and Gottfredson (1983) characterize it as one of the "brute facts of criminology" (p. 552). Age matters. It is not unusual—and may be a normal part of development—for adolescents to engage in rebellious, even delinquent, acts; but most people appear to "age out" of crime in their late teens and early 20s. In a seminal study, Moffitt (1993) distinguishes adolescent-limited offenders (large numbers of people who engage in antisocial behavior during their teenaged years) from life-course persistent offenders (a small population that displays early antisocial behavior and continues to do so across the life span). Loeber and his colleagues (2012) report that the age-crime curve is a function of IQ and impulsivity. Whether the decline in offending after the mid-20s is related to continuing brain development, particularly in the frontal lobes (Beckman, 2004); economic earning capacity (Lochner, 2004), the assumption of social responsibilities such as work and family (Farrington, 1986); or something else remains unknown.

There was substantial variation in age between the groups. While more than a quarter of the high-IQ society sample was 65+, only 2.2% of the control sam-

TABLE 16 Prevalence, incidence, and recency by age

		Age group					
		<25 (n = 339)	25–44 (n = 494)	45–64 (n = 256)	65+ (n = 82)	χ^2	p
Any offense last year	Once last year	15 (6.4)	15 (6.2)	9 (8.5)	4 (10.0)	34.07	8.67E-05
	2 to 5 last year	34 (14.5)	64 (26.3)	34 (32.1)	13 (32.5)		
	6 to 9 last year	14 (6.0)	28 (11.5)	15 (14.2)	2 (5.0)		
	10+ last year	172 (73.2)	136 (56.0)	48 (45.3)	21 (52.5)		
	Missing or None	104 (30.7)	251 (50.8)	150 (58.6)	42 (51.2)		
Any offense ever	Once ever	0 (0)	6 (1.4)	4 (1.8)	3 (4.1)	38.45	1.45E-05
	2 to 5 ever	5 (1.6)	24 (5.5)	21 (9.4)	6 (8.2)		
	6 to 9 ever	10 (3.3)	13 (3.0)	17 (7.6)	1 (1.4)		
	10+ ever	293 (95.1)	395 (90.2)	181 (81.2)	63 (86.3)		
	Missing or None	31 (9.1)	56 (11.3)	33 (12.9)	9 (11.0)		

NOTE: See table 13 for a description of table elements. Very small p values here are expressed in scientific notation (e.g., 8.67E-05 = .0000867).

ple, and no one in the university, incarcerated, or reassigned samples, belonged to this age group. Conversely, while more than half of the university sample was 25 or younger, this age group constituted less than 10% of the high-IQ society and incarcerated samples. Table 16 presents data from the study about prevalence, incidence, and recency by age. Consistent with other age-crime research, almost 70% of the <25 group reported an offense in the previous year, approximately half of those in the 25–44 and 65+ groups did so, and just over 40% of those in the 45–64 group did so. Those in the <25 group who reported an offense in the previous year reported a significantly higher incidence rate than the older groups. In terms of offenses ever committed, even though respondents in the 65+ group have had the longest time to accumulate offenses, the <25 group still reported the highest prevalence rate. The <25 group also reported significantly higher incidence rates than the older groups. This suggests that a greater percentage of young offenders might be committing greater numbers of offenses than older offenders. Alternatively, it could suggest that respondents from older groups have underestimated the prevalence and/or incidence of their offenses.

Ethnicity

Minorities are overrepresented in the criminal justice system in all Western countries (Tonry, 1997). In the United States, Hispanic males are imprisoned at approximately 2.4 times the rate of white males and African American males are incarcerated at 6.0 times the rate of white males (Carson, 2014). The cause of this overrepresentation, however, remains unknown. Disentangling the relationship between race and crime is difficult. Many criminologists are reluctant to discuss the intersection of race and crime for fear of appearing racist (Wright, 2009), and consequently the matter remains "mired in an unproductive mix of controversy and silence" (Sampson & Wilson, 2005, p. 177). Although early researchers like Lombroso believed that crime was racially determined, sociologically minded researchers attribute justice system overrepresentation to social factors such as structural discrimination, social disorganization, or transmission of a code of the street (Piquero, Piquero, & Stewart, 2015). Biosocial criminologists, on the other hand, relate it also to genetic traits (Wright, 2009; Wright & Morgan, 2015). Although not necessarily causal, co-occurring deficits in minority IQ scores and overrepresentation in criminal justice systems suggest a potential relationship and should be explored further.

Table 12 reveals that the samples were ethnically homogeneous. More than 90% of the index group and more than 60% of the control group identified as white. Although Asians comprised slightly more than one-fifth of the university sample, and although blacks comprised slightly more than one-quarter of the control sample, these ethnic categories were even more weakly represented across the study. Accordingly, analyses of prevalence and incidence rates by ethnicity were not conducted.

Nationality

Nationality is of criminological interest in at least three respects. First, in an international study of self-reported offending, behavior that is criminal and severely sanctioned in one country can be legal or decriminalized in another (e.g., possession of narcotics is a capital crime in Singapore but has been decriminalized in Portugal). Measuring subjects' nationalities controls for such regional variation. Second, countries of origin are correlated with measures of race and ethnicity, which have criminological dimensions. Third, nationality is often related to immigration status. New immigrants are arrested, convicted, and incarcerated at disproportionate rates (Tonry, 1997). Researchers attribute this overrepresentation to a number of factors: new immigrants often have lower levels of education and higher rates of unemployment, and they may not speak the local language. They often live in poor and disadvantaged communities marked by social disorganization (Marshall, 1997; Shaw & McKay, 1942). The convergence of immigration regulations and criminal law has prompted some scholars to write about "crimmigration" (e.g., Stumpf, 2006).

Although nationality is a meritorious variable for criminological inquiry, respondents in the current study did not always interpret the question as asking what country issued their passports. Rather, some respondents—particularly those in the university and control samples—understood the question as asking for additional ethnic detail. Thus, some US citizens of Irish descent answered, "Irish," for example, and some African Americans answered "African." Accordingly, the nationality data in table 12, while probably accurate for the high-IQ society and incarcerated samples, likely undercounts the percentage of US and UK responses in the university and control samples. Because of the distortion in the data, and the US and UK homogeneity of the samples, prevalence and incidence rates were not calculated by nationality.

Religion

Although religion has long been studied as a correlate of crime, the relationship between the two remains undertheorized. Akers (2010) rightly observed that religious institutions generally reinforce conformity to conventional norms, but even Lombroso (1876/2006) noted that "criminals and honest men attend church at almost the same rate" (p. 323). Indeed, Hirschi and Stark (1969) reported no relationship between religiosity and delinquency. In 1971, Knudten and Knudten concluded that more empirical work was needed before conclusions could be drawn. Recent research, however, suggests a consensus: religion and religious involvement exert a prosocial influence. In Johnson and Jang's (2011) systematic review of 270 studies, approximately 90% (244) reported an inverse or beneficial relationship between religion and measures of delinquency and crime; only 9% (24) reported no association or mixed findings; and only 2 studies reported a positive association between religion and antisocial outcomes. This might suggest a positive relationship between IQ and religiosity, since both are negatively correlated with delinquency and crime, but research indicates that IQ is *negatively* associated with religious belief and practice. In a 2013 meta-analysis by Zuckerman, Silberman, and Hall, correlations between intelligence and religious belief ranged between −.20 and −.25.

The current study bears out that finding. As noted in table 12, although less than 10% of the control group identified as atheist or agnostic ("none"), more than a third of the index group did so. On the other hand, 85% of the control group but less than half of the index group identified as Catholic or Christian. Other major world religions were weakly represented. Collectively, Buddhism, Hinduism, Islam, and Judaism accounted for less than 3% of the control group and less than 9% of the index group. Table 17 presents data about prevalence, incidence, and recency by religion. The table shows that at least half of all groups reported an offense in the previous year. Between 50% and 60% of those who professed no belief or who identified as Christian, Catholic, or Jewish reported an offense in the previous year; slightly more, approximately two-thirds, of those who identified as Hindu, Muslim, or other reported an offense in the previous year. Incidence rates were lowest among individuals with other religious beliefs and highest among Hindus, although these differences were not statistically significant. In terms of lifetime prevalence, Muslims, Christians, and Catholics all reported lifetime prevalence rates of approximately 90%, while atheists, Hindus, Jews, and those with other religious beliefs reported lower rates. Of those who reported an offense, Hindus, Jews, and atheists reported statistically significant higher incidence rates than other groups.

TABLE 17 Prevalence, incidence, and recency by religion

		Catholic (n = 175)	Christian (n = 592)	Hindu (n = 3)	Islam (n = 9)	Judaism (n = 32)	None (n = 252)	Other (n = 31)	χ^2	p
Any offense last year	Once last year	4 (4.3)	24 (8.1)	0 (0)	1 (16.7)	1 (5.3)	9 (6.2)	1 (5.0)	8.32	.9735
	2 to 5 last year	22 (23.7)	74 (24.9)	0 (0)	1 (16.7)	3 (15.8)	31 (21.2)	6 (30.0)		
	6 to 9 last year	8 (8.6)	30 (10.1)	0 (0)	0 (0)	1 (5.3)	16 (11.0)	2 (10.0)		
	10+ last year	59 (63.4)	169 (56.9)	2 (100)	4 (66.7)	14 (73.7)	90 (61.6)	11 (55.0)		
	Missing or None	82 (46.9)	295 (49.8)	1 (33.3)	3 (33.3)	13 (40.6)	106 (42.1)	11 (35.5)		
Any offense ever	Once ever	0 (0)	8 (1.6)	0 (0)	1 (12.5)	0 (0)	3 (1.3)	0 (0)	36.87	.0054
	2 to 5 ever	4 (2.5)	39 (7.5)	0 (0)	0 (0)	0 (0)	7 (3.0)	1 (3.5)		
	6 to 9 ever	13 (8.2)	23 (4.5)	0 (0)	0 (0)	0 (0)	4 (1.7)	2 (6.9)		
	10+ ever	141 (89.2)	447 (86.5)	3 (100)	7 (87.5)	31 (100)	221 (94)	26 (89.7)		
	Missing or None	17 (9.7)	75 (12.7)	0 (0.0)	1 (11.1)	1 (3.1)	17 (6.7)	2 (6.5)		

NOTE: See table 13 for a description of table elements.

Education

Educational achievement, along with occupational status and income, is a principal indicator of socioeconomic status (SES) (Adler et al., 1994). Although SES is not significantly related to self-reported offending (e.g., Polk, Frease, & Richmond, 1974), it is negatively and widely correlated with officially detected offenses (Ellis, Beaver, & Wright, 2009). The exact causal linkages between education and crime remain unknown. Hirschi (1969) famously suggests that school success establishes social bonds, as explained in chapter 6. Ehrlich (1975) suggests that educational attainment improves wages, which in turn lowers crime. Lochner (2004) suggests that education increases the costs of engaging in crime and of punishment. While sociologists typically relate crime and socioeconomic status with structural theories like social control, differential association, labeling, social disorganization, anomie, or class conflict (Parker & Mowen, 2015), biosocial criminologists relate it to intelligence, temperament, or environmental toxins (Walsh, Taylor, & Yun, 2015).

The study respondents were well educated. Nearly a quarter of the control group and nearly three-quarters of the index group had a college degree. Nearly half of the index group had a graduate degree. Table 18 presents data about offense prevalence, incidence, and recency by education level. With the exception of those reporting "some schooling" and "other" qualifications, at least half of all educational groups reported an offense in the previous year (e.g., fewer than 50% reported "none" for offenses last year). Incidence rates were higher among those with some college and other qualifications than among other groups, but these differences were not significant. Interestingly, in terms of lifetime prevalence, more of those with a professional degree or a PhD reported any previous offense than did other groups (e.g., the percentages of those with professional degrees or PhDs reporting "none" for offenses ever were only 3.6% and 5.6%, respectively). Those with some schooling and bachelor's degrees reported the greatest number of offenses per person, although these differences were not statistically significant.

Occupation

Like education and income, occupational status is a principal indicator of SES. And like education and income, occupational status is inversely associated with crime. "Neighborhoods with high rates of street crime are often neighborhoods with high rates of joblessness. Studies of burglars and robbers regularly show them to have poor employment records" (Wilson & Herrnstein, 1985, p. 312). But the linkages between work and crime are complex, especially at the macroeconomic level. While there is empirical support for Cantor and Land's (1985) model, suggesting that aggregate unemployment rates influence crime rates by influencing both offender motivation and the guardianship of criminal targets (Phillips & Land, 2012), others challenge the significance of unemployment rates. Although a

TABLE 18 Prevalence, incidence, and recency by education

		Some schooling (n = 31)	High school diploma or equivalent (n = 148)	Vocation or tech training (n = 35)	Some college (n = 443)	Bachelor's degree (n = 260)	Master's degree (n = 158)	PhD (n = 54)	Professional degree (n = 56)	Other (n = 25)	χ^2	p
Offense last year	Once last year	2 (13.3)	1 (1.3)	2 (10.5)	20 (8.0)	9 (6.5)	4 (5.1)	3 (9.4)	2 (6.9)	1 (11.1)	21.91	.5843
	2 to 5 last year	4 (26.7)	22 (29.3)	5 (26.3)	49 (19.6)	32 (23.2)	20 (25.3)	11 (34.4)	8 (27.6)	0 (0)		
	6 to 9 last year	1 (6.7)	3 (4.0)	2 (10.5)	23 (9.2)	15 (10.9)	8 (10.1)	2 (6.3)	5 (17.2)	2 (22.2)		
	10+ last year	8 (53.3)	49 (65.3)	10 (52.6)	158 (63.2)	82 (59.4)	47 (59.5)	16 (50.0)	14 (48.3)	6 (66.7)		
	Missing or None	16 (51.6)	73 (49.3)	16 (45.7)	193 (43.6)	122 (46.9)	79 (50.0)	22 (40.7)	27 (48.2)	16 (64.0)		
Offense ever	Once ever	0 (0)	0 (0)	0 (0)	8 (2.1)	2 (0.9)	1 (0.7)	1 (2.0)	1 (1.9)	0 (0)	21.43	.6134
	2 to 5 ever	1 (3.9)	11 (8.5)	2 (6.5)	19 (4.9)	9 (3.8)	6 (4.2)	3 (5.9)	3 (5.6)	2 (10.5)		
	6 to 9 ever	2 (7.7)	4 (3.1)	3 (9.7)	10 (2.6)	12 (5.1)	3 (2.1)	3 (5.9)	4 (7.4)	1 (5.3)		
	10+ ever	23 (88.5)	115 (88.5)	26 (83.9)	351 (90.5)	212 (90.2)	132 (93)	44 (86.3)	46 (85.2)	16 (84.2)		
	Missing or None	5 (16.1)	18 (12.2)	4 (11.4)	55 (12.4)	25 (9.6)	16 (10.1)	3 (5.6)	2 (3.6)	6 (24.0)		

NOTE: See table 13 for a description of table elements.

strong economy is frequently cited as an explanation for the crime drop of the 1990s, Levitt (2004) argues that low unemployment can explain only 2% of the decline in property crime and none of the reduction in violent crime and homicide. Fagan and Freeman (1999) find that the relationship between work and crime is multivalent, involving criminal returns, opportunity costs, punishment costs, social pressures, and personal preferences. Many offenders "double up," engaging in both crime and legal work. Crime and employment are not binaries, then, but exist upon a continuum. These findings echo Sutherland's (1940) groundbreaking address on white-collar crime. Employment and crime are not incommensurable. Sutherland's claim that respectable, employed, professionals can—and *do*—engage in criminal activity was a revelation. Today, however, it is known that white-collar crime is more costly and destructive (in terms of losses, injuries, and deaths) than all street crime combined (Coleman, 2005).

The current study coded job titles using the International Standard Classification of Occupations (ISCO-8; International Labour Organization, 2008) as well as an additional category for the unemployed. Almost half of the index group and almost one-quarter of the control group were unemployed: retirees, full-time students, or prisoners. Many of the respondents were professionals. Nearly one-quarter of the control group and more than a third of the index group listed a professional occupation. Managerial roles were also common: approximately 12% of the controls and 6% of index respondents held management or leadership roles. Almost a fifth of the control group held retail or sales positions, although this was far less common in the index group. Several ISCO-8 categories were underrepresented in both groups: agricultural work, machine operator jobs, crafts and trades, military jobs, and elementary employment (e.g., manual labor) were all uncommon. Given the very small sample sizes for these categories, analyses of prevalence and incidence rates by occupation were not conducted.

Income

Along with education and occupation, income is an indicator of SES. In their review, Ellis, Beaver, and Wright (2009) note that research has consistently reported a negative relationship between income and criminal behavior, except in the case of illegal drug use and possession, where no significant relationship between the variables exists. Despite this robust negative relationship between income and crime, a fascinating series of seven observations and experiments by Piff, Stancato, Côté, Mendoza-Denton, and Keltner (2012) suggests that high-SES subjects have higher rates of unethical behavior (i.e., lying, cheating, and stealing) than subjects with average or low SES. High-SES subjects also have higher rates of criminal offending. In two observations, using make, age, and appearance of vehicles as a proxy for income, Piff and his colleagues found that high-income vehicles were significantly less likely to yield to other vehicles and pedestrians, in violation of the California vehicular code.

Although missing data made analysis of prevalence and incidence rates unproductive in the current study, median annual incomes were calculated (converting foreign currencies to US dollars). Index participants reported slightly higher incomes than controls ($30,000 versus $26,000). Within the index group, there was terrific variation. Only one person in the incarcerated sample reported an annual income ($600); university respondents averaged $15,000; reassigned respondents averaged $31,750; and high-IQ society respondents averaged $40,000.

Sexual Orientation

In some jurisdictions, homosexual activity remains a crime (West & Green, 2006). Beyond the criminalization of the homosexual sexual act, however, there also appears to be a relationship between homosexuality and crime. In their systematic review, Ellis and his colleagues (2009) identified five articles reporting a positive association between homosexuality and criminal behavior (principally drug use), but they identified no articles reporting negative or nonsignificant associations.

As indicated in table 12, index and control respondents reported slightly higher rates of homosexuality and bisexuality than the estimated 1.7% of US adults who identify as lesbian or gay and the 1.8% who identify as bisexual (Gates, 2011). Homosexuals and bisexuals comprised a larger portion of the index group than the control group. Analyses of prevalence and incidence by sexual orientation were not conducted.

Marital Status

Marital status is another demographic variable with criminological consequences. Similar to the age-crime curve described above, many researchers have reported a desistance-linked "marriage effect" (i.e., an inverse relationship between offending and crime). The concept of the marriage effect emerges from Sampson and Laub's (1993) scholarship on criminal pathways and turning points across the life course. Marriage can inhibit crime through the forging of social bonds, through social control exercised by one's spouse, through limitation of leisure time outside the family (especially with criminal peers), or through changes in one's self-concept. The practical consequences of marriage on crime can be profound. Using counterfactual analysis, Sampson, Laub, and Wimer (2006) estimate a marriage-based reduction of 35% in the odds of crime. Barnes, Jorgensen, Pacheco, and TenEyck (2015) summarize the extant body of research: "Though there is some conflicting evidence, most studies indicate that marital status is inversely related to crime, especially for individuals who are attached to their spouse. . . . Some [studies] have found support but question the underlying causal processes, while others have reported results that are mixed or appear to stand in contrast to the marriage effect. Nevertheless, research . . . appears to suggest that marriage reduces crime" (p. 406).

TABLE 19 Comparison of demographics in high and low crime score quintiles

	High 20% $n = 246$	Low 20% $n = 244$
Mean IQ (estimated)	127.4	122.9
High-IQ group	41.1%	24.2%
Sex (% male)	61.1%	39.8%
Mean age (calculated)	34.7	40.0
Modal race/ethnicity	White (80.4%)	White (67.9%)
Modal nationality	USA (69.4%)	USA (69.6%)
Modal religion	None (18.7%)	None (24.6%)
Modal educational achievement	Some college	Some college
Modal occupation	Unemployed (19.2%)	Unemployed (13.4%)
Mean income	$29,224.80	$34,919.30
Modal sexual orientation	Heterosexual	Heterosexual
Modal marital status	Single	Married
Mean total offenses	1304.5 (Median: 725.0)	8.1 (Median: 5.0)
Crime score	≥8038.72	≤140.0

NOTE: Crime scores were calculated after right-limiting frequency counts ("ever") to 1,000 per offense and by applying the seriousness coefficients outlined in the technical appendix (appendix A).

Analyses of offense prevalence and incidence by marital status were not conducted in the current study, but table 12 reveals that there were differences between the index and control groups. Although single respondents comprised approximately 42% of both groups, more of the index group than the control group reported living with a partner, while more of the control respondents were married. Far more of the index respondents were separated or divorced, while far more of the controls were widowed.

ANTIPODES

Crime scores provide another means of examining demographic differences. Respondents were divided into quintiles by crime scores, and the demographics of the most criminal 20% were contrasted with those of the least criminal 20% (including the 14% of abstainers, respondents who reported no offenses at all). Table 19 provides a side-by-side comparison.

One might reasonably expect the most criminal respondents to differ dramatically from the least criminal respondents. Indeed, Vaughn, Fu, and their colleagues (2011) found that abstainers—individuals who have never consumed psychoactive substances (alcohol or other drugs) or engaged in delinquent or antisocial behavior—do differ from nonabstainers. Abstainers were significantly more likely to be female, Asian, or African American, and born outside the United States and less likely to be unemployed. In the current study, however, there were few demographic differences between the top and bottom quintiles. Table 19 reveals that the groups were comparable in terms of modal race (white), nationality (USA), religion (none), educational achievement (some college), occupation (unemployed—specifically, student), and sexual orientation (heterosexual). Remarkably, the most criminal respondents had higher—not lower—mean IQ scores than the least criminal respondents, and a greater percentage belonged to the high-IQ society sample. The IQ difference between the most and least criminal respondents was modest (4.5 points), but this result does not accord with research purporting a negative IQ-crime relationship. On the other hand, consistent with existing research, the most criminal respondents tended to be male, single, and younger and to earn less than the least criminal respondents.

MENTAL ILLNESS AND TREATMENT

As described in chapter 1, there is a long-standing association between genius and madness, particularly mood disorders (Jamison, 1993). In order to examine this relationship, the self-report survey asked respondents to indicate whether they had suffered from any form of mental illness (even mild forms) and to indicate whether they had ever received treatment from a psychologist, psychiatrist, or other mental-health professional. While these self-reports are subjective, and might not satisfy the diagnostic criteria set forth in the *Diagnostic and Statistical Manual of Mental Disorders* (*DSM-V*; American Psychiatric Association, 2013) or the International Classification of Diseases (World Health Organization, 2012), comparing self-diagnosed prevalence rates with *DSM-V* prevalence rates can indicate whether there is a potential association between genius and mental disorder in these samples. Table 20 describes the prevalence of self-diagnosed mental illness and mental-health treatment and indicates the most cited disorders.

Mental Illness

Across the study, 282 (23.1%) people reported a mental illness. Lifetime prevalence for any mental illness in the United States is estimated to be approximately 46.4% (Kessler et al., 2005). Of course, as indicated in table 20, index respondents reported a significantly higher rate than controls. The overall index rate was driven by the rates of the incarcerated (50.0%) and high-IQ society (40.0%) samples; rates were lower in the university (31.0%) and reassigned (35.7%) samples. All four index samples, however, reported a rate greater than twice that of the control group. Not all respondents who indicated that they had suffered from mental illness identified their disorder, and some identified more than one. Indeed, a handful identified three different disorders. Overwhelmingly, across both the index and control groups, depression was the most common complaint. Although respondents named 54 discrete complaints (reduced to categories and listed in appendix A) ranging from

TABLE 20 Rates of self-reported mental illness and mental health treatment in index and control groups

	High IQ (*n* = 460)	Control (*n* = 750)
Mental Illness	171 (37.2%)	111 (14.8%)
Depression	119 (57.2%)	65 (61.3%)
Bipolar Disorder	15 (7.2%)	9 (8.5%)
Anxiety	11 (5.3%)	10 (9.4%)
Obsessive-Compulsive Disorder	11 (5.3%)	3 (2.8%)
Other	52 (25.0%)	19 (17.9%)
Mental-Health Treatment	143 (31.1%)	119 (15.9%)
Depression	79 (45.9%)	83 (54.2%)
Bipolar Disorder	9 (5.2%)	8 (5.2%)
Anxiety	13 (7.6%)	18 (11.8%)
Marriage/Family/Relationship Counseling	13 (7.6%)	10 (6.5%)
Other	58 (33.7%)	34 (22.2%)

shyness and insomnia to antisocial personality disorder and dissociative disorder, depression constituted almost 60% of the complaints cited by the index group and more than 60% cited by the control group. Kessler and his colleagues (2005) report a lifetime prevalence rate of 16.6% for major depression. In comparison, only 65 (8.7%) respondents in the control group reported depression, but 119 (25.9%) of the index group did so. On the other hand, only 15 index respondents (3.3%) and 9 controls (1.2%) reported bipolar illness—rates lower than the 3.9% US lifetime prevalence rate for this mood disorder (Kessler et al., 2005). For anxiety-based disorders such as phobias, posttraumatic stress disorder (PTSD), obsessive-compulsive disorder, and the like, the lifetime prevalence rate is 28.8% (Kessler et al., 2005). However, only 27 (10.4%) index respondents and 20 (2.7%) controls reported this disorder.

The relationship between mental illness and crime has been studied at least since Lombroso (1876/2006), but their actual association is complex, as both are manifold phenomena. Until the 1990s, empirical research on the subject was scarce. A 1998 meta-analysis of recidivism in mainstream and mentally disordered populations concluded that the effect of mood disorders and psychoses on general and violent recidivism was statistically insignificant, although effect sizes for antisocial personality disorder were significant (ranging from .11 to .19 for general recidivism and .13 to .23 for violent recidivism; Bonta, Law, & Hanson, 1998). The authors conclude: "The results support the theoretical perspective that the major correlates of crime are the same, regardless of race, gender, class, and the presence or absence of a mental illness" (p. 139). Others (e.g., Hodgins, 1992) report an association between mental illness, mental handicap (retardation), and crime. Douglas, Guy, and Hart's (2009) meta-analysis of psychosis and interpersonal

TABLE 21 Prevalence, incidence, and recency by mental illness

		Yes ($n = 282$)	No ($n = 928$)	χ^2	p
Any offense last year	Once last year	9 (5.7)	34 (7.0)	3.33	.344
	2 to 5 last year	30 (19.0)	121 (24.9)		
	6 to 9 last year	14 (8.9)	46 (9.5)		
	10+ last year	105 (66.5)	285 (58.6)		
	Missing or None	124	442		
Any offense ever	Once ever	2 (0.8)	11 (1.3)	2.28	.5161
	2 to 5 ever	10 (3.9)	45 (5.5)		
	6 to 9 ever	8 (3.1)	34 (4.2)		
	10+ ever	237 (92.2)	728 (89.0)		
	Missing or None	25	110		

NOTE: See table 13 for a description of table elements.

violence concludes that "psychosis was reliably associated with a 49%-68% increased likelihood of violence" (p. 692).

Table 21 presents data about offense prevalence, incidence, and recency by mental illness. All respondents were pooled and divided by reported mental illness. A slightly higher proportion of those reporting a mental illness than those reporting no mental illness (56.0% versus 52.4%) also reported committing one or more offenses in the previous year. Incidence rates were higher among those reporting mental illness, although the differences were not significant. A similar pattern appears for lifetime prevalence and incidence: more of those reporting a mental illness than those reporting no mental illness (91.1% versus. 88.1%) also reported committing an offense in the past; and those reporting mental illness reported a greater number of offenses, although these differences were not significant.

Mental-Health Treatment

In all, 262 respondents indicated that they had received treatment from a psychologist, psychiatrist, or other mental-health professional. Prevalence rates for mental-health treatment were much higher in the index group—nearly twice as high—than in the control group. In both groups, most who received treatment received it for depression (consistent with the high prevalence of reported symptoms), although treatment for bipolar disorder, anxiety, or marital/family/relationship counseling was also common. While there was an association between reporting a mental illness and receiving treatment, not all of those who reported a mental illness received treatment, and not all of those who received treatment indicated that they had suffered from a mental illness. In the index group, two-thirds of those who reported a disorder received treatment (usually, although not always, for the disorder described), while one-third went without treatment. On the other hand, while most (90.0%) of those who indicated they did not suffer from a mental disorder also reported that they had received no treatment, 10.0% of those without mental illness had received treatment of some kind (often for depression, head injuries, drug addiction, PTSD, or marital/family/relationship counseling). The pattern was similar in the control group. Just under half (49.5%) of those reporting a disorder received treatment, while slightly more than half did not. Of those indicating no disorder, 90.0% did not receive treatment, while 10.0% reported receiving treatment (again, for depression, PTSD, or relationship counseling).

PERSONALITY MEASURES

Mainstream criminology has paid relatively little attention to the role of personality traits in crime, but contributions from biosocial criminology indicate that individual differences do influence behavior, including criminal behavior. Numerous well-known instruments have been developed to assess human personality, including the Minnesota Multiphasic Personality Inventory, the Myers-Briggs, the big-five test (OCEAN), and the revised Eysenck Personality Questionnaire (Eysenck & Eysenck, 1996). Because Eysenck published widely on intelligence and intelligence testing (1962, 1966), genius (1995), delinquency and criminality (1977; Eysenck & Gudjonsson, 1989), *and* personality (1967, 1970), the EPQ-R was an obvious choice for the current study's investigation of personality.

The EPQ-R is the successor to the Maudsley Personality Inventory (Eysenck, 1959) and the Eysenck Personality Inventory (EPI; Eysenck & Eysenck, 1964), which included a lie (L) scale to measure dissimulation. The EPQ differed from the EPI by adding a psychoticism (P) scale to the existing measures of neuroticism (N) and extraversion (E), thereby creating a personality inventory that assessed three independent axes of personality. As noted in chapter 2, Eysenck believed that these dimensions of temperament (P, N, and E)—along with intelligence—constitute the four major personality factors and can be used to better understand criminal behavior (Eysenck & Gudjonsson, 1989).

Those scoring highly on the extraversion scale are typically sociable, lively, active, assertive, sensation seeking, carefree, dominant, surgent, and venturesome (Eysenck & Gudjonsson, 1989). Eysenck (1977) suggests that extraverted individuals possess inhibited levels of arousal in the cortex, characterized as a "low idling speed" (p. 87), and that low levels of arousal leave extraverts hungry for external stimuli to maintain an optimal level of arousal, referred to as hedonic tone.

Individuals who score highly on the neuroticism scale are typically anxious, depressed, guilty, suffering from low self-esteem, tense, irrational, shy, moody, and emotional (Eysenck & Gudjonsson, 1989). Eysenck and Eysenck (1996) indicate that the term *emotionality* is functionally synonymous to *neuroticism*, and suggest, "if the high-N individual has to be described in one word, one might say that he is a worrier" (p. 5). Neuroticism has been associated with increased lability in the sympathetic branch of the autonomic nervous system, the portion of the brain responsible for "fight-or-flight" responses (Eysenck, 1977); because of lower activation thresholds in the limbic structures, neurotics exhibit greater sympathetic nervous system response than low-N individuals.

Individuals who score highly on the psychoticism scale are typically aggressive, cold, egocentric, impersonal, impulsive, antisocial, unempathic, and tough-minded (Eysenck & Gudjonsson, 1989). The P-axis actually more resembles the constellation of traits associated with psychopathy (Cleckley, 1982; DeLisi, 2009; Hare, 1980) than the impaired reality testing associated with the clinical psychoses of the *DSM-V*. Because *psychoticism* connotes associations that may not be appropriate for all high-P scorers, Eysenck and Eysenck (1996) indicate that *tough-mindedness* is an acceptable substitute in describing the P dimension of personality. It has been suggested that psychoticism may be linked to androgen levels (Blackburn, 1993) or a weakening of central nervous system homeostasis (Claridge, Robinson, & Birchall, 1985), but unequivocal evidence for the physiology of P has not been discovered. Indeed, the entire dimension of psychoticism remains in ambiguous theoretical territory. Howarth (1986) notes that it is unclear what elements of personality the heterogeneous P scale is tapping. Blackburn (1993) observes that by disaggregating traits of sociability and impulsivity—parts of extraversion in Eysenck's model—it is possible to describe the personalities of both primary and secondary psychopaths with no reliance on a P scale.

The EPQ-R's addiction subscale contains 32 items drawn from P, E, N, and L questions and has been used in studies of anorexics and bulimics, drug addicts, and alcoholics (Eysenck & Eysenck, 1996). Criminologists investigating illegal drug use could make good use of the addiction subscale. The EPQ-R's 34-item criminality scale includes 21 items from the addiction scale and was constructed by selecting the most diagnostic items from the P, E, and N scales. Because several items are overtly delinquent or antisocial (e.g., "Would you take drugs that may have strange or dangerous effects?" and "Do you enjoy practical jokes that can sometimes really hurt people?"), one would expect strong correlations between offending and criminality scores. Controls scored a mean of 9.01 and prisoners averaged 15.57, a significantly higher score (Eysenck & Eysenck, 1996).

Despite lingering theoretical disputes about the factors of personality and their neurological mechanisms, Eysenck's (1977) model of personality leads to a clear prediction about the relationship between personality and criminal offending: "In general terms, we would expect persons with strong antisocial inclinations to have high P, high E and high N scores; a similar expectation would be reasonable with respect to criminals" (p. 58). Overall, the evidence linking P to offending is strong (although problems remain in defining what P means), the evidence for a link between N and offending is good (although not unanimous), and the link between E and offending is equivocal.

In terms of psychoticism, "the broad position is that there is unanimous support for the contention that offenders will score highly on P" (Hollin, 1989, p. 56). Yet while most studies do report high P scores in delinquent and criminal populations, one such study (Farrington, Biron, & LeBlanc, 1982) cautions that including items in the P scale related to criminal attitudes (e.g., "Should people always respect the law?") can *create* the association between P and delinquency. The authors warn, "[I]t is only to be expected that criminals should have higher P scores. However, this does not mean that criminals are psychotic in any generally accepted sense of the word, or that we have learned anything about the personalities of criminals" (pp. 155–156).

The evidence linking neuroticism to crime is less robust than that linking psychoticism and crime, but still strong (Hollin, 1989). In their 1982 study, Farrington and his colleagues drew 16 comparisons between identified offenders and nonoffenders. In 9 of the 16 comparisons, offenders scored higher on P and N scales than nonoffenders, although there was no consistent association for E.

Evidence linking extraversion to criminal behavior is mixed. Perez and Torrubia (1985) used a sensation-seeking scale (containing both E and P items) and found a strong relationship between sensation-seeking (related to E) and antisocial behavior. Rushton and Chrisjohn (1981) found that self-reported delinquency correlates positively both with P and E, although there is no association between N and delinquency. Eysenck (1977) reported on two large-scale studies that compared prisoners and controls: one contrasted 1,301 prisoners and 1,392 controls and the other compared 569 prisoners to 595 controls. Both studies indicated that prisoners score significantly higher (p < .001) on scales of psychoticism, extraversion, and neuroticism. But in another study, Lane (1987) reported very different results between 60 delinquent students and 60 students without convictions (matched by age, sex, and social class). He found P to be predictive for criminality and positively correlated (.34) to the number of convictions, but he found that N was actually negatively correlated (−.35) to violence used in offending, and he found little difference in E between the groups.

Eysenck (1977) argues that neuroticism is a more relevant index of antisocial behavior in adults, while extraversion appears to be more relevant for juveniles. High N scores and offending are most strongly associated in measures of official delinquency, while high E scores and offending are most associated in measures of self-reported delinquency (Blackburn, 1993). This led Farrington and his colleagues (1982) to suggest that the relationship between high E scores and self-reported delinquency is a function of extraverted youths' tendency to boast about offending behavior (real or imagined). Extraversion as a trait is problematic because it includes dimensions of both sociability and impulsiveness, tapping both prosocial and potentially antisocial behaviors.

To differentiate these aspects of extraversion and to measure impulsiveness, venturesomeness, and empathy, the current study employed the 54-item Impulsiveness Questionnaire (IVE; Eysenck & Eysenck, 1996). Impulsiveness and venturesomeness correlate with each other (.24 in males, .11 in females), but they describe different traits. Impulsiveness measures the abnormal or pathological side of risk taking; it correlates with P (.46 for males, .45 for females) more than it correlates with E (.39 for males, .22 for females). The linkages between impulsivity and crime are strong (Block, 1995). Eysenck and McGurk (1980) report higher impulsivity scores in a sample of 641 delinquents than among controls; "Impulsiveness in and of itself predisposes a person toward offending" (Wilson & Herrnstein, 1985, p. 205; cf. Jackson & Beaver, 2013); "The impulsive or short-sighted person fails to consider the negative or painful consequences of his acts" (Gottfredson & Hirschi, 1990, p. 95). Shoda, Mischel, and Peake's (1990) study of impulse control in 4-year-olds suggests a link between impulsivity and later academic achievement. At age 18, the 4-year-olds who had most delayed gratification scored an average verbal SAT score of 610 and an average quantitative SAT score of 652, while those who had least delayed gratification scored 524 and 528, respectively. On the other hand, venturesomeness (i.e., healthy risk taking) correlates more with E (.37 for males, .22 for females) than with P (.22 for males, .11 for females). Eysenck and Eysenck (1996) explain, "Put another way, one could see impulsive individuals (of the P variety) as showing a complete lack of looking ahead at the consequences of their actions, while venturesome people (of the E type) exhibit more risk-taking behaviour, knowing fully that there is a risk involved" (p. 28).

The initial index group in the current study was provided with the EPQ-R and IVE instruments, and 358 participants returned these questionnaires. Because of copyright restrictions, EPQ-R and IVE questionnaires were not distributed to the control group, making index-versus-control comparisons impossible. Accordingly, table 22 compares respondents' psychoticism, extraversion, neuroticism, and lie scale scores to published norms (matched for age and sex).

Males reported aggregate psychoticism scores below age-matched norms. This, however, was an artifact of the samples: 11 male respondents who did not identify their age and 23 male respondents older than 70 were included in the total score. Because psychoticism diminishes with age, the inclusion of 70+ respondents depressed the aggregate score. If these 34 cases are omitted from the calculation, the total male P score increases to 7.21, a value greater than that of the norm (although not significantly so). Females produced aggregate psychoticism scores above norms. For females in the age 41–50 group, scores were significantly higher than norms. Again, the inclusion of 5 female respondents who were older than 70 and 7 respondents who did not identify their age influenced total P scores. Eliminating these 12 cases reduces the total P score to 6.33, but it nevertheless is

TABLE 22 EPQ–R scores for initial index respondents compared to norms (matched for sex and age)

Age	Psychoticism			Extraversion			Neuroticism			Lie Scale		
Males	Index	Norms		Index	Norms		Index	Norms		Index	Norms	
16–20	$n=11$ $x=7.81$ ± 4.00	$n=120$ $x=9.57$ ± 5.26	$t=0.2822$	$n=11$ $x=11.36$ ± 5.92	$n=108$ $x=15.97$ ± 5.26	$t=0.0071^{**}$	$n=11$ $x=8.91$ ± 5.17	$n=108$ $x=11.12$ ± 5.68	$t=0.2180$	$n=11$ $x=8.27$ ± 3.00	$n=108$ $x=5.37$ ± 4.18	$t=0.0270^{*}$
21–30	$n=63$ $x=8.76$ ± 3.57	$n=148$ $x=8.65\pm 4.56$	$t=0.8648$	$n=63$ $x=11.75$ ± 6.06	$n=64$ $x=14.50$ ± 5.64	$t=0.0091^{**}$	$n=63$ $x=10.33$ ± 5.58	$n=64$ $x=11.08$ ± 5.37	$t=0.4417$	$n=63$ $x=6.40$ ± 3.72	$n=64$ $x=5.53$ ± 3.39	$t=0.1707$
31–40	$n=31$ $x=7.39$ ± 3.50	$n=117$ $x=6.69$ ± 3.58	$t=0.3325$	$n=31$ $x=13.03$ ± 5.68	$n=53$ $x=11.92$ ± 5.67	$t=0.3894$	$n=31$ $x=9.68$ ± 5.44	$n=53$ $x=11.92$ ± 5.70	$t=0.0809$	$n=31$ $x=7.39$ ± 3.38	$n=53$ $x=6.66$ ± 3.59	$t=0.3610$
41–50	$n=48$ $x=6.27$ ± 3.76	$n=107$ $x=7.00$ ± 4.65	$t=0.3406$	$n=48$ $x=11.63$ ± 5.53	$n=55$ $x=11.91$ ± 5.09	$t=0.7896$	$n=48$ $x=9.23$ ± 5.90	$n=55$ $x=11.22$ ± 5.95	$t=0.0922$	$n=48$ $x=9.00$ ± 3.98	$n=55$ $x=7.04$ ± 3.87	$t=0.0129^{*}$
51–60	$n=36$ $x=6.89$ ± 3.60	$n=110$ $x=5.28$ ± 3.59	$t=0.0210^{*}$	$n=36$ $x=12.69$ ± 4.56	$n=69$ $x=8.94$ ± 5.75	$t=0.0010^{**}$	$n=36$ $x=8.75$ ± 6.29	$n=69$ $x=9.43$ ± 6.27	$t=0.5994$	$n=36$ $x=7.81$ ± 3.43	$n=69$ $x=9.14$ ± 4.29	$t=0.1105$
61–70	$n=38$ $x=5.84$ ± 3.19	$n=91$ $x=4.87$ ± 3.55	$t=0.1478$	$n=38$ $x=11.74$ ± 5.12	$n=59$ $x=8.68$ ± 5.71	$t=0.0087^{**}$	$n=38$ $x=5.11$ ± 4.56	$n=59$ $x=8.32$ ± 5.07	$t=0.0021^{**}$	$n=38$ $x=9.53$ ± 3.83	$n=59$ $x=10.05$ ± 3.65	$t=0.5033$
Total	$n=261$ $x=7.01$ ± 3.65	$n=693$ $x=7.19$ ± 4.60	$t=0.5700$	$n=261$ $x=11.78$ ± 5.58	$n=408$ $x=12.51$ ± 6.00	$t=0.1152$	$n=261$ $x=8.95$ ± 5.58	$n=408$ $x=10.54$ ± 5.81	$t=0.0005^{**}$	$n=261$ $x=8.05$ ± 3.87	$n=408$ $x=7.10$ ± 4.28	$t=0.0038^{**}$

(continued)

TABLE 22 *(continued)*

Age	Psychoticism			Extraversion			Neuroticism			Lie Scale		
Females												
16–20	n = 13 x = 6.15 ± 3.31	t = 0.4353	n = 203 x = 7.06 ± 4.11	n = 13 x = 14.31 ± 5.01	t = 0.4213	n = 161 x = 15.47 ± 4.99	n = 13 x = 17.23 ± 4.73	t = 0.0231*	n = 161 x = 14.03 ± 4.85	n = 13 x = 5.08 ± 2.22	t = 0.6879	n = 161 x = 5.45 ± 3.25
21–30	n = 43 x = 6.72 ± 3.59	t = 0.4099	n = 256 x = 6.20 ± 3.86	n = 43 x = 14.63 ± 5.17	t = 0.5768	n = 159 x = 14.17 ± 4.68	n = 43 x = 12.09 ± 5.41	t = 0.6054	n = 159 x = 12.53 ± 4.78	n = 43 x = 6.74 ± 3.93	t = 0.5356	n = 159 x = 6.33 ± 3.82
31–40	n = 5 x = 4.20 ± 3.42	t = 0.3249	n = 135 x = 5.87 ± 3.72	n = 5 x = 14.60 ± 5.41	t = 0.6599	n = 38 x = 13.55 ± 4.93	n = 5 x = 8.20 ± 3.83	t = 0.1353	n = 38 x = 11.71 ± 4.94	n = 5 x = 8.40 ± 3.65	t = 0.3697	n = 38 x = 6.79 ± 3.74
41–50	n = 11 x = 7.00 ± 3.90	t = 0.0178*	n = 109 x = 4.62 ± 3.05	n = 11 x = 10.45 ± 5.59	t = 0.2620	n = 50 x = 12.36 ± 4.95	n = 11 x = 11.00 ± 6.48	t = 0.9762	n = 50 x = 10.94 ± 5.92	n = 11 x = 6.18 ± 2.93	t = 0.1445	n = 50 x = 8.02 ± 3.88
51–60	n = 8 x = 4.88 ± 2.85	t = 0.4798	n = 102 x = 4.05 ± 3.21	n = 8 x = 13.88 ± 6.36	t = 0.9042	n = 45 x = 13.62 ± 5.47	n = 8 x = 12.63 ± 5.63	t = 0.5268	n = 45 x = 11.31 ± 5.36	n = 8 x = 6.88 ± 3.80	t = 0.2060	n = 45 x = 8.82 ± 3.97
61–70	n = 5 x = 6.40 ± 4.04	t = 0.1522	n = 73 x = 4.19 ± 3.26	n = 5 x = 15.40 ± 2.61	t = 0.1691	n = 41 x = 12.15 ± 5.08	n = 5 x = 13.00 ± 7.48	t = 0.2709	n = 41 x = 9.98 ± 5.51	n = 5 x = 9.20 ± 4.55	t = 0.2007	n = 41 x = 11.20 ± 3.09
Total	n = 97 x = 6.48 ± 3.67	t = 0.0677	n = 878 x = 5.73 ± 3.85	n = 97 x = 13.65 ± 5.22	t = 0.3861	n = 494 x = 14.14 ± 5.06	n = 97 x = 12.33 ± 5.98	t = 0.8138	n = 494 x = 12.47 ± 5.22	n = 97 x = 6.89 ± 3.60	t = 0.9816	n = 494 x = 6.88 ± 3.97

NOTE: Age groups do not sum to total sample sizes because some respondents did not identify age and some were older than 70. The *n* indicates the number of people in each sample, *x* indicates the average (mean) score and its standard deviation, and *t* indicates the amount of difference between the index scores and the norms. Norms are drawn from Eysenck & Eysenck, 1996.

* <.05 significance

** <.01 significance

higher than female norms. The respondents' high P scores are unexpected, given an inverse relationship between IQ and psychoticism:

> [P]sychoticism shows a negative correlation with intelligence . . . and psychoticism is one of the major determinants of antisocial behavior. . . . [I]t is difficult to know which is the more important variable, intelligence or psychoticism. . . . [C]orrelations between criminality and psychoticism tend to be higher . . . than those between criminality and intelligence (about .20); it is therefore arguable that psychoticism is the more important variable, although the correlation with intelligence is not high enough, when partialled out, to eliminate intelligence completely from the equation. (Eysenck & Gudjonsson, 1989, pp. 49–50)

High psychoticism scores are to be expected in innovators and iconoclasts, however. "The high-P scorer . . . is typically non-conformist and does not believe in society's rules and regulations. This attitude is also characteristic of the creative person and the genius" (Eysenck, 1995, p. 132).

Males in the current study produced extraversion scores below norms, especially among respondents 30 and younger, where scores were significantly lower. Males between 51 and 70, however, had significantly higher E scores than norms. If the 34 age-undefined cases are omitted, the total E score increases to 11.82 but remains below the norm. Females produced overall E scores below norms. They were higher than norms in four of the six age groups, but none of these differences was significant. Omitting the 12 age-undefined cases increases the total E score to 14.01, but this is still below the female norm.

Male neuroticism scores were below norms across all age groups, and they were significantly below norms within the age 61–70 group and in the aggregate. Eliminating the 34 age-undefined cases increases the total male N score to 9.15, but this is still significantly lower than the male norm. Aggregate female neuroticism scores were below norms as well, although they exceeded norms across four of the six age groups and were significantly higher in one of these. Omitting the 12 age-undefined cases increases the total N score to 12.61, a value greater than that of the norm (although still not statistically significant: $t = 0.7471$).

Lie scores (measuring conformity and dissembling on the questionnaire) were above norms for both males and females. For males, L scores were above norms in four of six age groups and were significantly greater than norms in the age 16–20, age 41–50, and aggregated groups. Omitting the 34 age-undefined cases reduces the total male L score to 7.92, although this value is still significantly greater than that of the norm ($t = 0.0166$). The possibility that respondents were dissimulating on the EPQ-R—faking being good—cannot be discounted. Aggregated female lie scores were above norms. In four of six age groups, they were lower than norms. Omitting the 12 age-undefined cases reduces the total female L score to 6.67, a value below that of the norm; this difference is not significant ($t = 0.6487$).

Addiction and criminality scores were calculated for respondents, but table 22 omits these because the EPQ-R does not provide age-graded norms for these scales. When respondent scores were compared to sex-based norms in the EPQ-R, males reported a mean addiction score of 10.81. This value is lower than the mean 11.60 of male controls and significantly lower ($t = 0.0001$) than the mean 19.83 reported by addicts. Females reported an addiction score of 12.63, slightly higher than the 12.61 reported by female controls but significantly lower ($t = 0.0001$) than the 20.25 reported by addicts. On the criminality scale, males reported a mean score of 9.47, a value greater than the 9.01 of controls but significantly lower ($t = 0.0001$) than the 15.57 reported by prisoners. Females reported a mean criminality score of 11.91. Criminality scores for female controls are not reported in the EPQ-R, but given the common content of the addiction and criminality scales, a score of 11.91—though higher than the male score—likely approximates a female norm.

In all, 260 males and 91 females returned Impulsivity Questionnaires. As indicated in table 23, both male and female respondents reported total impulsiveness (I) scores that were significantly lower than age- and sex-matched norms. This tendency was especially marked in young age groups, although some older respondents (60+ for males, 40+ for females) reported mean I scores that were greater than that of matched norms. Total venturesomeness scores were higher than norms for both males and females. Venturesomeness (V) was significantly higher for females. Young respondents had V scores close to—or even lower than—norms, but beyond 30 years old, males and females consistently reported scores that were higher than relevant norms. Males and females both reported total empathy (E) scores that were significantly below norms. Young (age 16–19) males reported E scores that were significantly higher than norms, but after age 50, male scores were consistently below norms; females reported E scores below norms in every age group (often significantly below norms).

In summary, males scored lower than published norms on measures of psychoticism, extraversion, neuroticism, impulsiveness, empathy, and addiction; they scored higher than norms on the lie scale and on measures of venturesomeness and criminality. Females scored lower than norms on measures of extraversion, neuroticism, impulsiveness, and empathy; they scored higher than norms on the lie scale and on measures of psychoticism, venturesomeness, and addiction. These results were not a function of including an incarcerated sample; even when those cases are omitted, the respondents' general personality profiles remain the same. Their high psychoticism and low empathy scores are intriguing, and the higher than average addiction (in females) and criminality (in males) subscale scores suggest that personality variables might play a meaningful role in explaining criminal behavior.

TABLE 23 IVE scores for index respondents compared to norms (matched for sex and age)

Age / Males	Impulsiveness Index	Impulsiveness Norms	Impulsiveness t	Venturesomeness Index	Venturesomeness Norms	Venturesomeness t	Empathy Index	Empathy Norms	Empathy t
16–19	n = 5, x = 7.40 ± 3.44	n = 73, x = 9.84 ± 4.13	t = 0.2015	n = 5, x = 7.40 ± 4.22	n = 73, x = 11.51 ± 3.34	t = 0.0106*	n = 5, x = 15.6 ± 1.14	n = 73, x = 12.47 ± 3.28	t = 0.0378*
20–29	n = 66, x = 5.58 ± 4.30	n = 97, x = 7.93 ± 4.12	t = 0.0006**	n = 66, x = 8.02 ± 3.59	n = 97, x = 10.31 ± 3.73	t = 0.0001**	n = 66, x = 10.92 ± 4.29	n = 97, x = 11.76 ± 3.17	t = 0.1527
30–39	n = 34, x = 6.41 ± 3.69	n = 69, x = 7.06 ± 4.20	t = 0.4444	n = 34, x = 9.29 ± 3.12	n = 69, x = 7.25 ± 3.70	t = 0.0068**	n = 34, x = 12.29 ± 3.40	n = 69, x = 11.87 ± 3.36	t = 0.5537
40–49	n = 41, x = 5.90 ± 4.07	n = 87, x = 6.08 ± 4.15	t = 0.8182	n = 41, x = 7.71 ± 3.80	n = 87, x = 7.08 ± 3.58	t = 0.3641	n = 41, x = 11.02 ± 2.63	n = 87, x = 11.82 ± 3.00	t = 0.1461
50–59	n = 39, x = 4.82 ± 3.56	n = 88, x = 5.38 ± 4.14	t = 0.4651	n = 39, x = 7.82 ± 3.06	n = 88, x = 6.16 ± 3.40	t = 0.0100**	n = 39, x = 10.21 ± 3.85	n = 88, x = 12.05 ± 3.14	t = 0.0053**
60–69	n = 33, x = 5.70 ± 4.50	n = 90, x = 5.14 ± 4.14	t = 0.5174	n = 33, x = 7.88 ± 3.19	n = 90, x = 5.66 ± 3.79	t = 0.0033**	n = 33, x = 10.42 ± 3.15	n = 90, x = 12.33 ± 3.78	t = 0.0108*
70–79	n = 26, x = 5.46 ± 3.82	n = 45, x = 3.91 ± 3.20	t = 0.0715	n = 26, x = 7.69 ± 4.09	n = 45, x = 4.47 ± 3.66	t = 0.0011**	n = 26, x = 10.77 ± 3.37	n = 45, x = 11.69 ± 3.43	t = 0.2770
80–89	n = 8, x = 5.63 ± 4.24	n = 7, x = 2.86 ± 3.60	t = 0.1993	n = 8, x = 7.25 ± 3.11	n = 7, x = 5.57 ± 3.42	t = 0.3371	n = 8, x = 10.13 ± 3.76	n = 7, x = 11.00 ± 3.12	t = 0.6370
No age recorded	n = 8	n = 3	—	n = 8	n = 3	—	n = 8	n = 3	—
Total	n = 260, x = 5.62 ± 4.00	n = 559, x = 6.55 ± 4.43	t = 0.0041**	n = 260, x = 7.88 ± 3.50	n = 559, x = 7.64 ± 4.25	t = 0.4275	n = 260, x = 11.22 ± 3.62	n = 559, x = 12.01 ± 3.31	t = 0.0021**

(continued)

TABLE 23 (continued)

Age	Impulsiveness			Venturesomeness			Empathy		
Females									
16–19	$n = 5$ $x = 7.00 \pm 6.44$	$n = 113$ $x = 9.73 \pm 4.64$	$t = 0.2076$	$n = 5$ $x = 9.60 \pm 2.88$	$n = 113$ $x = 9.55 \pm 3.38$	$t = 0.9741$	$n = 5$ $x = 10.80 \pm 2.17$	$n = 113$ $x = 14.53 \pm 2.87$	$t = 0.0050^{\star\star}$
20–29	$n = 46$ $x = 6.02 \pm 3.82$	$n = 191$ $x = 9.02 \pm 4.19$	$t = 0.0001^{\star\star}$	$n = 46$ $x = 7.87 \pm 3.66$	$n = 191$ $x = 8.69 \pm 3.91$	$t = 0.1975$	$n = 46$ $x = 11.22 \pm 3.89$	$n = 191$ $x = 14.39 \pm 2.87$	$t = 0.0001^{\star\star}$
30–39	$n = 7$ $x = 3.86 \pm 2.41$	$n = 101$ $x = 7.16 \pm 4.24$	$t = 0.0448^{\star}$	$n = 7$ $x = 8.71 \pm 2.43$	$n = 101$ $x = 6.24 \pm 3.58$	$t = 0.0758$	$n = 7$ $x = 12.14 \pm 3.80$	$n = 101$ $x = 14.17 \pm 3.19$	$t = 0.1105$
40–49	$n = 8$ $x = 6.00 \pm 4.75$	$n = 126$ $x = 5.57 \pm 4.02$	$t = 0.7720$	$n = 8$ $x = 8.13 \pm 2.95$	$n = 126$ $x = 5.19 \pm 3.34$	$t = 0.0165^{\star}$	$n = 8$ $x = 10.63 \pm 4.44$	$n = 126$ $x = 14.14 \pm 2.98$	$t = 0.0021^{\star\star}$
50–59	$n = 7$ $x = 4.29 \pm 2.43$	$n = 96$ $x = 7.08 \pm 4.21$	$t = 0.0872$	$n = 7$ $x = 7.86 \pm 4.45$	$n = 96$ $x = 4.74 \pm 2.81$	$t = 0.0078^{\star\star}$	$n = 7$ $x = 10.71 \pm 3.35$	$n = 96$ $x = 14.38 \pm 2.91$	$t = 0.0019^{\star}$
60–69	$n = 6$ $x = 6.33 \pm 4.63$	$n = 72$ $x = 5.78 \pm 3.20$	$t = 0.6971$	$n = 6$ $x = 6.00 \pm 3.22$	$n = 72$ $x = 3.75 \pm 2.52$	$t = 0.0429^{\star}$	$n = 6$ $x = 9.33 \pm 2.42$	$n = 72$ $x = 14.31 \pm 2.90$	$t = 0.0001^{\star\star}$
70–79	$n = 5$ $x = 5.46 \pm 3.82$	$n = 48$ $x = 5.38 \pm 3.94$	$t = 0.9656$	$n = 5$ $x = 9.40 \pm 3.78$	$n = 48$ $x = 3.31 \pm 2.66$	$t = 0.0001^{\star\star}$	$n = 5$ $x = 10.60 \pm 2.79$	$n = 48$ $x = 14.27 \pm 2.39$	$t = 0.0022^{\star\star}$
80–89	$n = 0$	$n = 9$ $x = 6.78 \pm 3.12$	—	$n = 0$	$n = 9$ $x = 3.67 \pm 2.49$	—	$n = 0$	$n = 9$ $x = 13.11 \pm 3.07$	—
No age recorded	$n = 6$	$n = 5$	—	$n = 6$	$n = 5$	—	$n = 6$	$n = 5$	—
Total	$n = 91$ $x = 5.49 \pm 3.84$	$n = 761$ $x = 7.48 \pm 4.42$	$t = 0.0001^{\star\star}$	$n = 91$ $x = 7.86 \pm 3.56$	$n = 761$ $x = 6.51 \pm 4.00$	$t = 0.0022^{\star\star}$	$n = 91$ $x = 10.93 \pm 3.70$	$n = 761$ $x = 14.32 \pm 2.92$	$t = 0.0001^{\star\star}$

NOTE: See table 22 for a description of table elements. One female respondent was older than 89 and is included in the total. Norms are drawn from Eysenck & Eysenck, 1996, p. 30.

* <.05 significance

** <.01 significance

INFLUENCES

In addition to collecting demographic details, data about mental illness and treatment, and EPQ-R and IVE scores, the study invited respondents to identify the books, films, and famous figures that had influenced their lives. These were not necessarily favorite books, films, and figures; rather, they were influential ones—ones that shaped character and potentially operated as turning points in respondents' lives. "How many a man has dated a new era in his life from the reading of a book" (Thoreau, 1854/2000, p. 170). Books, including works of fiction, have an enormous capacity to teach (Campbell, 1988). Films, too, have the potential to "shape dreams, aspirations, and attitudes in a way that does change who we are. Certainly, the movies change how we see ourselves" (Hofler, 2009, p. x). Famous figures—artists and scientists, scoundrels and saints—shape the course of human history (Hart, 1992). Our role models inspire us to be better people, encourage us to live fuller lives. "We identify with these characters, even if the story dates back thousands of years. We shed real tears over their setbacks and suffering. We try to emulate the greatness of the heroes and learn from the mistakes of the tragic figures" (Lazar, Karlan, & Salter, 2006, p. 1).

Respondents in the current study were asked to list up to three influential books, films, and famous figures (from history or popular culture) and to indicate briefly how each one exerted an influence in their lives. Many respondents left the question blank or affirmatively indicated "none." Many, however, provided thoughtful—even poignant—answers. Table 24 identifies the 10 most frequently listed books, films, and famous figures from the index and control groups.

The index and control lists have a great deal in common. For books, for example, both groups identified the Bible as the most influential work, and *To Kill a Mockingbird, The Catcher in the Rye,* and the Lord of the Rings series appeared in both lists. There were noteworthy differences, however. The index group listed two works by Ayn Rand (*Atlas Shrugged* and *The Fountainhead*), but these did not even qualify as honorable mentions in the control group list. The index group identified dystopian literature (e.g., *1984, Lord of the Flies,* and *Brave New World*) while the control group identified inspirational and religious titles (e.g., *Chicken Soup for the Soul, The Purpose Driven Life, The Da Vinci Code,* and the Left Behind series). These differences are consistent with differences in religious beliefs described previously. The control group also identified two titles (*Roots* and *The Autobiography of Malcolm X*) that may have particular salience for African American readers. While the index group was more than 90% white, the control group was more than 27% black.

Similar patterns emerge for influential films. While the top two films on the index list (the Star Wars films and *Schindler's List*) also appear on the control group list, the other eight listed titles do not. *The Passion of the Christ*—the top film on the control list—did not appear in the index list at all (because the index surveys

TABLE 24 Most influential books, films, and famous figures

	Index (*n* = 465)	Controls (*n* = 756)
Books	1. Bible (77)	1. Bible (171)
	2. *Atlas Shrugged* (11)	2. *To Kill a Mockingbird* (16)
	3. *To Kill a Mockingbird* (10)	3. Lord of the Rings series (10)
	4. *1984* (9)	4. *The Catcher in the Rye* (7)
	5. *Brave New World* (8)	5. *Roots* (7)
	6. *Lord of the Flies* (8)	6. *The Da Vinci Code* (6)
	7. *The Catcher in the Rye* (7)	7. *Chicken Soup for the Soul* (6)
	8. Lord of the Rings series (7)	8. *The Purpose Driven Life* (6)
	9. *The Fountainhead* (7)	9. *The Autobiography of Malcolm X* (6)
	10. *Nicomachean Ethics* (6)	10. Left Behind series (5)
Films	1. Star Wars films (13)	1. *The Passion of the Christ* (41)
	2. *Schindler's List* (12)	2. *The Color Purple* (21)
	3. *Gone with the Wind* (11)	3. *Roots* (12)
	4. *2001: A Space Odyssey* (10)	4. *Schindler's List* (10)
	5. *The Wizard of Oz* (10)	5. *Scarface* (9)
	6. *It's a Wonderful Life* (8)	6. *Malcolm X* (9)
	7. *Apocalypse Now* (8)	7. Star Wars films (8)
	8. *Gandhi* (7)	8. *Braveheart* (7)
	9. *Fantasia* (6)	9. *Forrest Gump* (7)
	10. *Star Trek* (6)	10. *The Shawshank Redemption* (7)
Famous Figures	1. Jesus Christ (36)	1. Jesus Christ (40)
	2. Albert Einstein (19)	2. Oprah Winfrey (21)
	3. Mahatma Gandhi (12)	3. Martin Luther King Jr. (20)
	4. John F. Kennedy (11)	4. Malcolm X (11)
	5. Martin Luther King Jr. (10)	5. John F. Kennedy (10)
	6. Richard Feynman (9)	6. Princess Diana (8)
	7. Abraham Lincoln (9)	7. George Bush (7)
	8. Winston Churchill (9)	8. Bill Clinton (7)
	9. Mother Theresa (7)	9. Mother Theresa (7)
	10. Thomas Jefferson (6)	10. Abraham Lincoln (6)

NOTE: Index data drawn in part from Oleson, 1999.

were collected in 1997, years before the 2004 control group surveys were distributed and before *The Passion of the Christ* was released). Controls also identified films related to black identity that the index group did not: *The Color Purple, Roots,* and *Malcolm X.*

Both groups emphasized that personal relationships were more influential than famous figures. Scores of respondents wrote in the following: parents, father, mother, siblings, brother, sister, grandparents, grandfather, grandmother, children, son, daughter, husband, wife, friend, foe, minister, teacher, military officer, scoutmaster, and community. More than a dozen named God. Table 25 does not include these answers, but they are not unimportant. They were clearly influential in the lives of the respondents. In terms of famous figures from history and popular culture, the index and control groups both identified Jesus Christ—convicted as a criminal, as noted in the introduction—as their most influential figure. Both groups also identified John F. Kennedy, Martin Luther King Jr. (another criminal), Abraham Lincoln, and Mother Theresa. But there were differences. The index list included two physicists: Albert Einstein and Richard Feynman. Einstein was an honorable mention on the control group list—several respondents identified him—but Feynman did not appear at all. On the other hand, Oprah Winfrey and Princess Diana—numbers two and six on the control group list—did not appear in the index list. Again, the timing of the survey distribution influenced these answers. When index respondents completed the questionnaire in 1997, Bill Clinton had not yet been impeached and George Bush was still a relatively unknown Texas governor.

SUMMARY

In all, 1,221 respondents completed and returned self-report questionnaires: 465 in the IQ 130+ index group and 756 in the control group. Index respondents and controls differed in their demographics. In addition to having higher IQ scores, the index group was proportionally more male, white, foreign, and unemployed. Fewer were heterosexual and proportionately more were separated, divorced, or living with a partner. They were older, were better educated, earned more, and were less religious. They were significantly more likely to report suffering from a mental illness, and a larger percentage of those who suffered from a mental illness also received mental-health treatment. The index and control groups identified many of the same influential books, films, and famous figures, but the index group was more influenced by dystopian literature and science while the control group was more influenced by African American identity and religious life.

Although the control group did not complete the EPQ-R, comparing index respondents to age- and sex-matched norms revealed that index respondents had higher than average measures of psychoticism, neuroticism, and venturesomeness. Females had higher than average measures of addiction and although males more closely resembled controls than prisoners on a scale for criminality, they had higher criminality scores. Respondents had lower than average measures of extraversion, impulsiveness, and empathy. Males had lower than average measures of addiction but higher than average lie scores, suggesting potential dissembling on the test, while females had lower than average lie scores.

4

The Offenses

[N]early all forms of antisocial behavior, especially crimes against persons or property and crimes that reflect impulsiveness, physical threat, or violence, are more apt to be committed by persons in the lower half of the IQ distribution.
—ARTHUR JENSEN, *THE G FACTOR: THE SCIENCE OF MENTAL ABILITY*, P. 297

As detailed in chapter 1, there is a consensus that delinquency and crime are associated with below-average intelligence. Specifically, proponents of this view argue that offenders and nonoffenders differ by approximately 8 to 10 IQ points. But such distinctions conflate occasional minor offenders (who scarcely differ from nonoffenders) and serious career criminals (Moffitt, Caspi, Silva, & Stouthamer-Loeber, 1995). These distinctions also treat crime as homogeneous, and fail to acknowledge that while many offenses may be correlated with low IQ, other crimes—especially those involving technical skills, planning, and professional opportunity—are associated with high IQ (Feldman, 1993; Wilson & Herrnstein, 1985). The current study attempts to disentangle these threads by disaggregating crime into nine offense types: (1) sexually oriented crimes, including prostitution, sexual assault, and rape; (2) violent crimes, including assault, kidnapping, and homicide; (3) drug crimes, including producing, buying, or selling cannabis, cocaine, or other illegal substances; (4) property crimes, including shoplifting, petty theft, and grand theft; (5) white-collar crimes, including insider trading, tax fraud, and engaging in trickery for financial gain; (6) professional misconduct, including plagiarism and fabricating scientific data; (7) vehicular offenses, including driving without a license and reckless driving; (8) justice system offenses, including resisting arrest, perjury, and failure to appear; and (9) a handful of other, miscellaneous offenses, such as counterfeiting, sedition, slander, and illegal gambling.

For each of these offense types, prevalence and incidence data are described, divided by index respondents and controls and by males and females, both for offenses committed within the year prior to the survey and for offenses ever committed. Prevalence rates are plotted against IQ ranges for index offenses, and material gleaned from follow-up interviews provides qualitative descriptions. Of course, as noted in chapter 3, the mean IQ of the control group lies within the gifted range, so this study is not so much a comparison between those with high and low IQs as it is between those with high and very high IQs. Still, if there *is* an inverse relationship between IQ and crime, prevalence rates should be higher in the control group than in the index group.

SEX CRIMES

The self-report questionnaire measured seven sexually oriented offenses, including prostitution, solicitation, sexual assault/rape, statutory rape, public indecency, and sexual harassment (both face-to-face and via telephone):

> Been paid for having sexual relations with someone.
>
> Paid someone for sexual relations.
>
> Had (or tried to have) sexual relations with someone against their will.
>
> Had sexual relations with someone under the legal age of consent (while over the age of consent yourself).
>
> Had sexual relations in a public place.
>
> Made sexual comments or advances toward someone that you knew were unwanted.
>
> Made obscene telephone calls, such as calling someone and saying dirty things.

These seven items are indicative, not exhaustive; left unmeasured, for example, were high-profile offenses such as sodomy (c.f., Bowers v. Hardwick, 1986; Lawrence v. Texas, 2003), incest (Bergelson, 2013), or the possession and distribution of child pornography (c.f., Paroline v. United States, 2014). A comprehensive review of the literature on sex crimes lies beyond the scope of this book, but several studies on the relationship between sex crimes and intelligence warrant mention. Below-average IQs have been reported among rapists (Ruff, Templer, & Ayers, 1976; Vera, Barnard, & Holzer, 1979), incest offenders (Langevin, Wortzman, Dickey, Wright, & Handy, 1988), and child molesters (Blanchard et al., 2007; Cantor et al., 2004). When Guay, Ouimet, and Proulx (2005) compared incarcerated sex offenders with nonsexual violent prisoners, they found that sex offenders had lower IQ scores (82.3 versus 89.1). When Cantor, Blanchard, Robichaud, and Christensen (2005) reanalyzed aggregated sex offender data, they too found that sex offenders had lower IQ scores than nonsexual offenders. They reported that offenders with adult victims had average IQ scores while those with child victims had below-average IQ scores. In their meta-analysis of sex offender neuropsychology, Joyal, Plante-Beaulieu, and de Chanterac (2014) concluded that "sex offenders as a group present significant and wide-ranging cognitive impairments compared with the general population"

TABLE 25 Sex offenses: prevalence, incidence, and recency by index and control groups and sex

		Index (n = 465)	Control (n = 756)	χ^2	p
Male	Never committed any sex offense	125 (37.5)	91 (31.5)	2.50	.1140
	Have committed a sex offense	208 (62.5)	198 (68.5)		
	Once last year	12 (34.3)	11 (20.4)	2.3589	.5013
	2 to 5 times last year	15 (42.9)	29 (53.7)		
	6 to 9 times last year	3 (8.6)	4 (7.4)		
	10+ times last year	5 (14.3)	10 (18.5)		
	Once ever	38 (18.5)	26 (14.7)	1.6046	.6583
	2 to 5 times ever	75 (36.4)	62 (35.0)		
	6 to 9 times ever	28 (13.6)	24 (13.6)		
	10+ times ever	65 (31.6)	65 (36.7)		
Female	Never committed any sex offense	54 (42.9)	200 (43.3)	0.01	.9307
	Have committed a sex offense	72 (57.1)	262 (56.7)		
	Once last year	7 (43.8)	15 (25.9)	2.9648	.3971
	2 to 5 times last year	6 (37.5)	20 (34.5)		
	6 to 9 times last year	1 (6.3)	9 (15.5)		
	10+ times last year	2 (12.5)	14 (24.1)		
	Once ever	14 (19.7)	37 (15.7)	1.4362	.6971
	2 to 5 times ever	28 (39.4)	102 (43.2)		
	6 to 9 times ever	8 (11.3)	35 (14.8)		
	10+ times ever	21 (29.6)	62 (26.3)		
Total	Never committed any sex offense	180 (38.7)	294 (38.9)	0.004	.9502
	Have committed a sex offense	285 (61.3)	462 (61.1)		
	Once last year	20 (37.0)	26 (23.0)	4.8183	.1856
	2 to 5 times last year	23 (42.6)	49 (43.4)		
	6 to 9 times last year	4 (7.4)	13 (11.5)		
	10+ times last year	7 (13.0)	25 (22.1)		
	Once ever	52 (18.4)	63 (15.2)	1.4236	.7000
	2 to 5 times ever	105 (37.2)	165 (39.8)		
	6 to 9 times ever	38 (13.5)	59 (14.2)		
	10+ times ever	87 (30.9)	128 (30.8)		

NOTE: See table 13 for a description of table elements.

(p. 166). Table 25 provides prevalence, incidence, and recency data for aggregated sex offenses for the current study's index and control groups by sex.

More than 60% of both the index and control respondents reported committing at least one of the seven listed sex offenses in the past. In terms of prevalence—the percentage of the sample indicating that they had committed the offense—a larger proportion of males than females reported a sex offense. A larger percentage of control group males than of index males reported sex offenses, but for females and for the aggregated total, the index group reported higher prevalence rates (none of these differences were significant, however). In terms of incidence—the total number of offenses committed by the sample—among those who reported a sex offense in the past, frequencies were higher in the control group both in the last year and ever. Index respondents were more likely to report a single offense; controls were more likely to report multiple offenses.

Although examining sex offenses by index and control groups reveals aggregated differences, it also is imperative to distinguish individual offenses. After all, while sex in public is a potentially "victimless" crime, rape is characterized as "the most serious violation of self," short of homicide (Coker v. Georgia, 1977, p. 597), and child molesters are despised and reviled more than murderers (Palmer, 2011). In the current study, one member of the incarcerated sample described his sexual offenses against children:

> "Sammie" was 8 when we first met, and I was 22. We still remain very close friends, even 33 years later, and have been a good influence on each other's lives. Sammie, who had been sexually active with girls even as a little boy, accepted me as a sexual partner when he was 16 and had left school; he stayed from time to time in my home. I had had no sexual contacts with anyone else between the ages of 15 and 30 and this was the first time I had ever had such an encounter with a person I cared about. I had somehow assumed that indefinite abstinence would bring me into line with what society expected, though all my fantasies were about boys.

He described systematically molesting Sammie's three younger brothers over the course of five years, each time at the boys' instigation, though he admitted that he made it easy for them to "make the final move." Sammie's household had been very irregular, sexually, and the offender was under the impression that the four brothers were sexually active with each other and other boys, although he was the only adult involved. He described his arrest: "I was so attached to these boys I was quite unable to extricate myself and in the end, I was arrested in 1977. Sammie was 22 by this time, and his brothers were 20, 16, and 12. Sammie and 'Brian' were also arrested and were very badly treated by the police, although in the end the director of public prosecutions would not allow them to be charged."

Another pedophile, a twice-convicted American child molester, described a similar set of circumstances in which he befriended and then seduced a group of "street kids" and some of their friends. He described his modus operandi:

> My M.O. was centered around fondling and fellatio with the boys, and with (one victim in my life) cunnilingus with a girl. I did not bribe any of my victims, but I did take them out on hiking trips, and paid them loads of attention and exposed them to nature, the water, the sand, trees, and forests. I intoxicated them with visual and aural and olfactory stimuli. . . . I was the seducer of children . . . the warped Pied Piper of Hamlin . . . and in the process, I have no idea how many minds I destroyed, crippled, ruining their innocence.

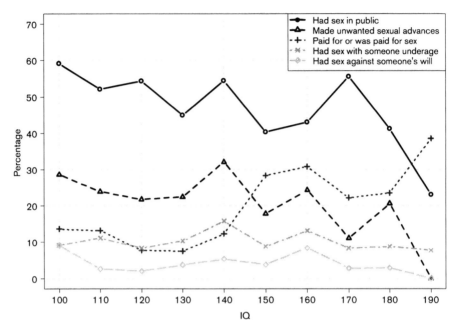

FIGURE 16. Prevalence rates for five measures of sex offenses by IQ.

When he was arrested the first time, police told him that they did not care what he did with the street boys—they were "garbage"—but he had made the grave mistake of molesting a policeman's son, and for that he would pay dearly. He served a four-year sentence, was released, and did not recidivate for three years. Yet when he was brought into the fold of a coworker's family, long-dormant habits reawakened. He grew close to all four of the family's children, but especially to 11-year-old twins, a boy and a girl. He seduced them, juggling them like jealous lovers for approximately one year, before the parents—his closest friends—discovered the secret. He attempted to take his own life while awaiting trial, but survived. In light of his prior record, the judge sentenced him to 20 to 40 years.

Figure 16 depicts the prevalence of five identified sex offenses by IQ band. For clarity of presentation, each graph point, plotted in 10-point increments, includes the IQ scores following the previous graph point (e.g., the IQ 120 point represents all scores between 111 and 120). Prevalence rates are displayed instead of incidence rates because IQ was not normally distributed across the samples: IQ 100 = 23; IQ 110 = 190; IQ 120 = 494; IQ 130 = 107; IQ 140 = 57; IQ 150 = 156; IQ 160 = 107; IQ 170 = 36; IQ 180 = 34; and IQ 190 = 12. To avoid a tangle of lines, obscene telephone calls were omitted from the figure and prostitution and solicitation were combined into a single measure. Figure 16 reveals that the most common sex offense was sex in public: that is, the area under this line is larger than that of any other offense. Most sex in public episodes were harmless and discrete, "quickies" committed in parked automobiles or in secluded woods. One American member of the high-IQ society reported having intercourse on the bow of a sailboat; another described receiving fellatio while driving across the country. A third described a representative situation. "I attempted to have sex at night on a beach once, but my girlfriend and I decided it was just too risky. I do find these risky things thrilling and stimulating, but when the potential consequences are too great, I can't risk it. There are times when the mind can over rule the loins!"

The relationship between IQ and prevalence rate for sex in public is negative. The slope and y-intercept of the linear regression trend line—predicting the amount of change in prevalence per unit of IQ change—is $y = -0.0251 + 0.6059$. Under a model that optimizes the data in a straight line, at IQ 100 (the y-axis) 60.59% of the sample would report sex in public; and for each 10-point unit of IQ increase, the percentage of subjects reporting sex in public would be expected to decrease by 2.51% (decreasing to a low of 38.0% at IQ 190, the right limit of the x-axis). As indicated in table 35, later in this chapter, the IQ-prevalence relationship is also negative for unwanted sexual offenses, statutory rape (underage sex), and sexual assault/rape (sex against someone's will). For solicitation (paying for sex) and prostitution (being paid for sex), however, the combined slope is positive: $y = +0.0276$. For each 10-point unit of IQ increase, prevalence increases by 2.76%. If a genius-level IQ interferes with the ability to communicate meaningfully with others (an idea explored in chapter 6), prostitution is one means of obtaining intimacy. Nearly one-third of the high-IQ sample—all of them male—reported paying for sex. Aggregating the prevalence rates of all seven sexual offenses, including the items not displayed in figure 16, and plotting them against IQ ranges, yields the prevalence line in figure 17.

Despite a downward turn at IQ 180–190, the trend line is slightly positive. For each 10-point unit of IQ increase, the prevalence of any lifetime sexual offense increases by 0.52%. Of course, this is a function of the high prevalence rates for solicitation; omitting this crime from the analysis would produce a slightly negative trend line. Nevertheless, contrary to the expectation of the leading literature on the IQ–general crime relationship and the IQ–sex crime relationship, lifetime prevalence of sex offenses appears to *increase* as IQ range increases.

VIOLENT CRIMES

The self-report questionnaire measured eight offenses related to violence, including assault (making a threat), battery (beating someone up), concealed weapons, building bombs, kidnapping, robbery, homicide, and attempted suicide:

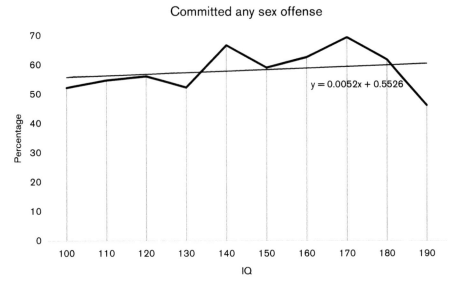

FIGURE 17. Prevalence rates for aggregated sex offenses by IQ. The trend line indicates a positive association between IQ and prevalence.

Used violence or the threat of violence to rob someone.

Carried a hidden weapon other than a plain pocketknife.

Made a serious threat that you meant to carry out.

Beaten someone up seriously enough that they required medical attention of any kind.

Killed another human being (excluding wartime situations).

Constructed a bomb or similar explosive device.

Held someone against their will (kidnapping).

Attempted suicide.

Here, too, these items are illustrative, not exhaustive. The study did not distinguish grades or types of homicide (Oleson, 2013), did not identify domestic violence or hate crime as discrete categories, and did not measure other violent crimes such as firearms violations or terrorism. Rape is often counted as a violent crime (FBI, 2015) but was recorded as a sexual offense in this study; blackmail (extortion) was counted as a miscellaneous offense.

The literature on violent crime lies beyond the scope of this book, but several studies on the association between intelligence and violence are noteworthy. Johansson and Kerr (2005) summarize the literature, writing, "On average, delinquents score eight IQ points lower than nondelinquents on standard intelligence tests and the relation between intelligence and criminality is stronger for violent than nonviolent offenses" (p. 357). Wilson and Herrnstein (1985) agree that violent crime, often impulsive and spontaneous, is associated with low IQ. Their suggestion is borne out in the research of Walsh (1987), who found that although bright-normal delinquents reported higher levels of property offending, dull-normal delinquents reported higher levels of violence; in the research of Heilbrun (1990), who found that high antisociality and low IQ were associated with the imposition of the death penalty in murder cases; and in the research of DeLisi, Piquero, and Cardwell (2014), who found that low IQ was a significant predictor of young offenders being charged with homicide. Macrolevel researchers also report a negative and significant association between IQ and violent crime at the county (Beaver & Wright, 2011), state (Bartels, Ryan, Urban, & Glass,, 2010; Templer & Rushton, 2011), and international (Rushton & Templer, 2009) levels. Researchers examining the relationship in the prison setting report that both individual and prison-unit IQs are significantly and negatively related to violent prison misconduct (Diamond, Morris, & Barnes, 2012). The relationship is not absolute, however. One study, using the data described in this book, reported a weak but positive correlation between IQ and the eight violent crimes (Oleson & Chappell, 2012).

Table 26 provides prevalence, incidence, and recency data for aggregated index and control groups. The index group reported a *higher*—not lower—prevalence rate of violent offenses than the control group (43.7% versus 38.2%), although this difference was not significant. Given the extant literature on IQ and violence, this finding is puzzling. Teasing the index and control groups apart by sex reveals that control males were significantly more likely than index males to report a violent offense (consistent with most research), while index females were significantly more likely than control females to report such an offense. The two relationships masked one another in the aggregate data. In terms of incidence rates, control group males reported more offenses than index males, although the finding was significant only for those offenses committed in the last year. Index females reported higher rates than controls, although this difference was not significant. Overall, controls reported more violent offenses than index respondents.

Figure 18 depicts the prevalence of six violent offenses by IQ: threat and battery (combined into a single measure), concealed weapon and bomb building (combined into a single measure), robbery, attempted suicide, kidnapping, and homicide. Homicides were relatively rare in this study: only 17 respondents reported a homicide. The most prevalent violent offense was the carrying of a concealed weapon and/ or the construction of explosive devices. Many respondents emphasized that their construction of explosive devices was harmless adolescent experimentation, and not the sort of conduct that would—at least before Columbine and 9/11—concern law enforcement officials. Some cases, however, were of enormous concern. One

TABLE 26 Violence offenses: prevalence, incidence, and recency by index and control groups and sex

		Index (n = 465)	Control (n = 756)	χ²	p
Male	Never committed any violence offense	189 (56.8)	137 (47.4)	5.43	.0198
	Have committed a violence offense	144 (43.2)	152 (52.6)		
	Once last year	9 (32.1)	11 (27.5)	5.3185	.1499
	2 to 5 times last year	12 (42.9)	14 (35.0)		
	6 to 9 times last year	4 (14.3)	2 (5.0)		
	10+ times last year	3 (10.7)	13 (32.5)		
	Once ever	38 (26.8)	34 (25.4)	7.8658	.0489
	2 to 5 times ever	49 (34.5)	32 (23.9)		
	6 to 9 times ever	16 (11.3)	11 (8.2)		
	10+ times ever	39 (27.5)	57 (42.5)		
Female	Never committed any violence offense	72 (57.1)	326 (70.6)	8.15	.0043
	Have committed a violence offense	54 (42.9)	136 (29.4)		
	Once last year	2 (20.0)	13 (40.6)	2.1645	.5390
	2 to 5 times last year	5 (50.0)	11 (34.4)		
	6 to 9 times last year	1 (10.0)	1 (3.1)		
	10+ times last year	2 (20.0)	7 (21.9)		
	Once ever	15 (27.8)	52 (42.3)	4.8174	.1857
	2 to 5 times ever	24 (44.4)	38 (30.9)		
	6 to 9 times ever	2 (3.7)	8 (6.5)		
	10+ times ever	13 (24.1)	25 (20.3)		
Total	Never committed any violence offense	262 (56.3)	467 (61.8)	3.53	.0604
	Have committed a violence offense	203 (43.7)	289 (38.2)		
	Once last year	11 (28.2)	24 (33.3)	6.2058	.1020
	2 to 5 times last year	18 (46.2)	25 (34.7)		
	6 to 9 times last year	5 (12.8)	3 (4.2)		
	10+ times last year	5 (12.8)	20 (27.8)		
	Once ever	53 (26.5)	87 (33.7)	7.5363	.0566
	2 to 5 times ever	76 (38.0)	70 (27.1)		
	6 to 9 times ever	18 (9.0)	19 (7.4)		
	10+ times ever	53 (26.5)	82 (31.8)		

NOTE: See table 13 for a description of table elements.

member of the incarcerated sample was a university student at the time of his arrest. A self-described "arrogant loner," he stole laboratory equipment from his university to construct multiple bombs. He described his "war against society":

> I was arrested in 1988 for a variety of violent crimes, for example, bomb making and planting, theft of poison. Nobody was hurt in my activities, though that was the intent. I would characterize my offenses as deriving from a "war against society," conducted with my younger brother and a friend. They both received noncustodial sentences and I got six (discretionary) life sentences as the ringleader. The bombs were home-

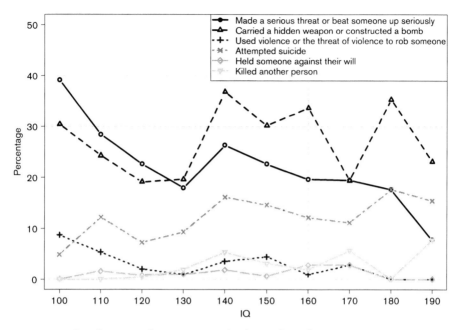

FIGURE 18. Prevalence rates for six measures of violence offenses by IQ.

made chemical devices made in conjunction with my hate campaign against society. At the time I desired nothing more than destruction and "revenge," for no apparent reason, and I felt powerful and important when building these things.

The slope of the trend line between IQ and the prevalence of concealed weapons/bomb construction is positive ($y = +0.0029x$). That is, for each 10-point unit of IQ increase, prevalence would be expected to increase by 0.29%. As indicated in table 35, later in this chapter, the linear relationship between IQ and lifetime prevalence is negative for robbery and threat/battery but positive for kidnapping, homicide, and attempted suicide.

Research on giftedness and suicide is equivocal (Farrell, 1989). While some indicate that IQ is positively correlated with higher than average rates of suicide (Hayes & Sloat, 1989; Lester, 2003; Voracek, 2004), others report a negative association (Gunnell, Harbord, Singleton, Jenkins, & Lewis, 2009). In the current study, one member of the high-IQ society described both his arrest for attempted suicide attempt and his five-week period of observation in a mental hospital, and he railed against the belief that suicide is synonymous with mental disorder:

If I have nothing to live for, must I be mentally ill if I want to stop this life and to say "good-bye"? I am not alone. We are many, who have no reason to go on, who have

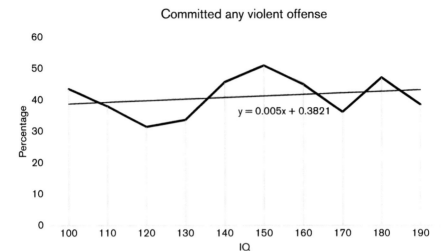

FIGURE 19. Prevalence rates for aggregated violence offenses by IQ. The trend line indicates a positive association between IQ and prevalence.

done our duties and are waiting only for that final border to cross. If I want my death to be easy and precious, I should have the right to decide my time and manner of death. Just me, myself, has the right to decide over my life; just me, myself, can know the truth and the reasons inside me. And it is not mental illness; it's the opposite.

Aggregating the prevalence rates of all eight violent offenses and plotting them against IQ ranges yields the prevalence line in figure 19 ($y = +0.0050x + 0.3821$). This suggests a *positive* relationship between IQ and lifetime prevalence of violent crime: for each 10-point unit of IQ increase, the prevalence of any lifetime violent offense would be expected to increase by 0.50%. This positive relationship is, in part, a function of a strong association between IQ and attempted suicide (which is arguably a victimless offense) and homicide (which has been challenged as not credible in self-report research). Still, this is an unexpected result given previously published research.

DRUG CRIMES

The self-report questionnaire measured 12 offenses related to drug crimes, including trafficking (smuggling alcohol, tobacco, or other drugs); producing drugs; buying, using, and selling (hard and soft) drugs; providing alcohol for minors; and public intoxication:

Used marijuana, cannabis, or hashish.

Bought marijuana, cannabis, or hashish.

Sold marijuana, cannabis, or hashish.

Used hard drugs such as heroin, cocaine, LSD, or ecstasy.

Bought hard drugs, such as heroin, cocaine, LSD, or ecstasy.

Sold hard drugs, such as heroin, cocaine, LSD, or ecstasy.

Manufactured or cultivated a controlled substance (drugs).

Taken pharmaceuticals prescribed for someone else.

Smuggled alcohol, tobacco, or food items (e.g., avoiding duty when crossing federal borders).

Smuggled illegal drugs or drug paraphernalia.

Bought or provided liquor for a minor.

Been drunk in a public place.

Although the questionnaire canvasses many categories related to drug crimes, it is not comprehensive. It does not, for example, examine the association between drug use and other crimes (like prostitution or theft) that can support a drug habit. Nor, beyond distinguishing between hard and soft drugs, does the questionnaire measure the use of any specific drugs. While driving under the influence is sometimes counted as a drug crime, it is categorized here as a vehicular crime.

A comprehensive survey of the literature on narcotics and drug policy would fill volumes, but a few studies on IQ and drugs merit mention. In their 2003 survey of the IQ-crime literature, Ellis and Walsh qualify their assessment of a robust, negative IQ-crime relationship, writing, "Regarding self reports pertaining exclusively to illegal drug use . . . a very uncertain pattern has been found, with only half of the 6 relevant studies reporting an inverse [IQ-crime] relationship" (p. 346). Indeed, Kellam, Ensminger, and Simon (1980) report a *positive* association between intelligence and self-reported drug use. Intelligence is positively correlated with alcohol abuse and dependence (Hatch et al., 2007; Kanazawa & Hellberg, 2010) and drug abuse (Fergusson, Horwood, & Ridder, 2005; Kanazawa & Hellberg, 2010; White & Batty, 2012; White, Gale, & Batty, 2012; see also McCracken, 2010). Whether related to sensation seeking (Raine, Reynolds, Venables, & Mednick, 2002), self-medication (Harris & Edlund, 2005), or other factors, when it comes to alcohol and drugs, individuals with high IQs appear to be *more* likely to engage in illegal activity than people with average IQs. One member of the incarcerated sample described one occasion during which he tried a designer drug:

In 1971, I did a profound overdose of something a friend of mine had "cooked up" in his amazingly complicated home lab. He called it "Near Mescaline," and it may have been one of the earliest "designer drugs" ever conjured. I did the equivalent of 40 big doses of the chemical. For two weeks, I experienced an artificially induced psychotic state, complete with internal voices telling me things, the end or stopping of time, and my reliving a constant audiovisual "loop" which content never changed. There was a part of me that *knew* I was insane, but I could not do anything about it.

He indicated that when he saw the hands of the clock move again, he knew that he was returning to sanity. Time and space once again meant something to him: "And my return to sanity, after I was able to process and experience the phenomenon of time, was so swift that I only recall that it hit me like an explosion, a physical blast. I recall crying simultaneously with my recognition of the passage of time, and I knelt and wept in front of the kitchen clock, with the same kind of awe and adoration I would surely have experienced had I seen the face of God."

Table 27 identifies the prevalence and incidence rates for drug offenses in the index and control groups by sex. Overall, more than 80% of index respondents and controls reported at least one drug offense in the past (cannabis offenses were especially frequent). Incidence figures are right-limited: several reports of "thousands" or "millions" of drug-use episodes had to be restricted to 1,000. Consistent with research asserting a positive association between IQ and drug use, the overall prevalence rate was higher in the index group than in the control group. This difference was not significant and was the product of larger, but still insignificant, differences between index and control females (82.5% versus 78.4%). Among males, on the other hand, controls reported slightly higher drug prevalence rates. Index respondents reported slightly higher incidence rates than controls in the previous year, while controls reported slightly higher lifetime incidence rates. None of the differences in incidence rates—male or female, last year or ever—were significant.

Figure 20 displays the prevalence of six drug offenses by IQ band: public intoxication, used/bought/sold soft drugs (cannabis) (three questionnaire items merged into a single measure), providing alcohol for a minor, used/bought/sold hard drugs (again, three items merged into a single measure for graphing purposes), smuggling alcohol or drugs (two questionnaire items merged), and producing drugs. To prevent a confusion of lines, the pharmaceuticals item is not included. The highest lifetime prevalence rates are recorded for public intoxication. Although rates exceed 50% between IQ 100 and IQ 180, they decline sharply at IQ 190. Consequently, the slope of the trend line is slightly negative: for each 10-point unit of IQ increase, the prevalence of any public intoxication offense would be expected to decrease by 0.24%. As indicated in table 35, later in this chapter, the linear relationship between IQ and lifetime prevalence is also negative for providing alcohol to a minor, hard drugs (i.e., used, bought, or sold hard drugs), and producing drugs. In contrast, the relationship is positive for soft drugs (i.e., used, bought, or sold soft drugs) and for smuggling alcohol or drugs.

TABLE 27 Drug offenses: prevalence, incidence, and recency by index and control groups and sex

		Index (n = 465)	Control (n = 756)	χ^2	p
Male	Never committed any drug offense	58 (17.4)	41 (14.2)	1.21	.2720
	Have committed a drug offense	275 (82.6)	248 (85.8)		
	Once last year	16 (16.3)	12 (14.5)	0.2381	.9712
	2 to 5 times last year	26 (26.5)	24 (28.9)		
	6 to 9 times last year	11 (11.2)	10 (12.1)		
	10+ times last year	45 (45.9)	37 (44.6)		
	Once ever	20 (7.6)	17 (7.9)	5.7809	.1228
	2 to 5 times ever	53 (20.1)	27 (12.6)		
	6 to 9 times ever	29 (11.0)	20 (9.3)		
	10+ times ever	162 (61.4)	151 (70.2)		
Female	Never committed any drug offense	22 (17.5)	100 (21.7)	1.05	.3045
	Have committed a drug offense	104 (82.5)	362 (78.4)		
	Once last year	6 (13.0)	23 (16.6)	2.1586	.5402
	2 to 5 times last year	16 (34.8)	49 (35.3)		
	6 to 9 times last year	3 (6.5)	17 (12.2)		
	10+ times last year	21 (45.7)	50 (36.0)		
	Once ever	8 (8.0)	24 (7.4)	1.4961	.6832
	2 to 5 times ever	26 (26.0)	67 (20.6)		
	6 to 9 times ever	10 (10.0)	37 (11.4)		
	10+ times ever	56 (56.0)	198 (60.7)		
Total	Never committed any drug offense	80 (17.2)	143 (18.9)	0.56	.4524
	Have committed a drug offense	385 (82.8)	613 (81.1)		
	Once last year	22 (14.8)	35 (15.8)	1.7644	.6227
	2 to 5 times last year	45 (30.2)	73 (32.9)		
	6 to 9 times last year	14 (9.4)	27 (12.2)		
	10+ times last year	68 (45.6)	87 (39.2)		
	Once ever	28 (7.6)	42 (7.7)	2.6809	.4435
	2 to 5 times ever	80 (21.6)	95 (17.5)		
	6 to 9 times ever	40 (10.8)	57 (10.5)		
	10+ times ever	222 (60.0)	350 (64.3)		

NOTE: See table 13 for a description of table elements.

As indicated in figure 21, prevalence rates of all 12 aggregated drug offenses (including pharmaceutical use, not displayed in figure 20) are high: across all IQ levels, lifetime prevalence exceeds 60%. The overall relationship between IQ and prevalence is positive ($y = +0.0133x + 0.6771$): for each 10-point unit of IQ increase, the prevalence of any lifetime drug offense would be expected to increase by 1.33%. This positive relationship is driven by strong positive associations between IQ and soft drug use and smuggling. This finding is consistent with previously published, although counterintuitive, research on IQ and substance use.

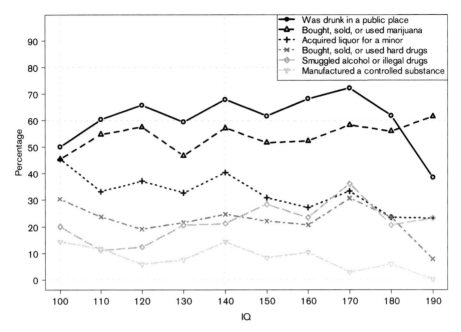

FIGURE 20. Prevalence rates for six measures of drug offenses by IQ.

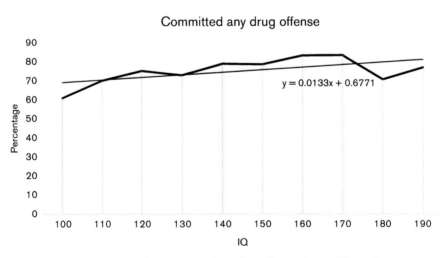

FIGURE 21. Prevalence rates for aggregated drug offenses by IQ. The trend line indicates a positive association between IQ and prevalence.

PROPERTY CRIMES

Property crime might not captivate the public imagination in the way that violent and sexual crimes do, but property crime is of terrific criminological importance. It constitutes approximately 88.1% of all the reported offenses in the Uniform Crime Reports and, in 2013, cost $16.6 billion (FBI, 2015). Accordingly, the self-report questionnaire measured 12 property offenses, including vandalism, arson, breaking and entering, pickpocketing, fencing and receiving, shoplifting and theft, motor-vehicle theft, taking goods or services without payment, and using someone's bank card or telephone without permission:

> Purposely damaged or destroyed property that did not belong to you.
>
> Stolen (or tried to steal) a motor vehicle, such as a car or motorcycle.
>
> Stolen (or tried to steal) things worth $5 or less (including petty shoplifting).
>
> Stolen (or tried to steal) things worth between $5 and $50.
>
> Stolen (or tried to steal) something worth more than $50.
>
> Picked someone's pocket or stolen (or tried to steal) from someone's purse.
>
> Knowingly bought, sold, or held stolen goods (or tried to do any of these things).
>
> Damaged property or real estate by lighting a fire (arson).
>
> Avoided paying for things such as movies, bus or subway rides, or food.
>
> Used another person's telephone or telephone card without their permission.
>
> Used another person's ATM (cashpoint) card without their permission.
>
> Broken into a building or vehicle (or tried to break in) to steal something or just to look around.

Although the questionnaire taps a range of offenses, it does not measure all property offenses. For example, burglary, an important form of property crime, is included in the breaking and entering item. Robbery, the taking of property by force, is counted as a violent crime; fraud, the taking of property by trickery, is counted as a white-collar offense.

The literature on property crime is extensive, but a few studies relating intelligence to property crimes bear mention. In their survey of the literature, Wilson and Herrnstein (1985) suggested that some offenders (like white-collar criminals) have IQs above most criminals, that other offenders (like violent and sex offenders) have lower IQs, and that "[i]n the center of the IQ distribution for offenders are found, not surprisingly, the high-frequency property offenders, such as the burglars and the auto thieves" (p. 165). In line with this claim, Walsh (1987) found that property offenders had higher IQs than violent offenders, although verbal IQs were low across the whole of his sample. Using aggregated data, IQ has been negatively and significantly associated with property crimes at the county (Beaver & Wright,

TABLE 28 Property offenses: prevalence, incidence, and recency by index and
control groups and sex

		Index (n = 465)	Control (n = 756)	χ^2	p
Male	Never committed any property offense	66 (19.8)	75 (26.0)	3.32	.0685
	Have committed a property offense	267 (80.2)	214 (74.1)		
	Once last year	14 (21.2)	11 (21.2)	0.4597	.9277
	2 to 5 times last year	29 (43.9)	20 (38.5)		
	6 to 9 times last year	8 (12.1)	7 (13.5)		
	10+ times last year	15 (22.7)	14 (26.9)		
	Once ever	24 (9.1)	17 (8.5)	2.2392	.5243
	2 to 5 times ever	72 (27.2)	44 (22.1)		
	6 to 9 times ever	40 (15.1)	28 (14.1)		
	10+ times ever	129 (48.7)	110 (55.3)		
Female	Never committed any property offense	25 (19.8)	157 (34.0)	9.26	.0023
	Have committed a property offense	101 (80.2)	305 (66.0)		
	Once last year	7 (24.1)	16 (20.3)	0.3286	.9546
	2 to 5 times last year	13 (44.8)	40 (50.6)		
	6 to 9 times last year	3 (10.3)	8 (10.1)		
	10+ times last year	6 (20.7)	15 (19.0)		
	Once ever	12 (12.0)	41 (14.6)	0.6689	.8805
	2 to 5 times ever	34 (34.0)	99 (35.4)		
	6 to 9 times ever	11 (11.0)	27 (9.6)		
	10+ times ever	43 (43.0)	113 (40.4)		
Total	Never committed any property offense	91 (19.6)	236 (31.2)	19.92	8.09E-06
	Have committed a property offense	374 (80.4)	520 (68.8)		
	Once last year	21 (21.4)	27 (20.6)	0.0329	.9984
	2 to 5 times last year	44 (44.9)	60 (45.8)		
	6 to 9 times last year	11 (11.2)	15 (11.5)		
	10+ times last year	22 (22.5)	29 (22.1)		
	Once ever	36 (9.7)	59 (12.3)	2.242	.5237
	2 to 5 times ever	107 (28.9)	143 (29.8)		
	6 to 9 times ever	51 (13.8)	55 (11.5)		
	10+ times ever	176 (47.6)	223 (46.5)		

NOTE: See table 13 for a description of table elements. Very small p values here are expressed in scientific notation (i.e., 8.09E-06 = .00000809).

2011) and state (Bartels et al., 2010) levels. Curiously, however, Gath, Tennent, and Pidduck (1971) found that bright delinquents asked for more offenses to be "taken into consideration," admitting to more priors than did average delinquents.

Table 28 identifies the prevalence and incidence rates for property offenses in the index and control groups by sex. Property offenses were prevalent. More than 60% of all groups (males, females, index, and controls) reported at least one property offense in the past. Across all three comparisons, index respondents reported higher prevalence rates than controls. The difference was not significant for males,

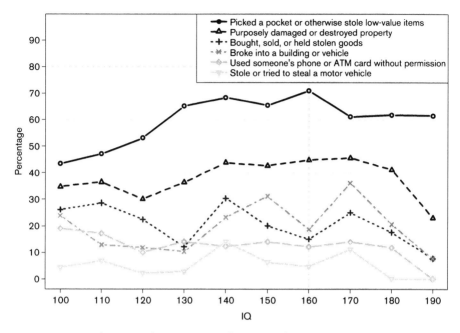

FIGURE 22. Prevalence rates for six measures of property offenses by IQ.

but it was highly significant for females and in the aggregated sample. Lifetime incidence rates were lower for male index respondents than controls but higher for female and aggregated index respondents than controls. For property offenses committed in the previous year, male controls reported slightly higher incidence rates than male index respondents. For females and aggregated respondents, incidence rates were slightly higher in the index than the control group. Differences in incidence rates were not significant.

Figure 22 displays the prevalence of six property offenses by IQ band: stealing (or trying to steal) something worth $5 or less (including petty shoplifting)/pick-pocketing or stealing from purses (two questionnaire items combined into a single measure), damaging or destroying property, buying or selling stolen goods, break-ing into a building or vehicle, using a telephone or ATM card without permission (two items combined into a single measure), and motor-vehicle theft. These are illustrative. For clarity of presentation, the questionnaire items for arson, high-value theft, and avoiding payment for goods and services are not represented. Petty theft was the most prevalent property offense. Above IQ 120, more than half the sample reported a petty theft/pickpocketing offense. Most examples involved stealing coins or pocket cash from one's own parents, taking chocolates from a shop, or stealing a magazine. One member of the high-IQ society, however, recounted an episode in which a shopkeeper's unwarranted accusation actually catalyzed his offending: "I was 14. I wanted to have a scout knife and I examined it long enough to make a shop assistant suspicious. He believed I had stolen the knife. I had not, however. He took me in a room and searched for the knife he thought I had stolen. I was so upset that I decided to steal the knife." Another member of the high-IQ society recounted the shame in being caught stealing after taking a job in a shop:

> One day on an impulse I took in 50 cents cash in payment for a tie and rang up "No Sale" on the cash register and put the 50 cents in my pocket. I thought no one was around in the store, but the owner's brother-in-law . . . spotted me. The owner took me aside later, asked me straight out if I had stolen 50 cents, and I admitted that I had. It was an earthshaking experience for me. I don't think the owner ever fully trusted me after that, and I knew it. That hurt far more than just getting caught. I have never stolen a cent from anyone ever in my life since.

The relationship between the lifetime prevalence of petty theft and IQ is positive ($y = +0.0194x + 0.4913$): for each 10-point unit of IQ increase, the lifetime prevalence of petty theft would be expected to increase by 1.94%. As indicated in table 35, later in this chapter, the linear relationship between IQ and lifetime prevalence is positive for two other graphed property offenses: damaging or destroying property, and breaking into a building or vehicle. However, the relationship is negative for motor-vehicle theft, buying or selling stolen goods, and using a telephone or ATM card without permission.

As indicated in figure 23, prevalence rates of all 12 aggregated property offenses (including those not displayed in figure 22) are high: as in the case of drug offenses, across all IQ levels lifetime prevalence exceeds 60%. The linear relationship between IQ and prevalence is positive ($y = +0.0206x + 0.6311$): for every 10-point unit of IQ increase, lifetime property offense prevalence would be expected to increase by 2.06%. Thus, the association between IQ and property offense prevalence is even stronger than that between IQ and drug offense prevalence.

WHITE-COLLAR CRIMES

The concept of white-collar crime is less than 100 years old (Sutherland, 1940), but the term has been incorporated into common parlance. In the public imagination, high-IQ crime *is* white-collar crime: offenses involving skill, planning, and the privilege of position. Research indicates that white-collar offenders do have IQs higher than those of controls (Raine et al., 2012). As noted in the introduction, the consequences of white-collar crime are grave. Criminologists have demonstrated that white-collar crime is far more injurious, in terms of physical harm, deaths, and financial losses, than all street crime combined (Coleman, 2005). Indeed, some white-collar crimes are so great in their scope or their consequences that they cease

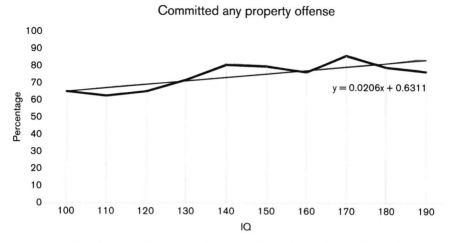

FIGURE 23. Prevalence rates for aggregated property offenses by IQ. The trend line indicates a positive association between IQ and prevalence.

to be understood as crimes (Reiman, 2001). One member of the high-IQ society described multiple counts of tax fraud but explained that they did not seem like real crimes: "More like taking a chance on a deduction that may or may not have been perfectly kosher. I think most people do that—tax advisers often suggest that if you think it might be a legit deduction just go ahead and take it. I don't remember any special feelings or consequences—it wasn't a case of doing something I knew was illegal as much as just a habit of taking all the deductions I thought I could."

The self-report questionnaire measured 10 white-collar offenses, including insider trading, espionage, unlawful surveillance, forgery, money laundering, fraud, tax fraud, copyright infringement, and cybercrime:

Used privileged information in making investment decisions.

Manipulated financial accounts in an illegal manner.

Sold or traded government or industrial secrets.

Intentionally misreported income information on your tax forms.

Broken into another computer (hacked).

Made unauthorized copies of commercial computer software.

Made copies of copyrighted records, tapes, or videocassettes.

Used an electronic device to eavesdrop or spy on someone.

Tricked (or tried to trick) a person, group, or company for financial gain (fraud).

Forged another person's signature on an official document, prescription, or bank check.

TABLE 29 White-collar offenses: prevalence, incidence, and recency by index and
control groups and sex

		Index (n = 465)	Control (n = 756)	χ^2	p
Male	Never committed any white-collar offense	66 (19.8)	107 (37.0)	22.81	1.79E-06
	Have committed a white-collar offense	267 (80.2)	182 (63.0)		
	Once last year	20 (18.4)	5 (11.1)	21.2832	9.19E-05
	2 to 5 times last year	52 (47.7)	9 (20.0)		
	6 to 9 times last year	16 (14.7)	6 (13.3)		
	10+ times last year	21 (19.3)	25 (55.6)		
	Once ever	16 (6.1)	12 (8.0)	23.46	.0294
	2 to 5 times ever	68 (26.1)	21 (13.9)		
	6 to 9 times ever	28 (10.7)	15 (9.9)		
	10+ times ever	149 (57.1)	103 (68.2)		
Female	Never committed any white-collar offense	30 (23.8)	187 (40.5)	11.81	5.89E-04
	Have committed a white-collar offense	96 (76.2)	275 (59.5)		
	Once last year	9 (21.4)	19 (20.7)	2.395	.4946
	2 to 5 times last year	18 (42.9)	31 (33.7)		
	6 to 9 times last year	4 (9.5)	6 (6.5)		
	10+ times last year	11 (26.2)	36 (39.1)		
	Once ever	3 (3.3)	25 (10.6)	4.8136	.1860
	2 to 5 times ever	25 (27.5)	66 (28.1)		
	6 to 9 times ever	12 (13.2)	29 (12.3)		
	10+ times ever	51 (56.0)	115 (48.9)		
Total	Never committed any white-collar offense	98 (21.1)	299 (39.6)	44.79	2.20E-11
	Have committed a white-collar offense	367 (78.9)	457 (60.5)		
	Once last year	29 (18.7)	24 (17.5)	17.1265	6.66E-04
	2 to 5 times last year	71 (45.8)	40 (29.2)		
	6 to 9 times last year	20 (12.9)	12 (8.8)		
	10+ times last year	35 (22.6)	61 (44.5)		
	Once ever	19 (5.3)	37 (9.6)	5.4366	.1425
	2 to 5 times ever	93 (26.1)	87 (22.5)		
	6 to 9 times ever	40 (11.2)	44 (11.4)		
	10+ times ever	204 (57.3)	218 (56.5)		

NOTE: See table 13 for a description of table elements. Very small p values here are expressed in scientific notation (e.g., 1.79E-06 = .00000179).

These offenses do not record all forms of white-collar crime. For example, bribery, identity theft, and racketeering are not measured. Violation of safety and environmental standards is coded as professional misconduct instead of white-collar crime; counterfeiting (analogous to forgery) is coded as a miscellaneous offense.

Table 29 identifies the prevalence and incidence rates for white-collar offenses in the index and control groups, by sex. More than half of all sample groups—male, female, and aggregate; index and control—reported at least one white-collar offense. Prevalence rates were significantly higher in all index groups than in corresponding control groups (78.9% versus 60.5% in the aggregated sample). Differences between index and control males, and between index and control females, were also significant. Among those reporting a white-collar offense in the last year, incidence rates were higher among controls (significantly higher among males and in the aggregated sample). Lifetime incidence rates were slightly (insignificantly) higher among male controls, among female index respondents, and among index respondents in the aggregated sample.

Figure 24 displays the prevalence of six white-collar offenses by IQ band: forgery, copyright violation (illegal copies of music or movies), illegal financial operations (money laundering), fraud, breaking into another computer (hacking), and using privileged investment information (insider trading). For clarity of presentation, four white-collar offenses are not pictured: espionage, tax fraud, illegal surveillance, and illegal software copying. By a considerable margin, the most prevalent white-collar offense in figure 24 is copyright violation. Between IQ 120 and IQ 180, more than half the respondents report at least one copyright violation offense. The slope of the trend line between IQ and the prevalence of copyright violation is positive ($y = +0.0206x + 0.4642$). That is, for each 10-point unit of IQ increase, prevalence would be expected to increase by 2.06%. The association between IQ and prevalence is positive for all of the other white-collar offenses described in figure 24 as well, as noted in table 35, later in this chapter.

As indicated in figure 25, lifetime prevalence rates for all 10 aggregated white-collar offenses (including those that not displayed in figure 24) are fairly high: they exceed 50% at all IQ levels except at IQ 110. The relationship between IQ and white-collar prevalence is positive ($y = +0.0293x + 0.4961$). This is the strongest positive linear relationship between IQ and prevalence in the study, indicating that for every 10-point unit of IQ increase, lifetime white-collar offense prevalence would be expected to increase by 2.93%.

PROFESSIONAL MISCONDUCT

The self-report questionnaire measured five offenses related to professional misconduct, including abuse of work privileges, the violation of safety or environmental standards, plagiarism, falsifying data, and academic cheating:

Violated safety or environmental standards.

Abused work privileges (e.g., personal telephone calls, personal e-mail, or personal use of the copy machine).

Plagiarized another person's work (used it without giving them credit).

Invented or altered research data.

Cheated on an examination or test.

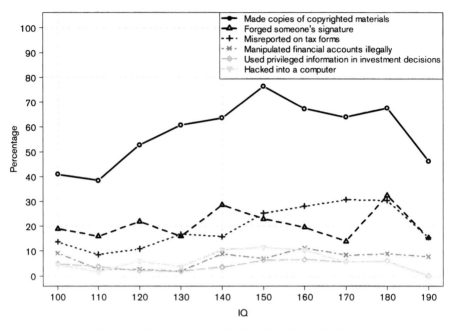

FIGURE 24. Prevalence rates for six measures of white-collar offenses by IQ.

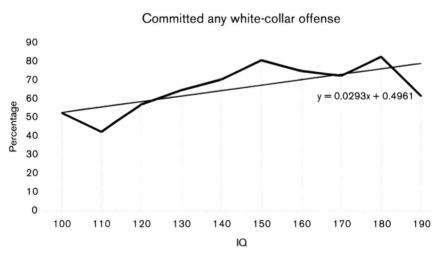

FIGURE 25. Prevalence rates for aggregated white-collar offenses by IQ. The trend line indicates a positive association between IQ and prevalence.

Some of these behaviors constitute criminal offenses, at least under certain conditions (e.g., 29 U.S.C. § 666[e] provides criminal penalties for any employer whose violation of the Occupational Health and Safety Act causes the death of an employee). Although his case is not representative, one member of the incarcerated sample described his own dramatic conviction for environmental offenses: "I am 50 years old. I have had no previous contact with any aspect of crime or the justice system, and I have been in prison for two and a half years. In real life, I'm a university lecturer, a renegade medic turned cell biologist, with about 100 scientific publications. I was arrested and charged with deliberately contaminating supermarket goods ... I was likewise charged, and again later convicted, for attempted murder."

Other misconduct offenses can lead to incarceration as well. For example, following a cheating scandal in 2015, Atlanta public school educators were sentenced, many to prison (Fantz, 2015). Other offenses can result in noncriminal professional sanctions (e.g., denunciation, retracted scholarship, loss of accreditation, suspension, or termination). Ward Churchill, known for his incendiary comments in the wake of the 9/11 attacks, was fired from the University of Colorado, Boulder, for plagiarism and falsification of data (Cheyfitz, 2009). In Europe, Diederik Stapel's (2014) falsification of data cost him his position as a social psychologist. Academic fraud is not uncommon (Broad & Wade, 1982; Klintworth, 2014), and its consequences can be great. For example, Sir Cyril Burt's twin research paved the way for Britain's tripartite educational system, but that entire system was undermined when Burt's data was denounced as fraudulent (e.g., Kamin, 1974; Mackintosh, 1995).

Table 30 identifies the prevalence and incidence rates for professional misconduct in the index and control groups by sex. Misconduct was widespread: more than 60% of all sample groups—male, female, and aggregate; index and control—reported at least one act of professional misconduct. Prevalence rates were significantly higher among index respondents than among corresponding controls (80.2% versus 72.1% in the aggregated sample). Among those reporting an act of professional misconduct in the last year, incidence rates were higher among index respondents than controls (although not significantly so); lifetime incidence rates were lower for female index respondents than female controls but were higher among male index respondents than male controls. In the aggregated sample, index respondents reported significantly higher lifetime incidence rates.

Figure 26 displays the prevalence of four professional misconduct offenses by IQ band: abuse of work privileges, plagiarism and cheating (merging two questionnaire items into a single measure), violation of safety or environmental standards, and falsification of research data. Abuse of work privileges was the most prevalent misconduct offense. Ubiquitous, it is often not treated as an offense, either by offenders or employers. One member of the high-IQ society explained that such behavior was condoned as de facto policy by management: "The abuse

TABLE 30 Professional misconduct: prevalence, incidence, and recency by index and control groups and sex

		Index (n = 465)	Control (n = 756)	χ^2	p
Male	Never committed any professional misconduct	70 (21.0)	92 (31.8)	9.39	.0022
	Have committed any professional misconduct	263 (79.0)	197 (68.2)		
	Once last year	13 (11.7)	5 (8.9)	5.9223	.1155
	2 to 5 times last year	41 (36.9)	21 (37.5)		
	6 to 9 times last year	7 (6.3)	10 (17.9)		
	10+ times last year	50 (45.1)	20 (35.7)		
	Once ever	22 (8.4)	14 (8.1)	2.4077	.4922
	2 to 5 times ever	57 (21.7)	44 (25.4)		
	6 to 9 times ever	21 (8.0)	19 (11.0)		
	10+ times ever	163 (62.0)	96 (55.5)		
Female	Never committed any professional misconduct	20 (15.9)	115 (24.9)	4.55	.0329
	Have committed a professional misconduct	106 (84.1)	347 (75.1)		
	Once last year	7 (14.9)	9 (7.1)	4.5778	.2055
	2 to 5 times last year	16 (34)	57 (44.9)		
	6 to 9 times last year	6 (12.8)	9 (7.1)		
	10+ times last year	18 (38.3)	52 (40.9)		
	Once ever	6 (5.8)	13 (4.3)	2.2949	.5135
	2 to 5 times ever	25 (24.3)	91 (30.2)		
	6 to 9 times ever	9 (8.7)	33 (11.0)		
	10+ times ever	63 (61.2)	164 (54.5)		
Total	Never committed any professional misconduct	92 (19.8)	211 (27.9)	10.19	.0014
	Have committed a professional misconduct	373 (80.2)	545 (72.1)		
	Once last year	20 (12.4)	14 (7.7)	3.8681	.2761
	2 to 5 times last year	58 (35.8)	78 (42.6)		
	6 to 9 times last year	13 (8.0)	19 (10.4)		
	10+ times last year	71 (43.8)	72 (39.3)		
	Once ever	28 (7.6)	27 (5.7)	7.8972	.0482
	2 to 5 times ever	82 (22.2)	135 (28.4)		
	6 to 9 times ever	30 (8.1)	52 (11.0)		
	10+ times ever	230 (62.2)	261 (55.0)		

NOTE: See table 13 for a description of table elements.

of work privileges consisted of using the company Xerox for duplicating my tax forms, using the phone for personal business, taking small amounts of office supplies home (sometimes inadvertently) and not returning them, and occasionally leaving the job for personal affairs. The situation was complicated by the fact that in my first technical job, these were considered fringe benefits (even by the management) and not abuses. When I first needed to take some time off for personal business, I asked my supervisor how to go about it. He said, 'Disappear.'"

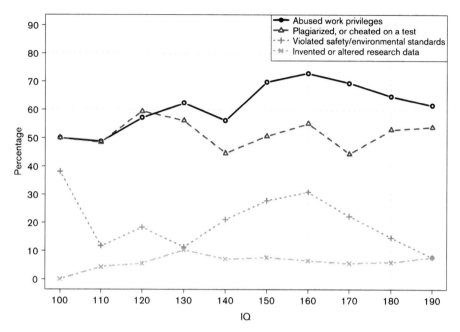

FIGURE 26. Prevalence rates for four measures of professional misconduct by IQ.

The slope of the trend line between IQ and the prevalence of abuse of work privileges is positive ($y = +0.0195x + 0.505$): for every 10-point unit of IQ increase, prevalence would be expected to increase by 1.95%. As noted in table 35, later in this chapter, the association between IQ and prevalence is also positive for falsification of research data but is negative for violation of safety or environmental standards and plagiarism/cheating.

As indicated in figure 27 lifetime prevalence rates for all five aggregated misconduct offenses are high: as is the case for drug and property offenses, lifetime prevalence exceeds 60% across all IQ levels. The relationship between IQ and lifetime prevalence of misconduct is positive ($y = +0.0212x + 0.6045$): for every 10-point unit of IQ increase, lifetime professional misconduct offense prevalence would be expected to increase by 2.12%.

VEHICULAR CRIMES

The self-report questionnaire measured four offenses related to vehicular crimes, including driving under the influence (DUI) of alcohol, driving without a license, using someone's vehicle without permission, and reckless driving:

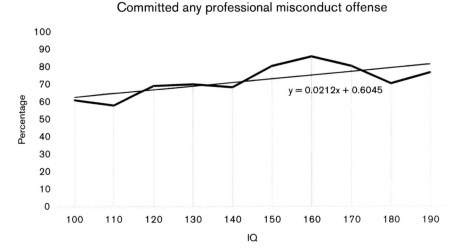

FIGURE 27. Prevalence rates for aggregated professional misconduct by IQ. The trend line indicates a positive association between IQ and prevalence.

> Consumed enough alcohol to put you over the legal limit and then driven a car.
>
> Driven a car without a license.
>
> Taken a vehicle for a ride (drive) without the owner's permission.
>
> Driven a car at unsafe speeds or in a reckless manner.

These items are illustrative, not comprehensive. The questionnaire does not measure mere speeding (an offense that virtually everyone who operates a vehicle has committed at least once), parking violations, or other traffic violations (e.g., failure to signal). It distinguishes taking a vehicle without permission (borrowing, without intent to steal) from motor-vehicle theft (counted in property offenses, described above). Vehicular homicide is counted as a violent offense. The DUI item (coded as a vehicular crime in this study and not a drug offense) does not specify any particular blood-alcohol content (levels vary by jurisdiction) and does not encompass nonautomobile violations (such as piloting an airplane or driving a boat under the influence).

A full review of vehicular crime lies beyond the scope of this book, but Smith and Kirkham (1982) find that intelligence is inversely correlated with driving violations. Low IQ drivers receive disproportionate numbers of speeding tickets and are overrepresented in intersection accidents. O'Toole (1990) reports that the motor-vehicle death rate for men with IQs between 85 and 100 is twice as high—and for

TABLE 31 Vehicular offenses: prevalence, incidence and recency by index and control groups and sex

		Index (n = 465)	Control (n = 756)	χ^2	p
Male	Never committed any vehicular offense	111 (33.3)	74 (25.6)	4.42	.0355
	Have committed a vehicular offense	222 (66.7)	215 (74.4)		
	Once last year	11 (18.0)	6 (9.7)	3.7816	.2860
	2 to 5 times last year	27 (44.3)	26 (41.9)		
	6 to 9 times last year	5 (8.2)	3 (4.8)		
	10+ times last year	18 (29.5)	27 (43.6)		
	Once ever	11 (5.0)	9 (4.8)	10.8638	.0125
	2 to 5 times ever	68 (30.6)	36 (19.4)		
	6 to 9 times ever	37 (16.7)	23 (12.4)		
	10+ times ever	106 (47.8)	118 (63.4)		
Female	Never committed any vehicular offense	49 (38.9)	154 (33.3)	1.35	.2450
	Have committed a vehicular offense	77 (61.1)	308 (66.7)		
	Once last year	6 (18.2)	22 (21.0)	1.6235	.6541
	2 to 5 times last year	16 (48.5)	42 (40.0)		
	6 to 9 times last year	4 (12.1)	9 (8.6)		
	10+ times last year	7 (21.2)	32 (30.5)		
	Once ever	3 (4.0)	28 (10.3)	4.3771	.2235
	2 to 5 times ever	18 (23.7)	78 (28.6)		
	6 to 9 times ever	11 (14.5)	35 (12.8)		
	10+ times ever	44 (57.9)	132 (48.4)		
Total	Never committed any vehicular offense	161 (34.6)	233 (30.8)	1.91	.1674
	Have committed a vehicular offense	304 (65.4)	523 (69.2)		
	Once last year	17 (17.9)	28 (16.8)	1.9185	.5895
	2 to 5 times last year	43 (45.3)	68 (40.7)		
	6 to 9 times last year	9 (9.5)	12 (7.2)		
	10+ times last year	26 (27.4)	59 (35.3)		
	Once ever	14 (4.6)	37 (8.1)	6.4367	.0922
	2 to 5 times ever	88 (29.1)	114 (24.8)		
	6 to 9 times ever	48 (15.9)	58 (12.6)		
	10+ times ever	152 (50.3)	250 (54.5)		

NOTE: See table 13 for a description of table elements.

men with IQs between 80 and 85, three times as high—as the rate for men with IQs between 100 and 115. "[P]eople with lower intelligence may have a poorer ability to assess risks and, consequently, may take more poor risks in their driving than more intelligent people" (1990, p. 220). People with low IQs also have high rates of other accidents (Gottfredson, 2005), prompting Gordon (1997) to characterize everyday life as an intelligence test.

Table 31 identifies the prevalence and incidence rates for vehicular offenses in the index and control groups by sex. Prevalence rates were high. More than 60%

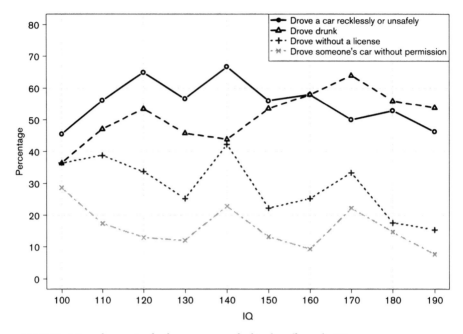

FIGURE 28. Prevalence rates for four measures of vehicular offenses by IQ.

of the respondents in all sample groups—male, female, and aggregate; index and control—reported at least one offense. Index respondents had lower prevalence rates than controls for vehicular offenses. These differences were not significant for females or in the aggregated samples, but they were significant for males. For vehicular offenses committed in the previous year, incidence rates were higher for controls than for index respondents, although none of these differences were significant. Lifetime incidence rates were significantly higher among male controls than among male index respondents, were higher (but insignificant) among females in the index group than among female controls, and, in the aggregated sample, were slightly and insignificantly higher for controls than for index respondents.

Figure 28 displays the prevalence rates of the four vehicular offenses by IQ band: reckless driving, driving under the influence of alcohol, driving without a license, and using a car without permission. Reckless driving was the most prevalent vehicular offense. The trend line between IQ and the prevalence of reckless driving has a negative slope ($y = -0.0059x + 0.5853$): that is, for every 10-point unit of IQ increase, prevalence would be expected to decrease by approximately 0.59%. As described in table 35, later in this chapter, the relationship between IQ and prevalence is also negative for driving without a license and for using a car with-

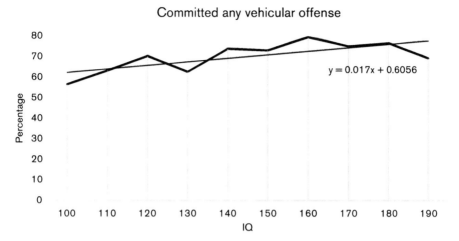

FIGURE 29. Prevalence rates for aggregated vehicular offenses by IQ. The trend line indicates a positive association between IQ and prevalence.

out permission but is positive for DUI (suggesting perhaps that DUI resembles a drug offense more than a vehicular offense). As indicated in figure 29, aggregated vehicular prevalence rates are high: as is the case for drug, property, and professional misconduct offenses, lifetime prevalence for vehicular offenses exceeds 60% across all IQ levels.

Driven by the strong positive association between IQ and DUI, the relationship between IQ and lifetime prevalence of vehicular offenses is also positive ($y = +0.0170x + 0.6056$): for every 10-point unit of IQ increase, lifetime prevalence would be expected to increase by 1.70% (see figure 29).

JUSTICE SYSTEM CRIMES

Feeley (1979) titled his classic study of a New Haven lower criminal court *The Process Is the Punishment*. He explained that even before a case reaches the judge for disposition and sentencing, simply becoming ensnared in the justice system imposes a number of pretrial costs upon defendants: fees to attorneys and bail bondsmen, wasted time, lost wages, and the like. Twenty-five years later, little had changed: the process was *still* the punishment (Bogira, 2005). Additionally, involvement with the justice system creates the possibility for new crimes against the administration of justice. After all, only after arrest can an offender be charged with resisting arrest, a decision that depends upon a host of factors (Kavanagh, 1997); only after parole can an offender be charged with a parole violation, an offense that returns approximately a quarter of US parolees to custody each year (Glaze & Bonczar, 2011). To learn more about such crimes, the self-report questionnaire measured seven offenses related (broadly) to the justice system, including draft dodging, sedition and insurrection, conspiracy (agreeing to a criminal act), resisting arrest, violating parole, perjury (lying under oath), and failure to appear:

> Taken steps to evade (dodge) a military draft or selective service.
>
> Instigated acts of rebellion against the government or agencies of the government.
>
> Made an agreement with other people to commit a criminal act.
>
> Resisted arrest.
>
> Violated the conditions of your parole.
>
> Knowingly lied while under oath.
>
> Failed to appear in court when ordered to do so by summons.

Although these offenses measure a range of justice-related crimes, they are not comprehensive. They do not, for example, include contempt of court, obstruction of justice, or malfeasance in elected office. Table 32 identifies the prevalence and incidence rates for justice system offenses in the index and control groups by sex. Prevalence rates were low. Less than 25% of the respondents in all sample groups— male, female, and aggregate; index and control—reported a justice system offense. A larger percentage of index females reported committing a justice system offense than female controls (11.9% versus 11.7%); but among males and the aggregated sample, controls reported higher prevalence rates than index respondents. None of these differences were significant. A similar pattern appears in incidence rates among those who reported a justice system offense. Females in the index group reported higher rates than female controls, both for offenses in the previous year and for offenses ever committed. Male controls reported higher rates than index males, both in the last year and ever. In the aggregated sample, index respondents reported higher incidence rates than controls for justice offenses in the last year but lower lifetime incidence rates than controls. None of the differences in incidence rates were significant.

Figure 30 displays the prevalence rates for the seven justice system offenses by IQ band. Conspiracy—making an agreement with other people to commit a criminal act—was the most prevalent justice system offense, especially above IQ 130. Nevertheless, the linear relationship between IQ and conspiracy is negative ($y = -0.0043x + 0.1551$): for every 10-point unit of IQ increase, prevalence would be expected to decrease slightly by approximately 0.43%. As described in table 35, later in this chapter, the relationship between IQ and prevalence is negative for perjury, resisting arrest, failure to appear, and parole violation; it is positive

TABLE 32 Justice system offenses: prevalence, incidence, and recency by index and control groups and sex

		Index (n = 465)	Control (n = 756)	χ^2	p
Male	Never committed any justice system offense	283 (85.0)	231 (79.9)	2.75	.0970
	Have committed a justice system offense	50 (15.0)	58 (20.1)		
	Once last year	5 (62.5)	5 (38.5)	1.1611	.5596
	2 to 5 times last year	2 (25.0)	5 (38.5)		
	6 to 9 times last year	0 (0)	0 (0)		
	10+ times last year	1 (12.5)	3 (23.1)		
	Once ever	17 (34.7)	14 (28.0)	0.6459	.8859
	2 to 5 times ever	12 (24.5)	15 (30.0)		
	6 to 9 times ever	5 (10.2)	5 (10.0)		
	10+ times ever	15 (30.6)	16 (32.0)		
Female	Never committed any justice system offense	111 (88.1)	408 (88.3)	0.0	.9466
	Have committed a justice system offense	15 (11.9)	54 (11.7)		
	Once last year	0 (0)	4 (33.3)	1.4583	.4823
	2 to 5 times last year	2 (66.7)	6 (50.0)		
	6 to 9 times last year	0 (0)	0 (0)		
	10+ times last year	1 (33.3)	2 (16.7)		
	Once ever	7 (46.7)	16 (34)	7.9149	.0478
	2 to 5 times ever	1 (6.7)	21 (44.7)		
	6 to 9 times ever	1 (6.7)	2 (4.3)		
	10+ times ever	6 (40.0)	8 (17.0)		
Total	Never committed any justice system offense	400 (86.0)	644 (85.2)	0.16	.6869
	Have committed a justice system offense	65 (14.0)	112 (14.8)		
	Once last year	5 (45.5)	9 (36.0)	0.2955	.8627
	2 to 5 times last year	4 (36.4)	11 (44.0)		
	6 to 9 times last year	0 (0)	0 (0)		
	10+ times last year	2 (18.2)	5 (20.0)		
	Once ever	24 (37.5)	30 (30.9)	5.1937	.1581
	2 to 5 times ever	13 (20.3)	36 (37.1)		
	6 to 9 times ever	6 (9.4)	7 (7.2)		
	10+ times ever	21 (32.8)	24 (24.7)		

NOTE: See table 13 for a description of table elements.

for draft dodging and insurrection. One member of the high-IQ society refrained from offenses that "might harm my fellow man. I do not hold the same beliefs about most governments and would have less compunction in those matters." As indicated in figure 31, prevalence rates for aggregated justice system offenses are low: lifetime prevalence does not exceed 25% at any IQ level.

The relationship between IQ and lifetime prevalence of justice offenses is negative ($y = -0.0048x + 0.1909$): for every 10-point unit of IQ increase, lifetime prevalence would be expected to decrease by approximately 0.48%.

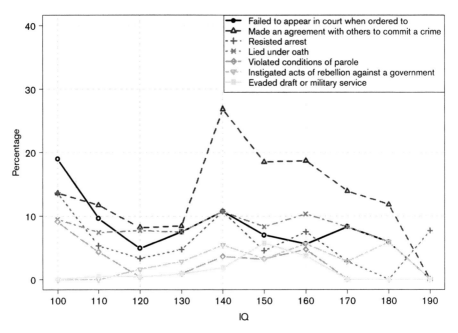

FIGURE 30. Prevalence rates for seven measures of justice system offenses by IQ.

Committed any justice system offense

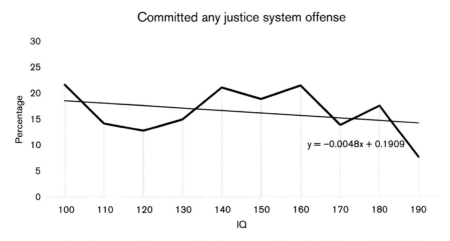

$$y = -0.0048x + 0.1909$$

FIGURE 31. Prevalence rates for aggregated justice system offenses by IQ. The trend line indicates a negative association between IQ and prevalence.

MISCELLANEOUS CRIMES

Finally, the self-report questionnaire included seven miscellaneous offenses, including counterfeiting, libel and slander, hunting and fishing without a license, blackmail, trespass, disorderly conduct, and gambling:

Counterfeited fine art or currency.

Spread false and injurious statements about someone, either orally or in print.

Fished or hunted without a license where one is required.

Blackmailed someone.

Intentionally trespassed on private or government property.

Been loud, rowdy, or unruly in a public place (disorderly conduct).

Gambled where it is illegal to do so.

Some of these offenses might have been categorized as other crime types (e.g., hunting and fishing without a license might be conceptualized as a justice system offense akin to evading a draft; blackmail, the use of a threat for gain, might be conceived as a violent crime). Because they did not fit neatly into the other eight offense categories, however, they were classified as miscellaneous crimes.

Table 33 provides prevalence and incidence rates in the index and control groups for aggregated miscellaneous offenses by sex. Prevalence rates were high. Across all sample groups—male, female, and aggregate; index and control—more than 60% reported at least one miscellaneous offense. Overall, index respondents reported a significantly higher prevalence rate than did controls (70.8% versus 64.2%). This was true of males, although this difference was not significant, but index females had a higher prevalence rate than female controls. A similar pattern appears in incidence rates among those who reported a miscellaneous offense. Index males reported lower incidence rates than male controls for offenses committed in the previous year and significantly lower rates for lifetime incidence. On the other hand, index females reported higher incidence rates than female controls for offenses in the previous year and significantly higher incidence rates for lifetime incidence. In the aggregated sample, index respondents reported lower rates than controls, both in the last year and ever. Differences in the aggregated sample were not significant.

Figure 32 displays the prevalence of six miscellaneous offenses, by IQ band: disorderly conduct, trespass, blackmail, gambling, injurious statements, and counterfeiting. Poaching (hunting or fishing without a license) is not displayed. Among these six miscellaneous offenses, trespassing was most prevalent, especially above IQ 130. The linear relationship between IQ and trespassing is positive ($y = +0.0100x + 0.3085$): for every 10-point unit of IQ increase, prevalence would be expected to increase by 1.00%. To the extent that IQ is correlated with sensation seeking (Raine et al., 2002) and novelty (Kanazawa, 2010), trespass may be

TABLE 33 Miscellaneous offenses: prevalence, incidence, and recency by index and control groups and sex

		Index (n = 465)	Control (n = 756)	χ^2	p
Male	Never committed any miscellaneous offense	91 (27.3)	86 (29.8)	0.45	.5028
	Have committed a miscellaneous offense	242 (72.7)	203 (70.2)		
	Once last year	16 (31.4)	9 (19.6)	6.3165	.0972
	2 to 5 times last year	20 (39.2)	12 (26.1)		
	6 to 9 times last year	3 (5.9)	4 (8.7)		
	10+ times last year	12 (23.5)	21 (45.7)		
	Once ever	28 (12.3)	14 (8.3)	12.6204	.0055
	2 to 5 times ever	83 (36.4)	45 (26.6)		
	6 to 9 times ever	27 (11.8)	13 (7.7)		
	10+ times ever	90 (39.5)	97 (57.4)		
Female	Never committed any miscellaneous offense	44 (34.9)	183 (39.6)	0.92	.3378
	Have committed a miscellaneous offense	82 (65.1)	279 (60.4)		
	Once last year	7 (21.9)	24 (31.6)	3.7112	.2944
	2 to 5 times last year	16 (50.0)	37 (48.7)		
	6 to 9 times last year	5 (15.6)	4 (5.3)		
	10+ times last year	4 (12.5)	11 (14.5)		
	Once ever	3 (3.9)	27 (11.6)	9.0685	.0284
	2 to 5 times ever	25 (32.5)	85 (36.6)		
	6 to 9 times ever	8 (10.4)	36 (15.5)		
	10+ times ever	41 (53.3)	84 (36.2)		
Total	Never committed any miscellaneous offense	136 (29.3)	271 (35.9)	5.64	.0175
	Have committed a miscellaneous offense	329 (70.8)	485 (64.2)		
	Once last year	24 (27.9)	33 (27.1)	1.8857	.5965
	2 to 5 times last year	36 (41.9)	49 (40.2)		
	6 to 9 times last year	9 (10.5)	8 (6.6)		
	10+ times last year	17 (19.8)	32 (26.2)		
	Once ever	31 (10.0)	41 (10.2)	0.4156	.9370
	2 to 5 times ever	108 (35.0)	132 (32.8)		
	6 to 9 times ever	35 (11.3)	49 (12.2)		
	10+ times ever	135 (43.7)	181 (44.9)		

NOTE: See table 13 for a description of table elements.

an attractive offense to people with high IQs. For all other miscellaneous offenses, however, the relationship is negative, as indicated in table 35, in the next section. The association between IQ and disorderly conduct is the most negative in the study. Consequently, the relationship between IQ and aggregate lifetime prevalence for miscellaneous offenses is also negative. The slope of the trend line is $y = -0.0081x + 0.6003$ (i.e., a 0.81% decrease in prevalence for every 10-point IQ increase), as illustrated in figure 33.

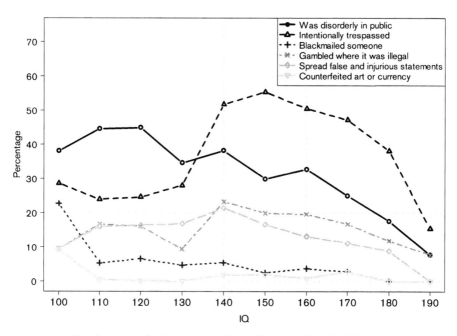

FIGURE 32. Prevalence rates for six measures of miscellaneous offenses by IQ.

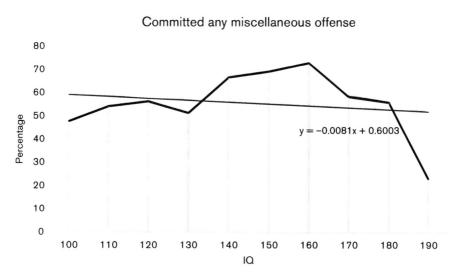

FIGURE 33. Prevalence rates for aggregated miscellaneous offenses by IQ. The trend line indicates a negative association between IQ and prevalence.

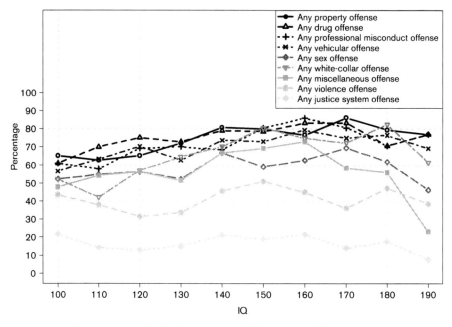

FIGURE 34. Prevalence rates for all nine aggregated offense types by IQ.

ALL CRIMES (AGGREGATE)

Combining disparate offenses can obfuscate their distinct and sometimes contradictory patterns. For this reason, the self-report offenses were analyzed by crime type: sex, violence, drugs, property, white-collar, misconduct, vehicular, justice system, and miscellaneous. For each of the nine offense types, the aggregate prevalence rates are plotted against IQ range in figure 34. Illustrations of this kind—a graph of graphs—are useful for interrogating the data by offense type and by IQ range (e.g., Are prevalence rates for each offense type high? Low? At any given IQ range, what offenses are most prevalent? Least? Are there visible differences between the left side of the distribution and the right?). However, the big question is whether there is a general relationship between IQ and propensity to commit crime. To that end, all 72 offenses were analyzed in the aggregate. In terms of general prevalence, 9 in 10 (88.9%, or 1,085) respondents reported committing at least one offense ever. More than half of the respondents (53.4%, or 652) reported committing at least one offense in the previous year. Some of these offenses were ubiquitous; others were rare. Table 34 lists the 72 offenses and indicates the percentage of the index and control groups who reported an offense.

TABLE 34 Prevalence and incidence rates for 72 offenses for index and control groups

	Index (n = 465)	Control (n = 756)
Sex		
Been paid for having sexual relations with someone	13 (2.8)	31 (4.1)
Paid someone for sexual relations	104 (22.4)	42 (5.6)
Had (or tried to have) sexual relations with someone against their will	22 (4.7)	19 (2.5)
Had sexual relations with someone under the legal age of consent (while over the age of consent yourself)	52 (11.2)	67 (8.9)
Made sexual comments or advances toward someone that you knew were unwanted	73 (15.7)	71 (9.4)
Had sexual relations in a public place	201 (43.2)	403 (53.7)
Made obscene telephone calls, such as calling someone and saying dirty things	41 (8.9)	127 (17.0)
Violence		
Used violence or the threat of violence to rob someone	12 (2.6)	22 (2.9)
Carried a hidden weapon other than a plain pocketknife	105 (22.6)	147 (19.5)
Made a serious threat that you meant to carry out	75 (16.1)	134 (17.8)
Beaten someone up seriously enough that they required medical attention of any kind	53 (11.4)	105 (13.9)
Killed another human being (excluding wartime situations)	14 (3.0)	3 (0.4)
Constructed a bomb or similar explosive device	55 (11.8)	31 (4.1)
Held someone against their will (kidnapping)	8 (1.7)	6 (0.8)
Attempted suicide	61 (13.2)	65 (8.7)
Drugs		
Used marijuana, cannabis, or hashish	250 (53.9)	412 (54.9)
Bought marijuana, cannabis, or hashish	141 (30.4)	243 (32.3)
Sold marijuana, cannabis, or hashish	62 (13.4)	109 (14.5)
Used hard drugs, such as heroin, cocaine, LSD, or ecstasy	106 (22.8)	139 (18.4)
Bought hard drugs, such as heroin, cocaine, LSD, or ecstasy	74 (15.9)	96 (12.7)
Sold hard drugs, such as heroin, cocaine, LSD, or ecstasy	23 (4.9)	47 (6.3)
Manufactured or cultivated a controlled substance (drugs)	39 (8.4)	57 (7.6)
Taken pharmaceuticals prescribed for someone else	124 (26.8)	321 (43.1)
Smuggled alcohol, tobacco, or food items (e.g., avoiding duty when crossing federal borders)	104 (22.4)	70 (9.3)
Smuggled illegal drugs or drug paraphernalia	43 (9.2)	42 (5.6)
Bought or provided liquor for a minor	147 (31.6)	267 (35.5)
Been drunk in a public place	299 (64.4)	472 (63.1)
Property		
Purposely damaged or destroyed property that did not belong to you	196 (42.2)	239 (31.9)
Stolen (or tried to steal) a motor vehicle, such as a car or motorcycle	29 (6.2)	26 (3.5)
Stolen (or tried to steal) things worth five dollars or less (including petty shoplifting)	297 (63.9)	357 (47.7)

(continued)

TABLE 34 *(continued)*

	Index (*n* = 465)	Control (*n* = 756)
Property		
Stolen (or tried to steal) things worth between $5 and $50	139 (29.9)	213 (28.4)
Stolen (or tried to steal) something worth more than $50.	77 (16.6)	110 (14.6)
Picked someone's pocket or stolen (or tried to steal) from someone's purse	52 (11.2)	58 (7.7)
Knowingly bought, sold or held stolen goods (or tried to do any of these things)	91 (19.6)	173 (23.1)
Damaged property or real estate by lighting a fire (arson)	32 (6.9)	22 (2.9)
Avoided paying for things such as movies, bus or subway rides, or food	233 (50.1)	275 (36.5)
Used another person's telephone or telephone card without their permission	55 (11.8)	82 (10.9)
Used another person's ATM (cashpoint) card without their permission	11 (2.4)	21 (2.8)
Broken into a building or vehicle (or tried to break in) to steal something or just to look around	115 (24.8)	86 (11.5)
White-Collar		
Used privileged information in making investment decisions	25 (5.4)	18 (2.4)
Manipulated financial accounts in an illegal manner	38 (8.2)	19 (2.6)
Sold or traded government or industrial secrets	4 (0.9)	2 (0.3)
Intentionally misreported income information on your tax forms	113 (24.4)	79 (10.5)
Broken into another computer (hacked)	41 (8.9)	35 (4.7)
Made unauthorized copies of commercial computer software	198 (42.9)	146 (19.6)
Made copies of copyrighted records, tapes, or videocassettes	276 (59.6)	344 (46.4)
Used an electronic device to eavesdrop or spy on someone	48 (10.4)	64 (8.6)
Tricked (or tried to trick) a person, group, or company for financial gain (fraud)	40 (8.6)	30 (4.0)
Forged another person's signature on an official document, prescription, or bank check	110 (23.8)	139 (18.7)
Professional Misconduct		
Violated safety or environmental standards	110 (23.7)	124 (16.7)
Abused work privileges (e.g., personal telephone calls, personal e-mail, or personal use of the copy machine)	315 (67.7)	407 (54.8)
Plagiarized another person's work (used it without giving them credit)	80 (18.3)	126 (16.9)
Invented or altered research data	41 (8.9)	33 (4.4)
Cheated on an examination or test	217 (46.9)	400 (53.8)
Vehicular		
Consumed enough alcohol to put you over the legal limit and then driven a car	251 (54.0)	377 (50.4)
Driven a car without a license	126 (27.2)	254 (33.8)
Taken a vehicle for a ride (drive) without the owner's permission	68 (14.6)	106 (14.1)
Driven a car at unsafe speeds or in a reckless manner	267 (57.4)	456 (61.2)

Justice System		
Taken steps to evade (dodge) a military draft or selective service	14 (3.0)	4 (0.5)
Instigated acts of rebellion against the government or agencies of the government	19 (4.1)	9 (1.2)
Made an agreement with other people to commit a criminal act	83 (17.9)	64 (8.6)
Resisted arrest	25 (5.4)	32 (4.3)
Violated the conditions of your parole	13 (2.8)	12 (1.6)
Knowingly lied while under oath	37 (8.0)	60 (8.0)
Failed to appear in court when ordered to do so by summons	33 (7.1)	49 (6.6)
Miscellaneous		
Counterfeited fine art or currency	6 (1.3)	4 (0.6)
Spread false and injurious statements about someone, either orally or in print	68 (14.7)	121 (16.2)
Fished or hunted without a license where one is required	95 (20.5)	194 (26.0)
Blackmailed someone	14 (3.0)	50 (6.7)
Intentionally trespassed on private or government property	222 (47.9)	182 (24.4)
Been loud, rowdy, or unruly in a public place (disorderly conduct)	138 (29.8)	328 (44.2)
Gambled where it is illegal to do so	87 (18.8)	111 (14.9)

NOTE: Self-report items are organized by offense type; see appendix B for the 72 items in their original questionnaire order. Numbers outside parentheses are prevalence counts (number of persons in the sample who reported an offense), and numbers inside parentheses are incidence counts (average number of offenses reported by those who reported an offense).

Although a negative linear association between IQ and crime would predict that prevalence rates would be generally lower in the index group than in the control group, this is not what was reported. In fact, index respondents reported *higher* prevalence rates on 50 of the 72 items, and on several serious items (e.g., fraud, homicide, kidnapping, arson, and breaking and entering) the index rate was more than twice that of controls. Lifetime prevalence for any offense was almost 10% higher in the index group (93.8%, or 436) than in the control group (84.7%, or 640). The oversampling of incarcerated participants in the index group accounts for some of these differences (particularly some of the low-frequency serious offenses), but it does not explain them in their entirety.

For 27 of the 49 offenses illustrated in this chapter's prevalence figures, the relationship between IQ and lifetime prevalence is negative, which is to say that as IQ increases, prevalence decreases, as predicted by most scholarship on IQ and crime. However, for 22 of the 49 illustrated offenses, the relationship is *positive*. As IQ increases, prevalence increases. The relationship between IQ and prevalence is even more remarkable when examining aggregated offenses by type. For seven of the nine offense types (i.e., sex, violence, drugs, property, white-collar, professional misconduct, and vehicular), the association between IQ and prevalence is positive. It is negative only for justice system offenses and miscellaneous offenses.

TABLE 35 Slope and *y*-intercept of offenses (most positive slope to most negative)

Committed any white-collar offense	$y = +0.0293x + 0.4961$
Paid someone for sexual relations or been paid for having sexual relations with someone	$y = +0.0276x + 0.0461$
Committed any misconduct offense	$y = +0.0212x + 0.6045$
Committed any property offense	$y = +0.0206x + 0.6311$
Made unauthorized copies of commercial computer software or of copyrighted records, tapes, or videocassettes	$y = +0.0206x + 0.4642$
Abused work privileges (e.g., personal telephone calls, personal e-mail, or personal use of the copy machine)	$y = +0.0195x + 0.505$
Picked someone's pocket or stolen (or tried to steal) from someone's purse, picked a pocket or otherwise stole items	$y = +0.0194x + 0.4913$
Consumed enough alcohol to put you over the legal limit and then driven a car	$y = +0.0192x + 0.4061$
Intentionally misreported income information on your tax forms	$y = +0.0188x + 0.0914$
Committed any vehicular offense	$y = +0.0170x + 0.6056$
Smuggled alcohol, tobacco, food items, illegal drugs, or drug paraphernalia	$y = +0.0139x + 0.1399$
Committed any drug offense	$y = +0.0133x + 0.6771$
Used, bought, or sold marijuana, cannabis, or hashish	$y = +0.0102x + 0.4854$
Intentionally trespassed on private or government property	$y = +0.0100x + 0.3085$
Attempted suicide	$y = +0.0097x + 0.0672$
Killed another human being (excluding wartime situations)	$y = +0.0056x - 0.0051$
Committed any sex offense	$y = +0.0052x + 0.5526$
Manipulated financial accounts in an illegal manner	$y = +0.0052x + 0.0395$
Committed any violent offense	$y = +0.0050x + 0.3821$
Invented or altered research data	$y = +0.0042x + 0.0371$
Broken into a building or vehicle (or tried to break in) to steal something or just to look around	$y = +0.0039x + 0.1747$
Instigated acts of rebellion against the government or agencies of the government	$y = +0.0032x + 0.0095$
Carried a hidden weapon other than a plain pocketknife or constructed a bomb or similar explosive device	$y = +0.0029x + 0.256$
Forged another person's signature on an official document, prescription, or bank check	$y = +0.0029x + 0.1899$
Purposely damaged or destroyed property that did not belong to you	$y = +0.0018x + 0.3693$
Broken into another computer (hacked)	$y = +0.0005x + 0.0565$
Used privileged information in making investment decisions	$y = +0.0004x + 0.0379$
Taken steps to evade (dodge) a military draft or selective service	$y = +0.0004x + 0.0107$
Held someone against their will (kidnapping)	$y = +0.0002x + 0.0102$
Cheated on an examination or test or plagiarized another person's work (used it without giving them credit)	$y = -0.0003x + 0.5173$
Gambled where it is illegal to do so	$y = -0.0012x + 0.1573$
Had sexual relations with someone under the legal age of consent (while over the age of consent yourself)	$y = -0.0017x + 0.1104$
Been drunk in a public place	$y = -0.0024x + 0.6191$
Stolen (or tried to steal) a motor vehicle, such as a car or motorcycle	$y = -0.0027x + 0.0668$
Had (or tried to have) sexual relations with someone against their will	$y = -0.0038x + 0.0617$

Counterfeited fine art or currency	$y = -0.0042x + 0.0404$
Made an agreement with other people to commit a criminal act	$y = -0.0043x + 0.1551$
Committed any justice system offense	$y = -0.0048x + 0.1909$
Knowingly lied while under oath	$y = -0.0053x + 0.1046$
Resisted arrest	$y = -0.0055x + 0.0903$
Driven a car at unsafe speeds or in a reckless manner	$y = -0.0059x + 0.5853$
Violated the conditions of your parole	$y = -0.0062x + 0.0605$
Used violence or the threat of violence to rob someone	$y = -0.0067x + 0.0653$
Committed any miscellaneous offense	$y = -0.0081x + 0.6003$
Used, bought, or sold hard drugs, such as heroin, cocaine, LSD, or ecstasy	$y = -0.0093x + 0.2748$
Violated safety or environmental standards	$y = -0.0102x + 0.2596$
Spread false and injurious statements about someone, either orally or in print	$y = -0.0108x + 0.1891$
Taken a vehicle for a ride (drive) without the owner's permission	$y = -0.0108x + 0.2207$
Manufactured or cultivated a controlled substance (drugs)	$y = -0.0110x + 0.1409$
Failed to appear in court when ordered to do so by summons	$y = -0.0115x + 0.1416$
Used another person's telephone, telephone card, or ATM (cashpoint) card without their permission	$y = -0.0117x + 0.1887$
Knowingly bought, sold or held stolen goods (or tried to do any of these things)	$y = -0.0140x + 0.2821$
Blackmailed someone	$y = -0.0161x + 0.1422$
Bought or provided liquor for a minor	$y = -0.0191x + 0.4317$
Made sexual comments or advances toward someone that you knew were unwanted	$y = -0.0207x + 0.3165$
Driven a car without a license	$y = -0.0218x + 0.4098$
Made a serious threat that you meant to carry out or beaten someone up seriously enough that they required medical attention of any kind	$y = -0.0226x + 0.3457$
Had sexual relations in a public place	$y = -0.0251x + 0.6059$
Been loud, rowdy, or unruly in a public place (disorderly conduct)	$y = -0.0349x + 0.5053$

The slope and *y*-intercept of these relationships are displayed in table 35, arranged from most positive to most negative.

Incidence rates—the average number of offenses reported per person reporting an offense—were *higher* among index respondents than controls, as well. Table 36 presents capped incidence rates for all nine offense types and aggregated offenses for the index and control groups. Across five offense types (sex, drugs, property, white-collar, and professional misconduct), index offenders reported more crimes per person than controls. For aggregated offenses, each index offender reported 95.5—almost 100—more offenses than controls. Indeed, the correlation between IQ and crime score (the sum of total offenses, capped at 1,000 per offense, with offenses multiplied by seriousness coefficients) is -0.02: in this study, there is almost no association between IQ score and the volume and severity of offending.

Table 37 presents the results of a binomial regression analysis (predicting lifetime prevalence for any crime, controlling for the effects of sex, age, ethnicity,

TABLE 36 Incidence rates and number of offenders for nine offense
types and aggregated offenses by index and control groups

Offense Type	Index ($n = 465$)	Control ($n = 756$)
Sex	19.9 ($n = 283$)	15.3 ($n = 417$)
Violence	27.2 ($n = 202$)	27.8 ($n = 260$)
Drugs	227.7 ($n = 373$)	194.8 ($n = 546$)
Property	48.1 ($n = 372$)	31.0 ($n = 484$)
White-Collar	57.5 ($n = 372$)	40.6 ($n = 396$)
Professional Misconduct	67.8 ($n = 375$)	42.2 ($n = 488$)
Vehicular	51.6 ($n = 350$)	54.6 ($n = 502$)
Justice System	10.5 ($n = 85$)	13.3 ($n = 103$)
Miscellaneous	35.3 ($n = 309$)	38.0 ($n = 407$)
Aggregated (All Offenses)	431.2 ($n = 442$)	335.7 ($n = 643$)

TABLE 37 Binomial regression predicting lifetime prevalence of any
offense

Variable	Coefficient	Standard Error
Intercept	2.355	0.372
Female	−0.316	0.227
Age (<25 as Reference)		
25–44	−0.071	0.262
45–64	−0.384	0.301
65+	−0.748	0.459
Ethnicity (White as Reference)		
Black	−0.569*	0.260
Other	0.033	0.433
Religion (Catholic as Reference)		
Protestant	0.489	0.660
Other	0.063	0.301
None	0.363	0.442
IQ Grouping (≤115 as Reference)		
116–129	−0.106	0.258
130+	0.731*	0.313

NOTE: When the regression analysis was conducted using IQ grouping, index/
control group, and high-IQ society/university/prison/control sample as variables,
only age (65+) and ethnicity (black) were significant terms. Because IQ, control
group, and sample are all collinear variables, tapping analogous measures, the
index/control group and sample variables were omitted.

* $p < .05$

religion, and IQ grouping). Holding other variables constant, only black ethnicity (which was negatively associated with offending) and IQ 130+ (which was positively associated with it) were significant predictors of committing an offense at any time. The regression analysis did not include all demographic variables that were collected in the study: nationality, education, occupation, income, sexual orientation, and marital status were not included. However, given the criminogenic relevance of the variables of sex and age (as described in chapter 3), it is remarkable that IQ 130+ was statistically predictive while these other variables were not.

SUMMARY

The negative linear relationship between IQ and crime presumed by many researchers would suggest that index group respondents, possessing a mean IQ of 148.7, should have lower prevalence rates—significantly lower prevalence rates— than controls and a mean IQ of 115.4. Respondents, however, did not report this result. Indeed, index respondents reported *higher* prevalence rates for 50 of 72 measured offenses. Across seven of the nine offense types—sex, violence, drug, property, white-collar, professional misconduct, and miscellaneous crimes—the index group's lifetime prevalence rates were higher than the control group's rates. For white-collar crimes, property offenses, and professional misconduct, they were *significantly* higher. If prevalence rates are analyzed by IQ instead of by index and control groups, the association between IQ and prevalence is further clarified. For sex, violent, drug, property, white-collar, professional misconduct, and vehicular offenses, the linear relationship between IQ and lifetime prevalence is positive. As IQ increases, so does prevalence. The relationship does not appear spurious: after controlling for other variables, IQ 130+ was a significant predictor of lifetime offense prevalence. Incidence rates in the study also defy conventional wisdom. Among respondents reporting an offense, lifetime incidence rates were higher for the index group than for the control group.

Of course, because offense types combined trivial and serious offenses into aggregated categories (e.g., sex in public and rape/attempted rape were both counted as sex offenses), higher prevalence rates might not necessarily signify greater criminality in any real sense. Perhaps index respondents recorded high rates of trivial and victimless offending, while controls recorded fewer—but far more serious—offenses. The data, however, do not support this hypothesis. Although the association between IQ and aggregated crime score is negative (i.e., those with higher IQs reported lower crime scores), the correlation is a mere −0.02. There is virtually no relationship between IQ and crime score (a measure of combined prevalence, incidence, and seriousness). If IQ and crime are inversely related, the strength of this negative relationship should be stronger. The inclusion of an incarcerated sample might help explain the high offense rates in the index group, but it cannot account for it entirely: there were only 30 respondents in the incarcerated sample (6.5% of the index group). The index group's lifetime prevalence rate was approximately 10% higher than that of the control group. Ultimately, the index respondents in this study reported more, not less, offending than controls.

Prosecution and Punishment

Alas, grant me madness. . . . Unless I am above the law, I am the most outcast of all outcasts.

—ALBERT CAMUS, *THE REBEL: AN ESSAY ON MAN IN REVOLT*, P. 70

Genius is often iconoclastic, inciting a reaction from the status quo. In the allegory of the cave (Hamilton & Cairns, 1989), Socrates warns that benighted men will rise against any enlightened soul who dares to utter the truth. Shaw (1957) quips, "If a great man could make us understand him, we should hang him" (p. 258). Swift similarly surmises, "When a true genius appears in the world, you may know him by this sign, that the dunces are all in confederacy against him" (in Eysenck, 1995, p. 11). Rhodes (1932) states it bluntly: "Society punishes the genius while he lives, even if its laws do not permit it to put him in gaol or execute him" (p. 37).

Empirical research bears out their claims: criminal punishment is not uncommon among the eminent. Among the 100 most influential figures in history (Hart, 1992), at least 16 were arrested, imprisoned, or executed; another 8 faced voluntary or involuntary exile; and others were engaged in unlawful revolutionary conduct. Table 38 outlines the criminality of Hart's 100. When Ellis (1927) analyzed 1,030 subjects drawn from the *Dictionary of National Biography*, 16.4% (160 of 975) of his male geniuses had been imprisoned on one or more occasions, and numerous others had escaped imprisonment only through voluntary exile. In contrast, in 2013, only 148 per 100,000 (or 0.148%) of the adults in England and Wales were incarcerated (Walmsley, 2016). Of course, Ellis measured a lifetime prevalence rate of incarceration among male British geniuses, while the 2013 English/Welsh rate describes the incarceration rate of men and women within a single year. Nevertheless, Ellis's lifetime imprisonment rate is *110 times* greater than the 2013 rate reported in England and Wales and therefore represents something greater than a cumulative average risk of incarceration over time. In his study of Swedish Mensa members, Persson (2007) reports elevated conviction rates too: "Participants were

TABLE 38 Criminality of 100 most influential figures in history

Rank	Name	Rank	Name
1	Muhammad	51	'Umar ibn al-Khattab
2	Isaac Newton	52	Asoka
3	**Jesus Christ**	53	St. Augustine
4	Buddha	54	Max Planck
5	**Confucius**	55	John Calvin
6	**St. Paul**	56	William T. G. Morton
7	Ts'ai Lun	57	William Harvey
8	Johann Gutenberg	58	Antoine Henri Becquerel
9	Christopher Columbus	59	Gregor Mendel
10	Albert Einstein	60	Joseph Lister
11	Karl Marx	61	Nikolaus August Otto
12	Louis Pasteur	62	Louis Daguerre
13	**Galileo Galilei**	63	**Joseph Stalin**
14	**Aristotle**	64	Rene Descartes
15	**Vladimir Lenin**	65	Julius Caesar
16	Moses	66	Francisco Pizarro
17	Charles Darwin	67	Hernando Cortes
18	Shih Huang Ti	68	Queen Isabella I
19	Augustus Caesar	69	William the Conqueror
20	Mao Tse-tung	70	Thomas Jefferson
21	Genghis Khan	71	Jean-Jacques Rousseau
22	Euclid	72	Edward Jenner
23	**Martin Luther**	73	Wilhelm Conrad Röntgen
24	Nicolaus Copernicus	74	Johann Sebastian Bach
25	James Watt	75	Lao Tzu
26	Constantine the Great	76	Enrico Fermi
27	George Washington	77	Thomas Malthus
28	Michael Faraday	78	**Francis Bacon**
29	James Clerk Maxwell	79	**Voltaire**
30	Orville Wright & Wilbur Wright	80	John F. Kennedy
31	**Antoine Laurent Lavoisier**	81	Gregory Pincus
32	Sigmund Freud	82	Sui Wen Ti
33	Alexander the Great	83	**Mani**
34	**Napoleon Bonaparte**	84	Vasco de Gama
35	**Adolf Hitler**	85	Charlemagne
36	William Shakespeare	86	Cyrus the Great
37	Adam Smith	87	Leonhard Euler
38	Thomas Edison	88	**Niccolo Machiavelli**
39	Antony van Leeuwenhoek	89	Zoroaster
40	Plato	90	Menes
41	Guglielmo Marconi	91	Peter the Great
42	Ludwig van Beethoven	92	Mencius
43	Werner Heisenberg	93	John Dalton
44	Alexander Graham Bell	94	Homer
45	Alexander Fleming	95	**Queen Elizabeth I**

46	Simon Bolivar	96	Justinian I
47	Oliver Cromwell	97	Johannes Kepler
48	John Locke	98	Pablo Picasso
49	Michelangelo	99	Mahavira
50	Pope Urban II	100	Niels Bohr

NOTE: Bold indicates the person's arrest, prosecution, and/or imprisonment by either secular or ecclesiastical authorities. Ranking data are drawn from Hart's *The 100* (1992).

asked asked whether they had ever been found guilty by a court of law of any kind of criminal behavior. Overall 10% answered yes and 90% no. . . . This result could be compared to Swedish crime statistics. Considering the entire population 18 years old and above (N = 7,199,337), 119,686 court rulings of varying kinds regarding crime with ensuing penalties were made. This means, in comparison to the research group, that 0.02% of all the Swedes were convicted of crime in 2006" (p. 27).

These findings indicate that genius may be prosecuted and punished at greater than average rates. One researcher even claims, "Gifted people are found in jail, just as they are everywhere else. However, they form a disproportionately larger portion of the prison population, perhaps as much as 20%. This is in contrast to the 3 to 5% of the general public who are gifted" (Streznewski, 1999, p. 264). The warden of the Los Angeles County Jail similarly writes, "The prison population IQ is higher than the non-prison population" ("Crime Doesn't Pay," 1961). Although provocative, these claims are difficult to reconcile with a substantial body of research indicating that the average IQ in prison is below the population mean of 100 (e.g., Beaver et al., 2013; Birmingham, Mason, & Grubin, 1996; Brown & Hartman, 1937; Diamond, Morris, & Barnes, 2012; Doll, 1920; Herrnstein & Murray, 1994; Stone, 1921). Some researchers interpret the below-average prison IQ as evidence of an inverse IQ-crime relationship, arguing that high-IQ offenders do not engage in crimes as frequently as those with average or low IQs. Others interpret the prison IQ as evidence of the differential detection hypothesis, suggesting that while offenders with high IQs evade detection, arrest, and conviction, offenders with low IQs are quickly apprehended. Others explain the prison IQ via the differential response hypothesis, suggesting that high-IQ offenders are treated differently than low-IQ offenders within the criminal justice system.

This chapter first describes the differential detection and differential reaction hypotheses. Second, in light of these hypotheses, it presents the rates of arrest and conviction reported within the current study. Third, the chapter explores the relationship between IQ and criminal culpability. Specifically, extrapolating from the US Supreme Court's holdings in *Atkins v. Virginia* (2002) and *Hall v. Florida* (2014), it asks whether genius criminals are *less* culpable than average offenders, *equally* culpable, or *more* culpable. Fourth and finally, it discusses the implications of IQ for the imposition of punishment. Although intelligence is associated with greater conditionability—an innate capacity for learning—and lower rates of prison disciplinary infractions, high IQ might also make prison more painful and isolating.

DIFFERENTIAL DETECTION/REACTION HYPOTHESES

Skeptics suggest that the low IQ–crime relationship is spurious and argue that below-average criminal IQs are either (1) the artifact of differences between offenders in their ability to get away with their crimes or (2) disparities in the treatment of low-IQ and high-IQ offenders. A number of researchers have explained the below-average IQ of known criminals by suggesting that high-IQ offenders evade detection, arrest, and conviction (e.g., Burt, 1955; Feldman, 1977; McCord, McCord, & Zola, 1959; Merrill, 1947; Murchison, 1926; Rutter & Giller, 1984; Stark, 1975; Sutherland, 1931). The empirical literature on the differential detection hypothesis is mixed. Murray and Herrnstein (1994) suggest that there *is* a differential detection effect but that, in the big picture, it does not matter:

> If intelligence has anything to do with a person's general competence, then it is not implausible that smart criminals get arrested less often because they pick safer crimes or because they execute their crimes more skillfully. But how much of a bias does this introduce into the data? Is there a population of uncaught offenders committing large numbers of crimes? The answer seems to be no. The crimes we can trace to the millions of offenders who do pass through the criminal justice system and whose IQs are known account for much of the crime around us, particularly the serious crime. There is no evidence for any other large population of offenders, and barely enough crime left unaccounted for to permit such a population's existence. (p. 243)

Many researchers conclude that there is no meaningful evidence to support the differential detection hypothesis (Ellis & Walsh, 2003; Miller, 2009). After all, crime is associated with low IQ in self-reported offending as well as in official statistics (Farrington, 1992). Indeed, in an elegant test of the differential detection hypothesis, Moffitt and Silva (1988) report no significant difference between the IQ scores of officially detected and undetected delinquents, although both groups had lower IQs than nondelinquent controls. The authors' result is "not consistent with the hypothesis that the IQ/delinquency relation is a spurious effect of differential police detection of low-IQ delinquents" (p. 332). Of course, in an effort to reduce "the chance of erroneous group assignment resulting from over-zealous self-report" (p. 331), Moffitt and Silva excluded subjects from their delinquent groups unless a parent, teacher, or police file corroborated their claims. Thus, a bright delinquent who successfully avoided the detection of parents, teachers, and police would have been excluded from the undetected delinquent sample. Presumably, such cases would be rare; accordingly, Moffitt and Silva's direct test of the differential detection hypothesis is considered to be the definitive study of the issue.

Other researchers, however, report evidence *for* differential detection. "[L]ow intelligence does not lead a boy into crime, although high intelligence may prevent him from going to a penal institution" (McCord, McCord, & Zola, 1959, p. 66). The negative relationship between IQ and offending is stronger for officially recorded offenses than for self-reported offending (Hirschi & Hindelang, 1977). When Murray and Herrnstein (1994) examined National Longitudinal Survey of Youth (NLSY) data, the mean IQ of individuals who were sentenced to a correctional facility was 93; of those convicted but not incarcerated, 100; of those booked but not convicted, 101; of those stopped by the police but not booked, 103, and of those with no police contact whatsoever, 106. In their reanalysis of NLSY data, Cullen, Gendreau, Jarjoura, and Wright (1997) found that IQ scores were not significantly related to self-reported offending but *were* significantly related to officially recorded offending. They concluded, "[I]ndependent of their actual levels of crime, 'cognitively disadvantaged' offenders are more likely to be jailed and processed in the system" (p. 396). Beaver and his colleagues (2013) reported a negative relationship between IQ and self-reported arrest and incarceration. Consistent with most IQ-crime research, they found an association between low IQ and offending; but after controlling for this, they *also* found that low IQ increased penetration into the criminal justice system, suggesting a differential detection effect. "[T]he fact that IQ has effects on criminal justice processing variables after the effects of self-reported delinquency are removed tends to suggest that IQ may have effects that are the result of differential detection" (p. 286).

Instead of—or in addition to—differential detection, some researchers suggest that differential *reaction* can explain the apparent inverse relationship between IQ and crime. They suggest that criminal justice officials treat low-IQ offenders differently than high-IQ offenders (Haarer, 1966; Mears & Cochran, 2013; Merrill, 1947). Menard and Morse (1984) express this view clearly: "If we eliminate the institutional reaction to IQ, the relationship between IQ and delinquency will be eliminated" (p. 1351). Of course, many IQ-crime researchers are skeptical about the differential reaction hypothesis. Jolliffe and Farrington (2010) explain: "There may be a relationship between intelligence and penetration into the criminal justice system, such that those with lower levels of intelligence are more likely to be convicted and imprisoned than those with higher levels of intelligence, but this might also reflect the relationship between low intelligence and an increase in the frequency or seriousness of offending" (p. 45).

Wilson and Herrnstein (1985) make the same argument, noting that crimes associated with low IQ (e.g., homicide, rape) have higher police clearance rates than offenses associated with high IQ (e.g., burglary, larceny). Thus, offense-based sorting, rather than reactions within the justice system, produces the low IQ–crime relationship. Hirschi and Hindelang (1977) are unequivocal in their rejection of the hypothesis: *"[T]he differential ability to avoid detection and the differential official reaction on the basis of IQ arguments are not supported by available evidence"* (pp. 582–583, emphasis in original).

Others, however, have found evidence supporting the differential reaction hypothesis. The findings of Beaver and his colleagues (2013) are consistent with the differential reaction hypothesis, and these researchers speculate that demeanor is a plausible mechanism by which low IQ might increase criminal justice penetration. Certainly, demeanor influences police decisions about whether to charge offenders with resisting arrest (Kavanagh, 1997). The ability to read behavioral cues of others and to react in socially appropriate ways—both positively associated with IQ—could influence an offender's ability to engender empathy in law enforcement officers and judges. Gath, Tennent, and Pidduck (1970) suggest that bright delinquents might be treated more leniently because of their greater ability to verbalize their problems. Further research is needed to ascertain whether low verbal intelligence, which is particularly implicated in delinquency and crime (Farrington & Welsh, 2007; Moffitt, 1993; West & Farrington, 1973), might limit the ability to communicate with justice system officials and thereby increase penetration into the criminal justice system. Examining self-reported rates of offending, arrest, and conviction in the current study—comparing index respondents to controls—sheds some light on the role of intelligence in criminal justice consequences.

SELF-REPORTED RATES OF ARREST
AND CONVICTION

Chapter 4 described self-reported prevalence and incidence rates in the index and control groups for nine different offense types. Using the same offense categories (i.e., sex, violence, drug, property, white-collar, professional misconduct, vehicular, justice system, and miscellaneous offenses), this chapter describes self-reported rates of arrest and conviction. All respondents who reported an arrest for a given crime also reported an equal or greater number of offenses (i.e., no one reported an arrest for an offense he or she had not committed, and no one reported a greater than 1:1 ratio of arrests to offenses). Convictions generally flowed from arrests, resembling a funnel in which some defendants are diverted out of the justice system while others are processed through it, as illustrated in figure 35.

That said, 28 respondents indicated that they had been convicted without a precipitating arrest (e.g., citations for minor infractions without being taken into custody) or reported more convictions than arrests (e.g., new charges laid after an arrest was made). Table 39 divides study respondents by index and control

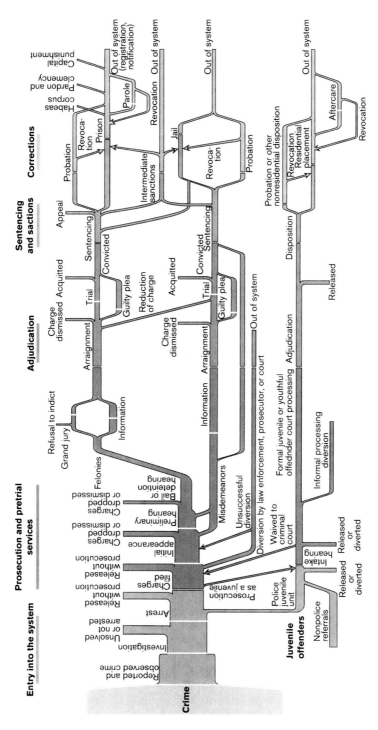

FIGURE 35. Diagram of US criminal justice system, from Bureau of Justice Statistics, 2015

TABLE 39 Arrests and convictions by offense type, index and control groups, and sex

	Males		Females		Total	
	Index ($n = 333$)	Control ($n = 289$)	Index ($n = 126$)	Control ($n = 462$)	Index ($n = 465$)	Control ($n = 756$)
Have committed a sex offense	208 (62.5)	198 (68.5)	72 (57.1)	262 (56.7)	285 (61.3)	462 (61.1)
Once arrested	3 (42.9)	1 (25.0)	0 (0)	0 (0)	3 (37.5)	1 (12.5)
2 to 5 times arrested	4 (57.1)	2 (50.0)	1 (100)	0 (0)	5 (62.5)	2 (25.0)
6 to 9 times arrested	0 (0)	0 (0)	0 (0)	1 (33.3)	0 (0)	1 (12.5)
10+ times arrested	0 (0)	1 (25.0)	0 (0)	2 (66.7)	0 (0)	4 (50.0)
Once convicted	3 (50.0)	0 (0)	0 (0)	0 (0)	3 (50.0)	0 (0)
2 to 5 times convicted	3 (50.0)	3 (100)	0 (0)	2 (66.7)	3 (50.0)	5 (71.4)
6 to 9 times convicted	0 (0)	0 (0)	0 (0)	0 (0)	0 (0)	0 (0)
10+ times convict	0 (0)	0 (0)	0 (0)	1 (33.3)	0 (0)	2 (28.6)
Have committed a violent offense	144 (43.2)	152 (52.6)	54 (42.9)	136 (29.4)	203 (43.7)	289 (38.2)
Once arrested	8 (44.4)	5 (41.7)	2 (50.0)	1 (100)	10 (45.5)	6 (46.2)
2 to 5 times arrested	7 (38.9)	5 (41.7)	0 (0)	0 (0)	7 (31.8)	5 (38.5)
6 to 9 times arrested	0 (0)	0 (0)	2 (50.0)	0 (0)	2 (9.1)	0 (0)
10+ times arrested	3 (16.7)	2 (16.7)	0 (0)	0 (0)	3 (13.6)	2 (15.4)
Once convicted	5 (33.3)	3 (42.9)	1 (33.3)	1 (100)	6 (31.6)	4 (50.0)
2 to 5 times convicted	9 (60.0)	3 (42.9)	2 (66.7)	0 (0)	12 (63.2)	3 (37.5)
6 to 9 times convicted	0 (0)	0 (0)	0 (0)	0 (0)	0 (0)	0 (0)
10+ times convict	1 (6.7)	1 (14.3)	0 (0)	0 (0)	1 (5.3)	1 (12.5)
Have committed a drug offense	275 (82.6)	248 (85.8)	104 (82.5)	362 (78.4)	385 (82.8)	613 (81.1)
Once arrested	11 (50.0)	5 (27.8)	1 (12.5)	3 (42.9)	12 (40.0)	8 (32)
2 to 5 times arrested	7 (31.8)	11 (61.1)	6 (75.0)	1 (14.3)	13 (43.3)	12 (48)
6 to 9 times arrested	2 (9.1)	0 (0)	0 (0)	0 (0)	2 (6.7)	0 (0)
10+ times arrested	2 (9.1)	2 (11.1)	1 (12.5)	3 (42.9)	3 (10.0)	5 (20.0)
Once convicted	7 (43.8)	5 (33.3)	0 (0)	3 (75.0)	7 (29.2)	8 (42.1)
2 to 5 times convicted	5 (31.3)	8 (53.3)	6 (85.7)	0 (0)	12 (50.0)	8 (42.1)
6 to 9 times convicted	1 (6.3)	1 (6.7)	0 (0)	0 (0)	1 (4.2)	1 (5.3)
10+ times convict	3 (18.8)	1 (6.7)	1 (14.3)	1 (25.0)	4 (16.7)	2 (10.5)
Have committed a property offense	267 (80.2)	214 (74.1)	101 (80.2)	305 (66.0)	374 (80.4)	520 (68.8)
Once arrested	14 (48.3)	3 (21.4)	3 (37.5)	9 (52.9)	17 (46.0)	12 (38.7)
2 to 5 times arrested	7 (24.1)	7 (50.0)	2 (25.0)	5 (29.4)	9 (24.3)	12 (38.7)
6 to 9 times arrested	1 (3.5)	3 (21.4)	1 (12.5)	0 (0)	2 (5.4)	3 (9.7)
10+ times arrested	7 (24.1)	1 (7.1)	2 (25.0)	3 (17.7)	9 (24.3)	4 (12.9)
Once convicted	12 (50.0)	4 (36.4)	2 (33.3)	5 (62.5)	14 (45.2)	9 (47.4)
2 to 5 times convicted	5 (20.8)	4 (36.4)	2 (33.3)	1 (12.5)	7 (22.6)	5 (26.3)
6 to 9 times convicted	2 (8.3)	2 (18.2)	1 (16.7)	0 (0)	3 (9.7)	2 (10.5)
10+ times convict	5 (20.8)	1 (9.1)	1 (16.7)	2 (25.0)	7 (22.6)	3 (15.8)
Have committed a white-collar offense	267 (80.2)	182 (63.0)	96 (76.2)	275 (59.5)	367 (78.9)	457 (60.5)

Once arrested	2 (28.6)	2 (66.7)	0 (0)	0 (0)	2 (20.0)	2 (40.0)
2 to 5 times arrested	2 (28.6)	0 (0)	2 (66.7)	0 (0)	4 (40.0)	0 (0)
6 to 9 times arrested	1 (14.3)	0 (0)	1 (33.3)	0 (0)	2 (20.0)	0 (0)
10+ times arrested	2 (28.6)	1 (33.3)	0 (0)	2 (100)	2 (20.0)	3 (60.0)
Once convicted	2 (33.3)	1 (20.0)	1 (33.3)	0 (0)	3 (33.3)	1 (16.7)
2 to 5 times convicted	1 (16.7)	1 (20.0)	2 (66.7)	0 (0)	3 (33.3)	1 (16.7)
6 to 9 times convicted	2 (33.3)	0 (0)	0 (0)	0 (0)	2 (22.2)	0 (0)
10+ times convict	1 (16.7)	3 (60.0)	0 (0)	1 (100)	1 (11.1)	4 (66.7)
Have committed professional misconduct	263 (79.0)	197 (68.2)	106 (84.1)	347 (75.1)	373 (80.2)	545 (72.1)
Once arrested	1 (100)	0 (0)	0 (0)	0 (0)	1 (100)	0 (0)
2 to 5 times arrested	0 (0)	0 (0)	0 (0)	0 (0)	0 (0)	0 (0)
6 to 9 times arrested	0 (0)	0 (0)	0 (0)	0 (0)	0 (0)	0 (0)
10+ times arrested	0 (0)	2 (100)	0 (0)	1 (100)	0 (0)	3 (100)
Once convicted	1 (100)	0 (0)	0 (0)	0 (0)	1 (100)	0 (0)
2 to 5 times convicted	0 (0)	2 (100)	0 (0)	0 (0)	0 (0)	2 (66.7)
6 to 9 times convicted	0 (0)	0 (0)	0 (0)	1 (100)	0 (0)	1 (33.3)
10+ times convict	0 (0)	0 (0)	0 (0)	0 (0)	0 (0)	0 (0)
Have committed a vehicular offense	222 (66.7)	215 (74.4)	77 (61.1)	308 (66.7)	304 (65.4)	523 (69.2)
Once arrested	9 (40.9)	6 (46.2)	0 (0)	6 (75.0)	9 (30.0)	12 (57.1)
2 to 5 times arrested	10 (45.5)	3 (23.1)	7 (87.5)	2 (25.0)	17 (56.7)	5 (23.8)
6 to 9 times arrested	0 (0)	1 (7.7)	0 (0)	0 (0)	0 (0)	1 (4.8)
10+ times arrested	3 (13.6)	3 (23.1)	1 (12.5)	0 (0)	4 (13.3)	3 (14.3)
Once convicted	7 (41.2)	6 (40.0)	0 (0)	8 (72.7)	7 (25.9)	14 (53.9)
2 to 5 times convicted	7 (41.2)	5 (33.3)	8 (88.9)	3 (27.3)	15 (55.6)	8 (30.8)
6 to 9 times convicted	0 (0)	2 (13.3)	0 (0)	0 (0)	0 (0)	2 (7.7)
10+ times convict	3 (17.7)	2 (13.3)	1 (11.1)	0 (0)	5 (18.5)	2 (7.7)
Have committed a justice system offense	50 (15.0)	58 (20.1)	15 (11.9)	54 (11.7)	65 (14.0)	112 (14.8)
Once arrested	7 (50.0)	2 (25.0)	1 (20.0)	3 (75.0)	8 (42.1)	5 (41.7)
2 to 5 times arrested	5 (35.7)	1 (12.5)	2 (40.0)	0 (0)	7 (36.8)	1 (8.3)
6 to 9 times arrested	0 (0)	2 (25.0)	0 (0)	0 (0)	0 (0)	2 (16.7)
10+ times arrested	2 (14.3)	3 (37.5)	2 (40.0)	1 (25.0)	4 (21.1)	4 (33.3)
Once convicted	7 (58.3)	3 (42.9)	0 (0)	1 (50.0)	7 (46.7)	4 (44.4)
2 to 5 times convicted	3 (25.0)	0 (0)	1 (33.3)	0 (0)	4 (26.7)	0 (0)
6 to 9 times convicted	2 (16.7)	2 (28.6)	0 (0)	0 (0)	2 (13.3)	2 (22.2)
10+ times convict	0 (0)	2 (28.6)	2 (66.7)	1 (50.0)	2 (13.3)	3 (33.3)
Have committed a miscellaneous offense	242 (72.7)	203 (70.2)	82 (65.1)	279 (60.4)	329 (70.8)	485 (64.2)
Once arrested	5 (38.5)	5 (50.0)	2 (50.0)	2 (50.0)	7 (41.2)	7 (50.0)
2 to 5 times arrested	5 (38.5)	4 (40.0)	1 (25.0)	2 (50.0)	6 (35.3)	6 (42.9)
6 to 9 times arrested	0 (0)	0 (0)	1 (25.0)	0 (0)	1 (5.9)	0 (0)
10+ times arrested	3 (23.1)	1 (10.0)	0 (0)	0 (0)	3 (17.7)	1 (7.1)
Once convicted	2 (28.6)	2 (33.3)	2 (66.7)	3 (75.0)	4 (40.0)	5 (50.0)
2 to 5 times convicted	4 (57.1)	3 (50.0)	1 (33.3)	0 (0)	5 (50.0)	3 (30.0)
6 to 9 times convicted	0 (0)	0 (0)	0 (0)	1 (25.0)	0 (0)	1 (10.0)
10+ times convict	1 (14.3)	1 (16.7)	0 (0)	0 (0)	1 (10.0)	1 (10.0)

(continued)

TABLE 39 *(continued)*

	Males		Females		Total	
	Index (*n* = 333)	Control (*n* = 289)	Index (*n* = 126)	Control (*n* = 462)	Index (*n* = 465)	Control (*n* = 756)
Have committed any of 72 listed offenses	319 (95.8)	253 (87.5)	117 (92.9)	387 (83.8)	442 (95.1)	643 (85.1)
Once arrested	22 (34.9)	13 (32.5)	1 (8.3)	5 (20.8)	23 (30.3)	18 (27.7)
2 to 5 times arrested	23 (36.5)	15 (37.5)	5 (41.7)	11 (45.8)	28 (36.8)	26 (40.0)
6 to 9 times arrested	4 (6.4)	5 (12.5)	3 (25.0)	2 (8.3)	7 (9.2)	7 (10.8)
10+ times arrested	14 (22.2)	7 (17.5)	3 (25.0)	6 (25.0)	18 (23.7)	14 (21.5)
Once convicted	17 (33.3)	11 (34.4)	0 (0)	7 (30.4)	17 (26.6)	18 (32.1)
2 to 5 times convicted	20 (39.2)	9 (28.1)	7 (58.3)	12 (52.2)	27 (42.2)	21 (37.5)
6 to 9 times convicted	2 (3.9)	4 (12.5)	2 (16.7)	0 (0)	4 (6.3)	4 (7.1)
10+ times convict	12 (23.5)	8 (25.0)	3 (25.0)	4 (17.4)	16 (25.0)	13 (23.2)

NOTE: Numbers outside parentheses are prevalence counts (number of persons in the sample who reported arrests or convictions) and numbers inside parentheses are incidence counts (average number of arrests or convictions reported by those who report them). Individual counts do not necessarily sum to totals because of missing data. Counts may not sum to 100% because of rounding.

groups as well as by sex. For each crime type, it identifies the offense prevalence rate (e.g., 61.3% of the index group and 61.1% of the control group reported a sex offense) and then identifies the number (prevalence) of respondents who reported an arrest or conviction for this type of offense, as well as the number (incidence) of arrests/convictions reported by those reporting arrests and convictions. For example, eight index respondents reported an arrest for sex crimes (37.5% of the eight reported a single arrest; 62.5% reported between two and five arrests). Six index respondents reported a conviction for sex offenses (half of them reported a single conviction; half reported between two and five convictions). Because of the relative infrequency (small cell counts) of arrests and convictions for most offense types, it was often impossible to calculate reliable statistical significance for the differences within male and female groupings. It was, however, possible to ascertain significance for differences in incidence rates between the total index and control groups. None of these differences, however, were statistically significant.

Conviction for a sex offense often carries enormous social stigma and can have profound legal consequences, including registering as a sex offender, residency restrictions, chemical castration, and civil commitment as a sexually violent predator (Human Rights Watch, 2007). Although lifetime prevalence rates for sex offenses were high (e.g., 61.3% of the index group and 61.1% of the control group reported one of the seven listed sex offenses), only a fraction of those engaging in these offenses were arrested for them. In fact, of the 285 index respondents reporting a sex offense, only 8 (2.8%) also reported an arrest for a sexual offense, and only 6 (2.1%) reported a conviction. Rates were even lower in the control group. Just 8 (1.7%) controls reporting a sex offense also reported an arrest, and only 7 (1.5%) reported a conviction. Index respondents who had been arrested for a sex offense reported fewer arrests per offender than did controls—half of whom reported 10+ arrests—although the difference between the groups was statistically insignificant (χ^2 = 7.29, p = .0633). That is, the chi-square statistic (χ^2), a measure of correspondence between observed and expected values, does not have a p value below .05, a common statistical threshold below which the observed result would not be expected to occur by chance. Because p = .0633 exceeds .05, the possibility that the differences between index and control groups were the result of random chance cannot be ruled out. Index respondents also reported fewer convictions than controls—half of the index respondents reported only one conviction for sex offenses, while none of the convicted controls reported a single conviction—but this difference was not significant either (χ^2 = 5.46, p = .0654). Males were more likely to report arrests and convictions for sex offenses. They accounted for 54.9% of those reporting a sex offense but 68.8% of arrestees and 69.2% of those convicted.

More than half (53.8%) of the US prisoners in state facilities are there for violent crimes (Carson, 2014). In the current study, lifetime prevalence for the eight listed violent offenses was lower than that for sex offenses: only 43.7% of the index group and only 38.2% of the control group reported a violent offense. Of the 203 index respondents who reported a violent offense, 22 (10.8%) also reported an arrest for a violent offense, and 19 (9.4%) reported a conviction. The index group, of course, included 30 respondents from the incarcerated sample, several of whom were serving sentences for violence. In the control group, rates were dramatically lower: only 13 (4.5%) of the 289 who reported a violent offense also reported an arrest, and only 8 (2.8%) reported an arrest. Among those who reported arrests or convictions for violence, the difference between index respondents and controls was insignificant, both for arrests (χ^2 = 1.31, p = .7279) and for convictions (χ^2 = 1.356, p = .4536). Again, males accounted for most arrests and convictions. They constituted just 60.1% of those reporting a violent offense but accounted for 85.7% of arrestees and 81.5% of those convicted.

The current phenomenon of mass incarceration is, to a great degree, an expression of the war on drugs. Approximately 16% of the US prisoners in state custody are there for drug crimes (Carson, 2014). In the current study, lifetime prevalence for drug offenses was high: 82.8% of the index group and 81.1% of the control group reported committing at least 1 of the questionnaire's 12 listed drug offenses. Arrest rates were fairly high in the index group (again, in part, because of the incarcerated sample). Of the 385 index respondents who reported a drug offense, 30 (7.8%) also reported an arrest for drugs, and 24 (6.2%) reported a conviction. One member of the index group, "Newton," was arrested for drug smuggling but found not guilty by reason of insanity. Newton defected to the United States from eastern Europe in the 1970s, working as a contractor for an American house builder. Together, Newton and the builder invested in an expensive house, hoping to strike it rich in California's speculative housing market, but when the market took an unexpected turn, the house was foreclosed upon. When investors came to ask about their capital, Newton realized that these men were members of an organized crime family who had been laundering drug money through the investment. Unable to repay them, Newton was given a choice: they could kill him as an example to others, or he could go to work for them, trafficking drugs until the debt was repaid.

So Newton became a smuggler, rationalizing his behavior by telling himself that no one was being hurt, by focusing on the glamor of James Bond–style night flights, sailing trips, and conspiratorial meetings. It was thrilling. Unfortunately, Newton's business partner had already approached the Drug Enforcement Agency (DEA) and informed on his partner's illicit enterprise. When Newton was approached by undercover DEA agents, he believed they were drug dealers of the highest class, polite and professional. He wrote, "After a few meetings, I did sell them one ounce of cocaine. Actually the snitch was supposed to do it himself, as the unwritten rules were, but he had excused himself at the very last minute and I had to do it myself, since I did not want to disappoint such nice people as they had appeared to be. And then, after they did pay me cash on delivery, I was feeling very safe and successful."

Another European, "Mr. S.," the head of the organized crime family, was the real target of the operation. Newton, unfamiliar with the art of trafficking, did not realize that uncut cocaine was such a valuable and illegal commodity, so when he met with the agents, he brought a whole kilogram of pure cocaine.

> The agent almost fainted when I laid a package of the size and shape of a loaf of bread on the restaurant table. He had to admit that he was some $48,000 short of the prize, since he brought only $2,000 with him. Since I didn't want to carry such a small package back and forth to and from the storage shed, where I had some 50 more of the same bags at the time [a further 100 kilos were being shipped to Newton while he was under investigation], I gave him the unit on credit, without even asking for those two grand.

The kilogram of cocaine had caught the DEA agent off guard, and Newton walked out of the meeting without being arrested. He continued about his business for two weeks, and then he went to an exclusive hotel to conclude the transaction with the agents: "When I stepped out of my car and waved at the 'drug dealer,' other DEA agents appeared on all sides. . . . [T]he clip of handcuffs was the last sound I remember before I fainted."

Newton regained consciousness in a police squad car, and upon arriving at the police station, he saw the crime boss, Mr. S., who had also been arrested. "At the very beginning of my jail time," wrote Newton, "I simply thought that I was dreaming, going through the nightmare dreams that disappear with the sunrise.

But there was an indictment and the charges coming instead." Initially, things looked grim for Newton. He was charged with drug trafficking and with gun smuggling, for shipping automatic weapons to Central America. But Mr. S. hired an excellent attorney on Newton's behalf, who had the charges reduced to possession of a controlled substance and conspiracy to sell a controlled substance. Newton wrote, "The gun charges were virtually unimportant, because it was becoming more . . . clear and certain, during the trial, that I was entrapped and persuaded by the undercover informant to modify legally purchased assault rifles." Seeing that Newton had become ensnared in a web of crime he did not altogether understand, the judge wanted to exercise clemency. The prosecutor was really interested in Mr. S. Therefore, together, the defense attorney and the judge exploited a recent car accident as a legal excuse. Because Newton had been in a coma and partially paralyzed for several months, the judge was able to justify an insanity plea. The prosecution's request for a 200-year prison sentence and a $1 million fine was reduced to 18 months in federal prison and a $10,000 fine.

Once he was serving time in Los Angeles county facilities, Newton considered becoming an informant, volunteering as a government witness in exchange for immunity—it had worked for his previous business partner, after all—but he refrained for three reasons: first, his attorney reassured him that he had a strong defense and would be out soon; second, his conscience would not allow it; and finally, Newton sincerely believed that his crime partners might have had him executed for such a betrayal.

Arrest and conviction rates for drugs were lower in the control group. Of the 613 controls who reported a drug offense, 25 (4.1%) also reported an arrest for drugs, and only 19 (3.1%) reported a drug conviction. Among those who reported arrests or convictions for drug offenses, the difference between index respondents and controls was insignificant, both for arrests ($\chi^2 = 2.91$, $p = .4058$) and for convictions ($\chi^2 = 0.97$, $p = .8097$). While males constituted 52.4% of those who reported a drug offense, they constituted 72.7% of those arrested for drugs and 72.1% of those convicted for drugs.

Property crimes are a staple of the criminal justice system: 18.8% of the US prisoners in state facilities are incarcerated for property offenses (Carson, 2014). In the current study, lifetime prevalence rates for property offenses were high, especially in the index group: 80.4% of the index group and 68.8% of the control group reported committing at least 1 of the 12 property crimes in the questionnaire. In the index group, of the 374 who reported a property crime, 37 (9.9%) also reported an arrest for property crime, and 31 (8.3%) reported a conviction. Rates were lower among controls: of the 520 who reported a property crime, 31 (6.0%) also reported an arrest, and 19 (3.7%) reported a conviction. Among males who reported arrests or convictions for property offenses, index males reported significantly more arrests ($\chi^2 = 8.41$, $p = .0383$), but the difference in the number of property convictions per convicted male was not significant (χ^2 = 2.26, p = .5200). The difference between total index respondents and controls was insignificant, both for property arrests (χ^2 = 2.91, p = .4062) and for convictions (χ^2 = 0.36, p = .9482). Males constituted 53.8% of those reporting a property offense, but they accounted for 63.2% of the arrests and 70.0% of the convictions for property crimes.

The risk of punishment for white-collar crime is generally low. One study indicated that out of every 100 suspects investigated by the Securities and Exchange Commission, 93 committed violations carrying criminal penalties but only 11 were selected for criminal treatment; only 6 were indicted; only 5 were convicted; and only 3 were sentenced to prison (Shapiro, 1985). White-collar offense prevalence was high in the current study, especially in the index group: 78.9% of the index group and 60.5% of the control group reported committing at least 1 of the 10 white-collar crimes listed in the questionnaire. Arrests and convictions, however, were rare. In the index group, of the 367 who reported a white-collar crime, only 10 (2.7%) also reported an arrest for white-collar crime, and 9 (2.5%) reported a conviction. Rates were even lower in the control group. Of the 457 who reported a white-collar crime, just 5 (1.1%) also reported an arrest, and only 6 (1.3%) reported a conviction. Among those who reported arrests or convictions for white-collar offenses, the difference between index respondents and controls was insignificant, both for arrests (χ^2 = 5.10, p = .1646) and for convictions (χ^2 = 5.42, p = .1437). Males constituted 54.5% of those reporting a white-collar offense, but they accounted for 66.7% of the corresponding arrests and 73.3% of the convictions.

Although cheating on a test or falsifying research data are unlikely to trigger a formal criminal sanction, the abuse of work privileges and safety/environmental violations *can* lead to criminal prosecution. Lifetime prevalence of professional misconduct was high in both groups: 80.2% of the index group and 72.1% of the control group reported committing at least one of the five professional misconduct offenses listed in the questionnaire. Arrests and convictions for misconduct offenses were rare. Of the 373 index respondents who reported professional misconduct, only 1 (0.3%) also reported one arrest for it; he also reported a single conviction. Of the 545 controls reporting misconduct, 3 (0.6%) also reported an arrest (all 3 reported 10+ arrests), and all 3 also reported multiple convictions. Counts were too infrequent to analyze for statistical significance, but controls reported dramatically higher incidence rates than index respondents for arrest and conviction. Males were underrepresented in arrests and convictions: they constituted 40.6% of those reporting a professional misconduct offense, but they constituted only 25.0% of arrests and convictions for misconduct. This was the only offense type in which females were overrepresented in arrests and convictions.

Lifetime prevalence for vehicular offenses was moderate: 65.4% of the index group and 69.2% of the control group reported committing at least one of the four listed vehicular offenses. In the index group, of the 304 who reported a vehicular offense, 30 (9.9%) also reported an arrest, and 27 (8.9%) reported a conviction. Rates were lower in the control group. Of the 523who reported a vehicular crime, 21 (4.0%) also reported an arrest, and 26 (5.0%) reported a conviction. Among those who reported arrests or convictions for vehicular offenses, index respondents reported greater incidence of arrests and convictions than controls, although these differences were insignificant, both for arrests (χ^2 = 6.74, p = .0807) and for convictions (χ^2 = 7.73, p = .0519). Males constituted only 52.8% of those who reported a vehicular offense but 68.6% of the arrests and 60.4% of the convictions for vehicular crimes.

Lifetime prevalence for justice system offenses was low: only 14.0% of the index group and only 14.8% of the control group reported committing any of the seven justice system offenses listed in the questionnaire. Arrests and convictions, however, were commonplace for these offenses. Criminality appeared to beget criminality. In the index group, of the 65 who reported a justice system offense, 19 (29.2%) also reported an arrest for a justice system crime, and 15 (23.1%) reported a conviction. This was, in part, a function of including respondents in the incarcerated sample. Rates were lower in the control group. Of the 112 who reported a justice system crime, 12 (10.7%) also reported an arrest and 9 (8.0%) reported a conviction. Among those who reported arrests or convictions for justice system offenses, controls reported larger numbers of arrests and convictions than index respondents. These differences were not significant, however, either for arrests (χ^2 = 5.91, p = .1159) or convictions (χ^2 = 3.75, p = .2894). Males constituted 61.0% of those who reported a justice system offense but 69.0% of arrests and 79.2% of convictions for justice system offenses.

Lifetime prevalence for miscellaneous offenses was high: 70.8% of the index group and 64.2% of the control group reported committing one or more of the seven miscellaneous offenses listed in the questionnaire. Arrests and convictions, however, were rare. In the index group, of the 329 who reported a miscellaneous offense, only 17 (5.2%) also reported an arrest, and just 15 (4.6%) reported a conviction. In the control group, of the 485 who reported a miscellaneous offense, 14 (2.9%) also reported an arrest, and 10 (2.1%) reported a conviction. Among those who reported arrests or convictions for miscellaneous offenses, index respondents reported larger numbers of arrests and convictions per person than controls. These differences were not significant, however, either for arrests (χ^2 = 1.73, p = .6312) or convictions (χ^2 = 1.61, p = .6569). Males were overrepresented in miscellaneous offense arrests and convictions: they constituted 54.7% of those reporting a miscellaneous offense but 74.2% of the corresponding arrests and 65.0% of the corresponding convictions.

Aggregating all offenses reveals high lifetime prevalence rates: 95.1% of the index group and 85.1% of the control group reported committing at least 1 of the 72 offenses listed on the questionnaire. Overall, arrests and convictions were uncommon. When asked if they had been arrested and/or convicted for *any* offense—including crimes not listed in the questionnaire—23.0% of the index group reported an arrest and 14.2% reported a conviction, a rate slightly higher than the 10% reported by Persson (2007). In comparison, 14.2% of the control group reported an arrest and 11.2% reported a conviction.

In the index group, of the 442 respondents who reported any of the 72 offenses, 76 (17.2%) also reported a corresponding arrest, and 64 (14.5%) reported a conviction. One might expect the inclusion of the incarcerated sample ($N = 30$) to inflate the arrest and conviction rates for the index group, but self-reported arrest and conviction rates in the incarcerated sample were surprisingly low (63.3% and 66.7%, respectively) because of missing data (blank answers). Even when the incarcerated sample was excluded, index respondents reported higher arrest and conviction rates than controls. In the control group, of the 643 respondents who reported any of the 72 offenses, only 65 (10.1%) also reported a corresponding arrest, and just 56 (8.7%) reported a corresponding conviction. Among those who reported arrests, index males reported more arrests per arrestee than male controls ($\chi^2 = 1.38$, $p = .7113$). Index females reported more arrests per arrestee than female controls ($\chi^2 = 2.38$, $p = .4971$). These differences in arrest frequencies were not significant. Among those who reported convictions, control males reported more convictions per person than index males ($\chi^2 = 2.72$, $p = .4371$). This difference was not significant. The higher rate of convictions among index females than female controls, however, was on the border of statistical significance ($\chi^2 = 7.77$, $p = .0510$). Males were overrepresented amid aggregated arrests and convictions: they constituted 52.7% of those reporting an offense but 73.0% of arrests and 69.2% of convictions. Arrests and convictions connote a dramatic response to serious crime, but these were often prosaic proceedings for minor offenses. One member of the high-IQ society described an arrest:

> I was arrested for not having paid a parking ticket. A policeman came into ... [my] office and took me into custody, took me to the local jail, fingerprinted me, and tossed me into a tank with a few unhappy drunks. My colleagues in the office immediately called the General Office, who sent an attorney down to get me out. It took about three hours. I later learned that a local judge had decided to crack down on "scofflaws" who didn't pay their parking tickets. . . . It was all straightened out by my paying a fine. But the arrest record had to remain, said the judge. . . . I've never forgotten those three hours inside a cage. It was terrifying.

Although table 39, earlier in the chapter, compares the numbers of arrests and convictions of males and females in the index and control groups, it does not contextualize these in light of the total number of reported offenses. For example, table 39 indicates that *all* index respondents who were arrested for sex crimes reported 5 or fewer arrests while *half* of the controls reporting an arrest for a sex crime reported 10 or more arrests. Without knowing the *total number* of sex crimes reported, it is difficult to determine whether the arrest differences between groups are meaningful. Table 40 provides information about the ratio of offenses to arrests and convictions.

TABLE 40 Ratio of offenses (O) to arrests (A) and convictions (C)

Sample	Sex	Violence	Drugs	Property	White-Collar	Misconduct	Vehicular	Justice	Miscellaneous	Total
High-IQ (n = 260)	O: 2349 (160) A: 5 (2) 1/469.8 C: 2 (1) 1/1174.5	O: 3277 (121) A: 19 (7) 1/172.5 C: 8 (4) 1/409.6	O: 37,432 (206) A: 16 (12) 1/2339.5 C: 11 (8) 1/3402.9	O: 7935 (205) A: 98 (15) 1/81.0 C: 74 (11) 1/107.2	O: 11,336 (203) A: 36 (4) 1/314.9 C: 28 (3) 1/404.9	O: 17,426 (212) A: 0 C: 0	O: 10,086 (195) A: 112 (21) 1/90.1 C: 104 (18) 1/97.0	O: 356 (44) A: 16 (8) 1/22.3 C: 17 (7) 1/20.9	O: 4887 (167) A: 9 (7) 1/543 C: 6 (4) 1/814.5	O: 95,084 A: 311 1/305.7 C: 250 1/380.3
University (n = 132)	O: 1176 (70) A: 4 (2) 1/294.0 C: 2 (1) 1/588.0	O: 1112 (41) A: 110 (5) 1/10.1 C: 4 (3) 1/278.0	O: 34,605 (104) A: 57 (9) 1/607.1 C: 30 (7) 1/1153.5	O: 4497 (108) A: 45 (8) 1/99.9 C: 25 (6) 1/179.9	O: 6399 (102) A: 10 (3) 1/639.9 C: 6 (3) 1/639.9	O: 4078 (109) A: 0 C: 0	O: 4192 (95) A: 21 (8) 1/199.6 C: 14 (6) 1/299.4	O: 296 (20) A: 16 (4) 1/18.5 C: 10 (2) 1/29.6	O: 3020 (88) A: 8 (3) 1/377.5 C: 2 (2) 1/1510	O: 59,375 A: 271 1/219.1 C: 93 1/638.4
Incarcerated (n = 30)	O: 1098 (22) A: 7 (4) 1/156.9 C: 7 (4) 1/156.9	O: 496 (20) A: 44 (10) 1/11.3 C: 41 (12) 1/12.1	O: 8661 (27) A: 53 (7) 1/163.4 C: 53 (8) 1/163.4	O: 4569 (27) A: 97 (11) 1/47.1 C: 79 (12) 1/57.8	O: 2503 (24) A: 26 (3) 1/96.3 C: 12 (3) 1/208.6	O: 1955 (23) A: 1 (1) 1/1955 C: 1 (1) 1/1955	O: 1929 (26) A: 29 (5) 1/66.5 C: 35 (7) 1/55.1	O: 210 (12) A: 22 (4) 1/9.5 C: 11 (3) 1/19.1	O: 1452 (26) A: 59 (7) 1/24.6 C: 34 (4) 1/42.7	O: 22,873 A: 338 1/67.7 C: 273 1/83.8
Reassigned (n = 43)	O: 1011 (31) A: 0 C: 0	O: 601 (20) A: 0 C: 0	O: 4222 (36) A: 2 (2) 1/2111 C: 1 (1) 1/4222	O: 896 (32) A: 3 (3) 1/298.7 C: 2 (2) 1/448.0	O: 1147 (27) A: 0 C: 0	O: 1953 (31) A: 1 (1) 1/1953 C: 0	O: 1864 (34) A: 3 (2) 1/621.3 C: 6 (2) 1/310.7	O: 34 (9) A: 1 (1) 1/34.0 C: 1 (1) 1/34.0	O: 1552 (28) A: 0 C: 0	O: 13,280 A: 10 1/1328.0 C: 10 1/1328.0
Aggregated Index (n = 465)	O: 5634 (283) A: 16 (8) 1/352.1	O: 5486 (202) A: 346 (22) 1/15.9	O: 84,920 (373) A: 128 (30) 1/663.4	O: 17,897 (372) A: 243 (37) 1/73.7	O: 21,385 (372) A: 72 (10) 1/297.0	O: 25,412 (375) A: 2 (2) 1/12,706	O: 18,071 (350) A: 165 (36) 1/109.5	O: 896 (85) A: 55 (17) 1/16.3	O: 10,911 (309) A: 76 (17) 1/143.6	O: 190,612 A: 1103 1/172.8

(continued)

TABLE 40 (continued)

Sample	Sex	Violence	Drugs	Property	White-Collar	Misconduct	Vehicular	Justice	Miscellaneous	Total
	C: 11 (6)	C: 53 (19)	C: 95 (24)	C: 180 (31)	C: 46 (9)	C: 1 (1)	C: 159 (33)	C: 39 (13)	C: 42 (10)	C: 626
	1/512.0	1/103.5	1/893.9	1/99.4	1/464.9	1/25,412	1/113.7	1/23.0	1/259.8	1/304.5
Control	O: 6370 (417)	O: 7224 (260)	O: 106,359 (546)	O: 15,007 (484)	O: 16,078 (396)	O: 20,583 (488)	O: 27,417 (502)	O: 1372 (103)	O: 15,456 (407)	O: 215,866
(n = 756)	A: 93 (8)	A: 94 (13)	A: 400 (25)	A: 335 (31)	A: 83 (6)	A: 70 (3)	A: 147 (23)	A: 411 (12)	A: 39 (14)	A: 1672
	1/68.5	1/76.9	1/265.9	1/44.8	1/193.7	1/294.0	1/186.5	1/3.3	1/396.3	1/129.1
	C: 51 (7)	C: 25 (8)	C: 323 (19)	C: 143 (19)	C: 103 (6)	C: 14 (4)	C: 101 (28)	C: 295 (10)	C: 63 (10)	C: 1118
	1/124.9	1/289.0	1/329.3	1/104.9	1/156.1	1/1470.2	1/271.5	1/4.7	1/245.3	1/193.1

NOTE: In each cell, O represents the total number of offenses committed by the sample by offense type. Following in parentheses is the number of respondents who reported committing one of the offenses. The letter A indicates the total number of reported arrests for the offense type by the sample, and the number in parentheses is the number of respondents reporting an arrest. The first fraction represents the ratio of arrests to offenses. C indicates the total number of convictions reported for the offense type by the sample, and the number in parentheses is the number of respondents reporting a conviction. The second fraction represents the ratio of convictions to offenses. Offenses were capped at 1,000 counts per each of the 72 offenses. Convictions do not always follow from arrests, and in some categories the number of convictions exceeds the number of arrests.

Data for all nine offense types and a total crime category are provided for all four index samples, as well as for the aggregated index group and the control group. Each cell contains several pieces of information. For example, the top left of table 40 indicates that the high-IQ society sample reported a total of 2,349 sex-coded offenses (committed by 160 members); five arrests (reported by 2 members of the sample), indicating that—on average—1 in every 469.8 sex offenses resulted in arrest; and two convictions (reported by 1 member of the sample), indicating that—on average—1 in every 1,174.5 sex offenses produced a conviction. By focusing on the numbers in parentheses in the table, it is possible to interpret the arrest and conviction data through a prevalence lens (e.g., 160 in the sample committed a sex crime, 2 were arrested, and 1 was convicted), but counting offenses—not just offenders—is a valuable way of comparing the relative risk of criminal justice sanctions between offense types and between the index and control groups.

Several features of table 40 stand out. First, members of the reassigned sample appear to be successful offenders. Across seven of the nine offense categories (all except for violent and justice system offenses), more than half of the sample reported offenses, but they reported no arrests or convictions for four crime types (sex, violence, white-collar, and miscellaneous offenses). Overall, they reported only 10 arrests and 10 convictions (a rate of one arrest/conviction per 1,328 offenses). Second, unsurprisingly, professional misconduct produced few arrests or convictions (especially in the index group). There were no reported arrests or convictions in the high-IQ society and university samples, only one arrest each in the incarcerated and reassigned samples, and only one conviction (in the incarcerated sample). Third, looking at *all* offenses, the aggregated index group was better able to avoid arrest and conviction than the control group. Although 1 in every 129.1 offenses resulted in an arrest for the control group, the index group was able to commit 172.8 offenses per arrest. The difference is even more striking for convictions: 1 in every 193.1 offenses resulted in a conviction in the control group, but the index group was able to commit 304.5 offenses per conviction. The data suggest that high-IQ respondents were more successful in their crimes than were controls.

Of course, given research indicating an association between low IQ and penetration into the criminal justice system (e.g., Beaver et al., 2013; Herrnstein & Murray, 1994), the index group (with a mean IQ of 148.7) *should* have reported less contact with the criminal justice system than the control group (with a mean IQ of 115.4). In the current study, however, index respondents reported *higher* prevalence rates of arrest (17.2% versus 10.1%) and conviction (14.5% versus 8.7%) than controls. In fact, members of the index group who reported an offense reported higher arrest rates than controls across eight of the nine offense types. For violent, white-collar, vehicular, and justice system offenses, the index arrest rate was twice that of the control rate. Only among professional misconduct offenses, where just four people in the study reported an arrest, did the control arrest rate exceed the index rate. The high arrest and conviction rates of the index group cannot be explained away as an artifact of the incarcerated sample for, even without the incarcerated respondents, the index group reported higher arrest and conviction rates than the control group.

Examining arrests and convictions as a function of total reported offenses, however, alters the perspective. After all, many respondents reported not just one offense, but many offenses; they reported not just one arrest or conviction, but multiple arrests and multiple convictions. In particular, the index group reported multiple offenses, but relatively few arrests and convictions; controls reported fewer offenses, but multiple counts of arrest and conviction. So, when examining offenses instead of offenders, a different picture emerges. As a function of total offenses, the index group had fewer arrests and convictions than the control group. They appeared to be slightly better at avoiding conviction once arrested (84.2% of those who had been arrested also reported a conviction in the index group, while the corresponding rate was 86.2% among controls). The high-IQ respondents got away with their offenses more often, providing support for the differential detection and differential reaction hypotheses. In light of this finding, a discussion of the implications of high IQ for criminal culpability may be warranted.

INVERTING *ATKINS*: CRIMINAL GENIUS AND CULPABILITY

Since at least the Hellenic period, criminal judges have recognized "psychiatric" conditions (Finkel, 1988). Under Roman law, insanity operated as a complete defense—like an animal, an insane person could not be held responsible in any way, although that person's "keeper" could be liable in tort (Milhizer, 2004). Early judges established rules to protect children, "lunatics" (the mentally ill), and "idiots" (the mentally retarded). The tenth-century laws of English king Æthelred treated those who did not choose their crime differently from those who did, and Æthelred's successor, Cnut, placed even more emphasis on mental states (Walker, 1968). In the thirteenth century, Henry de Bracton argued that offenders who lacked understanding of their actions were akin to animals and therefore should be treated leniently. In the seventeenth century, Sir Edward Coke differentiated the idiot who suffered from *fatuitas* (severe or profound retardation) from the idiot who suffered from *stultitia* (less severe impairment, but still below-average intelligence); and Hale (1800) devoted the fourth chapter of the *History of the Pleas of the Crown* to "the defect of ideocy, madness and lunacy, in reference to criminal offences and punishments" (p. 29). In the eighteenth century, Blackstone (1769/1841) decreed that "idiots and lunatics are not chargeable for their own acts, if committed when under these incapacities; no, not even for treason itself" (p. 16).

The US Supreme Court acknowledged the jurisprudential relevance of mental capacity in several cases involving capital punishment. In *Ford v. Wainwright* (1986), for example, the court prohibited the execution of the insane. In *Roper v. Simmons* (2005), the court prohibited the execution of defendants who were under 18 at the time of their crime. And in *Atkins v. Virginia* (2002), the court held that the Eighth Amendment of the Constitution prohibits the execution of mentally retarded defendants.

In *Atkins,* the majority reasoned that the execution of the mentally retarded failed to satisfy the two fundamental social purposes of the death penalty: retribution and deterrence. Retribution is served when parity exists between the most egregious of crimes (murder) and the most severe of punishments (death). Because the mentally retarded defendant has a "diminished ability to understand and process information, to learn from experience, to engage in logical reasoning, or to control impulses" (Atkins v. Virginia, 2002, p. 320), the retarded defendant *cannot* be sufficiently culpable to justify the death penalty. Deterrence is served when the increased punishment of one defendant inhibits the likelihood of offending in others. But the same limited cognitive abilities that reduce the culpability of the mentally retarded also make them less able to process information about the risk of execution. The mentally retarded are less deterred by capital punishment. The *Atkins* majority also expressed concerns about the risk of false confessions, the risk that juries would ascribe lack of remorse to retarded defendants based on their demeanor, and the risk that mental retardation could simultaneously operate as a mitigating factor but increase the perceived risk of future dangerousness (an aggravating factor used to justify the imposition of capital punishment). Citing increasing numbers of state legislatures that prohibited the execution of mentally retarded defendants, the views of professional and religious organizations, and public opinion polls, the *Atkins* majority concluded that there was sufficient evidence of a national consensus of what have previously been characterized as the "evolving standards of decency that mark the progress of a maturing society" (Trop v. Dulles, 356 U.S. 86, at 101, 1958) and struck down the practice. In 2014, in *Hall v. Florida,* the court clarified its decision in *Atkins* and ruled that diagnoses of mental retardation must be holistic and cannot rely on a bright-line threshold of IQ 70.

Extrapolating from the Supreme Court's logic in *Atkins* and *Hall* can shed light on the issue of culpability and cognition. After all, given the symmetrical nature of the intelligence distribution, the criminal genius (IQ ~>130) is as distant from the population IQ mean as the mentally retarded person (IQ ~<70). It is possible to invert the proportionality analysis employed in *Atkins* to evaluate the culpability of offenders with 130+ IQs and to understand whether the criminal genius should be (1) punished the *same* as everyone else, (2) punished *more,* or (3) punished *less.* Practical adjudication of criminal genius, however, could prove difficult:

If the alleged genius of a defendant were to become a factor in a criminal trial, the defense and prosecution would be compelled to prove their case in a trial before a judge and a jury. In a sense, we have a model of how this would work in the sanity trials following some criminal convictions. The legal justification for sanity trials, however, has long been sanctioned by law and tradition, and there are at least some standards which a judge and a jury can follow. But though a judge may think that he has a brain-twister as he works his way through the maze of contradictory reasonings of two opposing psychiatrists who have been called as witnesses by the prosecution and defense, this would be nothing as compared to the evidence given in a trial to determine whether or not a man was a genius. (Lipton, 1970, pp. 246–47)

The first approach to the punishment of the genius is—uncontroversially—to punish high-IQ offenders like everyone else. This approach, exemplifying the words etched upon the west pediment of the Supreme Court—"Equal Justice under Law" (Hennings, 1957)—treats intelligence as a threshold variable. All offenders who possess the requisite quantum of understanding are subjected to the same punishments. Thus, although they may commit identical crimes for very different reasons, the genius offender with an IQ score of 140, the average offender with an IQ score of 100, and the dull offender with an IQ score of 80 all receive the same punishment. This approach focuses upon offenses, not offenders. So long as an offender possesses enough intelligence to form the requisite guilty mind (*mens rea*) to commit a crime, his IQ score is irrelevant to matters of culpability and punishment. Thus, IQ operates like age: below a certain threshold, the quality assumes penological significance, but once that threshold is crossed, increases in the variable no longer matter. Under the court's holding in *Roper v. Simmons* (2005), the 17-year-old cannot be sentenced to death, but the 21-year-old is punished in the same way as is the 30-year-old, the 50-year-old, and the 70-year-old. This approach simplifies the adjudication of criminal sentences, but it ignores the influence that IQ exerts on retribution and deterrence. The defendant with a genius-level IQ, by definition, has an unusual capacity to engage in logical reasoning, to abstract principles from concrete events, and to process information. The genius may also be less impulsive (Lynam, Moffitt, & Stouthamer-Loeber, 1993). If that is so, under a proportionality analysis from *Atkins,* the genius might deserve *more* punishment for a criminal action.

Under the provisions of section 2.02 of the Model Penal Code (American Law Institute, 1985), offenders who engage in crimes purposefully are more culpable than offenders who do so knowingly, recklessly, or negligently. Purposefully choosing crime implies a kind of *scienter* (knowledge of the wrongfulness of the act) and a heightened *mens rea*. A similar rationale explains why first-degree murder is punishable by death under common law, while second-degree murder is not: a homicide committed in a willful, deliberate, and premeditated manner is intuitively more blameworthy than a murder that is committed impulsively. Because he is less impulsive, processes information more efficiently, and possesses greater foresight, the criminal genius's *mens rea* more resembles the highly culpable mental states of purpose or knowledge than the less culpable states of recklessness or negligence. The criminal genius who deliberately kills might transcend first-degree murder ("murder one") to approach something like "murder zero." Therefore, retributive principles might militate for punishing the genius *more* than offenders with average IQ scores. In terms of deterrence, since the genius is less impulsive and may be more aware of the costs and benefits associated with criminal conduct, increased punishment might successfully deter her. The genius, more than most, might be able to overcome bounded rationality (Korobkin & Ulen, 2000) and appreciate—in a way that many cannot—that a very long sentence multiplied by even a minimal risk of punishment is economically equivalent to a very brief sentence with a high risk of punishment. Of course, the genius may also appreciate that the risk of detection and punishment is low, especially for offenses with low rates of arrest. The genius may then choose crime, knowing that the likelihood of disappearing into the "dark figure" of undetected, unprosecuted, and unpunished crimes is great. Thus, in order to adequately deter genius criminals from exploiting differential detection, it may be necessary to punish them *more* severely than average offenders.

On the other hand, society might choose to punish the criminal genius *less*. Perhaps, heeding the Roman maxim *quod licet Jovi, non licet bovi* (what is permitted to Jupiter is forbidden to an ox), society should not punish the genius at all. In the *Politics,* Aristotle (350 BCE/1941) suggests that "legislation is necessarily concerned only with those who are equal in birth and capacity; and that for men of pre-eminent virtue there is no law—*they are themselves a law*" (p. 1195, emphasis added). Perhaps geniuses, knowing more and seeing farther, should not be subjected to criminal laws in the same way that other citizens are. Perhaps, if society's laws are blinkered and myopic, geniuses should be allowed to transgress them without penalty. It has been argued that geniuses, possessing superior moral reasoning and self-restraint, are more moral than others: "Morality depends on two things: (a) the ability to foresee and to weigh the possible consequences for self and others of different kinds of behavior; and (b) upon the willingness and capacity to exercise self-restraint. . . . Moral judgment, like business judgment, social judgment, or any kind of higher thought process, is a function of intelligence" (Terman, 1916, p. 11).

For decades, scholars have been interested in the relationships between intelligence, moral reasoning, and crime (e.g., Chassell, 1935; Westermarck, 1912). "A higher than average intelligence linked to a lower than average ethic is a positive menace to society" (Drews, in Sanderlin, 1979, p. 53). Kohlberg (1984) proposes an influential theory of moral maturation, distinguishing six levels of moral reasoning that span preconventional, conventional, and postconventional approaches (table 41).

TABLE 41 Stages of moral reasoning

Type	Stage	Description
Preconventional	1	Avoidance of punishment
	2	Desire for reward or benefit
Conventional	3	Anticipation of disapproval of others, whether real or imagined
	4	Anticipation of dishonor and guilt over concrete harm done to others
Postconventional	5	Concern about maintaining the respect of equals and the community, as well as concern for self-respect
	6	Adherence to universal principles

NOTE: Derived from Kohlberg, 1994, pp. 35–36.

Moral maturation theory suggests that because people with high IQs possess superior cognitive abilities, and because moral reasoning is a form of cognition, those with high IQs do not engage in crime because their moral decision making is more effective (Ellis & Walsh, 2003). Available research supports this claim, indicating that people with high IQs *do* engage in more sophisticated levels of moral reasoning (Karnes & Brown, 1980; Narváez, 1993): "While low IQ children uniformly exhibit immature moral thinking, those with high IQ scores can exhibit either mature or immature thinking" (Kohlberg, 1994, p. 45). Available research also suggests that offenders engage in lower levels of moral reasoning (Nelson, Smith, & Dodd, 1990; Stams et al., 2006). But Langdon, Clare, and Murphy (2011) found that adults with intellectual disability (mental retardation) are *less* likely to engage in illegal behavior, suggesting a curvilinear relationship (cf. Schwartz et al., 2015). After all, postconventional (stage five and six) moral reasoning is tethered not to laws but to universal principles (e.g., dignity, liberty, or sanctity of life) and sometimes produces conflicts between law and morality (Oleson, 2007a). Thoreau (1854/2000)—jailed for refusing to pay a poll tax—enjoined people to follow their internal sense of morality, even when it conflicts with the law. Many luminaries have been punished for making that choice: Socrates, Jesus Christ, Joan of Arc, Gandhi, and Martin Luther King Jr.

It might seem correct to punish these figures less, or not at all, than average criminals. But it is not always easy to distinguish the iconoclast from the criminal. When National Security Administration contractor Edward Snowden leaked classified documents about domestic US surveillance, some condemned him as a traitor who placed US lives at risk while others hailed him as whistleblower and a hero (Rall, 2015). Euthanasia activist "Dr. Death" Jack Kevorkian was convicted of second-degree murder in 1999 for his participation in the death of Thomas Youk, but he was hailed as "a medical hero" in the *British Medical Journal* (Roberts & Kjellstrand, 1996). Theodore Kaczynski was sentenced to eight terms of life imprisonment after accepting responsibility for the Unabomber crimes, but although he can be understood as a serial killer, his crimes also can be understood as actions of political necessity (Oleson, 2007b); Nathan Leopold and Richard Loeb believed that their thrill-kill murder of 14-year-old Bobby Franks would demonstrate that they were Nietzschean supermen, who lived beyond conventional categories of good and evil.

Perhaps, however, it is wrong to assume that any single approach to culpability applies equally to all criminal geniuses. Like the relationship between IQ and offending, the relationship between IQ and culpability might be curvilinear. Culpability could increase with IQ up to a point (e.g., 130 to 150) but decrease once IQ surpasses that level. If so, some geniuses should be punished the same as everyone else (or perhaps punished more, in light of retributive and deterrent considerations), but other geniuses might be excused for their crimes. The reason for excusing them, however, is not that they are like gods, operating above the law, but because their cognitive abilities render them functionally insane.

Although *Genetic Studies of Genius* rejected the stereotype of genius as pathological (Terman, 1926), other research shows that very high IQ scores are frequently associated with serious social and emotional problems (Dauber & Benbow, 1990; Janos, Fung, & Robinson, 1985; Kincaid, 1969; Winner, 2000). Being labeled "gifted" as a child is associated with midlife doubts about living up to one's potential and with diminished well-being at age 80 (Holahan & Holahan, 1999). Some researchers have raised the possibility that, like the relationship between IQ and crime, "the relationship between IQ and adjustment is curvilinear, changing from positive to negative at some point within the gifted range" (Grossberg & Cornell, 1988, p. 267). IQ scores of 160+ are associated with reduced self-esteem and increased risk of isolation, loneliness, and unhappiness (Gross, 1993). Even Terman, the unhesitating champion of high IQ, acknowledged that individuals with 170+ IQ scores frequently suffer from adjustment problems and confront "one of the most difficult problems of social adjustment that any human being is ever called upon to meet" (Burks, Jensen, & Terman, 1930, p. 265). Reanalyzing the Terman data, another study found that while only 13% of men with verbal intelligence scores below 98 were maladjusted, 25% of those with scores between 117 and 136 were, and 45% of men with scores greater than 175 were (Towers, 1990).

Towers (1988) theorizes that 160+ IQ geniuses face obstacles that 130–155 IQ geniuses do not because of the shape of the IQ distribution. People with IQs between 125 and 155 are more intelligent than most of their peers, allowing them to become confident leaders. There are also enough people in that IQ range to establish a cohort of giftedness. As Hollingworth (1942) notes, however, "[T]hose of 170 IQ and beyond are too intelligent to be understood by the general run of persons with whom they make contact. They are too infrequent to find congenial companions. They have to contend with loneliness and personal isolation" (p. 265). Herrnstein and Murray (1994) further elaborate this kind of cognitive stratification: "This does

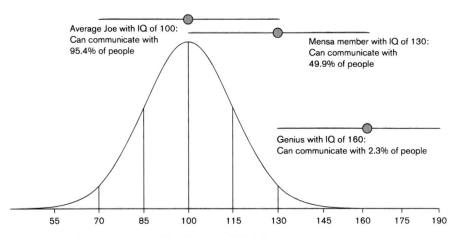

FIGURE 36. Communications gulf as function of IQ differences.

not mean that a member of the cognitive elite never crosses paths with a person with a low IQ, but the encounters that matter tend to be limited. The more intimate or more enduring the human relationship is, the more likely it is to be among people similar in intellectual level" (p. 25). Towers (1988) suggests a difference of roughly 30 IQ points, or two standard deviations, makes authentic communication between different levels of intelligence impossible.

If Towers is correct, by virtue of the shape of the IQ distribution (shown in figure 36), an average Joe with an IQ of 100 can communicate with 95% of people—that is, with others at the population mean of 100, plus or minus two standard deviations (μ +/− 2σ)—although half of those he encounters will be smarter than him. A Mensa member, on the other hand, with an IQ of 130 (μ + 2σ) can engage in genuine communication with 50% of people—everyone from the population mean of 100 up to those with a 160 IQ. She will be intellectually superior to almost 48% of them but still able to carry on authentic conversation with the 2% possessing higher IQ scores. Yet the individual with an IQ of 160 (μ + 4σ) can engage in genuine communication with less than 3% of human beings. Any such communication depends upon finding individuals with borderline genius intelligence (~130 IQ). Of course, the higher the IQ, the smaller the pool of individuals within two standard deviations. Individuals with IQ scores of 190+ (μ + 6σ or higher)—people like Francis Galton, Albert Einstein, or Nathan Leopold—could engage in genuine communication with only 0.003% of the population. Even given the effects of assortative association, the likelihood of meeting an intellectual equal would be remote (only one in a billion people possess such an IQ score). For William James Sidis, whose IQ was estimated to lie between 250 and 300 (μ + 10–13σ) (Wallace,

1986), genuine communication with another human being was statistically impossible (cf. Colman 1993).

In practice, excusing criminal conduct by reason of insanity simply because the defendant had a genius-level IQ would be difficult. The widely employed *M'Naghten* test asserts that a defendant is not guilty by reason of insanity if, "at the time of the committing of the act, the party accused was labouring under such a defect of reason, from disease of the mind, as not to know the nature and quality of the act he was doing, or if he did know it, that he did not know he was doing what was wrong" (M'Naghten's Case, 1843). Although the "disease of mind" element has been interpreted broadly in most jurisdictions, even courts that include mental defect (retardation) within the definition would be reluctant to include genius within its ambit. Many nineteenth-century degenerationists understood genius as mental disease, but thanks to the work of Terman and others, genius today connotes superior function and health, not pathology.

Establishing genius as a "disease of mind" is not necessarily a doomed endeavor, but it would require demonstrating that genius, the reciprocal state of mental retardation, can also result in maladaptive defects of communication, self-care, independent living, social/interpersonal skills, use of community resources, self-direction, functional academic skills, work, leisure, health, and safety (American Psychiatric Association, 2013). Furthermore, even if the disease prong of *M'Naghten* is established, the genius offender must also prove that he did not know the nature and quality of his actions or, if he did know them, did not know they were wrong. Of course, a high IQ would probably leave the genius criminal better equipped to appreciate the nature of her acts. The other wrongfulness prong may hold promise, however. If a court interprets the wrongfulness prong as requiring a lack of knowledge about *legal* wrongness, the insanity defense will almost certainly be precluded. Inasmuch as the genius possesses knowledge of the law but lacks an appropriate affective response to it, he resembles the psychopath (Cleckley, 1982; Hare, 1993) and, like the psychopath, would not be able to exploit his mental state as a legal defense (Mei-Tal, 2002). However, if demonstrating a lack of knowledge about *moral* wrongness can satisfy the wrongfulness prong, the genius may qualify. The genius may understand the wrongfulness of her actions in a manner alien to most people: she may know that her actions were technically illegal but, compelled by postconventional moral reasoning, may follow "higher laws" (Thoreau, 1854/2000). Understanding more and seeing farther than the rest of society, the genius's actions may be consistent with rationally derived moral principles but appear wrong, bizarre, irrational, and inexplicable to others.

In reality, a successful insanity defense on the basis of genius under *M'Naghten* is unlikely: it would require both the court's acceptance of genius as a mental disorder and satisfying the wrongfulness prong with moral knowledge. Nevertheless, in capital cases, high IQ has been introduced as mitigation evidence (e.g., Trepal v. State, 1993). The same psychological considerations that underlie the *Atkins* decision should apply with equal force in the case of the genius criminal. Even in noncapital cases, the cognitive differences of the high-IQ offender may justify reduced culpability. After all, given the symmetry of the normal curve, "[i]ndividuals who are mentally retarded or gifted share the burden of deviance from the norm, in both a development and a statistical sense" (Robinson, Zigler, & Gallagher, 2000, p. 1413). The genius with an IQ of 180 is as distant from the psychometric mean as is the "idiot" with an IQ of 20 (who was treated with leniency even under early English law).

CHALLENGES IN PUNISHING CRIMINAL GENIUS

Whether the judge chooses to punish the genius criminal the *same* as everyone else, to punish him *more,* or to punish him *less,* the high-IQ criminal's cognitive abilities have practical implications for the imposition of punishment. Courts impose punishments on the basis of several—sometimes competing—considerations. Punishment serves other collateral functions, but four cornerstone theories shape most penological thinking. Three of these theories of punishment are consequentialist in nature: deterrence (e.g., Zimring & Hawkins, 1973), incapacitation (e.g., Cohen, 1983), and rehabilitation (e.g., Ward & Maruna, 2007). These theories focus upon the prevention of future criminal acts. Of course, doing so raises thorny philosophical questions. Murphy and Coleman (1990) ask how the end of punishment can be prevention, since punishment is imposed after the crime has already occurred. In the *Protagoras,* Plato provides one answer: "In punishing wrongdoers, no one concentrates on the fact that a man has done wrong in the past, or punishes him on that account, unless taking blind vengeance like a beast. No, punishment is not inflicted by a rational man for the sake of the crime that has been committed—after all one cannot undo what is past—but for the sake of the future, to prevent either the same man or, by the spectacle of his punishment, someone else, from doing wrong again" (Hamilton & Cairns, 1989, p. 321).

But deterring the conduct of one person by punishing the behavior of another has been condemned as unjust (Olmsted, 1964). Accordingly, nonconsequentialists do not punish to influence contingent, future crimes; rather, they seek to redress past wrongs. The fourth theory of punishment—retribution—is related to deontological conceptions of duty and responsibility (von Hirsch, 1976). In a forceful characterization, Kant (1796/1887) explains:

> Even if a Civil Society resolved to dissolve itself with the consent of all its members—as might be supposed in the case of a People inhabiting an island resolving to separate and scatter themselves throughout the whole world—the last Murderer lying in

the prison ought to be executed before the resolution was carried out. This ought to be done in order that every one may realize the desert of his deeds, and that blood guiltiness may not remain upon the people; for otherwise they might all be regarded as participators in the murder as a public violation of Justice. (p. 198)

For much of the twentieth century, rehabilitation was out of favor. Indeed, in *Williams v. New York* (1949), the US Supreme Court proclaimed, "Retribution is no longer the dominant objective of the criminal law" (p. 248). But, "[o]ver the last quarter of the twentieth century and into the early part of the twenty-first century, retributivism has reestablished itself as the dominant theory behind criminal justice" (Haist, 2009, p. 799). In *Spaziano v. Florida* (1984), the Supreme Court announced that retribution "is an element of all punishments society imposes" (1p. 462).

Combining the four cornerstones of punishment can be difficult. A retrospective, deontological approach (retribution) to punishment may be irreconcilable with a prospective, consequentialist approach (deterrence, incapacitation, and rehabilitation; Robinson, 2001; Slobogin, 2009). Shaw (1977) describes the tension between retribution and rehabilitation with a wry syllogism: "Now, if you are to punish a man retributively, you must injure him. If you are to reform him, you must improve him. And men are not improved by injuries" (p. 287). Nevertheless, most judges take an eclectic approach to sentencing, employing no single approach but drawing upon all four.

Judges also limit punishment to what is necessary (e.g., 18 U.S.C. § 3553[a]). After all, punishment involves the deliberate imposition of pain (Hart, 1968). In *On Crimes and Punishments* (1764/1995), Beccaria argues "every act of authority of one man over another, for which there is not an absolute necessity, is tyrannical" (p. 17). Duff and Garland (1994) explain, "[T]o justify a system of punishment we must show not only that it does some good, or prevents some evil, but also that no available alternative practice would achieved as much or more good at lower cost" (p. 6).

In light of these considerations, the punishment of the criminal genius raises interesting issues. As a general matter, it should be easier to punish the high-IQ criminal than the average or dull offender: two of the hallmarks of intelligence are the ability to learn from experience and to think abstractly (Gottfredson, 1997). Even minor punishments—even the *threat* of punishment—should be sufficient to deter the genius from future criminal conduct. In Brecht's play *Galileo* (1966), when Pope Urban VIII instructs his Inquisitor not to torture the heretical physicist Galileo ("At the very most, he may be shown the instruments"), the Inquisitor replies ominously, "That will be adequate, Your Holiness. Mr. Galilei understands machinery" (p. 110).

Yet this same capacity for learning, abstract thought, and problem solving also makes the high-IQ prisoner a greater escape risk. Frank Lee Morris, the prisoner who led the 1962 escape of three prisoners from Alcatraz, had an IQ of 133 (McFadden, 2012). Richard Matt, one of the two "Shawshank" prisoners who escaped from Clinton Correctional Facility in 2015, was described as possessing "a genius IQ" (Michel, 2015). Many offenders assigned to high-security prison custody on the basis of sentence length, risk of disruption, or escape risk possess high IQ scores. As noted in chapter 1, Leavenworth penitentiary prisoners had aggregate IQ scores higher than enlisted World War I soldiers—even higher than the scores of their guards (Murchison, 1926). Today, many of the prisoners incarcerated in the federal supermax prison ADX Florence are terrorists, gang leaders, and kingpins, often with university degrees, deemed "too dangerous" to house in other Bureau of Prisons facilities.

Fortunately, in addition to possessing a capacity for abstract thinking, high-IQ offenders have sensitive and easily arousable autonomic nervous systems (Brooks, 1980; Eysenck & Gudjonsson, 1989; Gendreau & Suboski, 1971), usually making them efficiently conditioned and easily socialized. Braithwaite (1989) explains, "Persons deficient in conscience may turn out to be persons who for various reasons resist classical conditioning—they do not internalize rules as easily as others. Here is one basis for IQ as a correlate of crime. People whose constitution makes them low on conditionability will be both slow to learn (low IQ) and slow to develop a classically conditioned conscience. Criminals are people with autonomic nervous systems that respond more slowly and less vigorously to stimuli" (p. 36).

Empirical results bear out the theory. IQ is significantly and positively correlated with conditionability (e.g., Gendreau & Suboski, 1971). Diamond, Morris, and Barnes (2012) reported significant and negative relationships between both individual and unit-average IQ scores and violent prison misconduct. At the individual level, the authors found that an IQ increase of one standard deviation was associated with a 10% reduction in the odds of committing an act of violent misconduct; similarly, at the unit level, "individuals housed in a unit with a higher average IQ score were significantly less likely to engage in violent misconduct" (p. 119). IQ scores are negatively correlated with amount of personal space required per offender in prison; prisoners with low IQ scores require more space to avoid violence (Eastwood, 1985). Newberry and Shuker (2011) found that lower intellectual functioning was correlated with greater hostility, and they suggest that prison administrators might need to tailor different interventions to high- and low-IQ populations.

Because intelligence is important—possibly the most important factor—in performance of moderately or highly complex jobs (Gottfredson, 1997), high-IQ prisoners make excellent candidates for skilled prison labor, including clerical positions or trades (Streznewski, 1999; Zimmerman, 1949). High-IQ prisoners also are particularly well suited to postsecondary correctional education programs (Adams, 1969). American prisoners began taking college correspondence courses during the

1920s, but postsecondary programs did not become widespread throughout US prisons until the 1970s and 1980s. Such programs are useful mechanisms for maintaining prison order and can build literacy, social capital, and the capacity for empathy, reducing recidivism by as much as 55% (Tewksbury, Erikson, & Taylor, 2000). Nevertheless, in 1994, Congress enacted legislation that denied Pell Grant eligibility to all convicted felons in the United States (Page, 2004). After the ban, many prisons eliminated college programs: "in 1990, there were 350 higher education programs for inmates; by 1997, only 8 programs remained" (Mentor, 2005, p. 275). Thus, high-IQ prisoners may struggle to find—and fund—postsecondary education.

While the dismantling of postsecondary education programs may not trouble most prisoners—after all, even when prisoners were eligible for need-based Pell Grants, only 7.3% participated—they will be sorely missed by high-IQ prisoners. Intellectually gifted offenders may be best suited to use college programs to improve themselves (Adams, 1969). In his last preprison interview, Nathan Leopold—who later claimed to have mastered 27 languages in prison—commented upon the hardships of high-IQ prisoners like himself and his codefendant, Richard Loeb: "I suppose this wouldn't be so hard for some dull fellow with not much intelligence, and no imagination, and no real life behind him. That's what makes it hard for me and Dick, I suppose" (Higdon, 1999, p. 281).

Indeed, the same highly sensitive autonomic nervous system that makes the high-IQ criminal so conditionable may also make prison harder to endure. Intelligence may exacerbate the pains of imprisonment (Sykes, 1958). In "The Subjective Experience of Punishment" (2009), Kolber explains why offenders do not experience objectively identical punishments equally. First, he notes that prison sentences of equal duration can be *objectively* different: "One inmate may be sent to a facility that has large, individual prison cells with windows, while another is sent to a facility with small, shared cells with no natural light. Some prisons have higher rates of physical and sexual violence than others. Such variations in conditions reflect objectively observable features of punishment" (p. 188). Prison experiences can also be *subjectively* different. Kolber cites the case of Thomas Parker, a claustrophobic, arrested for sleeping on a highway. Confined in jail, he "fell into a frenzy" and was ordered to a "silence (solitary confinement) cell" (p. 190). En route, Parker struggled frantically with his jailers and injured himself. He died as a result of his injuries. While the high-IQ prisoner is distinguishable from the claustrophobe, his cognitive ability can also make incarceration a subjectively more painful experience (which has implications for parsimony and avoiding overpunishment).

Prisons are low-IQ environments (e.g., Diamond et al., 2012) and can be Hobbesian (cf. Crewe, Warr, Bennett, & Smith, 2014): weakness and vulnerability are exploited, violence and the threat of violence are instrumental tools, and prisoners align themselves with groups, finding security in confederacy. But the high-IQ prisoner, more than two standard deviations above most prisoners in terms of intelligence, and likely more intelligent than most correctional officers who operate the prison (e.g., Murchison, 1926), may not find peers. He might suffer—acutely— from the communication gulf proposed by Towers (1988, 1990). Although the high-IQ prisoner might find acceptance as a jailhouse lawyer (Milovanovic, 1988), in many cases, in a low-IQ environment where most inmates try to keep their heads down, giftedness can single the high-IQ prisoner out as different (cf. Janos et al., 1985). One high-IQ prisoner from the current study explained, "I never let fellow prisoners know just how smart I am. Rather than appreciate or admire such intelligence, they would despise me for it. I can't hide that I'm smart, so I intentionally make mistakes and give wrong answers to downplay how smart I really am. It hurts me badly to hide something I shouldn't have to hide."

Of course, it is not only other prisoners who can stigmatize the high-IQ prisoner. Prison administrators and correctional officers might also perceive high-IQ prisoners as presenting threats to institutional order and security. After all, innovation, novelty, and imagination are not valued in prison; routine, obedience, and compliance are. The same prisoner explained how his failure to conceal his intellectual abilities led to unwanted special treatment: "In the county jail, I was kept in a specially constructed eight-man cell alone. There were three video cameras directed into my cell and at least two guards watched the monitors 24 hours a day. I was escorted by a minimum of four guards. Why? Because my case was heinous? No. As one deputy testified, I was subjected to extraordinary security precautions because I was 'different.'" In most correctional settings, the high-IQ offender *will* be different. There are simply not enough high-IQ offenders to form a community. However, in 1948, the English government established an experimental facility ("approved school") for highly intelligent delinquents (Brooks, 1972, 1980; Simmons, 1956, 1962; Simmons & Davis, 1953). Housing as many as 48 boys between the ages of 14 and 18, Kneesworth Hall operated as a progressive experimental school for "bright" (115+ IQ) delinquents between 1949 and 1961. In 1985, the school was closed and the building was reopened as a psychiatric hospital.

Kneesworth staff believed that bright delinquents turned to crime because severe psychiatric disturbance overwhelmed the protective effects of high intelligence (Brooks, 1972; Simmons, 1956), a view shared by other researchers (e.g., Gath, Tennant, & Pidduck, 1970). Kneesworth teachers attempted to create a loving and nurturing community, a "haven" (Brooks, 1972, p. 40) and a home. The staff fostered a permissive ethos, guided by the view that "freedom is necessary for the child because only under freedom can he grow in his natural way" and that "freedom works best with clever children" (Neil, in Brooks, 1972, p. 29). The approach appeared to be successful in addressing the behavior of high-IQ delinquents. Although recidivism rates are generally high—more than 50% of those released return to prison within three years in many jurisdictions (Langan & Levin, 2002)—Kneesworth graduates fared well. Brooks (1972) traced the criminal histories of 135 Kneesworth graduates for 10 years and concluded that while 68 (50.4%) had been found guilty for something more than a minor misdemeanor, 67 (49.6%) had either "committed no offenses during the follow-up period" or had been "found guilty of only one minor misdemeanour" (p. 148). Although four of the five boys with IQ scores of 145+ belonged to the recidivist group, Brooks found no significant correlation between IQ scores and postrelease social readjustment.

SUMMARY

Most IQ-crime research suggests an inverse relationship between intelligence and involvement in the criminal justice system. Individuals possessing high IQs avoid contact with law enforcement, while those possessing below-average IQs are processed through the system in greater numbers and are overrepresented in correctional facilities. Noting that the inverse IQ-crime relationship is also supported in self-reported offending, some researchers suggest that high-IQ offenders simply do not engage in crimes as frequently as those with low IQs. Other researchers, however, characterize the IQ-crime relationship as spurious. They argue that the low IQ of known offenders is a function of differential detection (high-IQ offenders avoid detection and prosecution, while low-IQ offenders are identified and successfully prosecuted) and/or differential reaction (high-IQ offenders are treated more leniently than low-IQ offenders by officials with discretionary power in the criminal justice system). The empirical literature on the question is mixed: while the leading study on differential detection (Moffitt & Silva, 1988) found no support for the hypothesis, other researchers have reported corroborating evidence (e.g., Beaver et al., 2013; Cullen, Gendreau, Jarjoura, & Wright, 1997). The current study also provides support for the differential detection and differential reaction hypotheses (although the data do not provide a basis to determine which hypothesis is implicated). Although index respondents reported both higher arrest rates (17.2% versus 10.1%) and higher conviction rates (14.5% versus 8.7%) than controls, a different picture emerges when arrests and convictions are analyzed in light of the index group's greater number of total offenses. The index group got away with more crime than the control group. They reported more offenses per arrest (172.8 versus 129.1) and more offenses per conviction (304.5 versus 193.1) than controls.

The sentencing and incarceration of high-IQ offenders presents difficult penological challenges. The symmetrical, bell-shaped form of the IQ distribution means that the borderline genius offender with a 130+ IQ score is as distant from the population mean as the <70 IQ offender who is on the borderline of mental retardation. Given the discussion of criminal culpability and mental retardation in *Atkins v. Virginia*, the cognitive abilities of the genius could have implications for sentencing. If intelligence operates as a threshold quality like, for example, age, the genius should be punished like anyone else. On the other hand, if culpability is tied to *mens rea,* the foresight associated with higher IQs means the genius criminal might be more blameworthy and should be punished more severely. But a third, more speculative, approach is also possible: if the criminal genius's high IQ makes meaningful communication with others impossible, he might be functionally insane under the *M'Naghten* standard and therefore should be excused from criminal punishment. The criminal genius who is sentenced to prison may suffer more than other prisoners. Because high IQ is associated with greater nervous system sensitivity, the experience of prison—a low-IQ environment—may be subjectively more painful than for others. And because postsecondary education programs have been eliminated in the current era of mass and for-profit incarceration, high-IQ offenders who might have otherwise found a place in college programs could stand out—to their detriment—as different.

6

Explanations for High-IQ Crime

Among individuals at the upper end of the IQ spectrum, there may be a different explanation of offending that is needed.

—DANIEL P. MEARS AND JOSHUA C. COCHRAN, "WHAT IS THE EFFECT OF IQ ON OFFENDING?," P. 19

The quantitative data described in chapters 3 to 5 constitute the heart of the current study, but it is also valuable to examine the qualitative dimensions of high-IQ crime. Although quantitative data yield rich analyses, they do not convey a narrative. Patton (2002) explains: "Qualitative data describe. They take us, as readers, into the time and place of the observation so that we know what it was like to have been there. They capture and communicate someone else's experience of the world in his or her own words. Qualitative data tell a story" (p. 47). Qualitative methods offer a depth and a context that elude quantitative analysis (Tewksbury, 2009), providing rare "evidence of what it means, feels, sounds, tastes, or looks like to commit a particular crime" (Katz, 1988, p. 3).

To gather such evidence, participants who completed the self-report questionnaire were invited to participate in a follow-up interview. Of the 424 initial respondents, 198 volunteered, 44 of whom were purposively selected to describe the range of offending behaviors, from innocuous minor offending up through serious—even capital—crimes. The semistructured questions asked during the interviews are listed in appendix C. Additional qualitative data (e.g., e-mail, letters, poetry, and other written materials) were also collected from individuals who did not participate in follow-up interviews. Interviews were not conducted with members of the control group, so qualitative comparisons cannot be drawn between the index and control groups. Many of the 44 follow-up interviews were conducted face-to-face, but others were conducted over the telephone, via e-mail, or—in several cases— by written correspondence. I visited an incarcerated child molester, conducting an interview in a prison visitation room over two days, and interviewed several abstainers who claimed to have never committed an offense. Most of the described offenses were pedestrian in nature—behavior that would be unlikely to raise an eye-brow—but not all of it was. I interviewed a marijuana harvester, an armed robber, and a car thief. One respondent had been on the FBI's Ten Most Wanted list, and another had been arrested for building chemical bombs in a harrowing "war against society." As a rule, the interview participants were articulate, thoughtful, and reflex-ive—providing me with valuable insight into the linkages between their intelligence and their offending. I collected a substantial body of qualitative materials: interview transcripts, autobiographical sketches, written and e-mail correspondence, and sheaves of artwork.

While some interviewees claimed that they had committed no offenses, oth-ers reported extensive criminal histories. Most of the respondents making the lat-ter claims were prisoners, but not all were. Indeed, one of the most interesting series of interviews was conducted with "Faulkner," a 31-year-old professional who claimed to have killed 15 people, avoiding detection and arrest for these crimes (Oleson, 2004). After recounting Faulkner's story, this chapter examines a leading theory of the IQ-crime relationship (social bonds) using thematic analysis. The chapter concludes with a discussion of IQ as a protective factor, asking whether high IQ may cease to operate as a protective factor and, instead, function as a risk factor.

THE INTERVIEWS: "FAULKNER"

I met Faulkner through snowball sampling (Biernacki & Waldorf, 1981). Another high-IQ respondent thought that he would be an ideal participant in the study. I authorized this individual to share my e-mail address and telephone number, and Faulkner later called to suggest a meeting. We spoke on six separate occasions. I structured the interviews so that he could contact me, naming a time and location, while I had no means of contacting him. I deliberately avoided learning his name, his address, or place of business. I knew a great deal about his past but little about his present circumstances.

At our first interview, I was anxious. Faulkner remained suspicious and guarded, speaking knowledgeably about narcotics trafficking but only in generali-ties. It was not until our second meeting that—reassured I was not an undercover police officer—he began to open up. He began to describe his offenses and the antecedents that led him to the commission of his crimes. Later, his descriptions came to feel like a confession. He needed to talk about his history in order to make sense of it. Nichols (1995) argues, "Few motives in human experience are as powerful as the yearning to be understood. Being listened to means that we are taken seriously, that our ideas and feelings are known and, ultimately, that what we have to say matters" (p. 9). Although I could not absolve Faulkner of his sins, and although I was not equipped to provide psychotherapy, I could listen to him.

I could be his witness. Indeed, I wanted to listen to his story. I could help him try to understand how a sensitive, precocious teenager had become immersed in the underworld of organized crime. I wanted to understand this as well. Over time, I was able to sketch out Faulkner's life history.

Criminologists associate juvenile delinquency and adult criminal behavior with risk factors like low intelligence, socioeconomic deprivation, and poor parental supervision (West & Farrington, 1973), but Faulkner's demographics could not explain him. He sprang neither from slum nor broken home; rather, he grew up in the bosom of a nurturing middle-class family. His father—a religious man—was a civil servant. His mother was a schoolteacher who retired when Faulkner's sister was born. Faulkner's parents were unusually dedicated to their roles as caregivers. Disapproving of harsh or erratic discipline, they took pains to foster feelings of worth in their children. Faulkner still referred to his boyhood home as a safe and protected place: "I can always go home."

Faulkner reported a 162 IQ. As a child, he demonstrated precocious maturation. He spoke, read, and wrote earlier than other children. When he was six, a teacher placed a series of numbers on the classroom chalkboard. He intuitively substituted letters for the digits, cracked the code, and raised his hand to read the message aloud. But while this earned him the accolades of his teachers, his precocity also came with a cost. When he was nine, Faulkner qualified for a gifted education program. The only boy in his class to qualify, he was stigmatized for his giftedness (cf. Cross, Coleman, & Stewart, 1993). "Being the smart guy was bad." Accordingly, Faulkner cultivated a taste for heavy metal music, dressed in black t-shirts and jeans, and downplayed his intellectual abilities. Dissembling as a stigma management technique is not unusual (Foust & Booker, 2007; Winner, 1996). In fact, Gross (1993) found that most exceptionally gifted children deliberately underachieve for peer acceptance: "Several cannot recall a time in their lives when this has not been an automatic survival mechanism, accepted as a painful but necessary part of living" (pp. 275–276).

When Faulkner was 14, his father was transferred from a midwestern city to a small California town. Concurrent with that move, Faulkner made the decision to reinvent himself. He exchanged his heavy metal t-shirts for new wave fashion: bright colors and skinny ties. In doing so, Faulkner learned that there were many ways to be different. One could be smart without being a nerd. One had only to choose one's battles. At the age of 15, Faulkner was a high school honor student, averaging a 3.6 grade point average. But his teachers were indifferent. "No one cared," he explained. His teachers failed to cultivate his aptitudes, and he grew bored and impatient. Socially, he still struggled against the stigma of being too smart or too good. Although a helpful older girl had walked him through his first sexual encounter, adding a swagger to his step, Faulkner still felt nervous around girls and remained uncomfortable with the widespread underage drinking that plagued the community. Faulkner remained—fundamentally—the same bright but awkward boy that he had been at six years old.

At 17, while a high school junior, Faulkner went to visit a friend in a Los Angeles suburb. His friend suggested going to a nightclub that did not enforce the 21-year-old drinking age, and Faulkner reluctantly agreed. Arriving at the club, Faulkner realized that it was not what he had anticipated—it was not a "nightclub" at all—it was a sleazy bar. Still, he had arranged to meet his friend, so he ignored his apprehension and went inside. He was obviously out of place. The bar's patrons were working-class men who came to drink and forget their problems. Underage and dressed in flashy clothes, Faulkner stood out. An antagonistic man in his late 30s staggered up. Faulkner surveyed the room for his friend, but it was filled with unfamiliar faces. The drunk laughed at his clothes. He made fun of his age. Growing abusive, he began to shove Faulkner's shoulders, calling him names, trying to provoke a fight. "Leave me alone," Faulkner pleaded, trying to conceal rising fear. "What'samatter?" the drunk slurred. Faulkner searched the room for an understanding eye, but the other patrons looked away.

Unexpectedly, a large man moved through the room with surprising speed and agility. Before Faulkner completely understood what was happening, the mysterious stranger seized the drunk by the hair and bounced his face off of the bar. The stranger then half dragged, half carried the drunk to the door and expelled him into the parking lot. The other patrons ignored the entire incident. No one breathed a word. Faulkner remained visibly shaken, so his benefactor tried to put him at ease. He asked, "Can I buy you a drink?" and without waiting for an answer, ordered Faulkner a beer and a shot of whiskey. Unaccustomed to the bite of hard alcohol, Faulkner winced as he swallowed the whiskey but washed it back with the beer. The stranger introduced himself as Vincent, and the two began to talk. Faulkner told Vincent that he was a university student. Vincent's eyes sparkled at the lie, but he did not contradict Faulkner. Hours passed, and Faulkner's friend never arrived. After midnight, the two men gave up waiting. Vincent took Faulkner to an all-night diner and bought breakfast. When they rose to leave, Vincent tossed a $100 bill onto the table. Faulkner was impressed by the extravagance. He did not know who Vincent was but was anxious to find out. When Vincent offered Faulkner his business card, encouraging him to telephone the next time he was in Los Angeles, Faulkner tucked it safely away. He intended to do exactly that.

Months later, Faulkner returned to Los Angeles, visiting several of the universities to which he was applying. He also contacted Vincent (now "Vince") and arranged to meet Vince and some of Vince's friends for dinner. When they collected Faulkner in a high-end Mercedes, he found himself wondering again just who this man was. Vince introduced Faulkner to his beautiful wife, Jill, and Daniel, an employee in his security company.

Between visits to the campuses, Faulkner spent a great deal of time with Vince. Vince was an irreligious man, a pragmatist in everything he did; Faulkner, on the other hand, was governed by deeply ingrained Catholic values. Faulkner was keenly interested in Vince's money, his lifestyle, and his enigmatic business associates. Vince, in turn, was interested in Faulkner's mind, intrigued both by his beliefs and by the fact that he did not judge others by those beliefs. Faulkner began spending more time in Los Angeles, visiting Vince and Jill on weekends, staying in their expensive home, and assisting Vince with the security company. He also met the other regulars in Vince's home: Carlo, Mario, and Bunny. Carlo had been Vince's friend since childhood. Like Faulkner, he was an ardent Catholic but with a fiery temper. Mario had a phenomenal head for business, but no sense for people. Both Carlo and Mario shared Vince's dark Italian features and massive physique. Faulkner said that Vince, Carlo, and Mario each stood well over six feet high and weighed close to 250 pounds. Bunny's real name was Carol. When Faulkner met her, she was working as a stripper and dating one of Vince's employees. Later, Faulkner fell in love with her and planned a future with her.

Gradually, Faulkner was seduced into crime (cf. Katz, 1988). He recounted the first time Vince allowed him to carry a handgun. Faulkner described it as a coming-of-age moment, like a religious confirmation. The rigging for a shoulder holster had been draped across a chair in the security company's office, and Vince suggested that Faulkner try it on. That night, for the first time, Faulkner wore a concealed pistol. Vince and "the boys" appreciated Faulkner's quick mind and liked the fact that he did not permit himself to be afraid. Only eight years older than Faulkner, Vince took the younger man on like a little brother, inducting him into the mysteries of his lifestyle.

Faulkner finally understood that Vince was a career criminal who smuggled sizable volumes of cocaine and dealt opportunistically in stolen cars, assault rifles, and military ordnance. Although Vince dressed his operation in some of the trappings of the Mafia and talked about having individuals "whacked" or being "made guys," the 1983 Los Angeles cocaine market was a capitalist free-for-all, and Vince's crew had nothing to do with la Cosa Nostra. Their security operation did a legitimate business, but the company was primarily a front for smuggling. Carlo, Mario, and Danny functioned as Vince's principal agents, distributing to approximately 30 upper-level dealers. They moved a good product, purchasing up to 100 kilograms each week, making their operation one of the largest in the area at the time. They bought from two large South American cartels, paying between $5,000 and $25,000 per kilogram of high-grade cocaine and selling each kilo for anywhere between $20,000 and $50,000.

Faulkner asked Vince's wife what she thought of this. Jill was captivated by the life of easy money and glamour. She explained that Vince was "very powerful and scary, but not to me." In fact, she found it pleasing that Vince would kill for her.

It was proof of his loyalty and love. One night, Faulkner and Vince drove up the coast to a nightclub. As they left the club, on their way down an alley to the parking lot, two small-time criminals tried to rob them. The first robber pointed a pistol at Vince's face, but instead of handing over his wallet, Vince knocked the gun away and attacked the man. The second robber began to reach for his own weapon. Faulkner was wearing his shoulder holster and drew more quickly than the robber. Faulkner hesitated for an instant, then pulled the trigger, firing a single round.

"There was a lot of blood," Faulkner recalled. He was certain that he had killed the man, since at that time he believed, "If you get shot, you die." In truth, Faulkner had only wounded him. But the moment remained strange and surreal for Faulkner even as he told me about it, and he could scarcely remember Vince driving them home. Faulkner said that he could still see the image that had burned into his memory—the robber falling back while a red mist hung in the air. Faulkner said he was sick for hours. Even when there was nothing left to vomit, he wretched with dry heaves. And when Faulkner finally slept, he was plagued by panicky nightmares that "they" were coming after him. Vince exercised his talent for rationalizing. He blamed the victim and told Faulkner that "the guy was so stupid he'd gotten everything he'd had coming to him." He assured Faulkner that the man had lived, but made a joke of it: next time Faulkner would be a better shot and make a real kill. Like a proud father, Vince announced that Faulkner was "made" and rewarded him with the attentions of an upmarket call girl. Faulkner described his guilt and rationalization as "shedding his belief system."

Vince was grooming Faulkner for lieutenant status. He explained how to determine the purity of cocaine and showed Faulkner how to process currency transactions in Caribbean banks. He explained the border crossings that were easy to smuggle product through, where to conceal drugs in an automobile, and how to cross a police checkpoint. He constantly asked questions, challenging Faulkner to identify undercover policemen. Faulkner recalled one occasion where he managed to pick out a cop, only to later learn that he was a dirty cop, already on Vince's payroll. Still, Vince was impressed with Faulkner's observations.

The wealth of new knowledge made Faulkner arrogant. "The truth is that every intelligent man, as you know, dreams of being a gangster and of ruling over society by force alone" (Camus, 1957, p. 42). Faulkner was only 18, but he paid for his breakfasts with $100 bills, carried a concealed pistol, and could access hundreds of thousands of dollars in offshore accounts. He was convinced that he was invulnerable, and he was certain that Vince was. Faulkner also began dissociating the two immiscible aspects of his life, living as a high school senior during the week and a foot soldier in Vince's crew on weekends and stolen days. To maintain appearances, Faulkner enrolled as an undeclared freshman in a California university in September of 1984. Faulkner's parents were exceedingly proud, but Vince disapproved and told Faulkner to stop wasting time.

Faulkner struggled to maintain the façade of normality. When Faulkner's father sat down to fill out the financial aid paperwork required of each incoming student, Faulkner had far too much money in his savings account. Faulkner's father did not ask where the money had come from—did not want to know—and accepted the situation without question. But at the time of our interviews, Faulkner believed that his father had known then that something was amiss. Later that year, while visiting his parents during a school holiday, Faulkner accidentally left a pistol on his bed. When he came home, his mother asked him to explain. He said that he was holding it for a friend. Nothing more was said, although Faulkner wondered if she, too, had suspicions about his other life.

Faulkner was a disappointing college student. In this, he was not unique: many freshmen in Faulkner's class struggled to balance required coursework against newfound freedoms. But, it was not parties or women that made it difficult for Faulkner to concentrate; it was the smuggling and the killings. At the time of our interviews, Faulkner claimed to have killed 15 people. Such claims are not unprecedented. Although criminologists do not know a great deal about hit men, some literature exists on this population (MacIntyre, Wilson, Yardley, & Brolan, 2014). Gessen (1996) described a Moscow office manager who claimed to be a freelance killer in the booming crime markets of the former Soviet republics, Crowther (2001) described meeting a taxi driver who claimed to be a former gem dealer for the Mob with six hits under his belt, and Carlo (2006) described the confessions of a Mafia contract killer known as "the Iceman." Still, if Faulkner's story is true, then he has killed more people than Richard "Nightstalker" Ramirez, David "Son of Sam" Berkowitz, or "Boston Strangler" Albert DeSalvo (Hickey, 2016). While the term *serial killer* is typically to describe individuals compelled to kill for sexualized power-seeking reasons (Hickey, 2016; Norris, 1988), Faulkner qualifies as a serial killer under the law enforcement taxonomy proposed by Douglas, Burgess, Burgess, and Ressler (2006): "Serial murder was initially defined as three or more separate events in three or more separate locations with an emotional cooling-off period between homicides" (p. 96).

Understandably, Faulkner was reluctant to discuss the murders in detail. Although I took pains to ensure his anonymity, murder is a crime for which there is no statute of limitations (California Penal Code § 799) and for which—at least in California—the offender can be executed (California Penal Code § 190[a]). When the subject of killing was raised, Faulkner's voice trailed off and he turned his eyes away. He mumbled. He insisted that he killed only when it was necessary and emphasized that the majority of his victims were competitors in the narcotics trade. He had never killed an innocent individual, although he acknowledged that such killings are sometimes necessary. They are regrettable and reparations are made whenever possible, but "business is business" and casualties are an acceptable consequence of business. Ross Ulbricht, sentenced in 2015 to life in prison for creating and operating the Silk Road website, is alleged to have solicited the murders of people who threatened his operation, employing a similar rationale (Bearman & Hanuka, 2015a, 2015b). Killing, according to Faulkner, is an exercise in rationalization. Sykes and Matza (1957) explain that criminals are not constantly involved in criminality and do not conceive of themselves as "criminals." Rather, offenders drift back and forth between conventional and criminal behavior by invoking five powerful techniques of neutralization: denial of responsibility, denial of injury, denial of victim, condemnation of the condemners, and appeal to higher loyalties.

Faulkner employed analogous forms of rationalization to reduce the dissonance between his idea of himself (i.e., a good person, a good friend, a good Catholic) and his actions (i.e., drug trafficking, money laundering, murder). This rationalization allowed him to commit violent acts without conceiving of himself as a violent individual. Each time he killed, he convinced himself, "I had to," although the justification for this "obligation" grew increasingly flimsy. Faulkner identified five discrete stages:

Self-defense

Defense of others

Defense of livelihood

Defense of status quo

Defense of reputation

It was not just the first shooting that proved difficult for Faulkner. He claimed that the first couple of killings in each category were emotionally difficult.

In 1985, when Faulkner was busy studying freshman composition, Mario—Vince's employee with a head for business but little sense for people—was killed during a transaction that went awry. This precipitated a disastrous cascade of events. Vince did not make Mario's execution personal—it remained a matter of business—but he struck back hard, enforcing his infamous 10-to-1 rule. Vince farmed out contracts and waited for the bodies to pile up. But the situation escalated. Vince was, himself, shot in Los Angeles. Jill pleaded with her husband to retire, to take his money and get out of the business. Vince took Jill to Italy to recuperate and discuss retirement. Days after arriving, they were killed in Naples.

Faulkner refused to accept it. He had truly believed that Vince was invulnerable. Now Vince was dead, and Faulkner had to come to grips with his own vulnerability. At school, he fell behind in his coursework and failed tests. Professors asked if he had family problems. Faulkner tried to fill Vince's absence by assuming responsibility, but he lacked the requisite experience, connections, and confidence. Three days before he turned 20, Faulkner flew to Brazil for a deal. Bunny, Carlo, and Danny accompanied him. At the time of the meet, Faulkner telephoned

California to finalize some details with an attorney who worked for the security company and gathered up the drug money in a briefcase; after Bunny did her customary vest check, they set off. Faulkner said mirthlessly, "Things just went poorly after that." Faulkner's car was ambushed. He could not even tell where the shots were coming from, and before he could react, he was shot in the chest. He claimed that he was thrown back by the impact of the bullet and hit his head, losing consciousness. The others—Bunny, Carlo, and Danny—were killed.

Faulkner awoke to find himself handcuffed to the rail of a hospital bed. An armed federal policeman sat beside him. The policeman asked questions about Faulkner's identity, nationality, and the others' nationalities. When Faulkner did not reply, the policeman turned on a videotape, confiscated from a tourist as evidence. Initially, it was footage of a woman on holiday—but when bursts of automatic gunfire barked out, the frame jerked, and Faulkner saw Danny's lifeless body beside the car. He saw his own body, seemingly lifeless, lying nearby. He saw Carlo shot repeatedly, pinwheeling before he collapsed. And he saw Bunny shot once—just once, but fatally—in the head. He wished that he had died beside her. Faulkner looked away and noticed the briefcase in a chair across the room. He used most of the cash inside it to bribe the policeman. He used what remained to bribe an immigration official at the airport. His ribs were badly cracked and the flight into Mexico City was excruciating. When he examined his chest in an airport mirror, Faulkner saw three bruises radiating like dark stars. He boarded a red-eye to Los Angeles and arrived in the middle of the night without a single piece of baggage. From the airport, Faulkner called a college friend.

For months, Faulkner would awaken from nightmares, reach out for Bunny in the dark, and then remember that the nightmares were real. He was depressed and when he finally went to see one of the university psychologists, he learned that he fit most of the criteria for major depression and post-traumatic stress disorder (American Psychiatric Association, 2013). Faulkner considered seeking treatment, but the psychologist made him nervous. She asked too many questions, and he stopped going. Again, Faulkner relied upon dissociation, pretending that it had all happened to someone else. His academic marks improved, and although his grade point average remained stubbornly middle of the road, Faulkner graduated in 1988. After brief stints in retail and clerical work, he accepted a position with the sales department of a large corporation. He worked furiously at it, working harder and longer than anyone else in his division. Looking back, Faulkner believed that he was probably avoiding his past. He was promoted to a management position. At the time of our interviews, Faulkner was cautiously optimistic about his future. He still worked hard. He was involved with a woman that he had dated for two years. He hoped to go to graduate school for either a master's or a law degree.

I believe that Faulkner was candid with me. We enjoyed a strong rapport. He seemed interested in my research question and was comfortable with the publication of his criminal life story (as long as alterations to identifying names, dates, and places meant that his family and friends would not recognize him). But one question nagged me: *Was it true?* I tried to assess the reliability of Faulkner's story by revisiting the details of his narrative across several interviews. The specifics of his first shooting were consistent the first, second, and third times we talked about it, which left me convinced that he remembered the shooting as he recounted it. Faulkner also provided me with some documentation to corroborate his narrative. The printed screen from an Internet IQ test showed a 162 IQ. Newspaper clippings referred to shootings he had described. Still, I had no way of knowing that it was Faulkner who had completed the IQ test. I had no way of knowing if he simply invented stories to fit the newspaper accounts or if he had seen the story in a movie somewhere. It remained a fantastic narrative and, frankly, certain elements seemed too tidy. I wondered if he was protecting people. At the end of our sixth and final interview, I asked Faulkner if he was telling the truth. Before we shook hands and parted ways, he smiled and replied enigmatically, "I've been as honest as I can be."

My interviews with Faulkner were the most interesting I had, the ones that most elicited a "there but for the grace of God go I" response in me, but Faulkner was not the only individual to report a homicide ("Killed another human being [excluding wartime situations]"). Indeed, 4 others in the 44-person follow-up sample did so. Looking over the interview transcripts, I attempted to identify the themes that explained the patterns of offending in high-IQ populations.

EVALUATING THEORY: HIGH IQ AND SOCIAL BONDS

Qualitative research is underrepresented in criminological scholarship—one study found that, in leading criminology journals, only 11% of the articles employed qualitative methods (Buckler, 2008)—but qualitative analysis can be incredibly valuable in the development or testing of criminological theory. "[I]t is qualitative research and understandings that provide scholars with the insights to conceptualize issues and problems differently, thereby providing the foundation and building blocks for theoretical advancements, refinements and even initiations" (Tewksbury, 2009, p. 56). Thus, qualitative research may be useful in explicating the IQ-crime relationship, which, although well documented, remains undertheorized. One leading explanation, linking low IQ to crime through processes related to school achievement, draws upon control theory. Control theory inverts the question of why people commit crimes, asking instead what constrains us. "The question is, 'Why don't we do it?' There is much evidence that we would if we dared" (Hirschi, 1969, p. 34). Hirschi's early formulation of control theory—social bond theory—is particularly influential. Paternoster and Bachman (2010) do not exaggerate when they write, "[T]here have been literally hundreds of scholars who have commented on or empirically tested social bond theory" (p. 126). When Cooper, Walsh, and Ellis (2010) surveyed American Society of Criminology members, social control was one of the three preferred theories of crime (along with social learning and life course/developmental theories); previous surveys ranked control theory as *the* preferred theory of crime (Walsh & Ellis, 2004). Akers (1994) characterizes social bond theory as "the dominant theory of criminal and delinquent behavior for the past twenty-five years" (p. 115).

Control theory provides an elegant mechanism by which low IQ might lead to delinquency and crime. Hirschi's (1969) theory is founded upon four elements of the social bond: *attachment,* consisting of closeness to others, especially parents; *commitment,* consisting of self-interest that has been invested in social conformity; *involvement,* consisting of engagement in conventional activities that limit offending opportunities; and *belief,* consisting of assent to conventional social norms. The theory suggests, "The academically competent boy is more likely to do well in school and more likely as a result to like school. The boy who likes school is less likely to be delinquent" (p. 115); but low-IQ children who struggle with academic work will not value the institution of school (low commitment). Devaluing the institution, they will not invest time in school activities (low involvement) and will not value behaviors that promote school success (low belief). Without a connection to the institution, they will not form emotional relationships with teachers and peers (low attachment).

There is empirical support for control theory as an explanation for the IQ-crime relationship. Ward and Tittle (1994) evaluated two theories to explain the relationship: school performance (related to social bonds) and school reaction (related to labeling theory) and concluded that the school performance model better explained low-IQ delinquency. McGloin, Pratt, and Maahs (2006) analyzed National Longitudinal Study of Youth data to evaluate three competing explanations. The first, based upon Hirschi's theory, suggests that children with low IQ are less likely to succeed in school, and therefore they fail to form social bonds that deter criminal behavior. The second, related to the subcultural work of Cohen (1955), the differential association theory of Sutherland (Sutherland & Cressey, 1966), and the social learning theory of Akers (1998), suggests that children who cannot succeed in school (either because of low IQ or low socioeconomic status) will reject middle-class values, associate with delinquent peers, and adopt criminal values. The third, related to Gottfredson and Hirschi's (1990) theory of self-control, suggests that children with low IQ are more impulsive, more focused on immediate gratification, and less capable of appreciating the long-term consequences of their decisions. McGloin, Pratt, and Maahs found support for all three explanations of the IQ-delinquency relationship but concluded that poor school performance—a manifestation of social bond theory—exercised the largest effect.

Social bonds provide an explanation for the low IQ-crime relationship. Less obvious, however, is whether high IQ might also operate as a solvent upon social bonds. It seems counterintuitive that the same theory used to explain low-IQ crime could explain high-IQ crime, but the concept of an optimal IQ may provide the missing piece to this puzzle. As discussed in chapter 5, children with IQs between 130 and 150 have much in common with their average peers and are just superior enough to shine as natural leaders, but children with 150+ IQs often fail to form attachments. One respondent from the current study's high-IQ society sample explained, "A leader who thinks too much greater, faster, and deeper than his followers won't be understood well enough to be followed for long. And it's almost impossible for more intelligent folk to follow one whom they can outthink." Another respondent, this one from the incarcerated sample, noted that people with asymptotic IQs (at the low and high ends of the distribution) frequently struggle with relationships and psychosocial adjustment: "One possible explanation is that starting at an early age, people with high IQs have a hard time relating to and associating with people of average intelligence, since they operate at a different level of comprehension and interaction. As a result of this social dysfunction, highly intelligent people may be more inclined to experience a higher rate of psychological problems and, hence, criminal behavior later in life (similarly, there may be a high rate of personality disorders and criminality at the opposite end of the IQ scale)." If the relationship between IQ and social adjustment is curvilinear (Grant & Schwartz, 2011; Grossberg & Cornell, 1988), shifting from positive to negative somewhere around IQ 150, weakened social bonds might also help to explain criminal behavior among those with genius-level IQs. Social bond theory might be applied to adult offenders (e.g., Bouffard & Petkovsek, 2013) as well as adolescents. In the same way that Cohen's (1955) working-class boys rejected middle-class values, high-IQ subjects may choose delinquency and embrace oppositional values.

To ascertain whether social bond theory was affirmed, refuted, or extended within the current study, I used qualitative data analysis (QDA) software to analyze the interview transcripts and documentary materials. After the materials were entered into NVivo (Bazeley & Jackson, 2013), all data were systematically coded and the extracted elements were collated against the four components of Hirschi's (1969) model: attachment, commitment, involvement, and belief. The QDA involved more than merely combing interview transcripts for a few compelling examples; it entailed an iterative and comprehensive review of all collected qualitative data and Hirschi's theoretical work. This was necessary to ensure data homogeneity (i.e., coherence in data within themes) and data heterogeneity (i.e., distinctions between themes). But the investment of time and effort was warranted. Because the current study employed a theoretically driven, deductive approach to the data, thematic analysis (Guest, MacQueen, & Namey, 2012; Ryan & Bernard, 2003) made it possible to examine whether social bonds can explain high-IQ crime.

Attachment to Peers

Attachment involves meaningful relationships with others involving shared norms, emotional connectedness, and a sensitivity to each other's expectations. During this study's interviews, many respondents expressed a pervasive sense of alienation that related with a lack of attachment (cf. Roedell, 1984). Such feelings of alienation have been associated with delinquent behavior (e.g., Krueger et al., 1994). One high-IQ society member stated, "I hated school . . . I was not recognized for what I was." Participants expressed social difficulties in a range of relationships, including with parents, school peers, adult peers, intimates, and professional colleagues. Research shows that gifted people often feel like a minority of one (Lovecky, 1986; Torrence, 1961). Indeed, notes Farrell (1989), "the gifted often felt as though they were a distinct unit with no true peers" (p. 135). Widespread feelings of isolation and alienation in the current study were particularly striking in light of Persson's (2007) conclusion that "[f]eeling alienated when growing up especially seems conducive to later criminal behavior" (p. 21).

Many of the interview participants longed for human contact but struggled to attain it. One interviewee from the high-IQ society sample explained his feelings of social isolation: "[A]t school (even a school that selected based on intelligence) I felt terribly isolated. No doubt some of this was due to lack of social skills on my part. I have never had any "small talk"—i.e., I like to talk about serious, complex things or else keep silent. I can't keep the party going with a sequence of jokes (in fact, I'd prefer not to be there unless I can get drunk). This feeling of isolation comes back to me at social events, e.g., at local churches or meeting other parents." Another participant, from the incarcerated sample, articulated feelings of simultaneously desiring and rejecting social contact: "I have long exhibited attention-seeking behavior, and getting caught for my crimes certainly creates attention. Conversely, I have always been somewhat asocial: a paradoxical loner who at the same time rejects and desires social interaction. And having an ectomorphic build (5'6", 130lbs), I am drawn toward weapons—particularly firearms—as 'equalizers' and symbols of power."

Certainly, for individuals with high IQ scores, relationships play an essential role in psychosocial adjustment. Several participants reported difficulty in making friends, having too few friends, having friends who were older or younger than themselves, and rarely playing with other children (cf. Janos, Fung, & Robinson, 1985). Similarly, some of the participants described difficulties in forming and maintaining relationships with caregivers, friends, and intimate partners. For example, one high-IQ society member explained that being raised by family members with much lower IQ scores produced confusion that made social adjustment difficult: "Being raised by two aunts from early childhood, I was often confused by their prejudices, superstitions, and oddball reasons. With my IQ of maybe 150 or so, and theirs at 70 and 80 at most, I often had a difficult time adjusting to the world I found myself in. My personality must have been affected in ways I'm still unaware of."

Other participant focused on early relationships with caregivers as well (cf. McCord, 1991). A sex offender in the high-IQ society sample indicated that a dysfunctional relationship with his mother made it impossible to establish healthy relationships with women: "I am not the best one to discuss affairs of the heart, for I have had very poor experiences in that department, colored largely, as I now am aware, by my infantile experiences with my mother. The rage over her abuse and abandonment of me so severely impacted my relationships with women that real intimacy and enjoyment were simply out of the question." Most of his intimate relationships were with men. "The few heterosexual relationships I had," he noted, "were with women who were codependent, who had things in common with me, who were mixed up, lost, neurotic, and self-obsessing." Whether the participant's unsatisfying relationships with adult women led to the sexual molestation of young boys (and at least one young girl) is unknown. He did, however, associate his sexual offending with a lack of appropriate and fulfilling relationships: "The pedophilia was the ultimate act of desperation, to be *close* to someone, to *attempt* to be close to someone, who would *not*, could not, hurt me . . . whose love was unconditional and innocent . . . noncontrived . . . who idolized, loved, wanted, and needed my companionship" (emphasis in original).

Some interviewed persons indicated that they had engaged in acts of crime to neutralize stigma. Many of the respondents had been picked on by other children for their intellectual gifts, labeled as "nerds," "geeks," or "dorks." This is not unusual. Peterson and Ray (2006) report that 67% of gifted students experience bullying. One man from the incarcerated sample explained his theft of two bicycles in terms of rational choice (cf. Cornish & Clarke, 1987), justifying his decision as retribution for the stigma he endured: "I . . . noticed two lovely bicycles leaning against a garden wall. . . . I pulled up, opened the back doors, and threw the bikes in and drove away. I was feeling hungry at the time and they would be my meal ticket. It was greed—easy pickings. You can sell them at a give-away price. . . . At the time, I was feeling quite pleased with myself—people should be taught a lesson for rejecting me."

Another participant from the high-IQ society sample described engaging in acts of vandalism as a means of neutralizing stigma: "Well—I used to take great enjoyment in vandalizing school property. When I was angry at the school, angry at life in general, I would destroy property to satisfy myself. Also, I remember certain occasions some time ago when I would destroy school property to become more popular." This individual engaged in vandalism for personal gratification. Destroying school property felt good and ameliorated his feelings of anger. These actions, however, also enhanced his social standing with classmates and prompted him to destroy property even when he was not angry. For this individual (and others like him), offending became a means to overcome stigma and feelings of difference.

Gifted children who report feeling "different" have lower levels of self-esteem than those who do not feel this way (Janos et al., 1985). Given a robust association between low self-esteem and aggression, antisocial behavior, and delinquency (e.g., Donnellan, Trzesniewski, Robbins, Moffitt, & Caspi, 2005), feelings of difference have implications for criminal conduct. One member of the high-IQ society sample invoked themes of both alienation and low-self esteem (as well as the normal Sturm und Drang of adolescence) in explaining an attempted suicide: "I was 15, certain that the world hated me (and probably right), convinced I was stupid and no good (thanks, Mom), and just generally drowning in hormones and self-pity. Wrote a weepy 'you'll be sorry' note and tried, probably not very hard, to slit my wrists with a table knife. Who says the teens are the best years of your life? *Not!*" (emphasis in original).Another participant from the high-IQ sample speculated that early stigmatizing events had led to diminished self-esteem, as well as to self-defensive emotions, cognitions, and behaviors of superiority: "I have a gut feeling that this seeming isolation is largely self-imposed, or it is a residue from some kind of arrogance or feelings of superiority. Actually, what we used to call a 'superiority complex' in my youth has been largely recognized today to be a defense mechanism or related behavioral structure intended to compensate for feelings of gross inferiority. I myself believe that such 'complexities' are outcomes of toxic shaming experiences."

Commitment to Conventional Action

Commitment involves the weighing of costs and benefits of criminal behavior and evaluating whether such behavior will jeopardize current social standing or future success in conventional activities (e.g., academic achievement, employment, or community regard). Those who aspire to future success in conventional activities, or have already invested in conforming activities, take greater risks when they engage in criminal behavior because they effectively have "more to lose" and do not want to jeopardize their investment. Conversely, those with a lack of commitment to conformity can offend at "lower cost."

Given the association between IQ and middle-class values (Jensen, 1998), one would expect high levels of commitment in a gifted population. Certainly, in *Genetic Studies of Genius* (Burks, Jensen, & Terman, 1930; Holahan & Sears, 1995; Terman, 1926; Terman & Oden, 1947, 1959), Terman's subjects reported above-average levels of academic achievement, occupational prestige, and socially conforming behavior. In the current study, a few interview participants also expressed high levels of commitment. For example, one member from the high-IQ society indicated that she ceased the illegal manipulation of financial accounts because of the risk of social consequences:

When I was working for my ex-husband, I had to answer the phone, meet his clients, enter data, and type endless letters and forms. I also had to complete a complete track of the accounts (maths is not my forte!). The books had to balance at the end of the year, which involved a lot of jiggery-pokery of the computerized accounts. Ultimately my ex was responsible . . . I wouldn't do it again, because our tax office has now become very sophisticated and they always catch up with you in the end. I can't risk any financial shenanigans.

Many participants, however, expressed skepticism about the value of conventional pathways. They expressed *low* levels of commitment, which has implications for theories of crime based on social bonds: if people do not value social standing and conventional activities (like education and legitimate occupations), social bond theory predicts that offending behavior is more likely. One respondent from the incarcerated sample described how his frustrations with academia motivated him to drop out of graduate school and engage in a criminal lifestyle:

About my graduate school education . . . I had seen the hypocrisy of academia, the insanity, the mediocrity, and the personal ego games that even the most highly touted professional scholars repeatedly demonstrated in their daily actions and their written works. I was appalled at the low level of scholarship of doctoral theses and published dissertations, poorly contrived, poorly organized, poorly supported, and outrageously concluded with results related far from those factors upon which they had been allegedly based. . . . It was a lie, full of trickery, and I saw it repeatedly, and I lost faith in everything; in mankind, in God, in goodness, in the essential nature of humankind. I (who was already an entrenched agnostic and anti-establishmentarian) simply "turned on, tuned in, and dropped out" of society, taking on only meager jobs, menial jobs, low-echelon public service jobs that were support struts for my drug abuse lifestyle. In spite of myself, my work was (on merely "automatic" overdrive) always good enough to win me merit promotions, although the upscale movement meant nothing to me.

Because his career trajectory "meant nothing" to him, he could engage in sustained drug use without concern for professional consequences.

Another participant from the high-IQ sample indicated that gifted people engage in cost-benefit analyses to minimize the risk of undesirable social consequences, such as being fired or sent to prison (commitment), but they *do* engage in criminal behavior (especially hedonistic offenses, such as those involving sex and drugs):

Clearly the highly intelligent have the means to appreciate both costs and benefits and thus are less likely to take risks unnecessarily. Those that do take the risk of criminal activity may well be able to do it well and avoid being detected. The highly intelligent are less inclined toward the "defective" kind of impulsivity naturally, but their creative impulses may get out of hand occasionally, and they sometimes go berserk because of the pressure they're under from trying to adapt to a world full of idiots. Highly intelligent people are somewhat less inclined to use drugs than the general population (with the possible exception of "recreational" drug use; this probably applies to other illegal comfort-seeking behaviors, notably sexual offenses, as well).

He might be correct. Data from the current study are consistent with the differential detection hypothesis (see chapter 5), and his suggestion that high IQ is inversely related to impulsivity was also supported (see chapter 3). Index respondents also reported higher prevalence rates of sexual and drug offending than controls (see chapter 4).

Involvement in Conventional Activities

Akin to routine activity theory (e.g., Cohen & Felson, 1979), involvement is related to the opportunity to engage in criminal activity. When one spends significant time in prosocial endeavors like employment or schooling, there are correspondingly fewer opportunities to engage in acts of delinquency or crime. In the current study, several interview participants indicated that financial interests had motivated their crimes during periods of unemployment. One individual from incarcerated sample, a bank robber, described his naive but methodical plan to commit three robberies:

> Before the first robbery I had never committed a criminal offence. I was 43 years old when I robbed the first bank, whilst unemployed. Prior to that, I had an excellent career with a firm of management consultants, which came to an end through redundancy. I knew no criminals of whom I could ask advice. I carried out some research (a feasibility study) beforehand to establish the return from such an activity based on the method I intended to use. The method I used was simple, clever, depended on accurate timing, and required a strong heart. I was told by the detectives after being caught at the third bank that if I hadn't been caught that day, it was unlikely I would ever have been caught and would then have succeeded in getting away with three bank robberies. Which is extremely annoying, as I had already decided that the third one was going to be the last.

Another participant from the incarcerated sample also began to commit crimes while unemployed. Speaking of himself in the third person, he assuaged his initial pangs of conscience by telling himself that society deserved it—the denial of the victim—one of the five classic techniques of neutralization (Sykes & Matza, 1957): "He couldn't get a job and he was now 35 years old. He began to shoplift small articles, and at first he felt guilty. The guilt was only eased by the resentment he felt toward authorities. He was a hero whilst fighting for his country, now they didn't want to know him." This respondent's ability to temporarily neutralize inner checks against criminal behavior attenuated the strength of social bonds and subsequently opened the door to more serious offending.

Other participants in the study did not engage in crime because they were unemployed, but deliberately rejected prosocial, conventional activities—which seemed boring—to create the opportunities to engage in (more exciting) criminal activity. For example, one member of the incarcerated sample pursued illicit excitement by constructing a clandestine drug laboratory. By using his skills for illicit purposes, he was able to overcome the intolerable boredom associated with legitimate professional work: "I always score real high on the mechanical and verbal parts of aptitude tests. Thus far in life, this has meant that I can make a pretty good buck fixing things—just about anything—and without putting in a whole lot of hours per week. But, it was getting boring, and here was the chance to tinker with all the systems that make a clandestine speed lab run."

The allure of the laboratory lay in its illegality. There was something intellectually gratifying about designing and constructing an amphetamine lab, but the participant was using the same abilities and mechanical aptitudes that he had used in lawful employment. What distinguished the construction of the lab was its riskiness: the knowledge that, if caught, the existence of the lab would lead to criminal consequences. This individual speculated that many high-IQ offenders turn to crime as a form of resistance against boredom:

> As a general statement of why people who really don't need to commit crimes do so anyway, I would say that it represents a challenge. In today's rather humdrum world, there just ain't a whole lot of interesting things left to do—unless, perhaps, one can deal with immersing oneself in academia and getting involved with some sort of research. When you add the possibility of making a shitload of untaxed money to the pot, it can tempt quite a few of us. . . . I did it for the money and adventure. And I can say that there are quite a few similarly motivated in the federal prison system, where you tend to get a better class of criminal, if you will.

Like others, this respondent described multiple motives for his crimes. Profit played an obvious role, but excitement and adventure were key elements as well (cf. Katz, 1988). On the self-report questionnaire, one career criminal listed his occupation as "adventurer." The rejection of conventional work, even well-compensated work, in a bid to avoid boredom has consequences for involvement and exerts collateral influences on commitment and belief.

Belief

The stronger a person's belief in the shared values and norms of society, including adherence to law-abiding behavior, the less likely one is to deviate from those norms. Of course, one hallmark of gifted children is their independence of thought (Torrence, 1965; Winner, 1996). Although divergent thinking allows people with high IQs to form judgments free of undue social influence, it also implies greater nonconformity. If people lack a stake in social conformity and fail to assent to prevailing social norms, social bond theory predicts that offending is more likely. In the current study, participants expressed *low* levels of belief and related their rejection of social attitudes to three related themes: independence of thought, hypocrisy in the construction and enforcement of laws, and postconventional moral reasoning.

Several participants indicated that independence of thought separated them from others, which both fostered feelings of alienation (i.e., weakened bonds of attachment) and undermined any sense of shared beliefs. One individual from the high-IQ society sample explained, "The difference between people with a high and a low IQ might be that the ones with a high IQ have a well-developed capability of forming an opinion of their own, while the low-IQ people have to rely on opinions created by others. This last category is not bright enough to put two and two together until somebody else shows them how." His final sentence is hyperbolic, but research does indicate that the gifted have less need for external structure than people with average IQs (Dunn & Price, 1980). "Average persons have less of a desire to know ideas for their own sake. They substitute participation in social affairs for idea dominance or the preference for thinking and generating ideas" (Powell & Haden, 1984, p. 131). To the extent that people with high IQs are liberated from social conformity by virtue of independent judgment, they also may be free to engage in offending behaviors.

Some participants were deeply cynical about values and norms of society (e.g., lawful conduct), and they justified their lack of belief by pointing to hypocrisy in the construction and enforcement of laws—another one of Sykes and Matza's (1957) techniques of neutralization: condemning the condemners. For example, one participant from the high-IQ society sample had compiled a substantial file of newspaper clippings about elites who had engaged in crime. He explained,

> My "official misconduct" compilation is hardly brilliant; it's simply a collection of topical news stories. I have over 60 pages of similar reports, some of which are remarkably tabloid-like even though they were reported in reputable publications. An apt example involves Kendall Coffey, the US Prosecuting Attorney in Miami, who recently resigned amid allegations that he bit a topless dancer at a strip club. But do public officials receive the same sort of "justice" as the rest of the masses? After reading through the entire list of "official misconduct" it becomes apparent that the punishment meted out to police officers, mayors, senators, et cetera is extremely lenient except in the most egregious of cases.

Certainly, research suggests that a different standard of criminal justice exists for the wealthy, the connected, and the famous (Clarke, 2010; Taibbi, 2014). Some respondents in the current study were so fundamentally cynical about social values and norms that they verged upon nihilism: if human existence itself lacks meaning, the products of human existence (e.g., legal systems) are meaningless. As one person from the incarcerated sample commented, "I'd say geniuses commit crimes for the same reasons less gifted individuals do. There are at least two exceptions that come to mind. First, sometimes very intelligent people develop a disregard for laws because they all too easily see the hypocrisy of the people who make and enforce those laws. Second, it is common for very intelligent people to feel that their existence is ultimately meaningless. When you feel that there is no point to being, then it is not a very long stretch to the conclusion that man-made laws are also meaningless." If bonds of belief are attenuated at such a fundamental level, it is easy to see how criminal behavior would follow: according to William S. Burroughs (1992), the final words of Hassan i-Sabbah, founder of the secret order of eleventh-century Hashshashins (assassins), were "nothing is true, everything is permitted" (p. 149).

Several participants attributed weakened bonds of belief to differences in moral judgment. For example, one man from the high-IQ society sample indicated that although he had committed none of the 72 listed offenses, he *could have been* a master criminal, attributing his lawfulness to an internal moral compass: "In general, I can say that if I know something is unjust, against the law, or would hurt someone else, I would have no wish whatever to engage in it. It is my own conscience and integrity which prevent me from committing offenses. I'd rather put it positively: I am not tempted to transgress."

Of course, because postconventional thinking is keyed to universal principles instead of social norms, moral decisions can also conflict with prevailing laws (Oleson, 2007a). Some respondents echoed St. Augustine's claim that "an unjust law is no law at all" (in Murphy & Coleman, 1990, p. 11). For example, one woman in the university sample stated bluntly, "I would break and have broken laws that I deem to be unjust." One respondent from the incarcerated sample argued that the tension between independent moral judgment and current law might be particularly acute for people with high IQs: "In general, I believe that intelligent people are more individualistic and, hence, more inclined to question authority and challenge the status quo."

His claim is supported by empirical research: highly gifted people *are* especially likely to question authority (Webb, 1993). Questioning authority and rejecting prevailing laws, however, can transform the genius into a criminal and a rebel. As noted in chapter 1, many iconoclasts have been persecuted as criminals. Rhodes (1932) understood genius as quintessentially rebellious, a threat to the existing order. However, a respondent from the high-IQ society sample explained that while the exercise of independent moral judgment does not entail obedience to the law, neither does it necessarily constitute rebellion: "I think the focus isn't that we are rebelling against authority . . . we simply act in a manner consistent with our own self as the authority in our life. If you grasp the distinction. We do what we believe is right from resources within ourselves as opposed to rebelling against an authority that we consider inaccurate. We simply ignore authority, not rebel against it. From a standpoint of authority, that is said to be rebelling . . . but it simply is a false perspective."

Participants emphasized the independence of their own moral judgments while acknowledging the utility of law for the governance of society at large. Several people suggested that adherence to norms, rules, and laws was important for the general public but indicated that their own analyses of right and wrong were legitimate—possibly superior—alternatives to obedience to the law as written. Thus, to the extent that postconventional moral reasoning diverges from conventional social norms and laws, high IQ may attenuate social bonds related to belief and increase the likelihood of unlawful behavior.

In conclusion, the 44 respondents who participated in follow-up interviews articulated themes that aligned closely with the four components of the social bond outlined in Hirschi's (1969) theory. Specifically, many expressed weakened *attachment,* citing examples of stigmatization, isolation, and alienation. Some expressed weakened *commitment,* indicating skepticism about the value of conventional measures of achievement. A few expressed weakened *involvement,* noting that they had engaged in criminal actions during periods of unemployment or had rejected licit opportunities to engage in crime. And many expressed weakened *belief,* indicating that independence of thought, legal hypocrisy, and/or postconventional moral reasoning led them to think in socially discrepant ways. Although the thematic analysis of 44 interview transcripts and supplemental correspondence was exploratory in nature and cannot provide a definitive account of the causes of high-IQ crime, it does suggest that weakened social bonds might be implicated in adult high-IQ crime.

IQ: ALWAYS A PROTECTIVE FACTOR?

In light of research demonstrating an inverse association between IQ and delinquency/crime, some scholars have characterized low IQ as a "risk factor" for crime (e.g., Jolliffe & Farrington, 2010; Maguin & Loeber, 1996; McGloin, Pratt, & Maahs, 2004; Shader, 2001). Conversely, some have characterized high IQ as a "protective factor" (e.g., Fergusson & Lynskey, 1996; Kandel et al., 1988; Stattin, Romelsjo, & Stenbacka, 1997; Ttofi et al. 2016; White, Moffitt, & Silva, 1989). Experts sometimes disagree about what, precisely, constitutes a risk or protective factor (Shader, 2001). One view is that risk and protective factors simply represent opposite ends of a spectrum for a criminogenic variable (e.g., poor parental supervision is a risk factor; good parental supervision is a protective factor). Another approach is to distinguish promotive factors (variables that predict low probabilities of offending) from protective factors (variables that predict low probabilities of offending among persons exposed to risk factors; Farrington, Loeber, & Ttofi, 2012). Intelligence is an intriguing criminogenic variable because, at below-average levels, it is understood as a predictive risk factor for offending and because, at above-average levels, it is understood as a bona fide protective factor, reducing the likelihood of offending among high-risk populations (e.g., Kandel et al., 1988).

Although Portnoy, Chen, and Raine (2013) report that high IQ appears to protect against antisocial outcomes in the presence of risk factors, they also note that high IQ also helps criminals avoid detection and arrest: "Criminals with better executive functioning and high IQ, for example, would likely be better able to avoid getting caught by the police. . . . There is suggestive, though indirect, evidence that some biological protective factors may also be characteristic of successful criminals" (p. 296).

The materials analyzed in this chapter indicate that very high IQ operates more as a risk factor than a protective one. How can these qualitative descriptions be reconciled with solid research that identifies high IQ as a protective factor? At least three potential explanations exist. First, it is certainly possible that high IQ does operate as a protective factor but that—in some cases—other risk factors (e.g., serious emotional disturbance) overwhelm the protective effects of IQ. Crime occurs *in spite of* high IQ. As described in chapter 1, this is the view of several researchers who studied bright delinquents (e.g., Brooks, 1972; Gath, Tennent, & Pidduck, 1970, 1971; Simmons, 1956).

Second, IQ may mediate other criminogenic variables. The risk-needs-responsivity approach to criminal justice identifies eight principal risk factors: (1) antisocial attitudes, (2) antisocial peers, (3) antisocial cognition, (4) a history of antisocial behavior, (5) family and marital problems, (6) school or work difficulties, (7) lack of involvement in noncriminal leisure activities and recreation, and (8) substance abuse (Andrews & Bonta, 2015). Low intelligence is not counted as a risk factor but as a responsivity factor—relevant only insofar as it is a barrier to effective interventions. Given the suggestion of a gulf in communication that can occur when people are 30+ IQ points apart (Towers, 1990), high IQ might also operate as a responsivity factor—making it more difficult to ameliorate criminogenic risks.

Third, it is possible that the protective effects of high IQ are curvilinear. Given the mixed literature on high IQ and psychosocial adjustment outlined in chapter 1, IQ might operate as a protective factor up to a threshold level and then cease to either exert a protective effect or operate as an affirmative risk factor. Hollingworth (1942) warns, "If a parent would want his child to enjoy every advantage, he could not do better than wish the child to be endowed with an IQ not lower than 130 *or higher than 150*" (p. 265, emphasis added). If a sufficiently high IQ can strain social bonds, as the current study's qualitative analysis indicated, the relationship between IQ and protective effects might be curvilinear, switching direction from positive to negative. The current analysis cannot answer this question but suggests that further research is warranted.

SUMMARY

The qualitative data in this study augmented the quantitative analyses, providing phenomenological texture and detail of criminal activity that could not be measured with the self-report questionnaire. Follow-up interviews were conducted with 44 volunteers, selected to capture a broad spectrum of offenses and experiences. One of the most remarkable interview participants was Faulkner, who claimed to have killed 15 people in the course of his criminal career. I met with Faulkner on six occasions and assembled a basic life history of his experience. His account revealed something about the ways in which an individual can be seduced by the attractions of crime. Although other researchers also have uncovered homicides in self-report research, Faulkner's account of 15 homicides strained credulity. Still, even if he dissembled about some elements of his story, his narrative can help explain the phenomenon of high-IQ crime.

The other interviews also cast light on high-IQ crime. Employing Hirschi's (1969) theory of social bonds as a framework, the qualitative data were combed for themes relating to the four elements of the social bond: attachment, commitment, involvement, and belief. The data suggested that high-IQ individuals experience weakened bonds. Specifically, respondents described stigma and alienation that undermined attachment, skepticism about conventional measures of achievement that undermined commitment, unstructured time that compromised prosocial involvement, and an independence of thought that undermined belief. These qualitative data raise a provocative question: is high IQ always a protective factor, or—at some thresholds, or under some circumstances—might high IQ cease to operate as a protective factor and, potentially, begin to operate as a risk factor?

7

Discussion and Conclusion

Corruptio optimi pessima [the corruption of the best is the worst of all].
—ROMAN MAXIM

The media sometimes invoke the "criminal genius" ironically, as a variation on the "dumbest criminals" popularized in books (e.g., Butler & Ray, 2000) and television (Angus, 1996). But the term is also used in a nonironic sense. As noted in the introduction, the criminal genius is a much-cherished figure in literature, film, and television, with roots extending back to ancient myths and legends. That the criminal genius should capture the attention of the public is hardly surprising. The public's interest in crime is great and deep-seated. "[T]hey love crime, every one loves crime, they love it always" (Dostoevsky, 1881/1949, p. 451). The public's long-standing fascination with genius shows no sign of abating, either (Garber, 2002). Simonton (2013) has lamented that, after Einstein, original and innovative genius is extinct in the natural sciences; others wonder if genius is dead (Dobbs, 2006). But genius is not going quietly into that good night: according to WorldCat, an online global network of library content, more than 100 titles have been published on the subject of genius since 2006 alone. And, given the popularity of high-IQ antiheroes like *Breaking Bad*'s Walter White (Gilligan, 2008), *Sherlock*'s Jim Moriarty (McGuigan, 2010). and *Hannibal*'s eponymous Dr. Lecter (Fuller, 2013), public interest in the criminal genius appears to be flourishing (cf. Carlson, 2015).

Some social scientists continue to minimize the relevance of individual differences (Pinker, 2002). They dismiss IQ as a bogus construct or reject the association between low IQ and reported crime as spurious; but the strict environmentalist view that IQ is meaningless and that "anybody can learn anything" (Faris, 1961, p. 838) is no longer tenable. Genetics actually play a bigger role in human intelligence than does the environment (Gottfredson, 1997). Developments in neuroscience, genetics, and epidemiology are transforming criminology. "[T]he biological sciences have made more progress in advancing our understanding about behavior in the past 10 years than sociology has made in the past 50 years" (Robinson, 2004, p. 4). "The future is here," proclaimed one work on biosocial criminology (Vaughn & DeLisi, 2015, p. 636). Nevin's (2000) research, purporting a causal linkage between lead emissions and crime rates, has gone mainstream (e.g., Drum, 2013). Given breakthroughs in brain imaging (e.g., Jung & Haier, 2007), some have even speculated that paper-and-pencil IQ tests may soon be obsolete (Gupta, 2006). It soon may be possible to observe (and influence) brain function. Lombroso's (1876/2006) claim that crime is tied to brain morphology, derided throughout much of the twentieth century, is being vindicated. Using PET scans, Raine (2013) has been able to identify structural differences in the brains of psychopaths; and using transcranial magnetic stimulation, Dutton (2012) has experienced an induced state of temporary psychopathy in the lab.

The brain matters. Researchers continue to explore the contours of the IQ-crime relationship, building upon a substantial—and growing—body of scholarship about the linkages between cognitive deficits, criminal behavior, and involvement in the criminal justice system (e.g., Nedelec, Schwartz, & Connolly, 2015). Low general intelligence *(g)* is widely recognized as a robust correlate of crime; and slow executive function—involving decision making, memory, inhibitory control, and the regulation of behavior—is at least as important. Knowledge about the patterns of offending across the IQ distribution help to refine our understanding of the relationship between brain function and criminal behavior, but while much is known about those with below-average IQs, "the more 'gifted' offender has received relatively little attention" (Blackburn, 1993, p. 188).

Of course, researchers know that such offenders do exist. Media accounts of infamous high-IQ criminals such as Frank "Catch Me if You Can" Abagnale (Abagnale & Redding, 1980), "Mensa Murderer" George Trepal (Good & Goreck, 1995), and "Unabomber" Theodore Kaczynski (Chase, 2003) provide idiosyncratic information, and a number of studies of delinquency have focused on bright delinquents (e.g., Anolik, 1979; Cohn, 2009; Gath, Tennent, & Pidduck, 1970, 1971; Neihart, 2009). But, for all of the interest in the phenomenon, empirical information on high-IQ crime is scarce. This might be a function of frequency. Even if the IQ-crime relationship is spurious and high-IQ offenders commit crimes at the same rate as everyone else, people with 130+ IQs constitute only slightly more than 2% of the population, and less than 1 person in 2,000 has a 150+ IQ. Therefore, one would expect high-IQ offenders to account for only a fraction of total reported crime. Furthermore, if offenders with high IQs tend to engage in low-frequency, low-risk offenses such as forgery, bribery, and embezzlement, as theorized by Wilson and Herrnstein (1985), then recorded crimes of genius should be even rarer. And if high-IQ offenders engage in crimes such as workplace safety violations, industrial pollution, or too-big-to-fail financial fraud—antisocial behaviors that are not even conceived of as real "crimes" (Reiman & Leighton, 2013)—then the recorded crimes of genius should be still more rare. But criminologists know little about the dark figure of high-IQ crime, in part because they lack meaningful access to those whom Herrnstein and Murray (1994) call the "cognitive elite" (p. 47). Without research access to individuals who possess real power, privilege, and influence, criminologists interested in high-IQ crime have not been able to study up (Nader, 1972); accordingly, they have studied down, examining the vulnerable high-IQ populations that have been available (e.g., prison samples and adolescent delinquents).

KEY FINDINGS

The current study broke new ground by collecting self-report data from three heterogeneous index samples of high-IQ adults: members of an international high-IQ society (with an estimated mean IQ of 158.5), university students and staff from elite US and UK institutions (with an estimated mean IQ of 142.9), and prisoners from US and UK correctional facilities (with an estimated mean IQ of 145.2). The 465 index respondents provided a wealth of information about 17 demographic variables; information about the books, films, and famous figures that had influenced their characters; and prevalence, incidence, recency, arrest, and conviction data for 72 offenses. These 72 offenses were organized into nine offense types: (1) sex crimes, (2) violent crimes, (3) drug crimes, (4) property crimes, (5) white-collar crimes, (6) professional misconduct, (7) vehicular offenses, (8) justice system offenses, and (9) miscellaneous offenses. There were 358 index respondents who completed the revised Eysenck Personality Questionnaire (EPQ-R), and 44 index respondents were selected for follow-up interviews. Self-report data from the index group were contrasted with data from 765 controls (with an estimated mean IQ of 115.4).

The study's findings defied prevailing expectations about intelligence and crime. The literature positing an inverse relationship between IQ and offending suggests that a smaller percentage of the index group would report offenses than controls. Instead, index respondents reported *higher* prevalence rates for 50 of the 72 measured offenses. In fact, for seven of the nine general offense types—sex, violent, drug, property, white-collar, professional misconduct, and miscellaneous crimes—prevalence rates of the index group were higher than those of controls. For white-collar crimes, property offenses, and professional misconduct, they were *significantly* higher. Only for vehicular and justice system offenses did the control group report higher prevalence rates, and those differences were not statistically significant. This is illustrated in figure 37.

Collectively, the 465 people in the index group reported more than 190,000 offenses. Drugs, professional misconduct, and white-collar crime constituted the

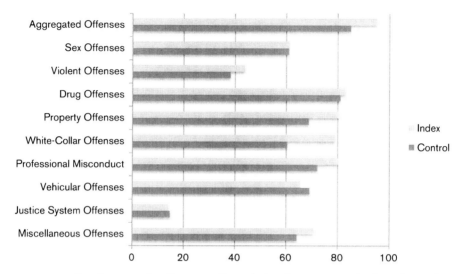

FIGURE 37. Prevalence rates by offense type. Figure depicts the percentage of index and control groups reporting at least one of the listed offenses within each offense type.

bulk of their crimes. The 756 people in the control group reported even more crime: more than 215,000 offenses. Almost half of these were drug crimes. Figure 38 depicts the total number of offenses by crime type for the index and control groups.

Index respondents who reported crimes reported more offenses per person (higher incidence rates) than did controls. This finding was not merely a function of including an incarcerated sample in the index group, nor was it a function of high rates of trivial offenses in the index group and lower rates of serious offenses in the control group. The overall correlation between IQ and crime score (a measure of combined prevalence, incidence, and offense seriousness) was −0.02. Although the *direction* of this relationship is consistent with most IQ-crime research, the magnitude of the relationship is very weak. There is almost no relationship between IQ and crime score. The very absence of a relationship is remarkable. The relationship between intelligence and crime does not appear to be simply negative and linear but rather something more complicated.

The data were consistent with the differential detection and differential reaction hypotheses, which suggest that bright offenders engage in crimes at rates comparable to those of others but avoid detection and/or are treated more leniently within the justice system. In the current study, although index respondents reported higher rates of arrest and conviction than controls, once the total number of arrests and convictions were contrasted against the total number of reported offenses, it became clear that the index group committed more offenses per arrest

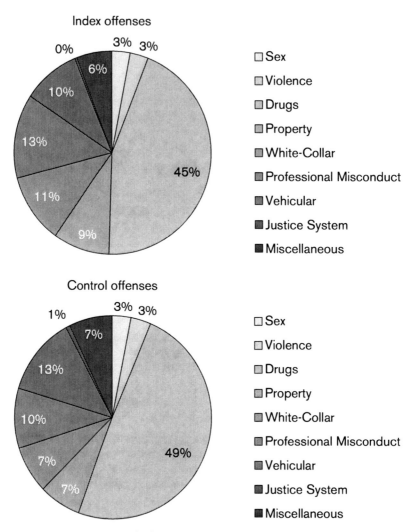

FIGURE 38. Composition of offense types by index and control groups. Offenses were capped at 1,000 counts per offense, which resulted in lower offense counts (notably in drug offenses).

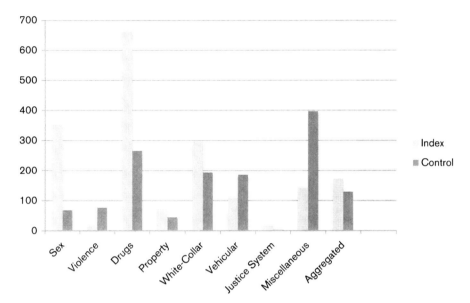

FIGURE 39. Offenses per arrest for index and control groups. Tall columns represent "success-ful" offending (many offenses with few arrests), while short columns represent offense types with relatively high rates of arrest. Justice system offenses in the control group are too small (1:3.3) to be visible in this figure, and professional misconduct offenses could not be displayed because the index ratio (1:12,706) rendered all other categories incomprehensible.

and more offenses per conviction than the control group. That is, the index group got away with more crime than the control group. Although this was not true for every offense category (e.g., violence, vehicular, and miscellaneous), it was true for sex crimes, drug crimes, white-collar crimes, professional misconduct, justice system crimes, and overall offending, as indicated in figure 39.

The high rates of prevalence, incidence, arrest, and conviction in the index group might be a function of sampling. In addition to having a mean IQ more than two standard deviations higher than the mean control group score (148.7 versus 115.4), a greater proportion of the index group was male (positively correlated with offending). The index participants were also older, better educated, better paid, less religious, and more likely to self-diagnose mental illness and to report mental-health treatment. Index respondents might have been better able to recall previous offenses and more inclined to count ambiguous events as offenses. These respond-ents were also noteworthy in terms of personality measures. Index respondents reported higher than average measures of psychoticism, neuroticism, and ven-turesomeness and lower than average measures of extraversion, impulsiveness, and empathy. High psychoticism, high neuroticism, and low empathy are consist-ent with Eysenck's (1977) theory of crime. Females reported higher than average addiction scores and males reported higher than average criminality and lie scale scores, suggesting the possibility of dissembling.

LIMITATIONS OF THE STUDY

This potential for falsehood was one of the great weaknesses of the current study. As a self-funded piece of doctoral research, the study was constrained by funding, available staff, time, and academic experience. It relied entirely upon self-reporting for multiple measures of offending: prevalence (whether the person ever committed the listed offense), incidence (how many times the person ever committed the listed offense), recency (the number of times the person committed the listed offense in the previous year), arrest, and conviction. The study also relied upon self-reporting for IQ and self-assessment of mental illness. Reliance upon self-reporting is not necessarily problematic. After all, the method boasts high measures of validity and reliability (Junger-Tas & Marshall, 1999). Even self-reported arrests correspond accurately with officially recorded arrests (Pollock, Menard, Elliott, & Huizinga, 2015). The instrument's content validity is strong (i.e., it taps a wide range of behaviors using relevant and plausible self-report items), but critics might—quite reasonably—challenge the study's findings because its questionnaire was neither validated against an external criterion (e.g., arrest records) nor analyzed for test-retest or split-half reliabilities. The study's findings, more preliminary than conclusive, must be interpreted in light of these concerns.

There are at least 11 other limitations to the current study. First, there are lingering questions about the representativeness of the three index samples. Although the inclusion of members of a high-IQ society, students from elite universities, and prisoners successfully drew from all three varieties of genius identified by Towers (1990)—outsiders, conformists, and dropouts—the study did not include a sample of high-IQ professionals who were not part of high-IQ societies. Thus, the study might reveal more about people who join high-IQ societies than provide a representative sample of all people with genius-level IQs.

Second, the study had modest response rates. The response rate for the index samples was low, possibly as low as 30.9%; because control group data were collected using a student-accessible PDF document, there is no way of knowing how many people considered participating in the study but chose not to do so. Therefore, nonresponse bias is a serious concern. Individuals who completed the survey might differ in systematic ways from those who chose not to complete the survey.

Third, and relatedly, because response rates were low, counts in some categories (e.g., arrests and convictions for specific offense types by sex) were too small to analyze with statistical techniques. Analyses were possible only when male and female data were pooled.

Fourth, because many participants did not know their IQ, scores were imputed (on the basis of *g*-loaded achievement test scores, educational achievement, or occupation). Imputed scores were founded upon reliable data (e.g., Hauser, 2002), but they operate only as estimates.

Fifth, the study did not measure other individual differences that might influence criminal behavior. Specifically, instruments to assess self-control (Tangney, Baumeister, & Boone, 2004), executive function (Kongs, Thompson, Iverson, & Heaton, 2000), emotional intelligence (Mayer, Caruso, & Salovey, 1999), or psychopathy (Hare, 1980) were not included. These attributes have profound implications for offending. The questionnaire also did not collect any information about sanctions or sentences associated with convictions (making it impossible to know if imposed penalties were correlated with IQ, as predicted by the differential reaction hypothesis).

Sixth, like many other surveys, missing data plagued the study. In particular, questions about age (birth date), income, and nationality were often left blank. Although the questionnaire included a column to affirmatively indicate that one had never engaged in a particular offense (see figure 15 in chapter 2), thereby distinguishing it from a question that one chose not to answer, only a fraction of the participants used this column. Most respondents simply left the boxes blank. Other answers were ambiguous. For example, if a person answered by marking an offense box with an X or a √ mark instead of a number, these were counted as a single offense, even if the individual had engaged in the behavior many times. Similarly, if a respondent wrote "a few," it was coded as 3 offenses; if "numerous" or "many," it was coded as 5. "Dozens" was coded as 12, "hundreds" as 100, and "thousands" as 1,000. Each offense was right-limited at 1,000, even for the participants who described their offenses as "∞." Such irregularities in reporting produced conservative counts and have the potential of undermining the accuracy of analyses.

Seventh, the index and the control data were collected seven years apart (1997 and 2004). Furthermore, the index data, collected in 1997, is now nearly 20 years old, raising questions about its enduring validity.

Eighth, although crime scores provided a means of comparing unlike offenses, the seriousness coefficients applied to offense counts are dated. *The Measurement of Delinquency* (Sellin & Wolfgang, 1964) is more than half a century old, and its assessments of offense seriousness reflect the biases of its era. More recent and more sophisticated approaches to the scaling of crime (Sherman, Neyroud, & Neyroud, 2016; Sweeten, 2012) might produce superior results.

Ninth, the purely quantitative approach to the 72 offenses—counting offenses committed in the previous year, offenses ever committed, arrests, and convictions—created the appearance of a concrete and unambiguous set of data (e.g., declaring that offender X committed 64 offenses). But because the listed offenses were not defined, questionnaire respondents might reasonably differ as to whether a given behavior satisfied the definition. The lack of specificity in terms proved to be an issue in the measurement of arrests and convictions. In follow-up interviews, it became clear that some individuals understood any form of detention imposed by law enforcement officials to be an "arrest" (e.g., a traffic stop), whereas others understood "arrest" as signifying only situations involving a full exercise of police power: *Miranda* rights, handcuffs, transport in a police car, mug shots, fingerprinting, police detention, and the filing of a criminal charge. Discrepancies in these definitions mean that reported arrest and conviction rates must be treated with caution.

Tenth, although personality data were collected for the index group, the EPQ-R was not distributed to the control group, making comparisons of personality traits impossible. Similarly, no qualitative interviews were conducted with members of the control group.

Eleventh, there was terrific variation in the 44 semistructured interviews that *were* conducted (within the index group). The interviews were conducted via different media, including e-mail, post, telephone, and face-to-face meetings. In-person interviews were conducted in a variety of settings, and they varied widely in duration and detail. They were useful for exploring the phenomenology of crime, but a tighter focus in interview questions and greater standardization across the interview situations would have permitted better comparisons to be drawn between participants. Looking back 20 years to the original collection of data, it is easy to see considerable limitations in the study. A dozen are identified above; there are certainly others.

STRENGTHS OF THE STUDY

In spite of the study's limitations, the research was groundbreaking. This is the first self-report study to examine intelligence and crime using an adult population with 130+ IQ scores. Murchison's (1926) comparison of Leavenworth prisoners and World War I soldiers debunked the myth of the feebleminded criminal but did little to unpack the relationship between IQ and offending. Terman's *Genetic Studies of Genius* (Burks, Jensen, & Terman, 1930; Holahan & Sears, 1995; Terman, 1926; Terman & Oden, 1947, 1959) provides an unprecedented vision of genius across the life span but devote little attention to crime. Studies of bright delinquents have shed important light on the etiology of gifted delinquency, but most of their subjects did not have genius-level IQs and their questionnaires did not include serious, adult crimes.

The current study, however, collected information from 465 adults with genius-level IQs of 130 or higher, measuring 72 different offenses, ranging in seriousness from minor, trivial offending to serious white-collar offenses and capital crimes. The study attempted to reveal the dark figure of high-IQ crime: it measured crimes that had ended in arrest and conviction, but it also measured offenses that had gone undetected, unsolved, and unpunished. Instead of simply measuring life-time prevalence with dichotomous yes/no questions, the self-report question-naire packed a huge amount of data into a small package, collecting prevalence, incidence, recency, arrest, and conviction data for 72 offenses. Instead of simply studying a prison sample, the study examined three different groups: high-IQ society members, university students from elite institutions, and a small group of prisoners. It also collected data from 756 controls. The study also included meas-ures of personality traits and incorporated 44 semistructured interviews. Instead of merely describing rates of prevalence and incidence without reference to *how* such events took place or what they *meant,* the study employed follow-up inter-views that added phenomenological context to the analyses. Qualitative analysis of the 44 follow-up interviews suggested that Hirschi's (1969) social bond theory is consistent with high-IQ offending. Interview participants described weakened elements of the social bond: attachment, commitment, involvement, and belief. For all of the study's limitations, the work described in this book constituted a seri-ous attempt to pierce the veil of elite crime and to grasp—even imperfectly—the essential qualities of high-IQ crime.

Thus, the study makes a novel contribution to the still-burgeoning literature on intelligence and crime. After a century of research, there is a consensus that IQ and executive function are important measures of individual difference and are related to crime. Furthermore, converging lines of evidence from neurology, biosocial criminology, studies of IQ and criminal justice processing, and big-data studies of IQ and crime rates all point to a robust association between low intelligence and crime (Nedelec et al., 2015). Even criminologists who reject IQ as a principal cause of crime acknowledge its association with offending (e.g., Caplan, 1965; Cullen, Gendreau, Jarjoura, & Wright, 1997).

On closer analysis, however, the specific shape of the IQ-crime relationship is less clear. The relationship between IQ and offending varies by offense type: IQ has been *positively* associated with drug use (White & Batty, 2012) and white-collar crime (Raine et al., 2012). Although low IQ is implicated in self-reported offending as well as crimes known to the police (West & Farrington, 1973), the inverse IQ-crime relationship appears to be stronger for known offenses than for self-reported ones. The article by Moffitt and Silva (1988) is frequently cited as a conclusive rebut-tal to suggestions of differential detection, but others have found support for the differential detection hypothesis. There is also uncertainty about *how* IQ is related to crime: "the mechanism that connects low intelligence and offending is still hotly debated" (Jolliffe & Farrington, 2010, p. 44). Leading explanations include moral reasoning (Neihart, 2009), school failure (Hirschi & Hindelang, 1977; McGloin, Pratt, & Maahs, 2004), impulsivity (Felson & Staff, 2006), social bonding (Hirschi, 1969), hemispheric functioning (Ellis & Walsh, 2003), evolutionary adaptation (Kanazawa, 2012), or inability to appreciate the consequences of actions (Wilson

& Herrnstein, 1985). Data from the current study cannot provide a conclusive answer about the shape of the IQ-crime relationship or definitively identify the mechanism through which IQ influences criminal behavior, but the research, measuring a little-studied population, can serve as a valuable data point in the larger inquiry.

HYPOTHESES FOR FUTURE TESTING

Future research might examine several questions and test several hypotheses related to high-IQ offending:

> The relationship between IQ and crime is often characterized as negative and linear, but other researchers have reported a curvilinear relationship, with peak offending in the low–average range and with low levels of offending in very high and very low IQ ranges (e.g., Mears & Cochran, 2013; Schwartz et al., 2015). The relationship between IQ and self-reported crime should be assessed, employing a representative sample of adults from across the IQ spectrum and measuring a full complement of offenses (not just delinquency and street crime). Particular attention should be paid to any distinct patterns of offending within the asymptotic tails of the IQ distribution.

> Although low intelligence is widely acknowledged as a robust correlate of delinquency and crime (e.g., Hirschi & Hindelang, 1977), the independent contribution of g should be separated from that of executive function (e.g., self-control) when examining the IQ-crime relationship. Measures of personality should also be included (especially dimensions of psychoticism/psychopathy). After controlling for personality and executive function, it is very possible that the strength of association between g and crime is much attenuated. To fully assess this question, the strength of these relationships should be measured across a variety of offenses, including crimes involving foresight and planning as well as those traditionally associated with impulsivity.

> It is often suggested that high-frequency, high-visibility crimes are associated with low IQ and that low-frequency, low-visibility crimes are more often associated with high IQ (e.g., Wilson & Herrnstein, 1985). Accordingly, the evidence for the differential detection and differential reaction hypotheses should be further examined using adults from across the IQ spectrum and by employing external measures of validity (e.g., arrest records, sentencing information).

> The PIQ > VIQ configuration, long associated with delinquency (Miller, 1987), should be further examined in the context of adult offending. In particular, the nature of the relationship between verbal ability and offending should be explored in the context of white-collar (and other elite) crimes. Additionally, the linkages between verbal intelligence, moral reasoning, and crime should be disentangled.

> Given evidence that white-collar crime is more costly and injurious than street crime (Coleman, 2005), the relationship between IQ and crime seriousness should be evaluated. Even if high-IQ offenders commit fewer crimes than offenders with low or

average IQs, if the former's offenses cause greater social harms (e.g., more victims, greater dollar losses) or entail greater law enforcement costs (e.g., eluding arrest, successful prison escapes), there might be a positive relationship between IQ and criminal harm/cost.

High IQ is widely understood as a protective factor, but research should determine whether it *always* operates as a protective influence or if, at certain levels or under certain conditions (e.g., when individuals have IQ scores above optimal levels), it could operate as a risk factor. Any conditions under which high IQ can function as a risk factor should be identified.

Hirschi's (1969) influential theory of social bonds suggests that boys with low IQ scores underperform in school, thereby weakening social bonds that would otherwise inhibit delinquency. Research might ascertain whether social bonds could also provide a theoretical explanation for high-IQ offending (via feelings of alienation).

IMPLICATIONS

Intelligence is understood as an important correlate of crime within criminology. Indeed, although the account of Lombroso's epiphany is probably apocryphal, it has been claimed that scientific criminology was born within the crucible of a brigand's skull: "This was not merely an idea, but a flash of inspiration. At the sight of that skull, I seemed to see all of a sudden, lighted up as a vast plain under a flaming sky, the problem of the nature of the criminal—an atavistic being who reproduces in his person the ferocious instincts of primitive humanity and the inferior animals" (Lombroso-Ferrero, 1911, p. xiv).

Lombroso's identification of the median occipital fossa (an abnormality observed in lower apes, rodents, and birds) in the criminal is echoed by contemporary neuroscientists' association of the cavum septum pellucidum with psychopathy (Fischman, 2011). Early researchers built upon Lombroso's theory of atavism, seeking to identify the criminal's physical type (e.g., Hooton, 1939; Sheldon, 1949), but others concluded that crime was the product of low IQ or "feeblemindedness" (Glueck & Glueck, 1930, 1934; Goring, 1919; Goddard, 1914; Terman, 1916). Later, led by Sutherland (1931), a number of sociologists challenged the link between low IQ and crime, and for decades intelligence was considered to be a spurious correlate of crime. "By mid-century, biological explanations for crime [such as IQ] were passé, disreputable, and perhaps even taboo. They were unthinkable and unmentionable" (Wright & Miller, 1998, p. 2). But IQ-crime research never really went away. Researchers continued to examine the link between cognition and crime (see, e.g., Caplan, 1965; Hirschi, 1969; Reiss & Rhodes, 1961; Shulman, 1951; West & Farrington, 1973; Woodward, 1955); and with the publication of "Intelligence and Delinquency: A Revisionist View" (Hirschi & Hindelang, 1977), the IQ-crime association enjoyed a proper renaissance. Intelligence was featured in *Crime and*

Human Nature (Wilson & Herrnstein, 1985) and focused upon in *The Bell Curve* (Herrnstein & Murray, 1994); intelligence was identified as an established correlate of crime in the *Handbook of Crime Correlates* (Ellis, Beaver, & Wright, 2009) and called "*the* quintessential biosocial variable" in the *Routledge International Handbook of Biosocial Criminology* (Nedelec et al., 2015, emphasis added).

Nevertheless, it is easy to understand why social scientists and policy makers might resist the suggestion that intelligence deficits are implicated in delinquency and crime. Pinker (2002) argues that people cling to notions of humans as blank slates because of four fundamental fears: *inequality* (the fear that innate individual differences may justify discrimination and oppression), *imperfectability* (the fear that if individual differences are innate, social interventions are doomed to fail), *determinism* (the fear that if behavior is caused by biology instead of choice, individuals are not responsible for their actions), and *nihilism* (the fear that understanding humans as biological organisms will strip meaning from experiences of beauty, morality, and love). If there is no association between IQ and crime, it is much easier to justify mass incarceration, draconian sentences, and overrepresentation of minorities in prisons and jails. In such a world, everyone has the same innate propensity to follow or defy the law, and crime can be understood as an exercise of choice, against which rational punishments are proportionately calibrated (Beccaria, 1764/1995; Bentham, 1789/1823). Of course, the law (as a human institution) does acknowledge some constraints on an individual's choice to engage in crime: legal defenses such as insanity, diminished capacity, provocation, and duress all recognize that biological abnormalities and environmental extremes can interfere with the free exercise of the will (Dressler, 2012). But the law usually operates in binaries, not continuums—a defendant is either insane or sane—and unless the defendant can prove extreme interference, the law presumes that crime is freely chosen. Packer (1968) ominously explains, "[T]he law treats man's conduct as autonomous and willed, not because it is, but because it is desirable to proceed as if it were" (pp. 74–75).

If, however, innate IQ differences exert a causal influence—directly or indirectly—on people's propensity to offend, then "equal justice under law," the maxim engraved into the west pediment of the US Supreme Court building, becomes complicated. For if crime is freely chosen by those with average or above-average IQ, but choice is constrained (making offending more likely) for those possessing below-average IQ, it is difficult to see how the law is either equal or just if it imposes the same punishment on both groups. Of course, IQ is not the only characteristic that implicates these concerns. Many other accidents of birth—for example, being born rich or poor, attractive or unattractive, male or female—raise analogous concerns of moral luck (Nagel, 1979; Williams, 1981). One response is to deny the association and to insist upon what Gottfredson (1994) describes as an "egalitarian fiction" (cf. Wright & Morgan, 2015). The alternative is to acknowledge the association. Progressives may want to recognize the hardships of limited intelligence in the context of criminal justice. Judicial decisions from the Supreme Court such as *Atkins v. Virginia* (2002) and *Hall v. Florida* (2014), as well as antecedents in early English common law, recognize that intellectual impairment has practical consequences for criminal blameworthiness. However, as noted, the law operates in binaries, and unless a defendant can demonstrate mental retardation in a capital case or is deemed unfit to stand trial (Pirelli, Gottdiener, & Zapf, 2011), low IQ does not normally serve an exculpatory function. On the contrary, low IQ could be used to justify oppressive measures. Writing of "natural criminals" and not the feebleminded as such, Lombroso (1876/2006) declared war against the criminal as an alien species: "Born criminals, programmed to do harm, are atavistic reproductions of not only savage men but also the most ferocious carnivores and rodents. This discovery should not make us more compassionate toward born criminals (as some claim), but rather should shield us from pity, for these beasts are members of not our species but the species of bloodthirsty beasts" (p. 348).

In light of the stability of IQ measures from childhood into adulthood (Deary, Pattie, & Starr, 2013), the ineffectiveness of social interventions to increase IQ (Wright & Boisvert, 2009), and the studies demonstrating that IQ at ages three and four are highly predictive of adult arrests (e.g., Denno, 1990; McCord & Ensminger, 1997; Stattin & Klackenberg-Larsson, 1993), it is not irrational to think that early measures of low IQ might be used to justify increased surveillance, preventive interventions, and labeling some children as "high risk." With only a little hyperbole, it is not difficult to imagine designations as "alphas," "betas" and "epsilons" in a brave new world (Huxley, 1932) of psychometrics. Nor is it impossible to imagine using neurological imaging of cognitive function to identify "criminals" before they actually commit a crime: the "precrime" of science fiction (Dick, 2002; McCulloch & Wilson, 2015). Already, the use of brain scans to identify early markers of psychopathy in children is raising equivalent questions (Fischman, 2011). And there is certainly a precedent for coercive interventions. The history of low IQ—of the "feebleminded"—is the history of eugenics (Gould, 1981; Kevles, 1985). Historically, in the name of sovereign interests, citizens with low IQs have been stripped of agency, personhood, even life itself (e.g., Rafter, 1997, 2008).

But a third possibility exists. Perhaps IQ *is* related to the propensity to engage in criminal activity but is neither linear (i.e., crime does not go down steadily as IQ goes up) nor equally implicated in all types of crime (Fox, 1946). Perhaps crime is ubiquitous, but while some crimes (visible ones, with obvious victims, and committed by the powerless) attract law enforcement attention and result in sanctions, other more subtle crimes (conducted by the powerful, beyond scrutiny, and without obvious victims) are committed with relative impunity. The rich might steal, but they steal big (Sutherland, 1940). The powerful might kill, but they kill with armies (Rostand, 1962). Those with high IQs might commit crimes—at least some crimes—at the same, or even higher, rates as those with average or below-average IQ scores, perhaps while avoiding detection. Although researchers sometimes treat the IQ-crime relationship as if it is linear, it is not. People with very low IQs are not hypercriminal, and not all people with very high IQs are abstainers. The relationship actually appears to be curvilinear (e.g., Mears & Cochran, 2013; Schwartz et al., 2015) and *not* because those with very low scores lack the ability to commit crime. Rather, something more interesting appears to be at work. Officially recorded crimes are correlated particularly with IQs in the 92–99 range, but the commission of crime occurs across the entirety of the IQ spectrum. Self-report research suggests that crime is the rule, not the exception. Although dated, Wallerstein and Wyle's 1947 study of "law abiding lawbreakers" revealed the prevalence of dark-figure offending: 99% of the "respectable people" in their study reported at least 1 of the 49 listed offenses, and 50% reported committing a felony. Porterfield's 1946 study of students at Texas Christian University corroborates Wallerstein and Wyle's findings: university students' self-reported offenses were every bit as serious—up to and including murder—as those committed by the delinquents processed by a local court. In the current study, participants with high IQs reported more crime than controls.

Thus, it may be the case that IQ *does* influence crime but exerts its influence obliquely, through the types of offenses that people commit and the disparate consequences that follow. Because IQ is positively correlated with measures of academic achievement, occupation, and income, individuals with high IQs enjoy greater opportunity to engage in offenses such as cheating, plagiarism, fraud, or insider trading. They are Sutherland's (1940) white-collar offenders and Mills's (1956) power elite. Of course, this does not mean that individuals with low IQs cannot commit acts of professional misconduct or white-collar offenses; they can, and they do. Nor does it mean that high-IQ offenders engage only in offenses requiring extraordinary intelligence or access to power. In the current study, nearly half of the offenses (44.6%) reported by the index group were drug related, and with few exceptions, these required no particular aptitude. But it does mean that even when offenders with high IQs *do* engage in street crimes, their cognitive abilities—their ability to think abstractly, anticipate consequences, and learn from experience—might help them avoid detection (e.g., the differential detection hypothesis). And because these same individuals also often possess high socioeconomic status, their engagement in street crime may be taken less seriously (e.g., Taibbi, 2014). Criminal acts like trespassing, public intoxication, driving under the influence of alcohol, drug possession, or sexual harassment might be forgiven as indiscretions when committed by a professional, but they can prosecuted to the full extent of the law when committed by "the poor, inept, and friendless" (Barnes & Teeter, 1959, p. 7). Those with high verbal IQs also might be able to communicate more effectively (Gath et al., 1970), cultivating empathy with officials in the criminal justice system and exploiting this rapport to avoid the consequences of their criminal actions (e.g., the differential reaction hypothesis).

Of course, this version of the IQ-crime relationship is a story that few want to hear. It has ugly implications. Not only does it mean that elites are just as likely to lie, cheat, and steal as anyone else—perhaps even more so (Piff, Stancato, Côté, Mendoza-Denton, & Keltner, 2012)—but it implies that our overcrowded prisons are filled, not with dangerous persons, but with unlucky people whose *real* crime was getting caught. Accordingly, attempts to examine dark-figure crime among elites are thwarted. Criminological research that studies up, not down, is obstructed. Erik Erikson once tried to console Stanley Milgram: "That pioneer work in this field is attacked as being unethical, unjustifiable, uninformative, or any other derogative dismissal is to be expected, simply because people like to shut their eyes to undesirable behavior" (in Milgram, 1974, p. 201). Gatekeepers deny access; professionals, perceiving risk without reward, refuse to participate (Fussell, 1983). And because research access to elites is denied, criminology's focus remains fixed on and misdirected to vulnerable populations (e.g., juvenile delinquents and convicted offenders). This is tragic. There might be an important relationship between IQ and criminal behavior, but until more research is conducted—using adult offenders across the IQ spectrum, measuring elite crime as well as street crime and status offenses—the contours of that relationship will remain unclear. The current study cannot provide a definitive answer about the role of high intelligence in criminal behavior, but it can—by providing a rare glimpse of self-reported offending in an extraordinary population—help to refine the question.

Technical Appendix

The devil is in the detail.
—ANONYMOUS PROVERB

This and the following appendixes augment chapter 2 by providing additional methodological detail. Appendix A outlines three broad aspects of the research: the construction of the self-report questionnaire, the scaling of offenses and implementation of the crime score, and the imputation of IQ scores. Appendix B provides a copy of the self-report questionnaire and appendix C describes the interview schedule.

CONSTRUCTION OF THE SELF-REPORT QUESTIONNAIRE

A cross-sectional self-report questionnaire was constructed after reviewing items listed in questionnaires of self-reported delinquency (SRD), including the 55 items in Porterfield's (1946) study of Texas university students; the 49 offenses measured by Wallerstein and Wyle (1947), the 21 items measured by Short and Nye (1957); the Richmond Youth Study (Hirschi, 1969); Riley and Shaw's (1985) national survey of British youth; the longitudinal Cambridge study of self-reported delinquency (West & Farrington, 1973); the National Youth Survey (Elliot & Huizinga, 1983); and the International Juvenile Self-Report Delinquency Survey (Junger-Tas, Terlouw, & Klein, 1994). These SRD instruments provided a foundation for the developed questionnaire: although the current survey was designed for adult respondents, many delinquency items were appropriated from existing studies (because the research measured lifetime prevalence and incidence rates, as well as offenses committed within the previous year). For example, 18 of the 72 final offense items (nos. 1, 2, 3, 4, 5, 7, 9, 10, 17, 19, 24, 27, 32, 33, 36, 66, 68, and 69) were drawn from the National Youth Survey (Elliott & Ageton, 1980, pp. 108–109). Other items were derived from Porterfield (1946) and Wallerstein and Wyle (1947), which facilitated direct comparisons between the current study and previously published data (Oleson, 2002). Other items were *not* drawn from existing SRD instruments and were derived through reviews of penal codes or generated through pilot testing. The sequence of offense items was designed to cluster offense types by category (e.g., questions 1 through 9 all relate to property offenses), but it also attempts to cultivate rapport with respondents by asking less sensitive questions before posing questions related to sexual offending, homicide, or attempted suicide. The precise sequence of offense items was finalized after pilot testing.

Because the self-report instrument was a postal questionnaire, developed to tap a literate population with superior intellectual ability, the questionnaire included detailed instructions for completing the offense section. Five empty boxes accompanied each of the 72 items. The first column ("Never") was included to distinguish an unanswered question from an affirmative disavowal of an offense. Only a small percentage of respondents took the trouble of ticking the boxes, however, so this measure was discarded in analyses. The second column ("Last Year") measured the number of offenses reported in the last year, while the third column ("Ever") measured the number of lifetime offenses (including those noted in column 2). Several respondents had *larger* numbers in column 2 than in column 3, however (in such cases, the larger number was used for both last year and ever measures). As noted in chapter 2, arrest and conviction (columns 4 and 5) were not defined, and in a number of cases, convictions were reported without arrests. Some respondents marked items with symbols (e.g., X or $\sqrt{}$), which were coded as 1 offense. Some respondents marked items with words: "a few" was coded as 3 offenses; "numerous" or "many" were coded as 5; "dozens" was coded as 12; "hundreds" was coded as 100; and "thousands" was coded as 1,000. All responses were truncated to 1,000 counts per offense item, which meant that answers of "2,500," "10,000," and "millions" were reduced to 1,000. This adjustment mostly affected drug offenses.

Because the questionnaire was exploratory in nature, several of the 17 demographic questions prompted free text responses rather than using preestablished categories. Three of these questions are described below. For example, the question about nationality produced 54 different responses:

1. African American
2. American
3. Australian
4. Austrian
5. Belgian
6. Bolivian
7. Brazilian

8. Canadian
9. Caribbean American
10. Chinese
11. Colombian
12. Cuban
13. Czech
14. Danish
15. Dominican
16. Dutch
17. Egyptian
18. European
19. Filipino
20. Finnish
21. French
22. German
23. Greek
24. Guyanese
25. Icelandic
26. Indian
27. Iranian
28. Irish
29. Israeli
30. Italian
31. Japanese
32. Jordanian
33. Kenyan
34. Lebanese
35. Mauritian
36. Mexican
37. Nicaraguan
38. Nigerian
39. Pakistan
40. Palauan
41. Palestinian
42. Panamanian
43. Polish
44. Puerto Rican
45. Russian
46. Sicilian
47. Singaporean
48. Spanish

49. Sri Lankan
50. Swedish
51. Taiwanese
52. Turkish
53. UK
54. Vietnamese

These responses were later collapsed into three groupings: US, UK, and other. Similarly, the religion question produced numerous nominal categories. These were clustered into the following eight broad groups:

1. None: Agnostic, Atheist, None
2. Catholicism: Catholic, Roman Catholic, Orthodox
3. Other Christian: Adventist, African Methodist Episcopal (AME), Anglican, Apostolic, Baptist, Christian, Congregational, Episcopalian, Holiness, Jehovah's Witness, Lutheran, Methodist, Mormon, Nazarene, Pentecostal, Presbyterian, Protestant, Quaker
4. Judaism: Jewish
5. Islam: Islamic
6. Buddhism: Buddhist
7. Hinduism: Hinduism
8. Other: Baha'i, Deism, Eclectic, No Preference, Nondenominational, Sikhism, Spiritual, Taoism, Theism, Theosophy, Undefined, Universal, Wiccan

The occupation question generated 64 response categories. These were sorted using the 10 categories of the International Standard Classification of Occupations (ISCO-8) (International Labour Organization, 2008) plus an additional category for the unemployed:

1. Unemployed: Disabled, Homemaker, Incarcerated, Retired, Student, Unemployed
2. Managers: Administration, Manager
3. Professionals: Accountant, Actuary, Analyst, Architect, Artist, Attorney, Cartographer, Chemist, Clergy, Consultant, Counselor, Dentist, Diver, Economist, Engineer, Filmmaker, Journalist, Marketer, Minister, Musician, Nurse, Optometrist, Pharmacist, Photographer, Physician, Physicist, Priest, Professor, Professional Speaker, Programmer, Psychologist, Researcher, Scientist, Singer, Social Worker, Statistician, Teacher, Veterinarian, Writer
4. Technicians and Associate Professionals: Contractor, Insurance, Mortician, Realtor, Technician
5. Clerical Support Workers: Bill Collector, Clerk, Human Resources, Postal Worker

6. Service and Sales Workers: Babysitter, Barber, Childcare, Cook, Corrections, Customer Service, Firefighter, Food Server, Government, Guard, Hairdresser, Handyman, Investigator, Loss Prevention, Personal Trainer, Police, Probation, Retail, Sales, Security
7. Skilled Agriculture, Forestry, and Fishery Workers: Farmer
8. Craft and Related Trades Workers: Builder, Carpenter, Construction, Electrician, Machinist, Mechanic, Pipefitter
9. Plant and Machine Operators, and Assemblers: Driver, Machine Operator
10. Elementary Occupations: Distribution, Merchandizer, Warehouse
11. Armed Forces Occupations: Military

Because respondents often provided only a one-word title, some guesswork was involved in categorizing ambiguous occupations into the ISCO-8 classification.

The questions related to mental illness and mental-health treatments also produced a wide range of narrative responses. Most of the responses related to depression, bipolar disorder, anxiety, or obsessive-compulsive disorder, so answers about mental illness were clustered into these categories. Treatment was related to depression, bipolar disorder, anxiety, or marriage/family/relationship counseling. Other complaints/treatments included ADD, ADHD, adjustment disorder, alcoholism, anger, antisocial personality disorder, coprolalia, dissociation, drug addiction, dyslexia, eating disorder, epilepsy, grief, hypochondria, insomnia, mercury poisoning, multiple personality disorder, narcissistic personality disorder, paranoia, phobias, psychosis, PTSD, schizoid personality disorder, schizophrenia, sexual abuse, shyness, stress, suicide attempt, trust disorder, and withdrawal.

SCALING OF OFFENSES AND IMPLEMENTATION OF THE CRIME SCORE

Given the enormous variation in the 72 measured self-report offenses, simply counting crimes would not suffice. Some offenses (e.g., cheating on a test or exam, plagiarism) are not even *crimes*. Some offenses are mere infractions (e.g., trespassing), while others are felonies (e.g., kidnapping, rape, and robbery)—even capital crimes (e.g., homicide). Therefore, as described in chapter 2, a mechanism to compare disparate offenses was developed. Appendix D of Sellin and Wolfgang's *The Measurement of Delinquency* (1964) lists 141 offenses used in the authors' scaling analysis; appendix E-4 presents the mean raw magnitude ratio scale scores obtained from 47 police officers and 37 university students for each of the 141 items. Since the police sample was larger, and because police scores reflected a greater internal consistency than the student scores, police estimations were applied to the self-report data without modification. Many items mapped directly onto Sellin and Wolfgang's questions, but others required estimation using the elements outlined in table 10. The 72 seriousness coefficients employed in the current study were: 1 (10.0), 2 (18.58), 3 (46.46), 4 (93.57), 5 (234.9), 6 (24.8), 7 (27.35), 8 (76.5), 9 (23.23), 10 (4.28), 11 (11.34), 12 (396.3), 13 (194.55), 14 (48.5), 15 (50.0), 16 (61.3), 17 (12.53), 18 (53.11), 19 (39.62), 20 (180.76), 21 (53.11), 22 (53.11), 23 (89.61), 24 (125.4), 25 (81.68), 26 (266.24), 27 (450.8), 28 (250.0), 29 (53.11), 30 (46.46), 31 (72.0), 32 (1.51), 33 (1.02), 34 (61.30), 35 (2.5), 36 (8.95), 37 (4.5), 38 (91.1), 39 (91.1), 40 (82.1), 41 (250.0), 42 (1.0), 43 (65.0), 44 (18.5), 45 (22.0), 46 (22.0), 47 (3.6), 48 (2.41), 49 (2.41), 50 (52.0), 51 (1.1), 52 (1.6), 53 (1.05), 54 (98.0), 55 (101.0), 56 (4.5), 57 (3.2), 58 (664.0), 59 (2.8), 60 (20.0), 61 (5.0), 62 (1.8), 63 (34.0), 64 (42.95), 65 (3.6), 66 (4.11), 67 (64.0), 68 (4.3), 69 (29.16), 70 (10.77), 71 (40.26), and 72 (6.2). As noted in chapter 2, the seriousness scores provided an objective basis for comparing different offense types, but the Sellin-Wolfgang scores might not correspond with contemporary views about what constitutes a serious crime. Accordingly, the current study's crime scores should be interpreted with caution.

IMPUTATION OF IQ SCORES

In addition to offense severity, other measures also had to be estimated in the research. While sampling from a 99.9% high-IQ society ensured that participants had IQs of 150+, most members of the university sample and control group did not report IQ scores. Therefore, it was necessary to impute IQ scores on the basis of other reported characteristics (e.g., academic achievement scores, education, and occupation).

Many members of the university sample did not report IQ scores but did report ACT, GMAT, GRE, LSAT, PSAT, or SAT scores. Because these tests are highly g-loaded, high-IQ societies often accept academic achievement tests or military selection tests for admission purposes. US Mensa, for example, accepts qualifying scores from approximately 200 different tests (Mensa, 2015). Similarly, many other high-IQ societies accept achievement scores as evidence of qualifying IQ (e.g., International Society for Philosophical Enquiry, 2015; Intertel, 2015; One in a Thousand Society, 2015; Poetic Genius Society, 2015). Calculation tables from de la Jara's (2015) IQ comparison website were employed for more precise estimates.

Of course, some members of the university sample did not report achievement test scores. In these cases, levels of educational achievement, academic field, or university selectivity were employed. Jensen (1980) reported that high school graduates possess a mean IQ of 110, students from average four-year universities score a 115 IQ, and persons receiving PhDs average a 130 IQ. Using Jensen's framework, master's degrees were estimated at 125. Herrnstein and Murray (1994) reported that students in elite professions such as law, medicine, dentistry, engineering, or chemistry average an IQ of 120; and they reported that graduates from the top 12 US universities (e.g., Harvard, Stanford, Yale, Princeton, Cal Tech, MIT,

Duke, Dartmouth, Cornell, Columbia, Chicago, and Brown) average an IQ of 140. This estimate of 140 was also applied to a few students with degrees from selective foreign universities such as Cambridge, Oxford, or the Sorbonne.

Some participants in the research (mostly within the control group) reported neither IQ nor achievement test score, neither educational achievement nor university major. In these cases, occupations were used to impute estimated IQ scores. These values were derived from Hauser (2002). Where both educational achievement and occupation were reported, education was used to generate an estimated IQ. This was because, in an analysis of cases within the current study where IQ, education, and occupation were all reported, educational achievement predicted IQ slightly better than occupation. Thus, in order of operations, credible IQ score or IQ percentage was recorded first. If multiple scores and/or percentages were reported, the highest of these was recorded. As needed, scores were adjusted into standardized scores with a mean of 100 and a standard deviation of 15. If IQ/IQ percentile was not reported, but membership in a high-IQ society was reported, the minimum IQ for admission into that society was assumed (e.g., IQ = 130 for Mensa, IQ = 150 for the International Society for Philosophical Enquiry). If, however, IQ/IQ percentile was not reported, then scores from g-loaded achievement tests were translated into IQ estimates and recorded. If neither IQ/IQ percentile nor achievement test score was reported, then educational achievement was used to impute an estimated IQ. The highest justifiable estimate was employed: for example, if a participant reported a master's degree (IQ = ~125) but also reported a bachelor's degree from Harvard University (IQ = ~140), then the score was recorded as a 140. Educational scores were used over occupational scores, however, even if the occupation might suggest a higher IQ than the education. Only if there was no record of IQ/IQ percentile, achievement test score, or educational achievement was occupation used to impute an estimated score.

Questionnaire

SECTION 1: DEMOGRAPHIC QUESTIONS

1. To which high-IQ societies do you now or have you previously belonged? (please list)
2. Do you know your IQ score or your IQ percentile? (please check one)
   ☐ Yes: My IQ is:
   I scored in the ___ IQ percentile.
   ☐ No
3. Usually, to qualify for membership in high-IQ societies, people have to document their intellectual ability with an IQ test score or with a similar examination of cognitive ability (e.g., an SAT or GRE score). If you remember the name of the test you took, please list it and your score in the space below.
   Test:
   Score:
4. Sex (please check one):
   ☐ Male
   ☐ Female
5. Ethnicity (please check the one that best describes you):
   ☐ Asian
   ☐ Black
   ☐ Latino
   ☐ White
   ☐ Other (please describe):

6. Nationality:
7. Religion:
8. Date of Birth (Month/Day/Year):
9. Occupation:
10. Annual Income (after taxes):
11. Sexual orientation (please check one):
    ☐ Heterosexual
    ☐ Homosexual
    ☐ Bisexual
12. Marital Status (please check one):
    ☐ Single
    ☐ Married
    ☐ Separated
    ☐ Divorced
    ☐ Unmarried, but living with partner
13. Highest academic level attained (please check one):
    ☐ Some schooling
    ☐ High school diploma or equivalent
    ☐ Vocational or technical training
    ☐ Some college
    ☐ Bachelor's degree
    ☐ Master's degree
    ☐ PhD
    ☐ Professional degree (JD, MD, etc.)
    ☐ Other:
14. Have you ever believed that you suffered from a form of mental illness, even a mild form? (please check one)
    ☐ Yes (please describe):
    ☐ No
15. Have you ever received actual treatment from a psychologist, psychiatrist, or other mental-health professional? (please check one)
    ☐ Yes. I was treated for:
    ☐ No
16. Have you ever been arrested? (please check one)
    ☐ Yes
    ☐ No
17. Have you ever been convicted of a crime? (please check one)
    ☐ Yes
    ☐ No

SECTION 2: SELF-REPORT QUESTIONS

A list of behaviors follows. To the right of each behavior, there are five boxes.

If you have **Never** engaged in the listed behavior, even as a child, please **check the box** in the first column.

If you have engaged in the listed behavior in the **Last Year,** please record the **total number of times** in the second column (estimate if necessary).

If you have **Ever** engaged in the listed behavior, please record the **total number of times** in the third column, including those offenses committed in the last year (estimate if necessary).

If you have ever been **Arrested** for the listed behavior, please record the **total number of times** in the fourth column (estimate if necessary).

If you have ever been **Convicted** for the listed behavior, please record the **total number of times** in the fifth column (estimate if necessary).

Examples:

If you have "purposely damaged or destroyed property that did not belong to you" twice in the last year, three times the year before that, being arrested once but never convicted, fill out the columns like those to the right.	**Nvr.**	**Lyr.** 2	**Evr.** 5	**Arr.** 1	**Con.** 0
If you have never "violated the conditions of your parole," then fill out the columns like those to the right.	**Nvr.** X	**Lyr.**	**Evr.**	**Arr.**	**Con.**

Again, it is very important that you answer these questions honestly. Your confidentiality is guaranteed.

	Nvr.	Lyr.	Evr.	Arr.	Con.
1. Purposely damaged or destroyed property that did not belong to you	☐	☐	☐	☐	☐
2. Stolen (or tried to steal) a motor vehicle, such as a car or motorcycle	☐	☐	☐	☐	☐
3. Stolen (or tried to steal) things worth $5 or less (including petty shoplifting)	☐	☐	☐	☐	☐
4. Stolen (or tried to steal) things worth between f$5 and $50	☐	☐	☐	☐	☐
5. Stolen (or tried to steal) something worth more than $50	☐	☐	☐	☐	☐
6. Picked someone's pocket or stolen (or tried to steal) from someone's purse	☐	☐	☐	☐	☐

7. Knowingly bought, sold or held stolen goods (or tried to do any of these things)	☐	☐	☐	☐	☐
8. Damaged property or real estate by lighting a fire (arson)	☐	☐	☐	☐	☐
9. Avoided paying for things such as movies, bus or subway rides, or food	☐	☐	☐	☐	☐
10. Been paid for having sexual relations with someone	☐	☐	☐	☐	☐
11. Paid someone for sexual relations	☐	☐	☐	☐	☐
12. Had (or tried to have) sexual relations with someone against their will	☐	☐	☐	☐	☐
13. Had sexual relations with someone under the legal age of consent (while over the age of consent yourself)	☐	☐	☐	☐	☐
14. Made sexual comments or advances toward someone that you knew were unwanted	☐	☐	☐	☐	☐
15. Had sexual relations in a public place	☐	☐	☐	☐	☐
16. Used violence or the threat of violence to rob someone	☐	☐	☐	☐	☐
17. Carried a hidden weapon other than a plain pocketknife	☐	☐	☐	☐	☐
18. Made a serious threat that you meant to carry out	☐	☐	☐	☐	☐
19. Beaten someone up seriously enough that they required medical attention of any kind	☐	☐	☐	☐	☐
20. Killed another human being (excluding wartime situations)	☐	☐	☐	☐	☐
21. Constructed a bomb or similar explosive device	☐	☐	☐	☐	☐
22. Used marijuana, cannabis, or hashish	☐	☐	☐	☐	☐
23. Bought marijuana, cannabis, or hashish	☐	☐	☐	☐	☐
24. Sold marijuana, cannabis, or hashish	☐	☐	☐	☐	☐
25. Used hard drugs such as heroin, cocaine, LSD, or ecstasy	☐	☐	☐	☐	☐
26. Bought hard drugs, such as heroin, cocaine, LSD, or ecstasy	☐	☐	☐	☐	☐
27. Sold hard drugs, such as heroin, cocaine, LSD, or ecstasy	☐	☐	☐	☐	☐
28. Manufactured or cultivated a controlled substance (drugs)	☐	☐	☐	☐	☐
29. Taken pharmaceuticals prescribed for someone else	☐	☐	☐	☐	☐
30. Smuggled alcohol, tobacco, or food items (e.g., avoiding duty when crossing federal borders)	☐	☐	☐	☐	☐

31. Smuggled illegal drugs or drug paraphernalia	☐	☐	☐	☐	☐
32. Bought or provided liquor for a minor	☐	☐	☐	☐	☐
33. Been drunk in a public place	☐	☐	☐	☐	☐
34. Consumed enough alcohol to put you over the legal limit and then driven a car	☐	☐	☐	☐	☐
35. Driven a car without a license	☐	☐	☐	☐	☐
36. Taken a vehicle for a ride (drive) without the owner's permission	☐	☐	☐	☐	☐
37. Driven a car at unsafe speeds or in a reckless manner	☐	☐	☐	☐	☐
38. Used privileged information in making investment decisions 39. Manipulated financial accounts in an illegal manner.	☐	☐	☐	☐	☐
40. Violated safety or environmental standards	☐	☐	☐	☐	☐
41. Counterfeited fine art or currency	☐	☐	☐	☐	☐
42. Abused work privileges (e.g., personal telephone calls, personal e-mail, or personal use of the copy machine)	☐	☐	☐	☐	☐
43. Sold or traded government or industrial secrets	☐	☐	☐	☐	☐
44. Intentionally misreported income information on your tax forms	☐	☐	☐	☐	☐
45. Used another person's telephone or telephone card without their permission	☐	☐	☐	☐	☐
46. Used another person's ATM (cashpoint) card without their permission	☐	☐	☐	☐	☐
47. Broken into another computer (hacked)	☐	☐	☐	☐	☐
48. Made unauthorized copies of commercial computer software	☐	☐	☐	☐	☐
49. Made copies of copyrighted records, tapes, or videocassettes.	☐	☐	☐	☐	☐
50. Used an electronic device to eavesdrop or spy on someone	☐	☐	☐	☐	☐
51. Plagiarized another person's work (used it without giving them credit)	☐	☐	☐	☐	☐
52. Invented or altered research data	☐	☐	☐	☐	☐
53. Cheated on an examination or test	☐	☐	☐	☐	☐
54. Taken steps to evade (dodge) a military draft or selective service	☐	☐	☐	☐	☐
55. Instigated acts of rebellion against the government or agencies of the government	☐	☐	☐	☐	☐

56. Made an agreement with other people to commit a criminal act	☐	☐	☐	☐	☐
57. Spread false and injurious statements about someone, either orally or in print	☐	☐	☐	☐	☐
58. Held someone against their will (kidnapping)	☐	☐	☐	☐	☐
59. Fished or hunted without a license where one is required	☐	☐	☐	☐	☐
60. Tricked (or tried to trick) a person, group, or company for financial gain (fraud)	☐	☐	☐	☐	☐
61. Resisted arrest	☐	☐	☐	☐	☐
62. Violated the conditions of your parole	☐	☐	☐	☐	☐
63. Blackmailed someone	☐	☐	☐	☐	☐
64. Knowingly lied while under oath	☐	☐	☐	☐	☐
65. Intentionally trespassed on private or government property	☐	☐	☐	☐	☐
66. Been loud, rowdy, or unruly in a public place (disorderly conduct)	☐	☐	☐	☐	☐
67. Attempted suicide	☐	☐	☐	☐	☐
68. Broken into a building or vehicle (or tried to break in) to steal something or just to look around	☐	☐	☐	☐	☐
69. Made obscene telephone calls, such as calling someone and saying dirty things	☐	☐	☐	☐	☐
70. Gambled where it is illegal to do so	☐	☐	☐	☐	☐
71. Forged another person's signature on an official document, prescription, or bank check	☐	☐	☐	☐	☐
72. Failed to appear in court when ordered to do so by summons	☐	☐	☐	☐	☐

SECTION 3: INFLUENCES

Please list your three most influential (in terms of shaping your character, not necessarily being your favorite) books, films, and famous figures (from history or popular culture). Please give this question a few moments of thought before answering, and say a word about how each item influenced you.

Books:
Films:

People:

Is there anything that we've missed?

This questionnaire was designed to help shed some light on the enigma of patterns of criminal behavior in intellectually gifted individuals. It has been carefully constructed and tested over many months, but there are bound to be oversights and omissions: offense items that should have been listed and were not, demographic questions that were not asked, or influences from sources other than books, films, and people that should have been asked about. If you have additional comments or criticism, please jot them down and share your ideas. Your feedback is very helpful and will be taken very seriously. Thank you very much for your cooperation in this project.

Interview Schedule

BEGIN BY BRIEFLY EXPLAINING THE RESEARCH

This research is being conducted in order to better understand the patterns of criminal behavior in the intellectually gifted. Although a great deal has been written about the relationship between IQ and crime, the patterns of offending in genius-level populations are still unexplored. This research project consists of two principal phases: the distribution of self-report questionnaires to exceptionally intelligent persons in high-IQ societies, in prestigious universities, or via the contact of colleagues; and secondly, the conduct of follow-up interviews. The purpose of these interviews is to augment the statistical findings of the questionnaires with qualitative (vs. quantitative) data and to collect narrative accounts of experiences with crime. While IQ is an important variable in this research, it is not the only variable being examined.

SECTION 1 QUESTIONS: INDIVIDUAL PERSPECTIVE AND PERSONAL DEMOGRAPHICS

How important do you think a person's IQ score actually is?

What other factors—other than IQ—are most important?

What are the three most important factors for a person?

On your questionnaire, you described your ethnicity as _____. Growing up, did you have a strong sense of ethnic identity?

Do you think that this ethnic identity (or lack thereof) has had an impact on your character?

You described your nationality as _____. Have you ever lived outside this country? If yes, ask where and when? For how long?

Have you ever traveled outside it? If yes, where to?

Would you ever want to live somewhere else? If yes, ask where and why?

You described your religion as _____. Would you say that you have strong religious beliefs? If 1 is no belief whatsoever and 10 is very deep religious belief, what number would best describe the strength of your religious beliefs?

Do your beliefs (or lack thereof) affect your behavior on a day-to-day basis? If yes, ask for an example.

You described your marital status as _____. Is this still accurate?

If not married, ask if currently involved with a significant other. If yes, for how long?

If married/divorced, ask how long married.

Do you have any children? If yes, ask number, sex, age.

Do you, yourself, have brothers or sisters? If yes, ask number, sex, age (establish birth order).

On your questionnaire, you described your occupation as _____. How long have you done this?

What jobs did you hold before this?

Ultimately, what job would you like to have?

What aspects make this particular job attractive to you?

You described your highest academic level as _____. Where did you go to school?

What kind of a student were you? Quiet? Mischievous? Popular? Shy? Hardworking? Underachiever?

What kind of grades did you get?

What were your favorite subjects?

Did you have any particular classes that were really influential? If yes, ask to describe what made them influential.

What class did you like least? Why?

If ticked questionnaire as homosexual or bisexual, ask if sexuality has been a difficulty. Are you open about it or is it something you've kept secret? Have your family and friends been supportive? Do you feel like your sexual orientation has been something that other people (would have) held against you? If yes, ask for an example.

If ticked questionnaire as suffering mental illness, ask if this is something that other people know about or if it is something you've kept secret?

Have your family and friends been supportive? Do you feel like this is
something that other people (would have) held against you? If yes, ask for
an example.

If ticked questionnaire as received mental health treatment, ask for details.
When was this? What sort of symptoms were you having? What kind of
treatment did you receive? Did it correct the problem? Do you still have
any symptoms?

If ticked questionnaire as arrested, ask for details. How many times? If more
than once, focus on the last offense. What offense were you arrested for?
When did this happen? What was the situation like?

If ticked questionnaire as convicted, ask for details. How many times
convicted? If more than once, focus on the last conviction? What offense
were you convicted for? When did this happen? What was the outcome—
did you serve probation or pay a fine or go to jail? What was the situation
like?

SECTION 2 QUESTIONS: SELF-REPORT

Offer the participant a blank questionnaire and ask him/her to look over the
offense index. Ask, Do you think you checked more or less boxes than the
average person would? Do you think you checked more or less boxes than
most high-IQ people would?

I'd like to talk to you now about just a few of the items you marked. Is
that okay? If yes, select between three and five offenses—at least one
of which is quite minor and the other of which are of particular
interest.

Beginning with the minor offense (to help build rapport), ask the participant
to describe the situation: Can you tell me a little about what happened?
Both in terms of what was actually happening in the situation, and also in
what you were thinking and feeling at the time. [This is essentially a
free-answer section, but probe for details as needed.]

What factors do you think led you do it?

What happened afterward?

Would you do it again?

Repeat with offenses of interest, limiting offense questions to a maximum of
five.

There are a number of items on the survey that you indicate you've never
done. What factors do you think are most important in preventing you
from committing these other offenses?

SECTION 3 QUESTIONS: INTERPRETATIVE QUESTIONS AND PLANS

What one thing in your life would you most like to go back and do differently if you could?

What one thing in your life have you been the most proud of?

Where do you see yourself a year from now? Five years from now?

Do you have any questions that you would like to ask me?

REFERENCES

Aamodt, M G. (2014, September 6). Serial killer statistics. Retrieved from http://maamodt
.asp.radford.edu/serial killer information center/project description.htm

Aamodt, M. G. (2015). Serial killer IQs. Retrieved from http://www.kidsiqtestcenter.com
/serial-killers-IQ.html

Abagnale, F. W., Jr., & Redding, S. (1980). *Catch me if you can.* New York, NY: Grosset &
Dunlap.

Academy of Criminal Justice Sciences. (2000). Code of ethics. Retrieved from http://www
.acjs.org/pubs/167_671_2922.cfm

Adams, J. (1980, November 18). Life of crime leads Abagnale to new career on side of law.
Bulletin Journal [Cape Girardeau, MO], A1.

Adams, S. (1969). Education and the career dilemma of high IQ prisoners. *Criminology,*
6(4), 4–12.

Adleman, R. H. (1973). *Alias big cherry.* New York, NY: Dial Press.

Adler, N. E., Boyce, T., Chesney, M. A., Cohen, S., Folkman, S., Kahn, R. L., & Syme, S. L.
(1994). Socioeconomic status and health: the challenge of the gradient. *American Psychologist,* 49(1), 15–24.

Adreon, F., & Witney, W. (Directors). (1956). *The adventures of Fu Manchu* [Television
series]. United States: NBC.

AFI. (2003). AFI's 100 years . . . 100 heroes and villains. Retrieved from http://www.afi
.com/100Years/handv.aspx

Agee, J., & Evans, W. (1969). *Let us now praise famous men.* Boston, MA: Houghton Mifflin.

Agnew, R. (1992). Foundation of a general strain theory of crime and delinquency. *Criminology,* 30(1), 47–87.

Akers, R. L. (1994). *Criminological theories.* Los Angeles, CA: Roxbury.

Akers, R. L. (1998). *Social learning and social structure: A general theory of crime and
deviance.* Boston, MA: Northeastern University Press.

Akers, R. L. (2010). Religion and crime. *Criminologist, 35*(6), 1–6.

Albert, R. S. (Ed.). (1992). *Genius and eminence* (2nd ed.). New York, NY: Pergamon Press.

Alfredson, D. (Director). (2010a). *The girl who kicked the hornet's nest* [Motion picture]. United States: Music Box Films.

Alfredson, D. (Director). (2010b). *The girl who played with fire* [Motion picture]. United States: Music Box Films.

Allain, M., & Souvestre, P. (1986). *Fantômas.* New York, NY: Ballantine Books.

American Anthropological Association. (1994). American Anthropological Association statement on "race" and intelligence. Retrieved from http://www.aaanet.org/stmts/race.htm

American Law Institute. (1985). *Model penal code: Official draft and explanatory notes; Complete text of model penal code as adopted at the 1962 Annual Meeting of the American Law Institute at Washington, D.C., May 24, 1962.* Philadelphia, PA: The Institute.

American Psychiatric Association. (2013). *Diagnostic and statistical manual of mental disorders* (5th ed.). Arlington, VA: American Psychiatric Association.

American Sociological Association. (2003). The importance of collecting data and doing social scientific research on race. Retrieved from http://www.asanet.org/images/press/docs/pdf/asa_race_statement.pdfAnderson, D. A. (1999). The aggregate burden of crime. *Journal of Law and Economics, 42*(2), 611–642.

Andreasen, N. C. (1987). Creativity and mental illness: Prevalence rates in writers and their first-degree relatives. *American Journal of Psychiatry, 144*(10), 1288–1292.

Andreasen, N. C. (2005). *The creating brain: The neuroscience of genius.* New York, NY: Dana Press.

Andrew, J. M. (1977). Delinquency: Intellectual imbalance? *Criminal Justice and Behavior, 4*(1), 99–104.

Andrews, D. A., & Bonta, J. (2015)). *The psychology of criminal conduct* (5th ed.). New York, NY: Routledge.

Andrews, D. A., Bonta, J., & Wormith, J. S. (2006). The recent past and near future of risk and/or need assessment. *Crime and Delinquency, 52*(1), 7–27.

Angus, S. (Director). (1996) *America's dumbest criminals* [Television series, 1996–2000]. United States [Produced for syndication].

Anolik, S. A. (1979). Personality, family, educational, and criminological characteristics of bright delinquents. *Psychological Reports, 44*(3), 727–734.

Antshel, K. M., Faraone, S. V., Maglione, K., Doyle, A. E., Fried, R., Seidman, L. J., & Biederman, J. (2010). Executive functioning in high-IQ adults with ADHD. *Psychological Medicine, 40*(11), 1909–1918.

Ardila, A., Pineda, D., & Rosselli, M. (2000). Correlation between intelligence test scores and executive function measures. *Archives of Clinical Neuropsychology, 15*(1), 31–36.

Aristotle. (1941). *The basic works of Aristotle* (R. McKeon, Trans.). New York, NY: Random House. (Original work written circa 350 BCE)

Asbury, H. (1928). *The gangs of New York: An informal history of the underworld.* New York, NY: Knopf.

Asinof, E. (1976). *The fox is crazy too.* New York, NY: Pocket Books.

Astin, A. W., & Boruch, R. F. (1970). A "link" system for assuring confidentiality of research data in longitudinal studies. *American Educational Research Journal, 7*(4), 615–624.

Atkins v. Virginia, 536 U.S. 304 (2002).

Baatz, S. (2008). *For the thrill of It: Leopold, Loeb, and the murder that shocked Jazz Age Chicago.* New York, NY: HarperCollins.

Babcock, W. L. (1895). On the morbid heredity and predisposition to insanity of the man of genius. *Journal of Nervous and Mental Disease, 20*(12), 749–769.

Baker, H. J., Decker, F. J., & Hill, A. S. (1929). A study of juvenile theft. *Journal of Educational Research, 20*(2), 81–88.

Ball, L. C. (2014). The genius in history: Historiographic explorations. In D. K. Simonton (Ed.), *The Wiley handbook of genius* (pp. 3–19). New York, NY: John Wiley & Sons.

Bamford, J. (2014, August). Edward Snowden: The untold story. *Wired.*

Bankston, C. L. (Ed.). (2007). *Great lives from history: Notorious lives* (3 Vols.). Pasadena, CA: Salem Press.

Barclay, J. (1999). A historical review of learning difficulties, remedial therapy and the rise of the professional therapist. In J. Swain & S. French (Eds.), *Therapy and learning difficulties: Advocacy, participation and partnership* (pp. 22–32). Oxford: Butterworth-Heinemann.

Barefoot v. Estelle, 463 U.S. 880 (1983).

Barnes, A. (2004). *Sherlock Holmes on screen: The complete film and TV history.* London: Reynolds & Hearn.

Barnes, H. E., & Teeters, N. K. (1959). *New horizons in criminology* (3rd ed.). Englewood Cliffs, NJ: Prentice-Hall.

Barnes, J. C., Jorgensen, C., Pacheco, D., & TenEyck, M. (2015). The puzzling relationship between age and criminal behavior: A biosocial critique of the criminological status quo. In K. M. Beaver, J. C. Barnes, & B. B. Boutwell (Eds.). *The nurture versus biosocial debate in criminology* (pp. 397–413). Thousand Oaks, CA: SAGE.

Barrett, W. P. (1991). *The trial of Joan of Arc.* Birmingham, AL: Notable Trials Library.

Bartels, J. M., Ryan, J. J., Urban, L. S., & Glass, L. A. (2010). Correlations between estimates of state IQ and FBI crime statistics. *Personality and Individual Differences, 48*(5), 579–583.

Baschetti, R. (2008). Genetic evidence that Darwin was right about criminality: Nature, not nurture. *Medical hypotheses, 70*(6), 1092–1102.

Bates, D. (2015, April 28). James Holmes trial: Accused "had obsession to kill since childhood." *London Evening Standard.* Retrieved from http://www.standard.co.uk/news/crime/aurora-shooting-james-holmes-had-obsession-to-kill-since-childhood-10208544.html

Baudelaire, C. (1980). *Oeuvres complètes.* Paris: Robert Laffont. (Original work published 1864)

Baxter, D. J., Motiuk, L. L., & Fortin, S. (1995). Intelligence and personality in criminal offenders. In D. H. Saklofske & M. Zeidner (Eds.), *International handbook of personality and intelligence* (pp. 673–686). New York, NY: Plenum Press.

Bazeley, P., & Jackson, K. (2013). *Qualitative data analysis with NVivo* (2nd ed.). Thousand Oaks, CA: SAGE.

BBC. (2014, June 26). Jimmy Savile NHS abuse victims aged five to 75. Retrieved from http://www.bbc.com/news/uk-28034427

Bearman, J., & Hanuka, T. (2015a). The rise and fall of Silk Road (part 1): Ross Ulbricht's journey from libertarian idealist to savage kingpin. *Wired, 23*(5), 90–97. Retrieved from https://www.wired.com/2015/04/silk-road-1

Bearman, J., & Hanuka, T. (2015b). The rise and fall of Silk Road (part 2): Ross Ulbricht's journey from drug kingpin to convicted criminal. *Wired, 23*(6), 82–89. Retrieved from http://www.wired.com/2015/05/silk-road-2

Beatty, S., Greenberger, R., Jimenez, P., & Wallace, D. (2008). *The DC Comics encyclopedia: The definitive guide to the characters of the DC universe* (rev. ed.). New York, NY: DK.

Beaver, K. M., Barnes, J. C., & Boutwell, B. B. (Eds.). (2015). *The nurture versus biosocial debate in criminology.* Thousand Oaks, CA: SAGE.

Beaver, K. M., DeLisi, M., Vaughn, M .G., Wright, J. P., & Boutwell, B. B. (2008). The relationship between self-control and language: Evidence of a shared etiological pathway. *Criminology, 46*(4), 939–970.

Beaver, K. M., & Nedelec, J. L. (2015). A biosocial explanation for male-female differences in criminal involvement. In K. M. Beaver, J. C. Barnes, & B. B. Boutwell (Eds.). *The nurture versus biosocial debate in criminology* (pp. 25–41). Thousand Oaks, CA: SAGE.

Beaver, K. M., Schwartz, J. A., Nedelec, J. L., Connolly, E. J., Boutwell, B. B., & Barnes, J. C. (2013). Intelligence is associated with criminal justice processing: Arrest through incarceration. *Intelligence, 41*(5), 277–288.

Beaver, K. M., Schwartz, J. A., Al-Ghamdi, M. S., Kobeisy, A. N., Dunkel, C. S., & van der Linden, D. (2014). A closer look at the role of parenting-related influences on verbal intelligence over the life course: Results from an adoption-based research design. *Intelligence, 46,* 179–187.

Beaver, K. M., Vaughn, M. G., Wright, J. P., DeLisi, M., & Howard, M. O. (2010).Three dopaminergic polymorphisms are associated with academic achievement in middle and high school. *Intelligence, 38*(6), 596–604.

Beaver, K. M., & Wright, J. P. (2011). The association between county-level IQ and county-level crime rates. *Intelligence, 39*(1), 22–26.

Beaver, K. M., Wright, J. P., & DeLisi, M. (2007). Self-control as an executive function: Reformulating Gottfredson and Hirschi's parental socialization thesis. *Criminal Justice and Behavior, 34*(10), 1345–1361.

Beaver, K. M., Wright, J. P., DeLisi, M., & Vaughn, M. G. (2012). Dopaminergic polymorphisms and educational achievement: Results from a longitudinal sample of Americans. *Developmental Psychology, 48*(4), 932–938.

Beccaria, C. (1995). *On crimes and punishments and other writings* (R. Bellamy, Ed., R. Davies & V. Cox, Trans.). New York, NY: Cambridge University Press. (Original work published 1764 as *Dei delitti e delle pene*)

Becker, G. (1978). *The mad genius controversy.* Beverly Hills, CA: SAGE.

Becker, H. S. (1963). *Outsiders: Studies in the sociology of deviance.* Glencoe, IL: Free Press.

Beckman, M. (2004). Crime, culpability, and the adolescent brain. *Science, 305*(5684), 596–599.

Bellair, P. E., McNulty, T. L., & Piquero, A. R. (2016). Verbal ability and persistent offending: A race-specific test of Moffitt's theory. *Justice Quarterly, 33*(3), 455–480.

Bellinger, D. C. (2012). A strategy for comparing the contributions of environmental chemicals and other risk factors to neurodevelopment of children. *Environmental Health Perspectives, 120*(4), 501–507.

Bentham, J. (1823). *An introduction to the principles of morals and legislation.* London: W. Pickering. (Original work published 1789)

Ben-Yehuda, N. (1980). The European witch craze of the 14th to 17th centuries: A sociologist's perspective. *American Journal of Sociology, 86*(1), 1–31.

Bergelson, V. (2013). Vice is nice but incest is best: The problem of a moral taboo. *Criminal Law and Philosophy, 7*(1), 43–59.

Bett, W. R. (1952). *The infirmities of genius.* London: Christopher Johnson.

Biderman, A. D., & Reiss, A. J. (1967). On exploring the "dark figure" of crime. *Annals of the American Academy of Political and Social Sciences, 374*(1), 1–15.

Biernacki, P., & Waldorf, D. (1981). Snowball sampling: Problems and techniques of chain referral sampling. *Sociological Methods and Research, 10*(2), 141–163.

Binder, A. (1988). Juvenile delinquency. *Annual review of psychology, 39*(1), 253–282.

Birmingham, L., Mason, D., & Grubin, D. (1996). Prevalence of mental disorder in remand prisoners: Consecutive case study. *British Medical Journal, 313*(7071), 1521–1524.

Bisbort, A. (2006). *"When you read this, they will have killed me": The life and redemption of Caryl Chessman, whose execution shook America.* New York, NY: Carroll & Graf.

Black, W. A. M., & Hornblow, A. R. (1973). Intelligence and criminality. *Australian and New Zealand Journal of Criminology, 6*(2), 83–92.

Blackburn, R. (1993). *The psychology of criminal conduct: Theory, research and practice.* New York, NY: John Wiley & Sons.

Blackstone, W. (1841). *Commentaries on the laws of England* (Book 4). New York, NY: W. E. Dean. (Original work published 1769)

Blanchard, R., Kolla, N. J., Cantor, J. M., Klassen, P. E., Dickey, R., Kuban, M. E., & Blak, T. (2007). IQ, handedness, and pedophilia in adult male patients stratified by referral source. *Sexual Abuse: A Journal of Research and Treatment, 19*(3), 285–309.

Blanco, M. (1996). On the make. *Varsity, 443,* 7.

Block, J. (1995). On the relation between IQ, impulsivity, and delinquency: Remarks on the Lynam, Moffitt, and Southamer-Loeber (1993) interpretation. *Journal of Abnormal Psychology, 104*(2), 395–398.

Bloom, H. (2002). *Genius: A mosaic of one hundred exemplary creative minds.* New York, NY: Warner Books.

Bloom, H. (Ed.). (2004). *Frankenstein: Bloom's major literary characters.* Broomall, PA: Chelsea House Publishers.

Bogira, S. (2005). *Courtroom 302: A year behind the scenes in an American criminal courthouse.* New York, NY: Alfred A. Knopf.

Bondio, M. G. (2006). From the "atavistic" to the "inferior" criminal type: The impact of the Lombrosian theory of the born criminal on German psychiatry. In P. Becker & R. F. Wetzell (Eds.), *Criminals and their scientists: The history of criminology in international perspective* (pp. 183–205). New York, NY: Cambridge University Press.

Bonta, J., Law, M., & Hanson, K. (1998). The prediction of criminal and violent recidivism among mentally disordered offenders: a meta-analysis. *Psychological Bulletin, 123*(2), 123–142.

Boring, E. G. (1923). Intelligence as the tests test it. *New Republic, 35,* 35–37.

Boruch, R. F. (1976). Strategies for eliciting and merging confidential social research data. In P. Nejelski (Ed.), *Social research in conflict with law and ethics* (pp. 83–109). Cambridge, MA: Ballinger.

Botelho, G. (2014, November 8). Pittsburgh professor convicted for fatally poisoning wife with cyanide. *CNN*. Retrieved from http://edition.cnn.com/2014/11/08/justice /pennsylvania-doctor-cyanide-poisoning

Bouffard, J. A., & Petkovsek, M. A. (2013). Testing Hirschi's integration of social control and rational choice: Are bonds considered in offender decisions? *Journal of Crime and Justice, 37*(3), 285–308.

Bourgois, P., & Schonberg, J. (2009). *Righteous dopefiend*. Berkeley: University of California Press.

Bousman, D. L. (Director). (2005). *Saw II* [Motion picture]. United States: Lionsgate Films.

Bousman, D. L. (Director). (2006). *Saw III* [Motion picture]. United States: Lionsgate Films.

Bousman, D. L. (Director). (2007). *Saw IV* [Motion picture]. United States: Lionsgate Films.

Bower, B. (1995). Criminal intellects. *Science News, 147*(15), 232–233, 239.

Bowers v. Hardwick, 478 U.S. 186 (1986).

Bowman, M. L. (1989). Testing individual differences in ancient China. *American Psychologist, 44*(3), 576–578.

Box, S. (1981). *Deviance, reality and society*. London: Holt, Rinehart and Winston.

Brabin, C. (Director). (1932). *The mask of Fu Manchu* [Motion picture]. United States: Metro-Goldwyn-Mayer.

Braithwaite, J. (1989). *Crime, shame and reintegration*. New York, NY: Cambridge University Press.

Branagh, K. (Director). (1994). *Mary Shelley's Frankenstein* [Motion picture]. United States: Tristar Pictures.

Brecht, B. (1966). *Galileo*. New York, NY: Grove Press.

Bridges, S. (1973). *Problems of the gifted child: IQ-150*. New York, NY: Crane, Russak.

Briggs, J. (1988). *Fire in the crucible: The alchemy of creative genius*. New York, NY: St. Martin's Press.

Brinch, C. N., & Galloway, T. A. (2012). Schooling in adolescence raises IQ scores. *Proceedings of the National Academy of Sciences, 109*(2), 425–430.

British Society of Criminology. (2015). Statement of ethics. Retrieved from http://www .britsoccrim.org/documents/BSCEthics2015.pdf

Broad, W., & Wade, N. (1982). *Betrayers of the truth: Fraud and deceit in the halls of science*. New York, NY: Simon and Schuster.

Broadhead, R. S., & Rist, R. C. (1976). Gatekeepers and the social control of social research. *Social Problems, 23*(3), 325–336.

Brooks, R. B. (1967). The highly intelligent delinquent. *Federal Probation, 31*, 43–46.

Brooks, R. B. (1972). *Bright delinquents: The story of a unique school*. Windsor, United Kingdom: National Foundation for Educational Research in England and Wales.

Brooks, R. B. (1980). Gifted delinquents. *Educational Research, 22*(3), 212–220.

Brown, A. W., & Hartman, A. A. (1937). Survey of the intelligence of Illinois prisoners. *American Institute of Criminal Law and Criminology, 28*(5), 707–719.

Bryman, A. (1988). *Quantity and quality in social research*. London: Unwin Hyman.

Buck v. Bell, 274 U.S. 200 (1927).

Buckler, K. (2008). The quantitative/qualitative divide revisited: A study of published research, doctoral program curricula, and journal editor perceptions. *Journal of Criminal Justice Education, 19*(3), 383–403.

Bulmer, M. (1986). *The Chicago school of sociology: Institutionalization, diversity, and the rise of sociological research*. Chicago, IL: University of Chicago Press.

Bunker, E. (2000). *Education of a felon*. New York, NY: St. Martin's Press.

Burdis, K., & Tombs, S. (2012). After the crisis. In S. Hall & S. Winlow (Eds.), *New directions in criminological theory* (pp. 276–291). New York, NY: Routledge.

Bureau of Justice Statistics. (2015). The justice system. Retrieved from http://www.bjs.gov/content/justsys.cfm

Burhan, N. A. S., Kurniawan, Y., Sidek, A. H., & Mohamad, M. R. (2014). Crimes and the bell curve: The role of people with high, average, and low intelligence. *Intelligence, 47,* 12–22.

Burks, B. S., Jensen, D. W., & Terman, L. M. (1930). *Genetic studies of genius*. Vol. 3, *The promise of youth: Follow-up studies of a thousand gifted children*. Stanford, CA: Stanford University Press.

Burroughs, W. S. (1992). *Nova express*. New York, NY: Grove Press.

Burt, C. (1955). *The subnormal mind* (3rd ed.). London: Oxford University Press.

Burt, C. H., & Simons, R. L. (2014). Pulling back the curtain on heritability studies: Biosocial criminology in the postgenomic era. *Criminology, 52*(2), 223–262.

Butler, D., & Ray, A. (2000). *The world's dumbest criminals*. Nashville, TN: Rutledge Hill Press.

Calder, D. (2013, November 6). 32 serial killers with high IQs. *St. Petersburg Conservative Examiner,* Retrieved from http://www.examiner.com/article/22-serial-killers-with-high-iqs

Campbell, J. (1988). *The power of myth*. New York, NY: Doubleday.

Camus, A. (1956). *The rebel: An essay on man in revolt*. New York, NY: Vintage Books.

Camus, A. (1957). *The fall*. London: Hamish Hamilton.

Cantor, D., & Land, K. C. (1985). Unemployment and crime rates in the post–World War II United States: A theoretical and empirical analysis. *American Sociological Review, 50*(3), 317–332.

Cantor, J. M., Blanchard, R., Christensen, B. K., Dickey, R., Klassen, P. E., Beckstead, A. L., ... Kuban, M. E. (2004). Intelligence, memory, and handedness in pedophilia. *Neuropsychology, 18*(1), 3–14.

Cantor, J. M., Blanchard, R., Robichaud, L. K., & Christensen, B. K. (2005). Quantitative reanalysis of aggregate data on IQ in sexual offenders. *Psychological Bulletin, 131*(4), 555–568.

Caplan, N. S. (1965). Intellectual functioning. In H. C. Quay (Ed.), *Juvenile Delinquency* (pp. 100–138). Princeton, NJ: Van Nostrand.

Caplan, N. S., & Powell, M. (1964). A cross comparison of average-and superior-IQ delinquents. *Journal of Psychology, 57*(2), 307–318.

Carlo, P. (2006). *The ice man: Confessions of a Mafia contract killer*. New York, NY: St. Martin's.

Carlson, A. L. (Ed.) (2015). *Genius on television: Essays on small screen depictions of big minds*. Jefferson, NC: McFarland.

Carlyle, T. (1966). *On heroes, hero-worship and the heroic in history*. Lincoln: University of Nebraska Press. (Original work published 1841)

Carpenter, R. C. (1967). 007 and the myth of the hero. *Journal of Popular Culture, 1*(2), 79–89.

Carroll, H. A. (1940). *Genius in the making*. New York, NY: McGraw-Hill.

Carson, E. A. (2014). *Prisoners in 2013*. Washington, DC: Bureau of Justice Statistics.

Cavani, L. (Director). (2002). *Ripley's game* [Motion picture]. United States: Fine Line Features.

Cattell, J. McK. (1903). A statistical study of eminent men. *Popular Science Monthly, 62*, 359–377.

Cattell, R. B. (1963). Theory of fluid and crystallized intelligence: A critical experiment. *Journal of educational psychology, 54*(1), 1–22.

Cernkovich, S. A., Giordano, P. C., & Pugh, M. D. (1985). Chronic offenders: The missing cases in self-report delinquency research. *Journal of Criminal Law and Criminology, 76*(3), 705–732.

Chabrol, C. (Director). (1990). *Dr. M* [Motion picture]. United States: Prism Entertainment.

Chan, D. W. (2001). The mad genius controversy: Does the East differ from the West? *Education Journal-Hong Kong-Chinese University of Hong Kong, 29*(1), 1–16.

Chase, A. (2003). *Harvard and the Unabomber: The education of an American terrorist*. New York, NY: W. W. Norton.

Chase, D. (Creator). (1999). *The Sopranos* [Television series, 1999–2007]. United States: HBO.

Chassell, C. F. (1935). *The relation between morality and intellect*. New York, NY: Columbia University, Teachers College, Bureau of Publications.

Chessman, C. (1954). *Cell 2455 death row*. Englewood Cliffs, NJ: Prentice-Hall.

Chessman, C. (1955). *Trial by ordeal*. Englewood Cliffs, NJ: Prentice-Hall.

Chessman, C. (1957). *The face of justice*. Englewood Cliffs, NJ: Prentice-Hall.

Chessman, C. (1960). *The kid was a killer*. Greenwich, CT: Gold Medal Books.

Cheyfitz, E. (2009). Framing Ward Churchill: The political construction of research misconduct. *Works and Days, 51*, 52–53.

Christie, A. (1992). *Appointment with death*. London: HarperCollins. (Original work published 1938)

Claridge, G., Robinson, D. L., & Birchall, P. (1985). Psychophysiological evidence of "Psychoticism" in schizophrenics' relatives. *Personality and Individual Differences, 6*(1), 1–10.

Clarke, A. C. (1968). *2001: A space odyssey*. New York, NY: New American Library.

Clarke, A. C. (1982). *2010: Odyssey two*. New York, NY: Del Rey.

Clarke, M. (2010). Celebrity justice: Prison lifestyles of the rich and famous. *Prison Legal News, 21*(7), 1–11.

Cleckley, H. (1982). *The mask of sanity* (6th ed.). St. Louis, MO: Mosby.

Clément, R. (Director). (1960). *Purple noon* [Motion picture]. United States: Times Film.

Cloward, R. E., & Ohlin, L. E. (1960). *Delinquency and opportunity*. New York, NY: Free Press.

Coates, T-N. (2015). *Between the world and me*. New York, NY: Spiegel & Grau.

Cohen, A. K. (1955). *Delinquent boys: The culture of the gang*. New York, NY: Free Press.

Cohen, J. (1983). Incapacitation as a strategy for crime control: Possibilities and pitfalls. *Crime and Justice, 5*, 1–84.

Cohen, L. E., & Felson, M. (1979). Social change and crime rate trends: A routine activity approach. *American Sociological Review, 44*(4), 588–608.

Cohn, S. (2009). Criminal gifted. In B. A. Kerr (Ed.), *Encyclopedia of giftedness, creativity, and talent* (pp. 221–223). Thousand Oaks, CA: SAGE.

Coker v. Georgia, 433 U.S. 584 (1977).

Coleman, J. W. (2005). *The criminal elite: Understanding white-collar crime* (6th ed.). New York, NY: Worth.

Colman, A.M. (1993). A supernatural IQ? Investigating a claim to an extraordinary IQ. *Skeptic, 7*(5), 12–13.

Condon, R. (1959). *The Manchurian candidate.* New York, NY: McGraw-Hill.

Conrad, J. (1902). The heart of darkness. In *Youth.* London: William Blackwood & Sons.

Conway, J. N. (2009). *King of Heists: The sensational bank robbery of 1878 that shocked America.* Guilford, CT: Lyons Press.

Cooper, J. A., Walsh, A., & Ellis, L. (2010). Is criminology moving to a paradigm shift? Evidence from a survey of the American Society of Criminology. *Journal of Criminal Justice Education, 21*(3), 332–347.

Coppola, F. (Director). (1979). *Apocalypse now* [Motion picture]. United States: United Artists.

Cornell, D. G. (1992). High intelligence and severe delinquency: Evidence disputing the connection. *Roeper Review 14*(4), 233–236.

Cornell, D. G., Delcourt, M. A. B., Bland, L. C., Goldberg, M. D., & Oram, G. (1994). Low incidence of behavior problems among elementary school students in gifted programs. *Journal for the Education of the Gifted, 18* (1), 4–19.

Cornish, D. B., & Clarke, R. V. (1987). Understanding crime displacement: An application of rational choice theory. *Criminology, 25*(4), 933–948.

Cowie, J., Cowie, V., & Slater, E. (1968). *Delinquency in girls.* London: Heinemann.

Cox, C. (1926). *Genetic studies of genius.* Vol. 2, *The early mental traits of three hundred geniuses.* Stanford, CA: Stanford University Press.

Cravens, H. (1992). A scientific project locked in time: The Terman genetic studies of genius, 1920s–1950s. *American Psychologist, 47*(2), 183–189.

Crewe, B., Warr, J., Bennett, P., & Smith, A. (2014). The emotional geography of prison life. *Theoretical Criminology, 18*(1), 56–74.

"Crime doesn't pay, but often brainy" (1961, June 8). *Chicago Daily Defender,* 23.

Cropley, A. J., & Cropley, D. H. (2011). Creativity and lawbreaking. *Creativity Research Journal, 23*(4), 313–320.

Cropley, A. J., Kaufman, J. C., & Runco, M. A. (2010). *The dark side of creativity.* New York, NY: Cambridge University Press.

Cropley, D. H., & Cropley, A. J. (2013). *Creativity and crime: A psychological analysis.* New York, NY: Cambridge University Press.

Cross, T. L., Coleman, L. J., & Stewart, R. A. (1993). The social cognition of gifted adolescents: An exploration of the stigma of giftedness paradigm. *Roeper Review, 16*(1), 37–40.

Crowther, H. (2001, June 13). Death and the madman: It's not impossible to evolve beyond revenge. *Independent Online.* Retrieved from http://www.indyweek.com/indyweek /death-and-the-madman/Content?oid=1183905

Csikszentmihalyi, M. (1996). *Creativity: Flow and the psychology of discovery and invention.* New York, NY: HarperCollins.

Cullen, F. T., Gendreau, P., Jarjoura, G. R., & Wright, J. P. (1997). Crime and the bell curve: Lessons from intelligent criminology. *Crime and Delinquency, 43*(4), 387–411.

Currie, R. (1974). *Genius: An ideology in literature.* London: Chatto & Windus.

Curry, C. (1902). Criminals and their treatment. *American Law Review, 36*(1), 10–35.

Dahl, J. (Director). (1994). *The last seduction* [Motion picture]. United States: October Films.

Daly, K., & Chesney-Lind, M. (1988). Feminism and criminology. *Justice Quarterly, 5*(4), 497–538.

Darrow, C. (1924). *Plea of Clarence Darrow August 22nd, 23rd and 25th 1924 in defense of Richard Loeb and Nathan Leopold Jr. on trial for murder.* Chicago, IL: Ralph Fletcher Seymour.

Darrow, C. (2012). *Attorney for the damned: Clarence Darrow in the courtroom* (A. Weinberg, Ed.). Chicago, IL: University of Chicago Press.

Darwin, C. R. (1870). *On the origin of species by means of natural selection.* New York, NY: D. Appleton. (Original work published 1859)

Darwin, C. R. (1875). *The descent of man and selection in relation to sex.* London: John Murray.

Dauber, S. L., & Benbow, C. P. (1990). Aspects of personality and peer relations of extremely talented adolescents. *Gifted Child Quarterly, 34*(1), 10–14.

Davidson, J. E. (2012). Is giftedness truly a gift? *Gifted Education International, 28*(3), 252–266.

Deary, I. J., Pattie, A., & Starr, J. M. (2013). The stability of intelligence from age 11 to age 90 years: The Lothian birth cohort of 1921. *Psychological Science, 24*(12), 2361–2368.

de Bono, E. (1976). *The greatest thinkers: The 30 minds that shaped our civilization.* New York, NY: G. P. Putnam's Sons.

De Falco, T., Brevoort, T., Darling, A., Sanderson, P., Teitelbaum, M., & Wallace, D. (2006). *The Marvel encyclopedia: The complete guide to the characters of the Marvel universe.* New York, NY: DK.

de la Jara, R. (2015). How to estimate your IQ based on your SAT or GRE scores. Retrieved from http://iqcomparisonsite.com/GREIQ.aspx

DeLisi, M. (2009). Psychopathy is the unified theory of crime. *Youth Violence and Juvenile Justice, 7*(3), 256–273.

DeLisi, M. (2015). Low self-control is a brain-based disorder. In K. M. Beaver, J. C. Barnes, & B. B. Boutwell (Eds.), *The nurture versus biosocial debate in criminology* (pp. 172–182). Thousand Oaks, CA: SAGE.

DeLisi, M., Piquero, A. R., & Cardwell, S. M. (2016). The unpredictability of murder juvenile homicide in the pathways to desistance study. *Youth Violence and Juvenile Justice, 14*(1), 26–42. DeLisi, M., Vaughn, M. G., Beaver, K. M., Wright, J. P. (2010). The Hannibal Lecter myth: Psychopathy and verbal intelligence in the Macarthur violence risk assessment study. *Journal of Psychopathology and Behavioral Assessment, 32*(2), 169–177.

Demme, J. (Director). (1991). *The silence of the lambs* [Motion picture]. United States: Orion Pictures.

Demme, J. (Director). (2004). *The Manchurian candidate* [Motion picture]. United States: Paramount Pictures.

Denno, D. W. (1990). *Biology and violence: From birth to adulthood.* New York, NY: Cambridge University Press.

Devlin, B., Daniels, M., & Roeder, K. (1997). The heritability of IQ. *Nature, 388*(6641), 468–471.

Dewan, S. (2010, February 19). Professor has no memory of shootings, lawyer says. *New York Times,* A8.

Diamond, B., Morris, R. G., & Barnes, J. C. (2012). Individual and group IQ predict inmate violence. *Intelligence, 40*(2), 115–122.

Dick, P. K. (2002). *Selected stories of Philip K. Dick.* New York, NY: Pantheon.

Dobbs, D. (2006). How to be a genius. *New Scientist, 191*(2569), 40–43.

Doherty, R. (Creator). (2013). *Elementary* [Television series, 2012–present]. United States: CBS.

Doleschal, E., & Klapmuts, N. (1973). Toward a new criminology. *Crime and Delinquency Literature, 5*(4), 607–626.

Doll, E. A. (1920). The comparative intelligence of prisoners. *Journal of the American Institute of Criminal Law and Criminology, 11*(2), 191–197.

Donnellan, M. B., Ge, X., & Wenk, E. (2000). Cognitive abilities in adolescent-limited and life-course-persistent criminal offenders. *Journal of Abnormal Psychology, 109*(3), 396–402.

Donnellan, M. B., Trzesniewski, K. H., Robins, R. W., Moffitt, T. E., & Caspi, A. (2005). Low self-esteem is related to aggression, antisocial behavior, and delinquency. *Psychological Science, 16*(4), 328–335.

Dostoevsky, F. (1950). *Crime and punishment* (Garnett, C., Trans.). New York, NY: Random House. (Original work published 1866)

Dostoevsky, F. (1949). *The brothers Karamazov* (C. Garnett, Trans.). New York, NY: Limited Editions Club. (Original work published 1881)

Douglas, J., & Olshaker, M. (1996). *Unabomber: On the trail of America's most-wanted serial killer.* New York, NY: Pocket Books.

Douglas, J., Burgess, A. W., Burgess, A. G., & Ressler, R. K. (2006). *Crime classification manual: A standard system for investigating and classifying violent crime* (2nd ed.). San Francisco, CA: Jossey-Bass.

Douglas, K. S., Guy, L. S., & Hart, S. D. (2009). Psychosis as a risk factor for violence to others: A meta-analysis. *Psychological Bulletin, 135*(5), 679–706.

Doyle, A. C. (2006). *The new annotated Sherlock Holmes.* Vol. 3, *The novels* (L. Klinger, Ed.). New York, NY: W. W. Norton. (Original work published 1887–1915)

Doyle, A. C. (2005). *The new annotated Sherlock Holmes.* Vol. 1, *The complete short stories* (L. Klinger, Ed.). New York, NY: W. W. Norton. (Original work published 1892–1893)

Dressler, J. (2012). Understanding criminal law (6th ed.). Danvers, MA: Matthew Bender.

Drum, K. (2013). America's real criminal element: Lead. *Mother Jones, 38*(1), 28–62.

DuBois, P. H. (1970). *A history of psychological testing.* Boston, MA: Allyn & Bacon.

Duff, R. A., & Garland, D. (Eds.). (1994). *A reader on punishment.* New York, NY: Oxford University Press.

Duffy, B. (1996). The mad bomber? *U.S. News and World Report, 120,* 28–36.

Dugdale, R. (1910). *The Jukes: A study in crime, pauperism, and heredity* (4th ed.). New York, NY: G. P. Putnam's Sons.

Duncan, M. G. (1996). *Romantic outlaws, beloved prisons: The unconscious meanings of crime and punishment.* New York: New York University Press.

Dunn, R. S., & Price, G. E. (1980). The learning style characteristics of gifted students. *Gifted Child Quarterly, 24*(1), 33–36.

Dutton, K. (2012). *The wisdom of psychopaths: What saints, spies, and serial killers can teach us about success.* New York, NY: Macmillan.

Eastwood, L. (1985). Personality, intelligence and personal space among violent and non-violent delinquents. *Personality and Individual Differences, 6*(6), 717–723.

Ehrlich, I. (1975). On the relation between education and crime. In F. T. Juster (Ed.), *Education, income, and human behavior* (pp. 313–338). New York, NY: McGraw-Hill. Retrieved from http://www.nber.org/chapters/c3702.pdf

Eisenman, R. (2008). Malevolent creativity in criminals. *Creativity Research Journal, 20*(2), 116–119.

Eisenstadt, J. M. (1978). Parental loss and genius. *American Psychologist, 33*(3), 211–223.

Elliott, D. S., & Ageton, S. S. (1980). Reconciling race and class differences in self-reported and official estimates of delinquency. *American Sociological Review, 45*(1), 95–110.

Elliott, D. S., & Huizinga, D. (1983). Social class and delinquent behavior in a national youth panel: 1976–1980. *Criminology, 21*(2), 149–177.

Ellis, H. (1927). *A study of British genius* (2nd ed.). London: Constable.

Ellis, L., Beaver, K., & Wright, J. (2009). *Handbook of crime correlates.* San Francisco, CA: Academic Press.

Ellis, L., & Walsh, A. (1999, July–August). Criminologists' opinions about causes and theories of crime and delinquency. *Criminologist, 24*, 1–6.

Ellis, L., & Walsh, A. (2003). Crime, delinquency and intelligence: A review of the worldwide literature. In H. Nyborg (Ed.), *The scientific study of general intelligence: Tribute to Arthur R. Jensen* (pp. 343–365). New York, NY: Pergamon.

Entertainment Weekly. (2008). The new classics: Books: The 100 best reads from 1993 to 2008. Retrieved from http://www.ew.com/article/2007/06/18/new-classics-books

Erikson, K. (1995). Commentary. *American Sociologist, 26*(2), 4–11.

Erickson, M. H. (1929). A study of the relationship between intelligence and crime. *Journal of the American Institute of Criminal Law and Criminology, 19*(4), 592–635.

Estabrook, A. H. (1916). *The Jukes in 1915* (No. 240). Washington, DC: Carnegie Institution of Washington.

Eysenck, H. J. (1959). *Manual of the Maudsley Personality Inventory.* London: University of London Press.

Eysenck, H. J. (1962). *Know your own I.Q.* London: Penguin Books.

Eysenck, H. J. (1966). *Check your own I.Q.* New York, NY: Penguin Books.

Eysenck, H. J. (1967). *The biological basis of personality.* Springfield, IL: C. C. Thomas.

Eysenck, H. J. (1970). *The structure of human personality.* London: Methuen.

Eysenck, H. J. (1977). *Crime and personality* (3rd ed.). London: Routledge and Kegan Paul.

Eysenck, H. J. (1995). *Genius: The natural history of creativity.* New York, NY: Cambridge University Press.

Eysenck, H. J., & Eysenck, S. B. G. (1964). *Manual of the Eysenck Personality Inventory.* London: University of London Press.

Eysenck, H. J., & Eysenck, S. B. G. (1996). *Manual of the Eysenck Personality Scales (EPS Adult).* London: Hodder and Stoughton.

Eysenck, H. J., & Gudjonsson, G. H. (1989). *The causes and cures of criminality.* London: Plenum Press.

Eysenck, S. B. G., & McGurk, B. J. (1980). Impulsiveness and venturesomeness in a detention centre population. *Psychological Reports, 47*(3f), 1299–1306.

Fagan, A. A. (2015). Sociological explanations of the gender gap in offending. In K. M. Beaver, J. C. Barnes, & B. B. Boutwell (Eds.), *The nurture versus biosocial debate in criminology* (pp. 10–24). Thousand Oaks, CA: SAGE.

Fagan, J., & Freeman, R. B. (1999). Crime and work. *Crime and Justice, 25,* 225–290.

Falconer, D. S. (1989). *Introduction to quantitative genetics.* London: Longman.

Fantz, A. (2015). Prison time for some Atlanta school educators in cheating scandal. *CNN.* Retrieved from http://www.cnn.com/2015/04/14/us/georgia-atlanta-public-schools-cheating-scandal-verdicts

Faris, R. E. L. (1961). Reflections on the ability dimension in human society. *American Sociological Review, 26*(6), 835–843.

Farrell, D. M. (1989). Suicide among gifted students. *Roeper Review, 11*(3), 134–139.

Farrington, D. P. (1986). Age and crime. *Crime and Justice, 7,* 189–250.

Farrington, D. P. (1989). Early predictors of adolescent aggression and adult violence. *Violence and Victims, 4*(2), 79–100.

Farrington, D. P. (1992). Explaining the beginning, progress and ending of antisocial behavior from birth to adulthood. In J. McCord (Ed.), *Facts, framework and forecasts: Advances in criminological theory* (Vol. 3, pp. 253–286). New Brunswick, NJ: Transaction.

Farrington, D. P., Biron, L., & LeBlanc, M. (1982). Personality and delinquency in London and Montreal. In J. Gunn & D. P. Farrington (Eds.), *Abnormal offenders, delinquency, and the criminal justice system* (pp. 121–148). New York, NY: Wiley.

Farrington, D. P., Loeber, R., & Ttofi, M. M. (2012). Risk and protective factors for offending. In B. C. Welsh & D. P. Farrington (Eds.), *The Oxford handbook of crime prevention* (pp. 46–69). New York, NY: Oxford University Press.

Farrington, D. P., Ohlin, L. E., & Wilson, J. Q. (1986). *Understanding and controlling crime.* New York, NY: Springer-Verlag.

Farrington, D. P., & Welsh, B. C. (2007). *Saving children from a life of crime: Early risk factors and effective interventions.* New York, NY: Oxford University Press.

Farrington, K. (1996). *Dark justice: The history of punishment and torture.* New York, NY: Reed International Books.

Fass, P. S. (1993). Making and remaking an event: The Leopold and Loeb case in American culture. *Journal of American History, 80*(3), 919–951.

FBI. (2015). Crime in the United States. Retrieved from http://www.fbi.gov/about-us/cjis/ucr/crime-in-the-u.s/2013/crime-in-the-u.s.-2013

Fears, J. R. (1978). Ο ΔΗΜΟΣ Ο ΡΩΜΑΙΩN Genius Populi Romani: A note on the origin of Dea Roma. *Mnemosyne, 31*(Fasc. 3), 274–286.

Feeley, M. M. (1979). *The process is the punishment: Handling cases in a lower criminal court.* New York, NY: Russell Sage Foundation.

Feist, G. J. (2014). Psychometric studies of scientific talent and eminence. In D. K. Simonton (Ed.), *The Wiley handbook of genius* (pp. 62–86). New York, NY: John Wiley & Sons.

Feldman, D. H. (1984). A follow-up of subjects scoring above 180 IQ in Terman's *Genetic Studies of Genius. Exceptional Children, 50*(6), 518–523.

Feldman, M. P. (1977). *Criminal behavior: A psychological analysis.* New York, NY: John Wiley & Sons.

Feldman, P. (1993). *The psychology of crime: A social science textbook.* New York, NY: Cambridge University Press.

Felson, R. B., & Staff, J. (2006). Explaining the academic performance-delinquency relationship. *Criminology, 44*(2), 299–320.

Ferguson, C. J., & Beaver, K. M. (2009). Natural born killers: The genetic origins of extreme violence. *Aggression and Violent Behavior, 14*(5), 286–294.

Fergusson, D. M., Horwood, L. J., & Ridder, E. M. (2005). Show me the child at seven II: Childhood intelligence and later outcomes in adolescence and young adulthood. *Journal of Child Psychology and Psychiatry, 46*(8), 850–858.

Fergusson, D. M., & Lynskey, M. T. (1996). Adolescent resiliency to family adversity. *Journal of Child Psychology and Psychiatry, 37*, 281–292.

Ferrell, J., & Hamm, M. S. (Eds.). (1998). *Ethnography at the edge: Crime, deviance, and field work.* Boston, MA: Northeastern University Press.

Feuillade, L. (Director). (1913a). *Fantômas in the Shadow of the Guillotine* [Motion picture]. United States: Gaumont.

Feuillade, L. (Director). (1913b). *Juve vs. Fantômas* [Motion picture]. United States: Gaumont.

Feuillade, L. (Director). (1913c). *The Murderous Corpse* [Motion picture]. United States: Gaumont.

Feuillade, L. (Director). (1914a). *The False Magistrate* [Motion picture]. United States: Gaumont.

Feuillade, L. (Director). (1914b). *Fantômas vs. Fantômas* [Motion picture]. United States: Gaumont.

Fincher, D. (Director). (1995). *Se7en* [Motion picture]. United States: New Line Cinema.

Fincher, D. (Director). (2011). *The girl with the dragon tattoo* [Motion picture]. United States: Columbia Pictures.

Finkel, N. (1988). *Insanity on trial.* New York, NY: Plenum Press.

Finnegan, W. (1998, March 16). Defending the Unabomber. *New Yorker,* 52–63.

Finocchiaro, M. A. (Ed.). (1989). *The Galileo affair: A documentary history.* Berkeley: University of California Press.

Firkowska-Mankiewicz, A. (2002). Intelligence (IQ) as a predictor of life success. *International Journal of Sociology, 32*(3), 25–43.

Fischman, J. (2011, June 12). Criminal minds. *Chronicle of Higher Education.* Retrieved from http://chronicle.com/article/Can-This-Man-Predict-Whether/127792.

Fleischer, R. (Director). (1959). *Compulsion* [Motion picture]. United States: Darryl F. Zanuck Productions.

Fleming, I. (1958). *Dr. No.* London: Jonathan Cape.

Fleming, I. (1959). *Goldfinger.* London: Jonathan Cape.

Fleming, I. (1961). *Thunderball.* London: Jonathan Cape.

Fleming, I. (1963). *On Her Majesty's secret service.* London: Jonathan Cape.

Fleming, I. (1964). *You only live twice.* London: Jonathan Cape.

Fleming, V. (Director). (1941). *Dr. Jekyll and Mr. Hyde* [Motion picture]. United States: Metro-Goldwyn-Mayer.

Flynn, J. R. (1987). Massive IQ gains in 14 nations: What IQ tests really measure. *Psychological Bulletin, 101*(2), 171–191.

Flynn, J. R. (2012). *Are we getting smarter: Rising IQ in the twenty-first century.* New York, NY: Cambridge University Press.

Ford v. Wainwright, 477 U.S. 399 (1986).

Foust, R. C., & Booker, K. (2007). The social cognition of gifted adolescents. *Roeper Review, 29*(5), 45–47.

Fox, V. (1946). Intelligence, race, and age as selective factors in crime. *Journal of Criminal Law and Criminology, 37*(2), 141–152.

Frankenheimer, J. (Director). (1962). *The Manchurian candidate* [Motion picture]. United States: United Artists.

Frankenheimer, J. (Director). (1996). *The island of Dr. Moreau* [Motion picture]. United States: New Line Cinema.

Franzen, M. D. (2000). *Reliability and validity in neuropsychological assessment.* New York, NY: Plenum.

Fraser, S. (Ed.). (1995). *The bell curve wars: Race, intelligence, and the future of America.* New York, NY: Basic Books.

Frears, S. (Director). (1996). *Mary Reilly* [Motion picture]. United States: Tristar Pictures.

Freud, S. (1964). *Leonardo da Vinci and a memory of his childhood* (A. Tyson, Trans.). New York, NY: Norton. (Original work published 1910)

Frey, M. C., & Detterman, D. K. (2004). Scholastic assessment or *g*? The relationship between the Scholastic Assessment Test and general cognitive ability. *Psychological Science, 15*(6), 373–378.

Friedman, N. P., Miyake, A., Corley, R. P., Young, S. E., DeFries, J. C., & Hewitt, J. K. (2006). Not all executive functions are related to intelligence. *Psychological Science, 17*(2), 172–179.

Friedman, N. P., Miyake, A., Young, S. E., DeFries, J. C., Corley, R. P., & Hewitt, J. K. (2008). Individual differences in executive functions are almost entirely genetic in origin. *Journal of Experimental Psychology: General, 137*(2), 201–225.

Fuller, B. (Writer). (2013). *Hannibal* [Television series, 2013–2016]. United States: NBC.

Fussell, P. (1983). *Class: A guide through the American status system.* New York, NY: Summit Books.

Galilei, G. (1953). *Dialogue concerning the two chief world systems* (S. Drake, Ed. & Trans.). Berkeley: University of California Press. (Original work published 1632)

Gallucci, N. T., Middleton, G., & Kline, A. (1999). Intellectually superior children and behavioral problems and competence. *Roeper Review, 22*(1), 18–21.

Galton, F. (1892). *Hereditary genius: An inquiry into its laws and consequences* (2nd ed.). New York, NY: Macmillan.

Garber, M. (2002, December). Our genius problem. *Atlantic.* Retrieved from http://www.theatlantic.com/magazine/archive/2002/12/our-genius-problem/308435

Gardner, H. (1983). *Frames of mind: The theory of multiple intelligences.* New York, NY: Basic Books.

Gardner, H. (1993). *Multiple intelligences: The theory in practice: A reader.* New York, NY: Basic Books.

Garland, A. F., & Zigler, E. (1999). Emotional and behavioral problems among highly intellectually gifted youth. *Roeper Review, 22*(1), 41–44.

Gates, G. J. (2011, April). How many people are lesbian, gay, bisexual, and transgender? Williams Institute. Retrieved from http://williamsinstitute.law.ucla.edu/research/census-lgbt-demographics-studies/how-many-people-are-lesbian-gay-bisexual-and-transgender

Gath, D., & Tennent, G. (1972). High intelligence and delinquency—a review. *British Journal of Criminology, 12*(2), 174–181.

Gath, D., Tennent, G., & Pidduck, R. (1970). Psychiatric and social characteristics of bright delinquents. *British Journal of Psychiatry, 116*(531), 151–160.

Gath, D., Tennent, G., & Pidduck, R. (1971). Criminological characteristics of bright delinquents. *British Journal of Criminology, 11*(3), 275–279.

Gauss, C. F. (1963). *Theory of the motion of the heavenly bodies moving about the sun in conic sections* (C. H. Davis, trans.). New York, NY: Dover. (Original work published 1809 as *Theoria motus corporum coelestium in sectionibus conicis solem ambientium*)

Gay, C. J. (1948). The blind look at an elephant: 10 experts, 25 "people" define "intelligence." *Clearing House, 22*(5), 263–266.

Geis, G., & Bienen, L. B. (1998). *Crimes of the century*. Boston, MA: Northeastern University Press.

Gemmill, W. N. (1915). Genius and eugenics. *Journal of the American Institute of Criminal Law and Criminology, 6*(1), 83–100.

Gendreau, P., & Suboski, M. D. (1971). Intelligence and age in discrimination conditioning of the eyelid response. *Journal of Experimental Psychology, 89*(2), 379–382.

Gessen, M. (1996). Moscow postcard: Prime suspect. *New Republic, 214*(15), 17–19.

Gibbs, N., Lacayo, R., Morrow, L., Smolowe, J., & Van Biema, D. (1996). *Mad genius: The odyssey, pursuit, and capture of the Unabomber suspect*. New York, NY: Warner Books.

Gibson, M. (2002). *Born to crime: Cesare Lombroso and the origins of biological criminology*. Westport, CT: Praeger.

Gilbert, G. M. (1950). *The psychology of dictatorship: Based on an examination of the leaders of Nazi Germany*. New York, NY: Ronald Press.

Gilbert, J. (2013). *Patched: The history of gangs in New Zealand*. Auckland: Auckland University Press.

Gilbert, L. (Director). (1967). *You only live twice* [Motion picture]. United States: United Artists.

Giles, F. (2001). *Napoleon Bonaparte: England's prisoner*. New York, NY: Carroll & Graf.

Gilligan, V. (Producer). (2008). *Breaking bad* [Television series, 2008–2013]. United States: AMC.

Gino, F., & Wiltermuth, S. S. (2014). Evil genius? How dishonesty can lead to greater creativity. *Psychological Science, 25*(4), 973–981.

Glaze, L. E., & Bonczar, T. (2011). *Probation and parole in the United States, 2010*. Washington, DC: Office of Justice Programs.

Glen, J. (Director). (1981). *For your eyes only* [Motion picture]. United States: United Artists.

Glueck, S., & Glueck, E. T. (1930). *500 criminal careers*. New York, NY: Alfred A. Knopf.

Glueck, S., & Glueck, E. T. (1934). *Five hundred delinquent women*. New York, NY: Alfred A. Knopf.

Goddard, H. H. (1912). *The Kallikak family: A study in the heredity of feeblemindedness*. New York, NY: Macmillan.

Goddard, H. H. (1914). *Feeble mindedness: Its causes and consequences*. New York, NY: Macmillan.

Goddard, H. H. (1915). *The criminal imbecile: An analysis of three remarkable murder cases*. New York, NY: Macmillan.

Goertzel, M. G., Goertzel, V., & Goertzel, T. G. (1978). *Three hundred eminent personalities*. San Francisco, CA: Jossey-Bass.

Goertzel, V., & Goertzel, M. G. (1962). *Cradles of eminence*. Boston, MA: Little, Brown.

Goffman, A. (2014). *On the run: Fugitive life in an American city.* Chicago, IL: University of Chicago Press.

Golan, M. (Director). (2002). *Crime and punishment* [Motion picture]. United States: Metro-Goldwyn-Mayer.

Goleman, D. (1980). 1,528 little geniuses and how they grew. *Psychology Today, 13*(9), 28–43.

Goleman, D. (1995). *Emotional intelligence.* New York, NY: Bantam Books.

Good, J., & Goreck, S. (1995). *Poison mind.* New York, NY: St. Martin's Paperbacks.

Gordon, R. A. (1997). Everyday life as an intelligence test: Effects of intelligence and intelligence context. *Intelligence, 24*(1), 203–320.

Goring, C. (1919). *The English convict: A statistical study* (Abridged ed.). London: HMSO.

Gottfredson, L. S. (1994). Egalitarian fiction and collective fraud. *Society, 31*(3), 53–59.

Gottfredson, L. S. (1997). Mainstream science on intelligence: An editorial with 52 signatories, history, and bibliography. *Intelligence, 24*(1), 13–23.

Gottfredson, L. S. (2005). Suppressing intelligence research: Hurting those we intend to help. In R. H. Wright & N. A. Cummings (Eds.), *Destructive trends in mental health: The well-intentioned path to harm* (pp. 155–186). New York, NY: Routledge.

Gottfredson, M. R., & Hirschi, T. (1990). *A general theory of crime.* Stanford, CA: Stanford University Press.

Gould, S. J. (1981). *The mismeasure of man.* New York, NY: W. W. Norton.

Gould, S. J. (1996). *The mismeasure of man* (Rev. ed.). New York, NY: W. W. Norton.

Grant, A. M., & Schwartz, B. (2011). Too much of a good thing: The challenge and opportunity of the inverted U. *Perspectives on Psychological Science, 6*(1), 61–76.

Graysmith, R. (1997). *Unabomber: A desire to kill.* Washington, DC: Regnery.

Greer, C., & McLaughlin, E. (2013). The Sir Jimmy Savile scandal: Child sexual abuse and institutional denial at the BBC. *Crime, Media, Culture, 9*(3), 243–263.

Greutert, K. (Director). (2009). *Saw VI* [Motion picture]. United States: Lionsgate Films.

Greutert, K. (Director). (2010). *Saw 3D* [Motion picture]. United States: Lionsgate Films.

Grieg, C. (2005). *Criminal masterminds: Evil geniuses of the underworld.* London: Capella.

Griffith, M. (Ed.). (1983). *Aeschylus: Prometheus Bound.* New York, NY: Cambridge University Press.

Gross, M. U. M. (1993). *Exceptionally gifted children.* New York, NY: Routledge.

Grossberg, I. N., & Cornell, D. G. (1988). Relationship between personality adjustment and high intelligence: Terman versus Hollingworth. *Exceptional Children, 55*(3), 266–272.

Grossman, L., & Lacayo, R. (2005). All-time 100 novels. *Time.* Retrieved from http://entertainment.time.com/2005/10/16/all-time-100-novels/slide/all

Grutter v. Bollinger, 539 U.S. 306 (2003).

Guay, J. P., Ouimet, M., & Proulx, J. (2005). On intelligence and crime: A comparison of incarcerated sex offenders and serious non-sexual violent criminals. *International Journal of Law and Psychiatry, 28*(4), 405–417.

Guest, G., MacQueen, K. M., Namey, E. E. (2012). *Applied thematic analysis.* Los Angeles, CA: SAGE.

Guinness World Records News. (2012). Sherlock Holmes awarded title for most portrayed literary human character in film and TV. Retrieved from http://www.guinnessworldrecords.com/news/2012/5/sherlock-holmes-awarded-title-for-most-portrayed-literary-human-character-in-film-tv-41743

Gunnell, D., Harbord, R., Singleton, N., Jenkins, R., & Lewis, G. (2009). Is low IQ associated with an increased risk of developing suicidal thoughts? *Social Psychiatry and Psychiatric Epidemiology, 44*(1), 34–38.

Gupta, S. (2006, September 12). Brainteaser: Scientists dissect mystery of genius. *CNN.* Retrieved from http://edition.cnn.com/2006/HEALTH/09/11/gupta.genius

Gusterson, H. (1997). Studying up revisited. *PoLAR: Political and Legal Anthropology Review, 20*(1), 114–119.

Haarer, D. L. (1966). Gifted delinquents. *Federal Probation, 30*(1), 43–46.

Hackl, D. (Director). (2008). *Saw V* [Motion picture]. United States: Lionsgate Films.

Hagan, F. E. (1993). *Research methods in criminal justice and criminology* (3rd ed.). New York, NY: Macmillan.

Haggard, P. (Director). (1980). *The fiendish plot of Dr. Fu Manchu* [Motion picture]. United States: Warner Bros.

Haist, M. (2009). Deterrence in a sea of "just deserts": Are utilitarian goals achievable in a world of "limiting retributivism"? *Journal of Criminal Law and Criminology, 99*(3), 789–821.

Hale, M. (1800). *History of the pleas of the Crown.* London: E. Rider.

Hall v. Florida, 572 U.S. ___, 34 S. Ct. 1986 (2014).

Hamblin, J. (2014, March 18). The toxins that threaten our brains. *Atlantic.* Retrieved from http://www.theatlantic.com/health/archive/2014/03/the-toxins-that-threaten-our-brains/284466

Hamilton, E., & Cairns, H. (Eds.). (1989). *Plato: The collected dialogues.* Princeton, NJ: Princeton University Press.

Hamilton, G. (Director). (1964). *Goldfinger* [Motion picture]. United States: United Artists.

Hamilton, G. (Director). (1971). *Diamonds are forever* [Motion picture]. United States: United Artists.

Hamilton, P. (1929). *Rope.* London: Constable.

Hamm, T. (2001). *Rebel and a cause: Caryl Chessman and the politics of the death penalty in postwar California, 1948–1974.* Berkeley: University of California Press.

Hanlon, R. E., Rubin, L. H., Jensen, M., & Daoust, S. (2010). Neuropsychological features of indigent murder defendants and death row inmates in relation to homicidal aspects of their crimes. *Archives of Clinical Neuropsychology, 25*(1), 1–13.

Hare, R. D. (1980). A research scale for the assessment of psychopathy in criminal populations. *Personality and Individual Differences, 1*(2), 111–119.

Hare, R. D. (1993). *Without conscience: The disturbing world of the psychopaths among us.* New York, NY: Guilford Press.

Harris, K. M., & Edlund, M. J. (2005). Self-medication of mental health problems: New evidence from a national survey. *Health Services Research, 40*(1), 117–134.

Harris, T. (1981). *Red dragon.* New York, NY: G. P. Putnam's Sons.

Harris, T. (1988). *The silence of the lambs.* New York, NY: St. Martin's Press.

Harris, T. (1999). *Hannibal.* New York, NY: Delacorte Press.

Harris, T. (2007). *Hannibal rising.* New York, NY: Random House.

Hart, H. L. A. (1968). *Punishment and responsibility: Essays in the philosophy of law.* New York, NY: Oxford University Press.

Hart, M. H. (1992). *The 100: A ranking of the most influential persons in history* (2nd ed.). New York, NY: Citadel Press.

Hartl, E. M., Monnelly, E. P., & Elderkin, R. D. (1982). *Physique and delinquent behavior: A thirty-year follow-up of William H. Sheldon's "Varieties of Delinquent Youth."* San Francisco, CA: Academic Press.

Harvey, S., & Seeley, K. R. (1984). An investigation of the relationships among intellectual and creative abilities, extracurricular activities, achievement, and giftedness in a delinquent population. *Gifted Child Quarterly, 28*(2), 73–79.

Haskell, D. (2002, April 11). Man claims killed Hitler to gain soul. UPI.com. Retrieved from http://www.upi.com/Top_News/2002/04/11/Man-claims-killed-Hitler-to-gain-soul/16021018544482

Hatch, S. L., Jones, P. B., Kuh, D., Hardy, R., Wadsworth, M. E. J., & Richards, M. (2007). Childhood cognitive ability and adult mental health in the British 1946 birth cohort. *Social Science and Medicine, 64*(11), 2285–2296.

Hattiangadi, N., Medvec, V. H., & Gilovich, T. (1995). Failing to act: Regrets of Terman's geniuses. *International Journal of Aging and Human Development, 40*(3), 175–185.

Hauser, R. M. (2002). *Meritocracy, cognitive ability, and the sources of occupational success.* Madison: Center for Demography and Ecology, University of Wisconsin. Retrieved from https://www.ssc.wisc.edu/cde/cdewp/98-07.pdf

Hayes, M. L., & Sloat, R. S. (1989). Gifted students at risk for suicide. *Roeper Review, 12*(2), 102–107.

Haynes, R. D. (2016). Whatever happened to the "mad, bad"scientist? Overturning the stereotype. *Public Understanding of Science, 25*(1), 31–44.

Headland, T. N., Pike, K., & Harris, M. (Eds.). (1999). *Emics and etics: The insider/outsider debate.* Newbury Park, CA: SAGE.

Hegel, G. W. F. (1956). *The philosophy of history* (J. Sibree, Trans.). New York, NY: Dover. (Original work published 1837 as *Vorlesungen über die Philosophie der Weltgeschichte*)

Heilbrun, A. B., Jr. (1990). Differentiation of death-row murderers and life-sentence murderers by antisociality and intelligence measures. *Journal of Personality Assessment, 54*(3–4), 617–627.

Hennings, T. C., Jr. (1957). Equal justice under law. *Georgetown Law Journal, 46*(1), 1–20.

Henkel, R. E. (1976). *Tests of significance.* Beverly Hills, CA: SAGE.

Herbert, F. (1982). *The white plague.* New York, NY: G. P. Putnam's Sons.

Hergenhahn, B. R. (1986). *An introduction to the history of psychology.* Belmont, CA: Wadsworth.

Herrnstein, R. J., & Murray, C. (1994). *The bell curve: Intelligence and class structure in American life.* New York, NY: Free Press.

Herschman, D. J., & Lieb, J. (1988). *The key to genius.* New York, NY: Prometheus Books.

Hickey, E. W. (2016). *Serial killers and their victims* (7th ed.). Boston, MA: Cengage Learning.

Higdon, H. (1999). *Leopold and Loeb: The crime of the century.* Chicago: University of Illinois Press.

Highsmith, P. (1955). *The talented Mr. Ripley.* New York, NY: Coward McCann.

Highsmith, P. (1970). *Ripley under ground.* New York, NY: Doubleday.

Highsmith, P. (1974). *Ripley's game.* New York, NY: Knopf.

Highsmith, P. (1980). *The boy who followed Ripley.* New York, NY: Lippincott & Crowell.

Highsmith, P. (1992). *Ripley under water.* New York, NY: Knopf.

Hindelang, M. J., Hirschi, T., & Weis, J. G. (1979). Correlates of delinquency: The illusion of discrepancy between self-report and official measures. *American Sociological Review, 44*(6), 995–1014.

Hirsch, N. D. M. (1931). *Genius and creative intelligence.* Cambridge, MA: Sci-Art.

Hirsch, W. (1896). *Genius and degeneration: A psychological study.* New York, NY: D. Appleton.

Hirschi, T. (1969). *Causes of delinquency.* Berkeley: University of California Press.

Hirschi, T., & Gottfredson, M. (1983). Age and the explanation of crime. *American Journal of Sociology, 89*(3), 552–584.

Hirschi, T., & Hindelang, M. J. (1977). Intelligence and delinquency: A revisionist review. *American Sociological Review, 42*(4), 571–587.

Hirschi, T., & Stark, R. (1969). Hellfire and delinquency. *Social Problems, 17*(2), 202–213.

Hitchcock, A. (Director). (1948). *Rope* [Motion picture]. United States: Warner Bros.

Hodges, A. (1983). *Alan Turing: The enigma.* London: Burnett Books.

Hodgins, S. (1992). Mental disorder, intellectual deficiency, and crime: Evidence from a birth cohort. *Archives of General Psychiatry, 49*(6), 476–483.

Hofler, R. (2009). *Variety's "the movie that changed my life": 120 celebrities pick the films that made a difference (for better or worse).* Boston, MA: Da Capo Press.

Hogh, E., & Wolf, P. (1983). Violent crime in a birth cohort: Copenhagen, 1953–1977. In K. T. Van Dusen and S. A. Mednick (Eds.), *Prospective studies of crime and delinquency* (pp. 249–267). Boston, MA: Kluwer-Nijhoff.

Holahan, C. K., & Holahan, C. J. (1999). Being labeled as gifted, self-appraisal, and psychological well-being: A life span developmental perspective. *International Journal of Aging and Human Development, 48*(3), 161–173.

Holahan, C. K., & Sears, R. R. (1995). *Genetic studies of genius. Vol. 6, The gifted group in later maturity.* Stanford, CA: Stanford University Press.

Holland, M. (2004). *The real trial of Oscar Wilde.* New York, NY: HarperCollins.

Hollin, C. R. (1989). *Psychology and crime: An introduction to criminological psychology.* London: Routledge.

Hollingworth, L. S. (1926). *Gifted children: Their nature and nurture.* New York, NY: Macmillan.

Hollingworth, L. S. (1942). *Children above 180 I.Q.* New York, NY: Harcourt, Brace, and World.

Hood, R., & Sparks, R. (1970). *Key issues in criminology.* New York, NY: World University Library.

Hooton, E. A. (1939). *The American criminal: An anthropological study.* Cambridge, MA: Harvard University Press.

Hornung, E. W. (1899). *The amateur cracksman.* London: Methuen.

Hornung, E. W. (1901). *The black mask.* London: Methuen.

Hornung, E. W. (1905). *A thief in the night.* London: Chatto & Windus.

Hornung, E. W. (1909). *Mr. Justice Raffles.* London: Smith, Elder.

Hough, M., & Mayhew, P. (1985). *Taking account of crime: Key findings from the 1984 British Crime Survey.* London: HMSO.

Howarth, E. (1986). What does Eysenck's psychoticism scale really measure? *British Journal of Psychology, 77*(2), 223–227.

Howe, M. J. A. (1999). *Genius explained.* New York, NY: Cambridge University Press.

Howell, N. (1990). *Surviving fieldwork: A report of the Advisory Panel on Health and Safety in Fieldwork.* Washington, DC: American Anthropological Association.

Howson, G. (1970). *Thief-taker general: The rise and fall of Jonathan Wild.* London: Hutchinson.

Hughes, J. (1980). *The philosophy of social research.* London: Longman.

Huizinga, D., & Elliott, D. S. (1986). Reassessing the reliability and validity of self-report delinquency measures. *Journal of Quantitative Criminology, 2*(4), 293–327.

Human Rights Watch. (2007, September). *No easy answers: Sex offender laws in the US.* Retrieved from https://www.hrw.org/sites/default/files/reports/us0907webwcover.pdf

Hunt, E. (2011). *Human intelligence.* New York, NY: Cambridge University Press.

Hunt, P. (Director). (1969). *On Her Majesty's secret service* [Motion picture]. United States: United Artists.

Huxley, A. (1932). *Brave new world.* London: Chatto & Windus.

Hyams, P. (1984). *2010: The year we make contact* [Motion picture]. United States: Metro-Goldwyn-Mayer.

Hyslop, T. B. (1925). *The great abnormals.* London: Philip Allan.

International Labour Organization. (2008). International standard classification of occupations. Retrieved from http://www.ilo.org/public/english/bureau/stat/isco/isco08/index.htm

International Society for Philosophical Enquiry. (2015). Qualifying scores. Retrieved from http://www.thethousand.com/admission/qualifying-scores

Intertel. (2015). Intertel qualifying test scores. Retrieved from http://www.intertel-iq.org/join.php

Irving, G. (Director). (1917). *Raffles, the amateur cracksman* [Motion picture]. United States: Hiller & Wilk.

Irwin, J. (1985). *The jail: Managing the underclass in American society.* Berkeley: University of California Press.

Iserson, K. V. (2002). *Demon doctors: Physicians as serial killers.* Tucson, AZ: Galen Press.

Israel, M., & Hay, I. (2011). Research ethics in criminology. In D. Gadd, S. Karstedt, & S. F. Messner (Eds.), *The SAGE handbook of criminological research methods* (pp. 500–514). Thousand Oaks, CA: SAGE.

Jackson, D. B., & Beaver, K. M. (2013). The influence of neuropsychological deficits in early childhood on low self-control and misconduct through early adolescence. *Journal of Criminal Justice, 41*(4), 243–251.

Jacobson, A. C. (1926). *Genius: Some revaluations.* Port Washington, NY: Kennikat Press.

Jacoby, R., & Glauberman, N. (Eds.). (1995). *The bell curve debate: History, documents, opinions.* New York, NY: Times Books.

Jacques, N. (1923). *Dr. Mabuse, master of mystery* (L. A. Clare, Trans.). London: George Allen & Unwin.

Jamison, K. R. (1993). *Touched by fire.* New York, NY: Free Press.

Jamison, K. R. (1995). Manic-depressive illness and creativity. *Scientific American, 272*(2), 46–51.

Janos, P. M., Fung, H. C., & Robinson, N. M. (1985). Self-concept, self-esteem, and peer relations among gifted children who feel "different." *Gifted Child Quarterly, 29*(2), 78–82.

Jensen, A. R. (1969). How much can we boost IQ and scholastic achievement? *Harvard Educational Review, 39*(1), 1–123.

Jensen, A. R. (1980). *Bias in mental testing.* New York, NY: Free Press.

Jensen, A. R. (1998). *The g factor: The science of mental ability.* Westport, CT: Praeger.

Johansson, P. (Director). (2011). *Atlas shrugged: Part I* [Motion picture]. United States: Atlas Distribution Company.

Johansson, P., & Kerr, M. (2005). Psychopathy and intelligence: A second look. *Journal of Personality Disorders, 19*(4), 357–369.

Johnson v. California, 543 U.S. 499 (2005).

Johnson, B. R., & Jang, S. J. (2011). Crime and religion: Assessing the role of the faith factor. In R. Rosenfeld, K. Quinet, & C. Garcia (Eds.), *Contemporary issues in criminological theory and research: The role of social institution; Papers from the American Society of Criminology 2010 Conference* (pp. 117–150). Boston, MA: Cengage Learning.

Jolliffe, D., & Farrington, D. P. (2010). Individual differences and offending. In E. McLaughlin & T. Newburn (Eds.), *The SAGE handbook of criminological theory* (pp. 40–55). Thousand Oaks, CA: SAGE.

Joyal, C. C., Beaulieu-Plante, J., & de Chantérac, A. (2014). The neuropsychology of sex offenders: A meta-analysis. *Sexual Abuse, 26*(2), 149–177.

Juda, A. (1949). The relationship between highest mental capacity and psychic abnormalities. *American Journal of Psychiatry, 106*(4), 296–307.

Jung, R. E., & Haier, R. J. (2007). The Parieto-Frontal Integration Theory (P-FIT) of intelligence: Converging neuroimaging evidence. *Behavioral and Brain Sciences, 30*(2), 135–154.

Junger-Tas, J., & Marshall, I. H. (1999). The self-report methodology in crime research. *Crime and Justice, 25,* 291–367.

Junger-Tas, J., Terlouw, G. J., & Klein, M. W. (Eds.). (1994). *Delinquent behavior among young people in the western world: First results of the international self-report delinquency study.* New York, NY: Kugler Publications.

Kaczynski, T. J. (2010). *Technological slavery: The collected writings of Theodore J. Kaczynski, a.k.a. "the Unabomber."* Port Townsend, WA: Feral House.

Kalat, D. (2001). *The strange case of Dr. Mabuse: A study of the twelve films and five novels.* Jefferson, NC: McFarland.

Kalin, T. (Director). (1992). *Swoon* [Motion picture]. United States: American Playhouse.

Kamin, L. J. (1974). *The science and politics of IQ.* New York, NY: Halstead Press.

Kanazawa, S. (2003). Why productivity fades with age: The crime-genius connection. *Journal of Research in Personality, 37*(4), 257–272.

Kanazawa, S. (2006). IQ and the wealth of states. *Intelligence, 34*(6), 593–600.

Kanazawa, S. (2012). *The intelligence paradox: Why the intelligent choice isn't always the smart one.* Hoboken, NJ: John Wiley & Sons.

Kanazawa, S., & Hellberg, J. E. (2010). Intelligence and substance use. *Review of General Psychology, 14*(4), 382.

Kandel, E., Mednick, S. A., Kirkegaard-Sorensen, L., Hutchings, B., Knop, J., Rosenberg, R., & Schulsinger, F. (1988). IQ as a protective factor for subjects at high risk for antisocial behavior. *Journal of Consulting and Clinical Psychology, 56*(2), 224–226.

Kant, I. (1887). *The philosophy of law: An exposition of the fundamental principles of jurisprudence as the science of right* (W. Hastie, Trans.). Edinburgh: T. & T. Clark. (Original work published 1796)

Kanuk, L., & Berenson, C. (1975). Mail surveys and response rates: A literature review. *Journal of Marketing Research, 12*(4), 440–453.

Kapnick, R., & Kelly, A. A. (1993). *Thinking on the edge: Essays by members of the International Society for Philosophical Enquiry.* Burbank, CA: Agamemnon Press.

Karnes, F. A., & Brown, K. E. (1980). Moral development and the gifted: An initial investigation. *Roeper Review, 3*(4), 8–10.

Katz, J. (1988). *Seductions of crime: Moral and sensual attractions in doing evil.* New York, NY: Basic Books.

Katz, J., & Abel, C. F. (1984). The medicalization of repression: Eugenics and crime. *Crime, Law and Social Change, 8*(3), 227–241.

Kaufman, A. S. (1976). Verbal-performance IQ discrepancies on the WISC-R. *Journal of Consulting and Clinical Psychology, 14*, 739–744.

Kaufman, A. S. (2009). *IQ testing 101.* New York, NY: Springer.

Kavanagh, J. (1997). The occurrence of resisting arrest in arrest encounters: A study of police-citizen violence. *Criminal Justice Review, 22*(1), 16–33.

Kearney, K. (1990). Leta Hollingworth's unfinished legacy: Children above 180 IQ. *Roeper Review, 12*(3), 181–188.

Keefe, P. R. (2013, February 11). A loaded gun: A mass shooter's tragic past. *New Yorker,* 70–77.

Kellam, S. G., Ensminger, M. E., & Simon, M. B. (1980). Mental health in first grade and teenage drug, alcohol, and cigarette use. *Drug and Alcohol Dependence, 5*(4), 273–304.

Kellner, D. (2013). Media spectacle and domestic terrorism: The case of the Batman/Joker cinema massacre. *Review of Education, Pedagogy, and Cultural Studies, 35*(3), 157–177.

Kenton, E. (Director). (1932). *The island of lost souls* [Motion picture]. United States: Paramount Pictures.

Kershner, I. (Director). (1983). *Never say never again* [Motion picture]. United States: United Artists.

Kessel, N. (1989). Genius and mental disorder: A history of ideas concerning their conjunction. In P. Murray (Ed.), *Genius: The history of an idea,* (pp. 196–212). Oxford: Basil Blackwell.

Kessler, R. C., Berglund, P., Demler, O., Jin, R., Merikangas, K. R., & Walters, E. E. (2005). Lifetime prevalence and age-of-onset distributions of DSM-IV disorders in the National Comorbidity Survey Replication. *Archives of General Psychiatry, 62*(6), 593–602.

Kevles, D. J. (1985). *In the name of eugenics: Genetics and the uses of human heredity.* New York, NY: Alfred A. Knopf.

Kincaid, D. (1969). A study of highly gifted elementary pupils. *Gifted Child Quarterly, 13*(4), 264–267.

Kinnell, H. G. (1983). Insanity and genius. *Psychiatric Bulletin, 7*(10), 188–189.

Kitsuse, J., & Cicourel, A. V. (1963). A note on the use of official statistics. *Social Problems, 2*(2), 131–139.

Klein, N. (2007). *The shock doctrine: The rise of disaster capitalism.* New York, NY: Picador.

Klintworth, G. K. (2014). *Giants, crooks and jerks in science.* Bloomington, IN: Xlibris.

Klockars, Carl B. (1979). Dirty hands and deviant subjects. In C. B. Klockars and F. W. O'Connor, (Eds.), *Deviance and decency: The ethics of research with human subjects.* Beverly Hills, CA: SAGE.

Knudten, R. D., & Knudten, M. S. (1971). Juvenile delinquency, crime, and religion. *Review of Religious Research, 12*(3), 130–152.

Kohlberg, L. (1984). *The psychology of moral development.* San Francisco, CA: Harper & Row.

Kohlberg, L. (1994). Stage and sequence: The cognitive-developmental approach to socialization. In B. Puka (Ed.), *Moral development: Defining perspectives in moral development* (pp. 1–135). New York, NY: Garland.

Kolber, A. J. (2009). The subjective experience of punishment. *Columbia Law Review, 109,* 182–236.

Kongs, S. K., Thompson, L. L., Iverson, G. L., & Heaton, R. K. (2000). *Wisconsin card sorting test—64 card version: Professional manual.* Odessa, FL: Psychological Assessment Resources.

Kooistra, P. (1989). *Criminals as heroes: Structure, power and identity.* Bowling Green, OH: Bowling Green State University Popular Press.

Koopmans, A. (2004). *Leopold and Loeb: Teen killers.* San Francisco, CA: Lucent Books.

Korobkin, R. B., & Ulen, T. S. (2000). Law and behavioral science: Removing the rationality assumption from law and economics. *California Law Review, 88*(4), 1051–1144.

Krapohl, E., Rimfeld, K., Shakeshaft, N. G., Trzaskowski, M., McMillan, A., Pingault, J. B., . . . Plomin, R. (2014). The high heritability of educational achievement reflects many genetically influenced traits, not just intelligence. *Proceedings of the National Academy of Sciences, 111*(42), 15273–15278.

Kretschmer, E. (1931). *The psychology of men of genius* (R. B. Cattell, Trans.). London: Kegan Paul, Trench, Trubner.

Kreuter, G. (1962). The vanishing genius: Lewis Terman and the Stanford study. *History of Education Quarterly, 2*(1), 6–18.

Krimsky, S., & Sloan, K. (Eds). (2011). *Race and the genetic revolution: Science, myth, and culture.* New York, NY: Columbia University Press.

Kroeber, A. L. (1944). *Configurations of cultural growth.* Berkeley: University of California Press.

Krohn, M. D., Thornberry, T. P., Gibson, C. L., & Baldwin, J. M. (2010). The development and impact of self-report measures of crime and delinquency. *Journal of Quantitative Criminology, 26*(4), 509–525.

Krueger, R. F., Schmutte, P. S., Caspi, A., Moffitt, T. E., Campbell, K., & Silva, P. A. (1994). Personality traits are linked to crime among men and women: Evidence from a birth cohort. *Journal of Abnormal Psychology, 103*(2), 328.

Kubrick, S. (Director). (1964). *Dr. Strangelove or: How I learned to stop worrying and love the bomb* [Motion picture]. United States: Columbia Pictures.

Kubrick, S. (Director). (1968). *2001: A Space Odyssey* [Motion picture]. United States: Metro-Goldwyn-Mayer.

Kunstler, W. M. (1961). *Beyond a reasonable doubt? The original trial of Caryl Chessman.* New York, NY: William Morrow.

Kurland, M. (1994). *A gallery of rogues: Portraits in true crime.* New York, NY: Macmillan.

Lagercrantz, D. (2015). *The girl in the spider's web* (G. Goulding, Trans.). London: MacLehose Press.

Lajoie, S. P., & Shore, B. M. (1981). Three myths? The over-representation of the gifted among dropouts, delinquents, and suicides. *Gifted Child Quarterly, 25*(3), 183–243.

Landrum, G. N. (1993). *Profiles of genius: Thirteen creative men who changed the world.* Buffalo, NY: Prometheus Books.

Landrum, G. N. (1994). *Profiles of female genius: Thirteen creative women who changed the world*. Amherst, NY: Prometheus Books.

Landrum, G. N. (1997). *Profiles of black success: Thirteen creative geniuses who changed the world*. Amherst, NY: Prometheus Books.

Landy, J. (2012). The devil, the master-criminal, and the reenchantment of the world (on *The Usual Suspects*). *Philosophy and Literature, 36*(1), 37–57.

Lane, D. A. (1987). Personality and antisocial behavior: A long-term study. *Personality and Individual Differences, 8*(6), 799–806.

Lang, F. (Director). (1922). *Dr. Mabuse: The gambler* [Motion picture]. United States: Universum Film.

Lang, F. (Director). (1928). *Metropolis* [Motion picture]. United States: Paramount Pictures.

Lang, F. (Director). (1933). *The testament of Dr. Mabuse* [Motion picture]. United States: Tudor Films.

Lang, F. (Director). (1960). *The 1,000 eyes of Dr. Mabuse* [Motion picture]. United States: Ajay Film.

Langan, P. A., & Levin, D. J. (2002). Recidivism of prisoners released in 1994. *Federal Sentencing Reporter, 15*(1), 58–65.

Langdon, P. E., Clare, I. C., & Murphy, G. H. (2011). Moral reasoning theory and illegal behaviour by adults with intellectual disabilities. *Psychology, Crime and Law, 17*(2), 101–115.

Lange-Eichbaum, W. (1931). *The problem of genius* (E. Paul & C. Paul, Trans.). New York, NY: Macmillan.

Langevin, R., Wortzman, G., Dickey, R., Wright, P., & Handy, L. (1988). Neuropsychological impairment in incest offenders. *Annals of Sex Research, 1*(3), 401–415.

Lareau, A., & Shultz, J. (1996). *Journey through ethnography: Realistic accounts of fieldwork*. Boulder, CO: Westview Press.

Larson, E. (2004). *The devil in the white city: Murder, magic, and madness at the fair that changed America*. New York, NY: Crown.

Larsson, S. (2008). *The girl with the dragon tattoo* (R. Keeland, Trans.). London: MacLehose Press.

Larsson, S. (2009a). *The girl who kicked the hornet's nest* (R. Keeland, Trans.). London: MacLehose Press.

Larsson, S. (2009b). *The girl who played with fire* (R. Keeland, Trans.). London: MacLehose Press.

Lawrence v. Texas, 539 U.S. 558 (2003).

Lazar, A., Karlan, D., & Salter, J. (2006). *The 101 most influential people who never lived*. New York, NY: HarperCollins.

Leary, T. (1990). *Flashbacks: A personal and cultural history of an era*. Los Angeles, CA: Jeremy P. Tarcher.

Leavesley, J. (2010). *Not your ordinary doctor*. Crows Nest, NSW: Allen & Unwin.

Leavitt, D. (2006). *The man who knew too much: Alan Turing and the invention of the computer*. New York, NY: W. W. Norton.

LeBor, A. (2009). *The believers: How America fell for Bernard Madoff's $65 billion investment scam*. London: Weidenfeld & Nicolson.

Lee, R. M. (1995). *Dangerous fieldwork: SAGE university papers series on qualitative research methods* (Vol. 34). Thousand Oaks, CA: SAGE.

Leigh, M. (Director). (1993). *Naked* [Motion picture]. United Kingdom: First Independent Films.

Leistedt, S. J., & Linkowski, P. (2014). Psychopathy and the cinema: Fact or fiction? *Journal of Forensic Sciences, 59*(1), 167–174.

Lélut, L. F. (1836). *Du demon de Socrate.* Paris: Trinquart, Libraire-Éditeur.

Lélut, L. F. (1846). *L'amulette de Pascal.* Paris: Chez J.-B. Bailliere.

Leo, R. A. (1995). Trial and tribulations: Courts, ethnography, and the need for an evidentiary privilege for academic researchers. *American Sociologist, 26*(1), 113–133.

Leo, R. A. (1996). The ethics of deceptive research roles reconsidered: A response to Kai Erikson. *American Sociologist, 27*(1), 122–128.

León-Carrión, J., & Ramos, F. J. C. (2003). Blows to the head during development can predispose to violent criminal behaviour: Rehabilitation of consequences of head injury is a measure for crime prevention. *Brain Injury, 17*(3), 207–216.

Leopold, N. F., Jr. (1958). *Life plus 99 years.* Garden City, NY: Doubleday.

Lerner, M. J. (1980). *The belief in a just world: A fundamental delusion.* New York, NY: Plenum Press.

Lester, D. (2003). National estimates of IQ and suicide and homicide rates. *Perceptual and motor skills, 97*(1), 206.

Levin, M. (1956). *Compulsion.* New York, NY: Simon and Schuster.

Levin, M. (1959). *Compulsion: A play by Meyer Levin.* New York, NY: Simon and Schuster.

Levine, S. Z. (2011). Elaboration on the association between IQ and parental SES with subsequent crime. *Personality and Individual Differences, 50*(8), 1233–1237.

Lévi-Strauss, C. (1955). The structural study of myth. *Journal of American Folklore, 68*(270), 428–444.

Levitt, S. D. (2004). Understanding why crime fell in the 1990s: Four factors that explain the decline and six that do not. *Journal of Economic Perspectives, 18*(1), 163–190.

Lewis, C. S. (1953). The humanitarian theory of punishment. *Res Judicatae, 6*(2), 224–230.

Lewis, R. B., Kitano, M. K., & Lynch, E. W. (1992). Psychological intensities in gifted adults. *Roeper Review, 15*(1), 25–31.

Lichtenstein, M., & Brown, A. W. (1938). Intelligence and achievement of children in a delinquency area. *Journal of Juvenile Research, 22,* 1–25.

Linder, D. (2002). The trial of Jesus: An account. Retrieved from http://law2.umkc.edu /faculty/projects/ftrials/jesus/jesusaccount.html

Lindsay, A. D. (1918). *Socratic discourses by Plato and Xenophon.* London: J. M. Dent & Sons.

Lindsay, J. (2004). *Darkly dreaming Dexter.* New York, NY: Doubleday.

Lindsay, J. (2005). *Dearly devoted Dexter.* New York, NY: Doubleday.

Lindsay, J. (2007). *Dexter in the dark.* New York, NY: Doubleday.

Lindsay, J. (2009). *Dexter by design.* New York, NY: Doubleday.

Lindsay, J. (2010). *Dexter is delicious.* New York, NY: Doubleday.

Lindsay, J. (2011). *Double Dexter.* New York, NY: Doubleday.

Lindsay, J. (2013). *Dexter's final cut.* New York, NY: Doubleday.

Lippmann, W. (1922a). The reliability of intelligence tests. *New Republic, 32,* 275–277.

Lippmann, W. (1922b). Tests of hereditary intelligence. *New Republic, 32,* 328–330.

Lipsitt, D., Buka, S., & Lipsett, L. (1990). Early intelligence scores and subsequent behavior. *American Journal of Family Therapy, 18,* 197–208.

Lipton, D. (1970). *The faces of crime and genius: The historical impact of the genius-criminal.* New York, NY: A. S. Barnes.

Lochner, L. (2004). Education, work, and crime: A human capital approach. *International Economic Review, 45*(3), 811–843.

Locke, J. (2002). *The second treatise of government: and, a letter concerning toleration.* Mineola, NY: Dover. (Original work published 1689)

Loeber, R., Menting, B., Lynam, D. R., Moffitt, T. E., Stouthamer-Loeber, M., Stallings, R., . . . Pardini, D. (2012). Findings from the Pittsburgh youth study: Cognitive impulsivity and intelligence as predictors of the age-crime curve. *Journal of the American Academy of Child and Adolescent Psychiatry, 51*(11), 1136–1149.

Lombroso, C. (1872). *Genio e follia.* Milan: Presso Gaetano Brigola.

Lombroso, C. (2006). *Criminal man.* (M. Gibson, N. Rafter, & M. Seymour, Trans.) Durham, NC: Duke University Press. (Original work published 1876 as *L'uomo delinquente*)

Lombroso, C. (1891). *The man of genius.* London: Walter Scott.

Lombroso, C. (1902). Why criminals of genius have no type. *International Quarterly, 6,* 229–240.

Lombroso-Ferrero, G. (1911). *Criminal man: According to the classification of Cesare Lombroso.* London: G. P. Putnam's Sons.

Lovecky, D. V. (1986). Can you hear the flowers singing? Issues for gifted adults. *Journal of Counseling and Development, 64*(9), 572–575.

Luban, D. (2005). Lawyers as upholders of human dignity (when they aren't busy assaulting it). *University of Illinois Law Review, 2005*(3), 815–845.

Lubinski, D., Webb, R. M., Morelock, M. J., & Benbow, C. P. (2001). Top 1 in 10,000: a 10-year follow-up of the profoundly gifted. *Journal of Applied Psychology, 86*(4), 718–729.

Ludwig, A. M. (1995). *The price of greatness: Resolving the creativity and madness controversy.* New York, NY: Guilford Press.

Ludwig, E. (1927). *Genius and character.* New York, NY: Harcourt, Brace.

Lynam, D., Moffitt, T., & Stouthamer-Loeber, M. (1993). Explaining the relation between IQ and delinquency: Class, race, test motivation, school failure, or self-control? *Journal of Abnormal Psychology, 102*(2), 187–196.

Lynn, R. (2001). *Eugenics: A reassessment.* Westport, CT: Praeger.

Lynn, R., & Vanhanen, T. (2002). *IQ and the wealth of nations.* Westport, CT: Praeger.

Lynn, R., & Vanhanen, T. (2006). *IQ and global inequality.* Augusta, GA: Washington Summit.

MacDonald, A. (1902). *A plan for the study of man* (57th Congress, 1st session, document no. 400). Washington, DC: Government Printing Office.

Machlin, M., & Woodfield, W. R. (1962). *Ninth life.* New York, NY: G. P. Putnam's Sons

Macintyre, B. (1997). *The Napoleon of crime: The life and times of Adam Worth, master thief.* New York, NY: Farrar, Straus, and Giroux.

MacIntyre, D., Wilson, D., Yardley, E., & Brolan, L. (2014). The British hitman: 1974–2013. *Howard Journal of Criminal Justice, 53*(4), 325–340.

Mack, T. (2012). The transmigrating evil genius: From Boothby to Rohmer to Fleming. *Journal of Literature and Art Studies, 2*(8), 751–757.

Mackintosh, N. (Ed.). (1995). *Cyril Burt: Fraud or framed?* New York, NY: Oxford University Press.

Madden, R. R. (1833). *The infirmities of genius* (Vol. 1). Philadelphia, PA: Carey, Lea, and Blanchard.

Maguin, E., & Loeber, R. (1996). Academic performance and delinquency. *Crime and Justice, 20,* 145–264.

Mahoney, A. R. (1980). Gifted delinquents: What do we know about them? *Children and Youth Services Review, 2*(3), 315–329.

Malinowski, B. (1954). *Magic, science, and religion.* New York, NY: Doubleday Anchor Books.

Maller, J. B. (1937). Juvenile delinquency in New York City: A summary of a comprehensive report. *Journal of Psychology, 3*(1), 1–25.

Mamoulian, R. (Director). (1931). *Dr. Jekyll and Mr. Hyde* [Motion picture]. United States: Paramount Pictures.

Manera, J. J. (Director). (2014). *Atlas shrugged: Who is John Galt?* [Motion picture]. United States: Atlas Distribution.

Manley, J. R. (1937, August 14). Where are they now? April fool! *New Yorker,* 22–26.

Mann, M. (Director). (1986). *Manhunter* [Motion picture]. United States: De Laurentis Entertainment Group.

Manos, J. Jr. (Creator). (2006). *Dexter* [Television series, 2006–2013]. United States: Showtime.

Margolin, L. (1993). Goodness personified: The emergence of gifted children. *Social Problems, 40*(4), 510–532.

Marioni, R. E., Davies, G., Hayward, C., Liewald, D., Kerr, S. M., Campbell, A., . . . Deary, I. J. (2014). Molecular genetic contributions to socioeconomic status and intelligence. *Intelligence, 44,* 26–32.

Marks, J. (1926). *Genius and disaster: Studies in drugs and genius.* Port Washington, NY: Kennikat Press.

Marshall, I. H. (Ed.). (1997). *Minorities, migrants, and crime: Diversity and similarity across Europe and the United States.* Thousand Oaks, CA: SAGE.

Mason, F. (2013). *The perfect crime: The real life crime that inspired Alfred Hitchcock's "Rope."* N.p.: Absolute Crimes.

May, R. (1975). *The courage to create.* New York, NY: W. W. Norton.

May, T. (1993). *Social research: Issues, methods, and process.* Philadelphia, PA: Open University Press.

Mayer, J. D., Caruso, D. R., & Salovey, P. (1999). Emotional intelligence meets traditional standards for an intelligence. *Intelligence, 27*(4), 267–298.

McCarthy, M. (1997). Nobel Prize winner Gajdusek admits child abuse. *Lancet, 349*(9052), 623.

McCord, J. (1991). Family relationships, juvenile delinquency, and adult criminality. *Criminology, 29*(3), 397–417.

McCord, J., & Ensminger, M. E. (1997). Multiple risks and comorbidity in an African American population. *Criminal Behaviour and Mental Health, 7*(4), 339–352.

McCord, W., McCord, J., & Zola, I. K. (1959). *Origins of crime: A new evaluation of the Cambridge-Somerville Youth Study.* New York, NY: Columbia University Press.

McCracken, C. B. (2010). Intellectualization of drug abuse. *Journal of the American Medical Association, 303*(19), 1894–1895.

McCulloch, J., & Wilson, D. (2015). *Pre-crime: Pre-emption, precaution and the future*. New York, NY: Routledge.

McDowall, D., & Loftin, C. (2007). What is convergence, and what do we know about it? In J. P. Lynch & L. A. Addington (Eds.), *Understanding crime statistics: Revisiting the divergence of the NCVS and UCR* (pp. 93–121). New York, NY: Cambridge University Press.

McFadden, R. D. (2012, June 10). Fate of 3 inmates who vanished from Alcatraz remains a mystery 50 years later. *New York Times*, A18.

McGloin, J. M., Pratt, T. C., & Maahs, J. (2004). Rethinking the IQ-delinquency relationship: A longitudinal analysis of multiple theoretical models. *Justice Quarterly, 21*(3), 603–635.

McGrew, K. (2009). CHC theory and the human cognitive abilities project: Standing on the shoulders of the giants of psychometric intelligence research. *Intelligence, 37*(1), 1–10.

McGue, M. (1997). The democracy of the genes. *Nature, 388*(6641), 417–418.

McGuigan, P. (Director). (2010). *Sherlock* [Television series, 2010–present]. England: BBC.

McKeown, R. E., Cuffe, S. P., & Schulz, R. M. (2006). US suicide rates by age group, 1970–2002: An examination of recent trends. *American Journal of Public Health, 96*(10), 1744.

McKernan, M. (1989). *The amazing crime and trial of Leopold and Loeb*. Birmingham, AL: Notable Trials Library. (Original work published 1924)

McLaren, R. B. (1993). The dark side of creativity. *Creativity Research Journal, 6*(1–2), 137–144.

McMahon, D. M. (2013). *Divine fury: A history of genius*. New York, NY: Basic Books.

McTiernan, J. (Director). (1988). *Die hard* [Motion picture]. United States: Twentieth Century Fox.

McTiernan, J. (Director). (1995). *Die hard with a vengeance* [Motion picture]. United States: Twentieth Century Fox.

Mears, D. P., & Cochran, J. C. (2013). What is the effect of IQ on offending? *Criminal Justice and Behavior, 40*(11), 1280–1300.

Mei-Tal, M. (2002). The criminal responsibility of psychopathic offenders. *Israel Law Review, 36*(2), 103–121.

Mello, M. (1999). *The United States of America versus Theodore John Kaczynski: Ethics, power and the invention of the Unabomber*. New York, NY: Context Books.

Mello, M. (2000). The non-trial of the century: Representations of the Unabomber. *Vermont Law Review, 24*(2), 417–535.

Melnick, M. D., Harrison, B. R., Park, S., Bennetto, L., & Tadin, D. (2013). A strong interactive link between sensory discriminations and intelligence. *Current Biology, 23*(11), 1013–1017.

Menard, S., & Morse, B. J. (1984). A structuralist critique of the IQ-delinquency hypothesis: Theory and evidence. *American Journal of Sociology, 89*(6), 1347–1378.

Mendes, S. (Director). (2015). *SPECTRE* [Motion picture]. United States: Columbia Pictures.

Mensa. (2015). Qualifying test scores. Retrieved from http://www.us.mensa.org/join/testscores/qualifyingscores

Mentor, K. (2005). Education. In M. Bosworth (Ed.), *Encyclopedia of prisons and correctional facilities*. (pp. 274–279). Thousand Oaks, CA: SAGE.

Merrill, M. A. (1947). *Problems of child delinquency*. New York, NY: Houghton Mifflin.

Merton, R. K. (1961). Social problems and sociological theory. In R. K. Merton & R. A. Nisbet (Eds.), *Contemporary social problems: An introduction to the sociology of deviant behavior* (pp. 697–737). New York, NY: Harcourt, Brace, and World.

Meyer, J. P. (2012, August 10). James Holmes' University of Illinois application offers no hint of mental issues. *Denver Post.* Retrieved from http://www.canoncitydailyrecord.com/news /colorado/ci_21286187/holmes-university-illinois-application-offers-no-hint-mental

Michel, L. (2015, June 9). Escaped killer's son shares memories of his notorious father. *Buffalo News.* Retrieved from http://www.buffalonews.com/city-region/escaped-killers-son-shares-memories-of-his-notorious-father-20150609

Michel, L., & Herbeck, D. (2001). *American terrorist: Timothy McVeigh and the Oklahoma City bombing.* New York, NY: Harper.

Milgram, S. (1974). *Obedience to authority: An experimental view.* New York, NY: Harper & Row.

Milhizer, E. R. (2004). Justification and excuse: What they were, what they are, and what they ought to be. *St. John's Law Review, 78*(3), 725–1257.

Miller, C. D. (2010, February 9). Rodney Alcala, alleged serial killer with genius IQ, to match wits with Calif. justice system. *CBS News.* Retrieved from http://www.cbsnews.com/news /rodney-alcala-alleged-serial-killer-with-genius-iq-to-match-wits-with-calif-justice-system

Miller, E. (1994). Intelligence and brain myelination: A hypothesis. *Personality and Individual Differences, 17*(6), 803–833.

Miller, J. M., & Tewksbury, R. (Eds.). (2001). *Extreme methods: Innovative approaches to social science research.* Boston, MA: Allyn & Bacon.

Miller, L. (1987). Neuropsychology of the aggressive psychopath: An integrative review. *Aggressive Behavior, 13*(3), 119–140.

Mills, C. W. (1956). *The power elite.* New York, NY: Oxford University Press.

Milovanovic, D. (1988). Jailhouse lawyers and jailhouse lawyering. *International Journal of the Sociology of Law, 16*(4), 455–475.

Milton, J. (1998). *Paradise lost.* (A. Fowler, Ed.). New York, NY: Longman. (Original work published 1667)

Minghella, A. (Director). (1999). *The talented Mr. Ripley* [Motion picture]. United States: Miramax.

Missett, T. C. (2013). Exploring the relationship between mood disorders and gifted individuals. *Roeper Review, 35*(1), 47–57.

M'Naghten's case, U.K.H.L. J16 (19 June 1843).

Moffitt, T. E. (1993). Adolescence-limited and life-course-persistent antisocial behavior: a developmental taxonomy. *Psychological Review, 100*(4), 674–701.

Moffitt, T. E., Caspi, A., Silva, P. A., & Stouthamer-Loeber, M. (1995). Individual differences in personality and intelligence are linked to crime. In J. Hagan (Ed.), *Current perspectives on aging and the life cycle* (Vol. 4, *Delinquency and disrepute in the life course: Contextual and dynamic analyses,* pp. 1–34). Greenwich, CT: JAI Press.

Moffitt, T. E., & Silva, P. A. (1988). IQ and delinquency: A direct test of the differential detection hypothesis. *Journal of Abnormal Psychology, 97*(3), 330–333.

Monk-Turner, E., Oleson, J., Cortez, P., Dean, D., Kracke, C., Harmon, J., . . . Trach, G. (2006). Gender disparity in criminal offenses among persons of high IQ. *International Journal of Offender Therapy and Comparative Criminology, 50*(5), 506–519.

Montour, K. (1977). William James Sidis, the broken twig. *American Psychologist, 32*(4), 265–279.

Moore, A., & Gibbons, D. (1987). *Watchmen.* New York, NY: DC Comics.

Mora, G. (1964). One hundred years from Lombroso's first essay: Genius and insanity. *American Journal of Psychiatry, 121*(6), 562–571.

Moreau, J. J. (1859). *La psychologie morbide dans ses rapports avec la philosophie de l'histoire, ou de l'influence des névropathies sur le dynamisme intellectuel.* Paris: Libraire Victor Masson.

Morning, A. (2014). And you thought we had moved beyond all that: Biological race returns to the social sciences. *Ethnic and Racial Studies, 37*(10), 1676–1685.

Moyser, G. (1988). Non-standardized interviewing in elite research. In R. Burgess (Ed.), *Studies in qualitative methodology* (Vol. 1, pp. 109–136). Greenwich, CT: JAI Press.

Mucchielli, L. (2006). Criminology, hygienism, and eugenics in France, 1870–1914: The medical debates on the elimination of "incorrigible" criminals. In P. Becker & R. F. Wetzell (Eds.), *Criminals and their scientists: The history of criminology in international perspective* (pp. 207–229). New York, NY: Cambridge University Press.

Murchison, C. (1926). *Criminal intelligence.* Worcester, MA: Clark University Press.

Murdoch, S. (2007). *IQ: A smart history of a failed idea.* Hoboken, NJ: John Wiley & Sons.

Murphy, J. G., & Coleman, J. L. (1990). *Philosophy of law: An introduction to jurisprudence* (Rev. ed.). San Francisco, CA: Westview Press.

Murphy, K. M., & D'Angelo, R. Y. (1963). The intelligence factor in the criminality of women. *American Catholic Sociological Review, 24*(4), 340–347.

Murray, P. (Ed.). (1989). *Genius: The history of an idea.* New York, NY: Basil Blackwell.

Nader, L. (1972). Up the anthropologist: Perspectives gained from studying up. In D. Hymes (Ed.), *Reinventing anthropology* (pp. 284–309). New York, NY: Random House.

Nagel, T. (1979). *Mortal questions.* New York, NY: Cambridge University Press.

Narváez, D. (1993). High achieving students and moral judgment. *Journal for the Education of the Gifted, 16*(3), 268–279.

Nasar, S. (1998). *A beautiful mind.* New York, NY: Simon and Schuster.

National Center for Education Statistics. (2013). Degree granting institutions: Enrollment by sex and age. Retrieved from https://nces.ed.gov/programs/digest/mobile/Enrollment_DGI_Enrollment_by_Sex_and_Age.aspx

Nedelec, J. L, Schwartz, J. A., & Connolly, E. J. (2015). Intelligence as the quintessential biosocial variable: An examination of etiological factors and associations with criminal offending and criminal justice processing. In M. DeLisi & M. G. Vaughn (Eds.), *The Routledge international handbook of biosocial criminology* (pp. 463–485). New York, NY: Routledge.

Neihart, M. (1999). The impact of giftedness on psychological well-being: What does the empirical literature say? *Roeper Review, 22*(1), 10–17.

Neihart, M. (2009). Growing up smart and criminal. In D. Ambrose & T. Cross (Eds.), *Morality, Ethics, and Gifted Minds* (pp. 313–325). New York, NY: Springer.

Neill, R. W. (Director). (1942). *Sherlock Holmes and the secret weapon* [Motion picture]. United States: Universal Pictures.

Neill, R. W. (Director). (1945). *The woman in green* [Motion picture]. United States: Universal Pictures.

Neisser, U., Boodoo, G., Bouchard, T. J., Jr., Boykin, A. W., Brody, N., Ceci, S. J., . . . Urbina, S. (1996). Intelligence: Knowns and unknowns, *American Psychologist, 51*(2), 77–101.

Nejelski, P., & Lerman, P. (1971). A researcher-subject testimonial privilege: What to do before the subpoena arrives. *Wisconsin Law Review, 1971*(4), 1085–1148.

Nelson, J. R., Smith, D. J., & Dodd, J. (1990). The moral reasoning of juvenile delinquents: A meta-analysis. *Journal of Abnormal Child Psychology, 18*(3), 231–239.

Nevin, R. (2000). How lead exposure relates to temporal changes in IQ, violent crime, and unwed pregnancy. *Environmental Research, 83*(1), 1–22.

Newberry, M., & Shuker, R. (2011.) The relationship between intellectual ability and the treatment needs of offenders in a therapeutic community prison. *Journal of Forensic Psychiatry and Psychology, 22*(3), 455–471.

Nichols, M. P. (1995). *The lost art of listening: How learning to listen can improve relationships*. New York, NY: Guilford Press.

Nicholson, R. A., & Kugler, K. E. (1991). Competent and incompetent criminal defendants: A quantitative review of comparative research. *Psychological Bulletin, 109*(3), 355–370.

Nietzsche, F. (1911). *Thus spake Zarathustra: A book for all and none* (T. Common, Trans.). New York, NY: Macmillan. (Original work published 1885)

Nisbet, J. F. (1900). *The insanity of genius and the general inequality of human faculty physiologically considered* (4th ed.). London: Grant Richards.

Nisbett, R. E. (2009). *Intelligence and how to get it*. New York, NY: W. W. Norton.

Nisbett, R. E., Aronson, J., Blair, C., Dickens, W., Flynn, J., Halpern, D. F., & Turkheimer, E. (2012). Intelligence: New findings and theoretical developments. *American Psychologist, 67*(2), 130–159.

Nitzsche, J. C. (1975). *The genius figure in antiquity and the middle ages*. New York, NY: Columbia University Press.

Nordau, M. (1895). *Degeneration* (5th ed.). New York, NY: D. Appleton.

Norman, A. D., Ramsay, S. G., Martray, C. R., & Roberts, J. L. (1999). Relationship between levels of giftedness and psychosocial adjustment. *Roeper Review, 22*(1), 5–9.

Normandeau, A. (1970). Crime indices for eight countries. *Revue internationale de police criminelle, 234*, 15–18.

Norris, J. (1988). *Serial killers*. New York, NY: Doubleday Books.

Norton, M. B. (2002). *In the devil's snare: The Salem witchcraft crisis of 1692*. New York, NY: Alfred A. Knopf.

Nye, F. I., & Short, J. F. (1957). Scaling delinquent behavior. *American Sociological Review, 22*, 326–331.

Ochse, R. (1990). *Before the gates of excellence: The determinants of creative genius*. New York, NY: Cambridge University Press.

Oden, M. H. (1968). The fulfillment of promise: 40 year follow-up of the Terman gifted group. *Genetic Psychology Monographs, 77*, 3–93.

Office for National Statistics. (2014). *Crime in England and Wales, year ending June 2014*. London: Office for National Statistics.

Ogilvie, J. M., Stewart, A. L., Chan, R. C. K., & Shum, D. K. (2011). Neuropsychological measures of executive function and antisocial behavior: A meta-analysis. *Criminology, 49*(4), 1063–1107.

Oleson, J. C. (1997). A dangerous activity: Writers as a sub-type of criminal genius? *Prison Writing, 11*, 80–90.

Oleson, J. C. (1999a). Extreme criminology. *Forensic Update, 59*, 22–27.

Oleson, J. C. (1999b). A question of influences: An analysis of literary, cinematic, and personal influences in two samples of exceptionally intelligent individuals. *Telicom, 12*(31), 24–31.

Oleson, J. C. (2002). The worst of all: A study of offending in high IQ populations. *Caribbean Journal of Criminology and Social Psychology, 7*(1–2), 44–88.

Oleson, J. C. (2003). The celebrity of infamy: A review essay of five autobiographies by three criminal geniuses. *Crime, Law and Social Change, 40*(4), 391–408.

Oleson, J. C. (2004). Sipping coffee with a serial killer: On conducting life history interviews with a criminal genius. *Qualitative Report, 9*(2), 192–215.

Oleson, J. C. (2005). Evil the natural way: The chimerical utopias of Henry David Thoreau and Theodore John Kaczynski. *Contemporary Justice Review, 8*(2), 211–228.

Oleson, J. C. (2006). Contemporary demonology: The criminological theories of Hannibal Lecter, part two. *Journal of Criminal Justice and Popular Culture, 13*(1), 29–49.

Oleson, J. C. (2007a). The Antigone dilemma: When the paths of law and morality diverge. *Cardozo Law Review, 29*(2), 669–702.

Oleson, J. C. (2007b). "Drown the world": Imperfect necessity and total cultural revolution. *Unbound: Harvard Journal of the Legal Left, 3*, 19–116.

Oleson, J. C. (2009). The insanity of genius: Criminal culpability and right-tail psychometrics. *George Mason Law Review, 16*(3), 587–641.

Oleson, J. C. (2013). Dissecting the serial killer: Toward a typology of serial homicide. In D. Dabney (Ed.), *Crime types: A text reader* (2nd ed., pp. 57–69). Belmont, CA: Wadsworth.

Oleson, J. C., & Chappell, R. (2012). Self-reported violent offending among subjects with genius-level IQ scores. *Journal of Family Violence, 27*(8), 715–730.

Oleson, J. C., & MacKinnon, T. (2015). Seeing *Saw* through the criminological lens: Popular representations of crime and punishment. *Criminology, Criminal Justice, Law and Society, 16*(1), 35–50.

Olmsted, A. S. (1964). Suppose we change the subject. *Federal Probation, 28*(3), 10–12.

One in a Thousand Society. (2015). Membership. Retrieved from http://www.oathsociety.com/membership.html

Oplev, N. A. (Director). (2010). *The girl with the dragon tattoo* [Motion picture]. United States: Music Box Films.

Oppenheim, A. (1992). *Questionnaire design, interviewing and attitude measurement*. New York: Pinter.

O'Toole, B. I. (1990). Intelligence and behaviour and motor vehicle accident mortality. *Accident Analysis and Prevention, 22*(3), 211–221.

Packer, H. L. (1968). *The limits of the criminal sanction*. Stanford, CA: Stanford University Press.

Padovan, A. (1902). *The sons of glory: Studies in genius*. New York, NY: Funk and Wagnalls.

Page, J. (2004). Eliminating the enemy: The import of denying prisoners access to higher education in Clinton's America. *Punishment and Society, 6*(4), 357–378.

Palmer, B. (2011, November 15). Are child molesters really the most hated people in prison? *Slate*. Retrieved from http://www.slate.com/articles/news_and_politics/explainer/2011/11

/jerry_sandusky_out_on_bail_are_child_molesters_tormented_in_american_prisons_.
html

Palys, T., & Lowman, J. (2002). Anticipating law: Research methods, ethics, and the law of privilege. *Sociological Methodology, 32*(1), 1–17.

Parker, F. J. (1975). *Caryl Chessman: The red light bandit.* Chicago, IL: Nelson Hall.

Parker, K. F., & Mowen, T. (2015). A sociological analysis of social class. In K. M. Beaver, J. C. Barnes, & B. B. Boutwell (Eds.), *The nurture versus biosocial debate in criminology* (pp. 75–90). Thousand Oaks, CA: SAGE.

Parnell, P. C., & Kane, S. C. (Eds.). (2003). *Crime's power: Anthropologists and the ethnography of crime.* New York, NY: Palgrave.

Paroline v. United States, 572 U.S. ___, 134 S. Ct. 1710 (2014).

Paternoster, R., & Bachman, R. (2010). Control theories. In E. McLaughlin & T. Newburn (Eds.), *The SAGE handbook of criminological theory* (pp. 114–138). Thousand Oaks, CA: SAGE.

Paternoster, R., & Triplett, R. (1988). Disaggregating self-reported delinquency and its implications for theory. *Criminology, 26*(4), 591–626.

Patton, M. Q. (2002). *Qualitative research and evaluation methods* (3rd ed.). Thousand Oaks, CA: SAGE.

Paulhus, D. L., Lysy, D. C., & Yik, M. S. (1998). Self-report measures of intelligence: Are they useful as proxy IQ tests? *Journal of Personality, 66*(4), 525–554.

Payment, S. (2004). *The trial of Leopold and Loeb: A primary source account.* New York, NY: Rosen.

Perez, J., & Torrubia, R. (1985). Sensation seeking and antisocial behaviour in a student sample. *Personality and Individual Differences, 6*(3), 401–403.

Pernick, M. S. (2002). Taking better baby contests seriously. *American Journal of Public Health, 92*(5), 707–708.

Persson, R. S. (2007). The myth of the anti-social genius: a survey study of the socio-emotional aspects of high-IQ individuals. *Gifted and Talented International, 22*(2), 19–34.

Peter, L. J. (1977). *Peter's quotations: Ideas for our time.* London: Bantam Books.

Peterson, J. S., & Ray, K. E. (2006). Bullying and the gifted: Victims, perpetrators, prevalence, and effects. *Gifted Child Quarterly, 50*(2), 148–168.

Phillips, J., & Land, K. C. (2012). The link between unemployment and crime rate fluctuations: An analysis at the county, state, and national levels. *Social Science Research, 41*(3), 681–694.

Pietrusza, D. (2003). *Rothstein: The life, times, and murder of the criminal genius who fixed the 1919 World Series.* New York, NY: Carroll & Graf.

Piff, P. K., Stancato, D. M., Côté, S., Mendoza-Denton, R., & Keltner, D. (2012). Higher social class predicts increased unethical behavior. *Proceedings of the National Academy of Sciences, 109*(11), 4086–4091.

Pinker, S. (2002). *The blank slate: The modern denial of human nature.* New York, NY: Viking.

Piquero, N. L., Piquero, A. R., & Stewart, E. S. (2015). Sociological viewpoint on the race-crime relationship. In K. M. Beaver, J. C. Barnes, & B. B. Boutwell (Eds.), *The nurture versus biosocial debate in criminology* (pp. 43–54). Thousand Oaks, CA: SAGE.

Pirelli, G., Gottdiener, W. H., & Zapf, P. A. (2011). A meta-analytic review of competency to stand trial research. *Psychology, Public Policy, and Law, 17*(1), 1–53.

Pittman, B. (Director). (1995). *Harrison Bergeron* [Motion picture]. United States: Showtime Networks.

Plante-Beaulieu, J., & de Chanterac, A. (2013). The neuropsychology of sexual offenders: A meta-analysis. *Sexual Abuse: A Journal of Research and Treatment, 26*(2), 149–177.

Platt, T., & Takagi, P. (1979). Biosocial criminology: A critique. *Crime and Social Justice, 11*, 5–13.

Plomin, R. (1999). Genetics and general cognitive ability. *Nature, 402*, C25–C29.

Poetic Genius Society. (2015). Membership qualifications. Retrieved June 1, 2015 from http://www.poeticgenius.com/qualifications.htm

Polk, K., Frease, D., & Richmond, F. L. (1974). Social class, school experience, and delinquency. *Criminology, 12*(1), 84–96.

Pollard-Gott, L. (2009). *The fictional 100: Ranking the most influential characters in world literature and legend.* New York, NY: iUniverse.

Pollock, W., Menard, S., Elliott, D. S., & Huizinga, D. H. (2015). It's official: Predictors of self-reported vs. officially recorded arrests. *Journal of Criminal Justice, 43*(1), 69–79.

Polsky, N. (1969). *Hustlers, beats, and others.* Garden City, NY: Anchor Books.

Porterfield, A. (1946). *Youth in trouble.* Fort Worth, TX: Leo Potishman Foundation.

Portnoy, J., Chen, F. R., & Raine, A. (2013). Biological protective factors for antisocial and criminal behavior. *Journal of Criminal Justice, 41*(5), 292–299.

Powell, P. M., & Haden, T. (1984). The intellectual and psychosocial nature of extreme giftedness. *Roeper Review, 6*(3), 131–133.

Prentice, N. M., & Kelly, F. J. (1963). Intelligence and delinquency: A reconsideration. *Journal of Social Psychology, 60*, 327–337.

Previc, F. H. (1999). Dopamine and the origins of human intelligence. *Brain and Cognition, 41*(3), 299–350.

Prins, H. (1986). *Dangerous behaviour, the law, and mental disorder.* London: Tavistock.

Proper, D. (2004). The incomprehensible crime of Leopold and Loeb: "Just an experiment." In F. Y. Bailey & S. Chermak (Eds.), *Famous American crimes and trials* (Vol. 3, pp. 63–86). Westport, CT: Praeger.

Putch, J. (Director). (2012). *Atlas shrugged II: The strike* [Motion picture]. United States: Atlas Distribution.

Quart, A. (2006). *Hothouse kids: The dilemma of the gifted child.* New York, NY: Penguin Press.

Quay, H. C. (1987). Intelligence. In H. C. Quay (Ed.), *Handbook of juvenile delinquency* (pp. 106–117). New York, NY: Wiley.

Rafter, N. H. (Ed.). (1988). *White trash: The eugenic family studies, 1877–1919.* Boston, MA: Northeastern University Press.

Rafter, N. H. (1997). *Creating born criminals.* Chicago: University of Illinois Press.

Rafter, N. H. (2008). Criminology's darkest hour: Biocriminology in Nazi Germany. *Australian and New Zealand Journal of Criminology, 41*(2), 287–306.

Rafter, N. H., & Brown, M. (2011). *Criminology goes to the movies: Crime theory and popular culture.* New York: New York University Press.

Raine, A. (1993). *The psychopathology of crime: Criminal behavior as a clinical disorder.* San Diego, CA: Academic Press.

Raine, A. (2013). *The anatomy of violence: The biological roots of crime.* New York, NY: Random House.

Raine, A., Laufer, W. S., Yang, Y., Narr, K. L., Thompson, P., & Toga, A. W. (2012). Increased executive functioning, attention, and cortical thickness in white-collar criminals. *Human Brain Mapping, 33*(12), 2932–2940.

Raine, A., Reynolds, C., Venables, P. H., & Mednick, S. A. (2002). Stimulation seeking and intelligence: A prospective longitudinal study. *Journal of Personality and Social Psychology, 82*(4), 663.

Rall, T. (2015). *Snowden.* New York, NY: Seven Stories Press.

Rand, A. (1957). *Atlas shrugged.* New York, NY: Penguin Books.

Raskin, E. (1936). Comparison of scientific and literary ability: A biographical study of eminent scientists and men of letters of the nineteenth century. *Journal of Abnormal and Social Psychology, 31*, 20–35.

Ratliff, E. (2016, March 3–April 27). The mastermind [Seven-part online article]. Retrieved from https://mastermind.atavist.com

Ratner, B. (Director). (2002). *Red dragon* [Motion picture]. United States: Universal Pictures.

Reiman, J. (2001). *The rich get richer and the poor get prison* (6th ed.). Boston, MA: Allyn & Bacon.

Reiman, J., & Leighton, P. (2013). *The rich get richer and the poor get prison* (10th ed.). New York, NY: Routledge.

Reinl, H. (Director). (1966). *The return of Dr. Mabuse* [Motion picture]. United States: Ajay Film.

Reiss, A. J., & Rhodes, A. (1961). The distribution of juvenile delinquency in the social class structure. *American Sociological Review, 26*(5), 720–732.

Reiterman, T., & Jacobs, J. R. (1982). *Raven: The untold story of the Reverend Jim Jones and his people.* New York, NY: E. P. Dutton.

Rhodes, H. T. F. (1932). *Genius and criminal.* London: John Murray.

Rich, M. (2014). Genetics and the unsettled past: The collision of DNA, race, and history; Race and the genetic revolution: Science, myth, and culture. *New Genetics and Society, 34*(4), 449–453.

Richards, K. (2011). Negotiating power and access and being called 'kid': Interviewing elites in criminological research. In L. Bartels & K. Richards (Eds.), *Qualitative criminology: Stories from the field* (pp. 68–79). Annandale, NSW: Hawkins Press.

Riley, D., & Shaw, M. (1985). *Parental supervision and juvenile delinquency.* London: HMSO.

Risch, N., Burchard, E., Ziv, E., & Tang, H. (2002). Categorization of humans in biomedical research: Genes, race and disease. *Genome Biology, 3*(7), 1–12.

Ritchie, G. (Director). (2011). *Sherlock: A game of shadows* [Motion picture]. United States: Warner Bros.

Roach, J. (Director). (1997). *Austin Powers: International man of mystery* [Motion picture]. United States: New Line Cinema.

Roach, J. (Director). (1999). *Austin Powers: The spy who shagged me* [Motion picture]. United States: New Line Cinema.

Roach, J. (Director). (2002). *Austin Powers in Goldmember* [Motion picture]. United States: New Line Cinema.

Roberts, J., & Kjellstrand, C. (1996). Jack Kevorkian: A medical hero. *British Medical Journal, 312*(7044), 1434.

Robertson, J. S. (Director). (1920). *Dr. Jekyll and Mr. Hyde* [Motion picture]. United States: Paramount Pictures.

Robinson, M. (2004). *Why crime? An integrated systems theory of antisocial behavior.* Upper Saddle River, NJ: Prentice Hall.

Robinson, N. M., Zigler, E., & Gallagher, J. J. (2000). Two tails of the normal curve: Similarities and differences in the study of mental retardation and giftedness. *American Psychologist, 55*(12), 1413.

Robinson, P. H. (2001). Punishing dangerousness: Cloaking preventive detention as criminal justice. *Harvard Law Review, 114*(5), 1429–1456.

Rockwell, J. G. (1927). Genius and the I.Q. *Psychological Review, 34*(5), 377–384.

Roe, A. (1952). A psychologist examines sixty-four eminent scientists. *Scientific American, 187*, 21–25.

Roedell, W. C. (1984). Vulnerabilities of highly gifted children. *Roeper Review, 6*(3), 127–130.

Roeg, N. (Director). (1993). *Heart of darkness* [Motion picture]. United States: Turner Network Television.

Rohmer, S. (1997). *The insidious Dr. Fu-Manchu.* Mineola, NY: Dover. (Original work published 1913)

Rohmer, S. (1916). *The Return of Dr. Fu-Manchu.* New York, NY: A. L. Burt.

Rohmer, S. (1931). *Daughter of Fu Manchu.* London: Cassell.

Rohmer, S. (1936). *President Fu Manchu.* Garden City, NY: Doubleday, Doran.

Rohmer, S. (1960). *Emperor Fu Manchu.* London: Herbert Jenkins.

Root-Bernstein, R., & Root-Bernstein, M. (1999). *Sparks of genius: The 13 thinking tools of the world's most creative people.* New York, NY: Houghton Mifflin.

Roper v. Simmons, 543 U.S. 551 (2005).

Rose, S. (2009). Darwin 200: Should scientists study race and IQ? No: Science and society do not benefit. *Nature, 457*(7231), 786–788.

Rostand, J. (1962). *The substance of man.* New York, NY: Doubleday.

Rothe, D. L., & Friedrichs, D. O. (2006). The state of the criminology of crimes of the state. *Social Justice, 33*(1), 147–161.

Rowe, D. C. (1994). *The limits of family influence: Genes, experience, and behavior.* New York, NY: Guilford Press.

Ruff, C. F., Templer, D. I., & Ayers, J. L. (1976). The intelligence of rapists. *Archives of sexual behavior, 5*(4), 327–329.

Runnion, M. (1982, December 20). A former quiz kid explains why the best and brightest tots are not always the happiest. *People,* 107. Retrieved from http://www.people.com/people/archive/article/0,,20083838,00.html

Rushton, J. P. (1995). *Race, evolution, and behavior: A life history perspective.* New Brunswick, NJ: Transaction.

Rushton, J. P., & Chrisjohn, R. D. (1981). Extraversion, neuroticism, psychoticism, and self-reported delinquency: Evidence from eight separate samples. *Personality and Individual Differences, 2*(1), 11–20.

Rushton, J. P., & Templer, D. I. (2009). National differences in intelligence, crime, income, and skin color. *Intelligence, 37*(4), 341–346.

Russell, S. (2002). *Lethal intent.* New York, NY: Pinnacle Books.

Rutter, M., & Giller, H. (1984). *Juvenile delinquency: Trends and perspectives.* New York, NY: Guilford Press.

Rutter, M., Tizard, J., & Whitmore, K. (1970). *Education, health, and behavior: Psychological and medical study of child development.* New York, NY: Wiley.

Ryan, G. W., & Bernard, H. R. (2003). Techniques to identify themes. *Field Methods, 15*(1), 85–109.

Sacks, P. (1999). *Standardized minds: The high price of America's testing culture and what we can do to change it.* Cambridge, MA: Perseus Books.

Samenow, S. E. (1984). *Inside the criminal mind.* New York, NY: Times Books.

Sampson, R. J., & Laub, J. H. (1993). *Crime in the making: Pathways and turning points through life.* Cambridge, MA: Harvard University Press.

Sampson, R. J., Laub, J. H., & Wimer, C. (2006). Does marriage reduce crime? A counterfactual approach to within-individual causal effects. *Criminology, 44*(3), 465–508.

Sampson, R. J., & Wilson, W. J. (2005) Toward a theory of race, crime, and urban inequality. In S. L. Gabbidon & H. T. Greene (Eds.), *Race, crime and justice: A reader* (pp. 177–189). New York, NY: Routledge.

Sanderlin, O. (1979). *Gifted children: How to identify and teach them.* New York, NY: A. S. Barnes.

Sands, S. (2009). *Behind the mask: A true story of obsession and savage genius.* New York, NY: St. Martin's Paperbacks.

San Juan, E., & McDevitt, J. (2013). *Hitchcock's villains: Murderers, maniacs, and mother issues.* Lanham, MD: Scarecrow Press.

Sarbin, T. R. (1969). *The myth of the criminal type* (Monday Evening Papers No. 18). Middletown, CT: Center for Advanced Studies, Wesleyan University.

Sargent, J. (Director). (1998). *Crime and punishment* [Motion picture]. United States: NBC.

Scarce, R. (1995). Scholarly ethics and courtroom antics: Where researchers stand in the eyes of the law. *American Sociologist, 26*(1), 87–112.

Scarce, R. (2005). *Contempt of court: A scholar's battle for free speech from behind bars.* New York, NY: AltaMira Press.

Schaefer, B. E. (1993). Sherlock Holmes and some astronomical connections. *Journal of the British Astronomical Association, 103*(1), 30–34.

Schechter, H. (1994). *Depraved: The definitive true story of H. H. Holmes, whose grotesque crimes shattered turn-of-the-century Chicago.* New York, NY: Pocket Books.

Schlesinger, J. (2012). *The insanity hoax: Exposing the myth of the mad genius.* Ardsley-on-Hudson, NY: Shrinktunes Media.

Schneider, W. J., & McGrew, K. S. (2012). The Cattell-Horn-Carroll model of intelligence. In D. Flanagan & P. Harrison (Eds.), *Contemporary intellectual assessment: Theories, tests, and issues* (3rd ed., pp. 99–144). New York: Guilford.

Schwartz, J. A., Savolainen, J., Aaltonen, M., Merikukka, M., Paananen, R., & Gissler, M. (2015). Intelligence and criminal behavior in a total birth cohort: An examination of functional form, dimensions of intelligence, and the nature of offending. *Intelligence, 51,* 109–118.

Schwarz, O. L. (1947). *Average man against superior man.* New York, NY: Philosophical Library.

Scott, C. (1961). Research on mail surveys. *Journal of the Royal Statistical Society, 124*(2), 143–195.

Scott, R. (Director). (2001). *Hannibal* [Motion picture]. United States: Metro-Goldwyn-Mayer.

Seagoe, M. V. (1975). *Terman and the gifted.* Los Altos, CA: William Kaufmann.

Sears, F. (Director). (1955). *Cell 2455, death row* [Motion picture]. United States: Columbia Pictures.

Sears, R. R. (1977). Sources of life satisfaction in the Terman gifted men. *American Psychologist, 32*(2), 119–128.

Seeley, K. R. (1984). Giftedness and juvenile delinquency in perspective. *Journal for the Education of the Gifted, 8*(1), 59–72.

Seligman, D. (1994). *A question of intelligence: The IQ debate in America.* New York, NY: Citadel Press.

Sellers, A. V. (1926). *The Leopold-Loeb case.* Brunswick, GA: Classic Publishing.

Sellin, T., & Wolfgang, M. E. (1964). *The measurement of delinquency.* New York: John Wiley & Sons.

Serebriakoff, V. (1965). *IQ: A Mensa analysis and history.* London: Hutchinson.

Serebriakoff, V. (1985). *Mensa: The society for the highly intelligent.* London: Constable.

Serebriakoff, V. (1995). How the Mensa IQ level was established. *Mensa International Journal, 384,* 28.

Sexton, D. (2001). *The strange world of Thomas Harris: Inside the mind of the creator of Hannibal Lecter.* London: Short Books.

Shader, M. (2001). *Risk factors for delinquency: An overview.* Washington, DC: US Department of Justice, Office of Justice Programs, Office of Juvenile Justice and Delinquency Prevention.

Shapiro, S. P. (1985). The road not taken: The elusive path to criminal prosecution for white collar offenders. *Law and Society Review, 19*(2), 179–217.

Shaplen, R. (1960). *Kreuger: Genius and swindler.* New York, NY: Alfred A. Knopf.

Sharkey, P. (2010). The acute effect of local homicides on children's cognitive performance. *Proceedings of the National Academy of Sciences of the United States of America, 107*(11), 733–738.

Sharp, D. (Director). (1965). *The face of Fu Manchu* [Motion Picture]. United States: Seven Arts Pictures.

Sharp, E. (1972). *The IQ cult.* New York, NY: Coward, McCann & Geoghegan.

Shaw, C. R., & McKay, H. D. (1942). *Juvenile delinquency in urban areas.* Chicago, IL: University of Chicago Press.

Shaw, G. B. (1908). *The sanity of art.* London: New Age Press.

Shaw, G. B. (1957). *Man and superman.* London: Penguin Books.

Shaw, G. B. (1977). Imprisonment. In G. Ezorsky (Ed.), *Philosophical perspectives on punishment* (pp. 281–299). Albany: State University of New York Press.

Sheldon, W. H. (1949). *Varieties of delinquent youth: An introduction to constitutional psychiatry.* New York, NY: Harper & Brothers.

Shelley, M. W. (1869). *Frankenstein; or, The modern Prometheus.* Boston, MA: Sever, Francis. (Original work published 1818)

Shenk, D. (2010). *The genius in all of us: Why everything you've been told about genetics, talent, and IQ is wrong.* New York, NY: Doubleday.

Sherman, L., Neyroud, P. W., & Neyroud, E. (2016, April 3). The Cambridge Crime Harm Index: Measuring total harm from crime based on sentencing guidelines. *Policing.* Advance online publication. doi:10.1093/police/paw003

Shockley, W. (1972). Dysgenics, geneticity, raceology: A challenge to the intellectual responsibility of educators. *Phi Delta Kappan, 53*(5), 297–307.

Shoda, Y., Mischel, W., & Peake, P. K. (1990). Predicting adolescent cognitive and self-regulatory competencies from preschool delay of gratification. *Developmental Psychology, 26*(6), 978–986.

Short, J. F., Jr., & Nye, F. I. (1957). Reported behavior as a criterion of deviant behavior. *Social Problems, 5*(3), 207–213.

Shulman, H. M. (1951). Intelligence and delinquency. *Journal of Criminal Law and Criminology, 41*(6), 763.

Shurkin, J. N. (1992). *Terman's kids: The groundbreaking study of how the gifted grow up.* Boston, MA: Little, Brown.

Shyamalan, M. N. (Director). (2000). *Unbreakable* [Motion Picture]. United States: Touchstone Pictures.

Siler, T. (1999). *Think like a genius: The ultimate user's guide for your brain.* New York, NY: Bantam.

Simmons, M. M. (1956, March 2). Disproving Bentham: From a correspondent. *Times Educational Supplement,* 271.

Simmons, M. M. (1962, January 26). Intelligent delinquents. *Times Educational Supplement,* 129.

Simmons, M. M., & Davis, R. (1953). Experiment at Kneesworth Hall. *British Journal of Delinquency, 4,* 109–122.

Simons, R. L. (1978). The meaning of the IQ-delinquency relationship. *American Sociological Review, 43*(2), 268–270.

Simonton, D. K. (1976). Biographical determinants of achieved eminence: A multivariate approach to the Cox data. *Journal of Personality and Social Psychology, 33*(2), 218–226.

Simonton, D. K. (1984). *Genius, creativity, and leadership: Historiometric inquiries.* Cambridge, MA: Harvard University Press.

Simonton, D. K. (1988). *Scientific genius: A psychology of science.* New York, NY: Cambridge University Press.

Simonton, D. K. (1990). *Psychology, science, and history: An introduction to historiometry.* New Haven, CT: Yale University Press.

Simonton, D. K. (1994). *Greatness: Who makes history and why.* New York, NY: Guilford Press.

Simonton, D. K. (1998). Historiometric methods in social psychology. *European Review of Social Psychology, 9*(1), 267–293.

Simonton, D. K. (1999). *Origins of genius: Darwinian perspectives on creativity.* New York, NY: Oxford University Press.

Simonton, D. K. (2003). Qualitative and quantitative analyses of historical data. *Annual Review of Psychology, 54*(1), 617–640.

Simonton, D. K. (2006). Presidential IQ, openness, intellectual brilliance, and leadership: Estimates and correlations for 42 US chief executives. *Political Psychology, 27*(4), 511–526.

Simonton, D. K. (2009). *Genius 101.* New York, NY: Springer.

Simonton, D. K. (2011). *Great flicks: Scientific studies of cinematic creativity and aesthetics.* New York, NY: Oxford University Press.

Simonton, D. K. (2013). After Einstein: Scientific genius is extinct. *Nature, 493,* 602.

Simonton, D. K. (2014). *The Wiley handbook of genius*. Chichester, United Kingdom: John Wiley & Sons.

Simpson, G. (2008). "Stop calling it aggression": War as crime. *Current Legal Problems, 61*(1), 191–228.

Singer, B. (Director). (1995). *The usual suspects* [Motion picture]. United States: Gramercy Pictures.

Sirotkina, I. (2002). Mad genius: The idea and its ramifications. *Intellectual News, 10*(1), 91–98.

Skal, D. J. (1998). *Screams of reason: Mad science and modern culture*. New York, NY: W. W. Norton.

Skinner v. Oklahoma, 316 U.S. 535 (1942).

Skogan, W. G. (1977). Dimensions of the dark figure of unreported crime. *Crime and Delinquency, 23*(1), 41–50.

Slobogin, C. (2009). Introduction to the symposium on the Model Penal Code's sentencing proposals. *Florida Law Review 61*(4), 665–682.

Sluka, J. A. (1995). Reflections on managing danger in fieldwork: Dangerous anthropology in Belfast. In C. Nordstrom & A. C. G. M. Robben (Eds.), *Fieldwork under fire: Contemporary studies of violence and survival*. Berkeley: University of California Press.

Smith, D. I., & Kirkham, R. W. (1982). Relationship between intelligence and driving record. *Accident Analysis and Prevention, 14*(6), 439–442.

Smith, K., Taylor, P., & Elkin, M. (2013). *Crimes detected in England and Wales, 2012/13*. London: National Archives.

Smithyman, S. D. (1979). Characteristics of "undetected" rapists. In W. H. Parsonage (Ed.), *Perspectives on victimology* (pp. 99–120). London: SAGE.

Snider, B. (1990, November 4). The most dangerous man alive. *San Francisco Examiner, Image*, 47–54.

Snyder, Z. (Director). (2009). *Watchmen* [Motion picture]. United States: Warner Bros.

Snyderman, M., & Rothman, S. (1987). Survey of expert opinion on intelligence and aptitude testing. *American Psychologist, 42*(2), 137–144.

Solotaroff, I. (1997, August). America's greatest living criminal genius sends his regards. *Esquire*, 72–76.

Sonenschein, D. (2001). On having one's research seized. In J. M. Miller & R. Tewksbury (Eds.), *Extreme methods: Innovative approaches to social science research* (pp. 209–215). Boston, MA: Allyn & Bacon.

Souvestre, E., & Allain, M. (1916). *Fantômas*. New York, NY: Brentano's.

Souvestre, E., & Allain, M. (1917a). *The exploits of Juve*. New York, NY: Brentano's.

Souvestre, P., & Allain, M. (1917b). *Messengers of evil*. New York, NY: Brentano's.

Souvestre, P., & Allain, M. (1918a). *A nest of spies*. New York, NY: Brentano's.

Souvestre, P., & Allain, M. (1918b). *A royal prisoner*. New York, NY: Brentano's.

Spaziano v. Florida, 468 U.S. 447 (1984).

Spearman, C. (1927). *The abilities of man*. New York, NY: Macmillan.

Spielberg, S. (Director). (2002). *Catch me if you can* [Motion picture]. United States: DreamWorks.

Spottiswoode, R. (Director). (2005). *Ripley under ground* [Motion picture]. England: Isle of Man Film.

Sprenger, A. (1861). *Das leben und die lehre des Mohammad* (Vol. 1). Berlin: Nicolaische Verlagsbuchhandlung.

Stams, G. J., Brugman, D., Deković, M., van Rosmalen, L., van der Laan, P., & Gibbs, J. C. (2006). The moral judgment of juvenile delinquents: A meta-analysis. *Journal of Abnormal Child Psychology, 34*(5), 692–708.

Stapel, D. (2014). *Faking science: A true story of an academic fraud* (N. J. L. Brown, Trans.). Retrieved from https://errorstatistics.files.wordpress.com/2014/12/fakingscience-20141214.pdf

Stark, R. (1975). *Social problems.* New York, NY: Random House.

Starrett, V. (1943, December 26). Books alive. *Chicago Sunday Tribune,* D12.

Stattin, H., & Klackenberg-Larsson, I. (1993). Early language and intelligence development and their relationship to future criminal behavior. *Journal of Abnormal Psychology, 102*(3), 369–378.

Stattin, H., Romelsjo, A., & Stenbacka, M. (1997). Personal resources as modifiers of the risk for future criminality: An analysis of protective factors in relation to 18-year-old boys. *British Journal of Criminology, 37*(2), 198–223.

Stern, A. (2005). *Eugenic nation: Faults and frontiers of better breeding in modern America.* Berkeley: University of California Press.

Sternberg, R. J. (1985). *Beyond IQ: A triarchic theory of human intelligence.* New York, NY: Cambridge University Press.

Sternberg, R. J. (2003). *Wisdom, intelligence, and creativity synthesized.* New York, NY: Cambridge University Press.

Stevenson, R. L. (1886). *Strange case of Dr Jekyll and Mr Hyde.* London: Longmans, Green.

Stiles, A. (2009, April). Literature in mind: H. G. Wells and the evolution of the mad scientist. *Journal of the History of Ideas,* 317–339.

Stone, C. P. (1921). A comparative study of the intelligence of 399 inmates of the Indiana reformatory and 653 men of the United States Army. *Journal of the American Institute of Criminal Law and Criminology, 12*(2), 238–257.

Stone, I. F. (1988). *The trial of Socrates.* Boston, MA: Little, Brown.

Stone, J. W. (1990). *Report of the trial of Professor John W. Webster* (2nd ed.). Birmingham, AL: Notable Trials Library. (Original work published 1850)

Stone, O. (Director). (1987). *Wall Street* [Motion picture]. United States: Twentieth Century Fox.

Strenze, T. (2007). Intelligence and socioeconomic success: A meta-analytic review of longitudinal research. *Intelligence, 35*(5), 401–426.

Streznewski, M. K. (1999). *Gifted grownups: The mixed blessings of extraordinary potential.* New York, NY: John Wiley & Sons.

Stross, C. (2006). *The Jennifer morgue.* New York, NY: Penguin.

Stumpf, J. P. (2006). The crimmigration crisis: Immigrants, crime, and sovereign power. *American University Law Review, 56*(2), 367–419.

Stuntz, W. J. (2011). *The collapse of American criminal justice.* Cambridge, MA: Harvard University Press.

Sturtz, J. (1995). Crimson criminals. *Swoon, 1*(7), 42–47.

Stuss, D. T., & Benson, D. F. (1986). *The frontal lobes.* New York, NY: Raven Press.

Subotnik, R. F., Karp, D. E., & Morgan, E. R. (1989). High IQ children at midlife: An investigation into the generalizability of Terman's genetic studies of genius. *Roeper Review,* 11(3), 139–144.

Sudiker, B. (2003). *Born evil or born genius: The leading cause of crime and turmoil in today's world.* New York, NY: S.P.I. Books.

Sudman, S., & Bradburn, N. M. (1973). Effects of time and memory factors on response in surveys. *Journal of the American Statistical Association, 68*(344), 805–815.

Sutherland, E. H. (1931). Mental deficiency and crime. In K. Young (Ed.), *Social Attitudes* (pp. 357–375). New York, NY: Holt.

Sutherland, E. H. (1940). White-collar criminality. *American Sociological Review, 5*(1), 1–12.

Sutherland, E. H., & Cressey, D. R. (1966). *Principles of criminology* (7th ed.). Philadelphia, PA: J. B. Lippincott.

Sweeten, G. (2012). Scaling criminal offending. *Journal of Quantitative Criminology, 28*(3), 533–557.

Sykes, G. M. (1958). *The society of captives: A study of a maximum security prison.* Princeton, NJ: Princeton University Press.

Sykes, G. M., & Matza, D. (1957). Techniques of neutralization. *American Sociological Review, 22*(6), 664–670.

Tabibnia, G., Satpute, A. B., & Lieberman, M. D. (2008). The sunny side of fairness preference for fairness activates reward circuitry (and disregarding unfairness activates self-control circuitry). *Psychological Science, 19*(4), 339–347.

Taibbi, M. (2014). *The divide: American injustice in the age of the wealth gap.* New York, NY: Spiegel & Grau.

Tangney, J. P., Baumeister, R. F., & Boone, A. L. (2004). High self-control predicts good adjustment, less pathology, better grades, and interpersonal success. *Journal of Personality, 72*(2), 271–324.

Tarantino, Q. (Director). (2009). *Inglourious basterds* [Motion picture]. United States: Universal Pictures.

Tarnopol, L. (1970). Delinquency and minimal brain dysfunction. *Journal of Learning Disabilities, 3,* 200–207.

Tartt, D. (1992). *The secret history.* New York, NY: Alfred A. Knopf.

Taylor, D. (Director). (1977). *The island of Dr. Moreau* [Motion picture]. United States: American International Pictures.

Taylor, I., Walton, P., & Young, J. (1973). *The new criminology: For a social theory of deviance.* Boston, MA: Routledge and Kegan Paul.

Teitelbaum, L. E. (1983). Spurious, tractable, and intractable legal problems: A positivist approach to law and social science research. In R. F. Boruch & J. S. Cecil (Eds.), *Solutions to Ethical and Legal Problems in Social Research* (pp. 11–48). New York, NY: Academic Press.

Templer, D. I., & Rushton, J. P. (2011). IQ, skin color, crime, HIV/AIDS, and income in 50 US states. *Intelligence, 39*(6), 437–442.

Tennenbaum, A. N. (1992). The crisis in criminology. *Telos: A Quarterly Journal of Critical Thought, 92,* 51–62.

Tennent, G., & Gath, D. (1975). Bright delinquents: A three-year follow-up study. *British Journal of Criminology, 15*(4), 386–390.

Terman, L. M. (1916). *The measurement of intelligence.* New York, NY: Houghton Mifflin.

Terman, L. M. (1917). The intelligence quotient of Francis Galton in childhood. *American Journal of Psychology, 28*(2), 209–215.

Terman, L. M. (1926). *Genetic studies of genius.* Vol. 1, *Mental and physical traits of a thousand gifted children* (2nd ed.). Stanford, CA: Stanford University Press.

Terman, L. M., & Oden, M. H. (1947). *Genetic studies of genius.* Vol. 4, *The gifted child grows up: Twenty-five years' follow-up of a superior group.* Stanford, CA: Stanford University Press.

Terman, L. M., & Oden, M. H. (1959). *Genetic studies of genius.* Vol. 5, *The gifted group at mid-life: Thirty-five years' follow-up of the superior child.* Stanford, CA: Stanford University Press.

Tewksbury, R. (2009). Qualitative versus quantitative methods: Understanding why qualitative methods are superior for criminology and criminal justice. *Journal of Theoretical and Philosophical Criminology, 1*(1), 38–58.

Tewksbury, R., Erickson, D. J., & Taylor, J. M. (2000). Opportunities lost: The consequences of eliminating Pell grant eligibility for correctional education students. *Journal of Offender Rehabilitation, 31*(1–2), 43–56.

Theakston, G. (Director). (2002). *Sherlock: Case of evil* [Motion picture]. United States: USA Network.

Theodore, J. (2007). *Evil summer: Babe Leopold, Dickie Loeb, and the kidnap-murder of Bobby Franks.* Carbondale: Southern Illinois University Press.

Thoreau, H. D. (2000). *The annotated Walden: Walden; or, life in the woods* (P. V. D. Stern, Ed.). New York, NY: Barnes & Noble. (Original work published 1854)

Thornberry, T. P., & Krohn, M. D. (2000). The self-report method for measuring delinquency and crime. *Criminal Justice, 4*(1), 33–83.

Thorndike, E. L. (1914). Units and scales for measuring educational products. *Proceedings of a Conference on Educational Measurements. Indiana University Bulletin, 12*(10), 128–141.

Tonry, M. (1997). Ethnicity, crime, and immigration. *Crime and Justice, 21*, 1–29.

Torrence, E. P. (1961). Problems of highly creative children. *Gifted Child Quarterly, 5*(2), 31–34.

Torrence, E. P. (1965). *Gifted children in the classroom.* New York, NY: Macmillan.

Towers, G. M. (1988). IQ and the problem of social adjustment. *Vidya, 98*, 5–9.

Towers, G. M. (1990). The outsiders. *LUCID: The Mensa Truth SIG Dialogue, 10*(2), 6–16.

Trahan, L. H., Stuebing, K. K., Fletcher, J. M., & Hiscock, M. (2014). The Flynn effect: A meta-analysis. *Psychological Bulletin, 140*(5), 1332–1360.

Traynor, M. (1996). Countering the excessive subpoena for scholarly research. *Law and Contemporary Problems, 59*(3), 119–148.

Trepal v. State, 621 So. 2d 1361, 1363 (Fla. 1993).

Trop v. Dulles, 356 U.S. 86 (1958).

Trost, A., & Kravetsky, V. (2013). *100 people with the highest IQs in history.* N.p.: A&V, printed by CreateSpace.

Truman, J. L., & Langton, L. (2014). *Criminal victimization, 2013.* Washington, DC: Bureau of Justice Statistics.

Tsanoff, R. A. (1949). *The ways of genius.* New York, NY: Harper & Brothers.

Ttofi, M. M., Farrington, D. P., Piquero, A. R., Lösel, F., DeLisi, M., & Murray, J. (2016). Intelligence as a protective factor against offending: A meta-analytic review of prospective longitudinal studies. *Journal of Criminal Justice*. Advance online publication. doi:10.1016/j.jcrimjus.2016.02.003

Tucker, W. H. (2002). *The funding of scientific racism: Wickliffe Draper and the Pioneer Fund.* Chicago: University of Illinois Press.

Tulchin, S. H. (1939). *Intelligence and crime.* Chicago, IL: University of Chicago Press.

Türck, H. (1914). *The man of genius.* Berlin: Wilhem Borngräber Verlag.

Vakhtin, A. A., Ryman, S. G., Flores, R. A., & Jung, R. E. (2014). Functional brain networks contributing to the Parieto-Frontal Integration Theory of intelligence. *NeuroImage, 103,* 349–354.

Valliant, P. M., & Bergeron, T. (1997). Personality and criminal profile of adolescent sexual offenders, general offenders in comparison to nonoffenders. *Psychological Reports, 81*(2), 483–489.

Van Ash, C., & Rohmer, E. S. (1972). *Master of villainy: A biography of Sax Rohmer* (R. E. Briney, Ed.). London: Tom Stacey.

van Dijk, J., van Kesteren, J., & Smit, P. (2007). *Criminal victimization in international perspective: Key findings from the 2004–2005 ICVS and EU ICS.* Den Haag, the Netherlands: Wetenschapppelijk Onderzoek-en Documentalcentrum.

Van Hoffmann, E. (1990). *A venom in the blood.* New York, NY: Donald I. Fine.

Van Onselen, C. (2007). *The fox and the flies: The secret life of a grotesque master criminal.* New York, NY: Walker.

Vary, A. B. (2010, June 1). The 100 greatest characters of the last 20 years: Here's our full list! *Entertainment Weekly.* Retrieved from http://www.ew.com/article/2010/06/01/100-greatest-characters-of-last-20-years-full-list

Vaughn, M. G., & DeLisi, M. (2015). Biosocial criminology: The future is here. In M. DeLisi & M. G. Vaughn (Eds.), *The Routledge international handbook of biosocial criminology* (pp. 636–643). New York, NY: Routledge.

Vaughn, M. G., DeLisi, M., Gunter, T., Fu, Q., Beaver, K. M., Perron, B. E., & Howard, M. O. (2011). The severe 5%: A latent class analysis of the externalizing behavior spectrum in the United States. *Journal of Criminal Justice, 39*(1), 75–80.

Vaughn, M. G., Fu, Q., Wernet, S. J., DeLisi, M., Beaver, K. M., Perron, B. E., & Howard, M. O. (2011). Characteristics of abstainers from substance use and antisocial behavior in the United States. *Journal of Criminal Justice, 39*(3), 212–217.

Vera, H., Barnard, G. W., & Holzer, C. (1979). The intelligence of rapists: New data. *Archives of Sexual Behavior, 8*(4), 375–377.

Vold, G. B., & Bernard, T. J. (1986). *Theoretical criminology* (3rd ed.). New York, NY: Oxford University Press.

von Hirsch, A. (1976). *Doing justice: The choice of punishments.* New York, NY: Hill & Wang.

Vonnegut, K. (1968). Harrison Bergeron. In *Welcome to the monkey house* (pp. 7–13). New York, NY: Delacorte Press.

von Sternberg, J. (Director). (1935). *Crime and punishment* [Motion picture]. United States: Columbia Pictures.

Voracek, M. (2004). National intelligence and suicide rate: An ecological study of 85 countries. *Personality and Individual Differences, 37*(3), 543–553.

Wade, N. (2014). *A troublesome inheritance: Genes, race and human history.* New York, NY: Penguin Books.

Waits, C., & Shors, D. (1999). *Unabomber: The secret life of Ted Kaczynski; His 25 years in Montana*. Helena, MT: Helena Independent Record and Montana Magazine.

Walker, B. G. (1983). *The woman's encyclopedia of myths and secrets*. New York, NY: Harper & Row.

Walker, N. (1968). *Crime and insanity in England*. Vol., 1, *The historical perspective*. Edinburgh: University of Edinburgh Press.

Wallace, A. (1986). *The prodigy*. New York, NY: E. P. Dutton.

Wallace, D. (2014). *DC Comics: Super-villains: The complete visual history*. San Rafael, CA: Insight Editions.

Wallerstein, J. S., & Wyle, C. J. (1947, March–April). Our law-abiding law-breakers. *National Probation*, 107–112.

Walmsley, R. (2016). *World prison population list* (11th ed.). London: Institute for Criminal Policy Research. Retrieved from http://www.prisonstudies.org/sites/default/files/resources/downloads/world_prison_population_list_11th_edition.pdf

Walsh, A. (1987). Cognitive functioning and delinquency: Property versus violent offenses. *International Journal of Offender Therapy and Comparative Criminology, 31*(3), 285–289.

Walsh, A., & Ellis, L. (1999). Political ideology and American criminologists' explanations for criminal behavior. *Criminologist, 24*(6), 1, 14, 26–27.

Walsh, A., & Ellis, L. (2004). Ideology: Criminology's Achilles' heel? *Quarterly Journal of Ideology, 27*(1–2), 1–25.

Walsh, A., Petee, T. A., & Beyer, J. A. (1987). Intellectual imbalance and delinquency comparing high verbal and high performance IQ delinquents. *Criminal Justice and Behavior, 14*(3), 370–379.

Walsh, A., Taylor, C. Y., & Yun, I. (2015). The role of intelligence and temperament in interpreting the SES-crime relationship. In K. M. Beaver, J. C. Barnes, & B. B. Boutwell (Eds.), *The nurture versus biosocial debate in criminology* (pp. 91–106). Thousand Oaks, CA: SAGE.

Walsh, A., & Wright, J. P. (2015). Rage against reason: Addressing critical critics of biosocial research. *Journal of Theoretical and Philosophical Criminology, 7*(1), 61–72.

Walz, R. (2000). *Pulp surrealism: Insolent popular culture in early twentieth-century Paris*. Berkeley: University of California Press.

Wan, J. (Director). (2004). *Saw* [Motion picture]. United States: Lionsgate Films.

Ward, D. A., & Tittle, C. R. (1994). IQ and delinquency: A test of two competing explanations. *Journal of Quantitative Criminology, 10*(3), 189–212.

Ward, T., & Maruna, S. (2007). *Rehabilitation*. New York, NY: Routledge.

Wasserman, J. D. (2003). Assessment of intellectual functioning. In J. R. Graham & J. A. Naglieri (Eds.), *Handbook of psychology*. Vol. 10, *Assessment psychology* (pp. 417–442). Hoboken, NJ: Wiley.

Weber, C. O., & Guilford, J. P. (1926). Character trends versus mental deficiency in the problem of delinquency. *Journal of Criminal Law and Criminology, 16*(4), 610–672.

Webb, J. T. (1993). Nurturing social-emotional development of gifted children. In K. A. Heller, F. J. Monks, and A. H. Passow (Eds.), *International handbook for research on giftedness and talent* (pp. 525–538). Oxford: Pergamon Press.

Webber, P. (Director). (2007). *Hannibal rising* [Motion picture]. United States: Metro-Goldwyn-Mayer.

Wechsler, D. (1939). *The measurement of adult intelligence*. Baltimore, MD: Williams & Witkins.

Wechsler, D. (1955). *The range of human capacities* (2nd ed.). Baltimore, MD: Williams & Wilkins.

Weindling, P. (2001). The origins of informed consent: the international scientific commission on medical war crimes, and the Nuremberg Code. *Bulletin of the History of Medicine, 75*(1), 37–71.

Weisberg, R. W. (1986). *Creativity: Genius and other myths*. New York, NY: W. H. Freeman and Company.

Wells, H. G. (1896). *The island of Dr. Moreau: A possibility*. New York, NY: Stone & Kimball.

Wenders, W. (Director). (1977). *The American friend* [Motion picture]. United States: New Yorker Films.

Werker, A. (Director). (1939). *The adventures of Sherlock Holmes* [Motion picture]. United States: Twentieth Century Fox.

Wertham, F. (1954). *Seduction of the innocent*. New York, NY: Rinehart.

West, D. J. (1967). *The young offender*. London: Penguin Books.

West, D. J., & Farrington, D. P. (1973). *Who becomes delinquent?* London: Heinemann.

West, D. J., & Green, R. (Eds.). (1997). *Sociolegal control of homosexuality: A multi-nation comparison*. New York, NY: Plenum Press.

West, S. (Director). (1997). *Con air* [Motion picture]. United States: Buena Vista Pictures

Westermarck, E. (1912). *The origin and development of the moral ideas* (Vols. 1 & 2). London: Macmillan and Co., Limited.

Whale, J. (Director). (1931). *Frankenstein* [Motion picture]. United States: Universal Pictures.

Whale, J. (Director). (1935). *The bride of Frankenstein* [Motion picture]. United States: Universal Pictures.

Whedon, J. (Director). (2008). *Dr. Horrible's sing-along blog* [Motion picture]. United States: Hulu.

Wheen, F. (2004). *The irresistible con: The bizarre life of a fraudulent genius*. London: Short Books.

White, J., & Batty, G. D. (2012). Intelligence across childhood in relation to illegal drug use in adulthood: 1970 British Cohort Study. *Journal of Epidemiology and Community Health, 66*, 767–774.

White, J., Gale, C. R., & Batty, G. D. (2012). Intelligence quotient in childhood and the risk of illegal drug use in middle age: The 1958 National Child Development Survey. *Annals of Epidemiology, 22*(9), 654–657.

White, J. L., Moffitt, T. E., & Silva, P. A. (1989). A prospective replication of the protective effects of IQ in subjects at high risk for juvenile delinquency. *Journal of Consulting and Clinical Psychology, 57*(6), 719–724.

White, R. D. (Ed.). (2012). *Climate change from a criminological perspective*. New York, NY: Springer.

Wilkinson, R., & Pickett, K. (2009). *The spirit level: Why greater equality makes societies stronger*. New York, NY: Bloomsbury Press.

Willerman, L., Schultz, R., Rutledge, J. N., & Bigler, E. D. (1991). In vivo brain size and intelligence. *Intelligence, 15*(2), 223–228.

Williams, A., Head, V., & Prooth, S. (2010). *Criminal masterminds (True crime): Evil geniuses of the world of crime.* Eastbourne, United Kingdom: Canary Press.

Williams, B. (1981). *Moral luck: Philosophical papers, 1973–1980.* New York, NY: Cambridge University Press.

Williams, T., Dunlap, E., Johnson, B. D., & Hamid, A. (1992). Personal safety in dangerous places. *Journal of Contemporary Ethnography, 21*(3), 343–374.

Williams v. New York, 337 U.S. 241 (1949).

Wilson, J. Q., & Herrnstein, R. J. (1985). *Crime and human nature.* New York, NY: Simon and Schuster.

Winchester, S. (1998). *The professor and the madman: A tale of murder, insanity, and the making of the "Oxford English Dictionary."* New York, NY: HarperCollins.

Winner, E. (1996). *Gifted children: Myths and realities.* New York, NY: Basic Books.

Winner, E. (2000). The origins and ends of giftedness. *American Psychologist, 55*(1), 159–169.

Winslow, R. W., & Gay, P. T. (1993). The moral minorities: A self-report study of low-consensus deviance. *International Journal of Offender Therapy and Comparative Criminology, 37*(1), 17–27.

Winter, P. (1961). *On the trial of Jesus.* Berlin: Walter de Gruyter.

Wirthwein, L., & Rost, D. H. (2011). Giftedness and subjective well-being: A study with adults. *Learning and Individual Differences, 21*(2), 182–186.

Witney, W., & English, J. (Directors). (1940). *Drums of Fu Manchu* [Motion picture]. United States: Republic Pictures.

Wolff, S. (2004). Ways into the field and their variants. In U. Flick, R. V. Kardoff, & I. Steinke (Eds.), *A companion to qualitative research* (pp. 195–202). Thousand Oaks, CA: SAGE.

Wolfgang, M. E. (1976). Ethical issues of research in criminology. In P. Nejelski (Ed.), *Social research in conflict with law and ethics* (pp. 25–34). Cambridge, MA: Ballinger.

Wolfgang, M. E., Figlio, R. M., & Sellin, T. (1972). *Delinquency in a birth cohort.* Chicago, IL: University of Chicago Press.

Wood, S. (Director). (1939). *Raffles* [Motion picture]. United States: United Artists.

Woodward, M. (1955). The role of low intelligence in delinquency. *British Journal of Delinquency, 5*(4), 281–303.

Wootton, B. (1959). *Social science and social pathology.* New York, NY: Macmillan.

World Health Organization. (2012). International classification of diseases (ICD-10). Retrieved from http://www.who.int/classifications/icd/en

Wright, J. P. (2009). Inconvenient truths: Science, race, and crime. In A. Walsh & K. M. Beaver (Eds.), *Biosocial criminology: New directions in theory and research* (pp. 137–153). New York, NY: Routledge.

Wright, J. P., & Boisvert, D. (2009). Intelligence and crime. In J. M. Miller (Ed.), *21st century criminology: A reference handbook* (pp. 93–100). Thousand Oaks, CA: SAGE.

Wright, J. P., & Morgan, M. A. (2015). Human biodiversity and the egalitarian fiction. In K. M. Beaver, J. C. Barnes, & B. B. Boutwell (Eds.), *The nurture versus biosocial debate in criminology* (pp. 55–73). Thousand Oaks, CA: SAGE.

Wright, R., Decker, S. H., Redfern, A. K., & Smith, D. L. (1992). A snowball's chance in hell: Doing fieldwork with active residential burglars. *Journal of Research in Crime and Delinquency, 29*(2), 148–161.

Wright, R. A., & Miller, J. M. (1998). Taboo until today? The coverage of biological arguments in criminology textbooks, 1961 to 1970 and 1987 to 1996. *Journal of Criminal Justice, 26*(1), 1–19.

Yablonsky, L. (1965). Experiences with the criminal community. In A. Goulder & S. M. Miller (Eds.), *Applied sociology: Opportunities and problems* (pp. 55–73). New York, NY: Free Press.

Yancy, D. (2007). *The Unabomber.* San Francisco, CA: Lucent Books.

Yoakum, C. S., & Yerkes, R. S. (Eds.). (1920). *Army mental tests.* New York, NY: Henry Holt.

Yoder, A. H. (1894). The study of the boyhood of great men. *Pedagogical Seminary, 3*(1), 134–156.

Young, J. (2011). *The criminological imagination.* Malden, MA: Polity.

Young, T. (Director). (1962). *Dr. No* [Motion picture]. United States: United Artists.

Young, T. (Director). (1963). *From Russia with love* [Motion picture]. United States: United Artists.

Young, T. (Director). (1965). *Thunderball* [Motion picture]. United States: United Artists.

Zeleny, L. D. (1933). Feeble-mindedness and criminal conduct. *American Journal of Sociology, 38*(4), 564–576.

Zimmerman, J. (1949). The convict lease system in Arkansas and the fight for abolition. *Arkansas Historical Quarterly, 8*(3), 171–188.

Zimring, F. E., & Hawkins, G. J. (1973). *Deterrence: The legal threat in crime control.* Chicago, IL: University of Chicago Press.

Zuckerman, M., Silberman, J., & Hall, J. A. (2013). The relation between intelligence and religiosity a meta-analysis and some proposed explanations. *Personality and Social Psychology Review, 17*(4), 325–354.

INDEX

In this index, "criminal genius study" in main headings and "the study" in subheadings refer specifically to the study conducted for this book. Other studies of criminal genius(es) and of crimes committed by persons of high intelligence are listed as "crime research" or "research" in both main and subheadings. Figures and tables are indicated by *f* and *t* in italics. Italics are also used for names of fictional characters.

CPSIA information can be obtained
at www.ICGtesting.com
Printed in the USA
LVOW08*1443040117

519722LV00001B/5/P